SPARK 2014 User's Guide

Release 19.0w

AdaCore and Altran UK Ltd

Feb 13, 2018

CONTENTS

GETTING STARTED WITH SPARK

We begin with a very simple guide aimed at getting new users up and running with the SPARK tools. A small SPARK example program will be used for illustration.

Note: The online version of this User's Guide applies to the latest development version of the SPARK toolset. If you're using an official release, some of the described features may not apply. Refer to the version of the SPARK 2014 User's Guide shipping with your release, available through *Help → SPARK* in GPS and GNATbench IDEs, or under `share/doc/spark` in your SPARK installation.

As a prerequisite, it is assumed that the SPARK tools have already been installed. As a minimum you should install:

- SPARK Pro or SPARK Discovery
- GPS or the GNATbench plug-in of Eclipse

SPARK Pro is the most complete toolset for SPARK. SPARK Discovery is a reduced toolset that still allows to perform all analyses presented in this User's Guide, but is less powerful than SPARK Pro. Compared to SPARK Pro, SPARK Discovery:

- only comes with one automatic prover instead of three
- does not integrate the static analyzer CodePeer
- does not generate counterexamples for failed proofs
- has limited proof support for programs using modular arithmetic or floating-point arithmetic
- comes without a lemma library for more difficult proofs

Note that GPS is not strictly required for SPARK as all the commands can be invoked from the command line, or from Eclipse using the GNATbench plug-in, but the instructions in this section assume that GPS is being used. If you are a supported user, you can get more information on how to install the tools in "AdaCore Installation Procedures" under the "Download" tab in GNAT Tracker, or by contacting AdaCore for further advice.

The key tools that we will use in this example are GNATprove and GPS. To begin with, launch GPS with a new default project and check that the *SPARK* menu is present in the menu bar.

Note: For SPARK 2005 users, this menu will appear under the name *SPARK 2014*, to avoid any confusion with the existing *SPARK* menu for SPARK 2005 toolset.

Now open a new file in GPS and type the following short program into it. Save this file as `diff.adb`.

```
1  procedure Diff (X, Y : in Natural; Z : out Natural) with
2    SPARK_Mode,
3    Depends => (Z => (X, Y))
```

```
4   is
5   begin
6      Z := X - X;
7   end Diff;
```

The program is intended to calculate the difference between X and Y and store the result in Z. This is reflected in the aspect Depends which states that the output value of Z depends on the input values of X and Y, but, as you may have noticed, there is a bug in the code. Note the use of aspect SPARK_Mode to identify this as SPARK code to be analysed with the SPARK tools. To analyze this program, select *SPARK → Examine File* from the menu in GPS. GNATprove executes in flow analysis mode and reports:

```
diff.adb:1:20: warning: unused variable "Y"
diff.adb:1:36: info: initialization of "Z" proved
diff.adb:3:03: medium: missing dependency "null => Y"
diff.adb:3:24: medium: incorrect dependency "Z => Y"
```

These warnings are informing us that there is a discrepancy between the program's contract (which says that the value of Z is obtained from the values of X and Y) and its implementation (in which the value of Z is derived only from the value of X, and Y is unused). In this case the contract is correct and the code is wrong, so fix the code by changing the assignment statement to Z := X - Y; and re-run the analysis. This time it should report no warnings or errors.

Having established that the program is free from flow errors, now let's run the tools in proof mode to check for run-time errors. Select *SPARK → Prove File* from the menu in GPS, and click on Execute in the resulting dialog box. GNATprove now attempts to show, using formal verification, that the program is free from run-time errors. But it finds a problem and highlights the assignment statement in red, reporting:

```
diff2.adb:1:37: info: initialization of "Z" proved
diff2.adb:6:11: info: overflow check proved
diff2.adb:6:11: medium: range check might fail
```

This means that the tools are unable to show that the result of subtracting one Natural number from another will be within the range of the type Natural, which is hopefully not too surprising! There are various ways in which this could be addressed depending on what the requirements are for this subprogram, but for now let's change the type of parameter Z from Natural to Integer. If the analysis is re-run with this change in place then GNATprove will report no errors or warnings. All checks are proved so we can be confident that no exceptions will be raised by the execution of this code.

This short example was intended to give a flavor of the types of analysis that can be performed with the SPARK tools. A more in-depth example is presented later in *SPARK Tutorial*.

INTRODUCTION

SPARK 2014 is a programming language and a set of verification tools designed to meet the needs of high-assurance software development. SPARK 2014 is based on Ada 2012, both subsetting the language to remove features that defy verification, but also extending the system of contracts and aspects to support modular, formal verification.

The new aspects support abstraction and refinement and facilitate deep static analysis to be performed including flow analysis and formal verification of an implementation against a specification.

SPARK 2014 is a much larger and more flexible language than its predecessor SPARK 2005. The language can be configured to suit a number of application domains and standards, from server-class high-assurance systems (such as air-traffic management applications), to embedded, hard real-time, critical systems (such as avionic systems complying with DO-178C Level A).

A major feature of SPARK 2014 is the support for a mixture of proof and other verification methods such as testing, which facilitates in particular the use of unit proof in place of unit testing; an approach now formalized in DO-178C and the DO-333 formal methods supplement. Certain units may be formally proven and other units validated through testing.

SPARK 2014 is supported by various tools in the GNAT toolsuite:

- the GNAT compiler
- the GPS integrated development environment
- the GNATtest tool for unit testing harness generation
- the GNATprove tool for formal program verification

In the rest of this document, we'll simply say SPARK to refer to SPARK 2014.

The remainder of this document is structured as follows:

- *Installation of GNATprove* goes through the installation steps on different platforms.
- *Identifying SPARK Code* describes the various means to identify the part of the program in SPARK that should be analyzed.
- *Overview of SPARK Language* provides an overview of the SPARK language.
- *SPARK Tutorial* gives an introduction to writing, testing and proving SPARK programs.
- *Formal Verification with GNATprove* describes the use of the GNATprove formal verification tool.
- *Applying SPARK in Practice* lists the main objectives and project scenarios for using SPARK.

INSTALLATION OF GNATPROVE

In general, you will need to install a recent version of GNAT toolchain (that supports Ada 2012 syntax) to compile SPARK programs. You will need to install one toolchain for each platform that you target, for example one toolchain for native compilation on your machine and one toolchain for cross compilation to an embedded platform.

For analyzing SPARK programs, we recommend to first install GPS and then install GNATprove under the same location. Alternatively, you can install the GNATbench plug-in for Eclipse instead of GPS, using the Eclipse installation mechanism. The same version of GPS or GNATbench can support both native and cross compilations, as well as SPARK analysis.

If you choose to install GNATprove in a different location, you should also modify the environment variables GPR_PROJECT_PATH (if you installed GNAT). On Windows, edit the value of GPR_PROJECT_PATH under the Environnement Variables panel, and add to it the value of <GNAT install dir>/lib/gnat and <GNAT install dir>/share/gpr (so that SPARK can find library projects installed with GNAT) and <SPARK install dir>/lib/gnat (so that GNAT can find the SPARK lemma library project installed with SPARK, for details see *Manual Proof Using SPARK Lemma Library*). On Linux/Mac with Bourne shell, use:

```
export GPR_PROJECT_PATH=<GNAT install dir>/lib/gnat:<GNAT install dir>/share/gpr:
↪<SPARK install dir>/lib/gnat:$GPR_PROJECT_PATH
```

or on Linux/Mac with C shell:

```
setenv GPR_PROJECT_PATH <GNAT install dir>/lib/gnat:<GNAT install dir>/share/gpr:
↪<SPARK install dir>/lib/gnat:$GPR_PROJECT_PATH
```

See below for detailed installation instructions of GPS and GNATprove.

3.1 System Requirements

Formal verification is complex and time consuming, so GNATprove will benefit from all the speed (CPU) and memory (RAM) that can be made available. A minimum of 2 GB of RAM per core is recommended. More complex analyses will require more memory. A recommended configuration for running GNATprove on large systems is an x86-64 machine running Linux 64bits or Windows 64bits with at least 8 cores and 16 GB of RAM. Slower machines can be used to analyze small subsystems, but a minimum of 2.8Ghz CPU and 2 GB of RAM is required.

In addition, if you want to use the integration of CodePeer static analysis in GNATprove (switch --codepeer=on) you will need approximately 1 GB of RAM per 10K SLOC of code. In other words, in order to analyze 300K SLOC of code with CodePeer, you will need a 64bits configuration with at least 30 GB of RAM. Note that these numbers will vary depending on the complexity of your code. If your code is very simple, you will need less memory. On the other hand if your code is very complex, then you will likely need more memory.

3.2 Installation under Windows

If not already done, first run the GPS installer by e.g. double clicking on *gps-<version>-i686-pc-mingw32.exe* and follow the instructions.

Note: If you're using GNAT GPL instead of GNAT Pro, you should run instead the GNAT GPL installer, which installs GPS.

Then similarly run the GNATprove installer, by e.g. double clicking on *spark-<version>-x86-windows-bin.exe*.

You should have sufficient rights for installing the package (administrator or normal rights depending on whether it is installed for all users or a single user).

3.3 Installation under Linux/Mac

If not already done, you need to extract and install the GPS compressed tarball and then run the install, e.g.:

```
$ gzip -dc gps-<version>-<platform>-bin.tar.gz | tar xf -
$ cd gps-<version>-<platform>-bin
$ ./doinstall
```

Then follow the instructions displayed.

Note: If you're using GNAT GPL instead of GNAT Pro, you should install instead the GNAT GPL package, which installs GPS.

Then do the same with the SPARK tarball, e.g.:

```
$ gzip -dc spark-<version>-<platform>-bin.tar.gz | tar xf -
$ cd spark-<version>-<platform>-bin
$ ./doinstall
```

Note that you need to have sufficient rights for installing the package at the chosen location (e.g. root rights for installing under /opt/spark).

IDENTIFYING SPARK CODE

In general a program can have some parts that are in SPARK (and follow all the rules in the SPARK Reference Manual), and some parts that are full Ada 2012. Pragma or aspect `SPARK_Mode` is used to identify which parts are in SPARK (by default programs are in full Ada).

This section contains a simple description of pragma and aspect `SPARK_Mode`. See *Pragma SPARK_Mode* for the complete description.

Note that GNATprove only analyzes parts of the code that are identified as being in SPARK using pragma or aspect `SPARK_Mode`.

4.1 Mixing SPARK Code and Ada Code

An Ada program unit or other construct is said to be "in SPARK" if it complies with the restrictions required to permit formal verification given in the SPARK Reference Manual. Conversely, an Ada program unit or other construct is "not in SPARK" if it does not meet these requirements, and so is not amenable to formal verification.

Within a single Ada unit, constructs which are "in" and "not in" SPARK may be mixed at a fine level in accordance with the following two general principles:

- SPARK code shall only reference SPARK declarations, but a SPARK declaration which requires a completion may have a non-SPARK completion.

- SPARK code shall only enclose SPARK code, except that SPARK code may enclose a non-SPARK completion of an enclosed SPARK declaration.

More specifically, non-SPARK completions of SPARK declarations are allowed for subprogram declarations, package declarations, task type declarations, protected type declarations, private type declarations, private extension declarations, and deferred constant declarations. [Strictly speaking, the private part of a package, a task type or a protected type is considered to be part of its completion for purposes of the above rules; this is described in more detail below].

When a non-SPARK completion is provided for a SPARK declaration, the user has an obligation to ensure that the non-SPARK completion is consistent (with respect to the semantics of SPARK) with its SPARK declaration. For example, SPARK requires that a function call has no side effects. If the body of a given function is in SPARK, then this rule is enforced via various language rules; otherwise, it is the responsibility of the user to ensure that the function body does not violate this rule. As with other such constructs (notably pragma Assume), failure to meet this obligation can invalidate any or all analysis (proofs and/or flow analysis) associated with the SPARK portion of a program. A non-SPARK completion meets this obligation if it is semantically equivalent (with respect to dynamic semantics) to some notional completion that could have been written in SPARK.

The SPARK semantics (specifically including flow analysis and proof) of a "mixed" program which meets the aforementioned requirement are well defined - they are the semantics of the equivalent 100% SPARK program. For the semantics of other "mixed" programs refer to the Ada Reference Manual.

In the case of a package, a task type, or a protected type, the specification/completion division described above is a simplification of the true situation. For instance, a package is divided into 4 sections, not just 2: its visible part, its private part, the declarations of its body, and the statement list of its body. For a given package and any number N in the range 0 .. 4, the first N sections of the package might be in SPARK while the remainder is not.

For example, the following combinations may be typical:

- Package specification in SPARK. Package body not in SPARK.

- Visible part of package specification in SPARK. Private part and body not in SPARK.

- Package specification in SPARK. Package body almost entirely in SPARK, with a small number of subprogram bodies not in SPARK.

- Package specification in SPARK, with all subprogram bodies imported from another language.

- Package specification contains a mixture of declarations which are in SPARK and not in SPARK. The latter declarations are only visible and usable from client units which are not in SPARK.

Task types and protected types are similar to packages but only have 3 sections instead of 4. The statement list section of the body is missing.

Such patterns are intended to allow for application of formal verification to a subset of a program, and the combination of formal verification with more traditional testing (see *Applying SPARK in Practice*).

4.2 Project File Setup

The project file is used to identify coarsely which parts of a program are in SPARK. To get more details on project file setup, see section *Setting Up a Project File*.

4.2.1 Setting the Default SPARK_Mode

There are two possible defaults:

1. No value of SPARK_Mode is specified as a configuration pragma. In that case, only the parts of the program explicitly marked with SPARK_Mode => On are in SPARK. This default is recommended if only a small number of units or subprograms are in SPARK.

2. A value of SPARK_Mode => On is specified as a configuration pragma. In that case, all the program should be in SPARK, except for those parts explicitly marked with SPARK_Mode => Off. This mode is recommended if most of the program is in SPARK.

Here is how to specify a value of SPARK_Mode => On as a configuration pragma:

```
project My_Project is
   package Builder is
      for Global_Configuration_Pragmas use "spark.adc";
   end Builder;
end My_Project;
```

where spark.adc is a configuration file containing at least the following line:

```
pragma SPARK_Mode (On);
```

4.2.2 Specifying Files To Analyze

By default, all files from a project are analyzed by GNATprove. It may be useful to restrict the set of files to analyze to speedup analysis if only a subset of the files contain SPARK code.

The set of files to analyze can be identified by specifying a different value of various project attributes in the mode used for formal verification:

- `Source_Dirs`: list of source directory names
- `Source_Files`: list of source file names
- `Source_List_File`: name of a file listing source file names

For example:

```
project My_Project is

  type Modes is ("Compile", "Analyze");
  Mode : Modes := External ("MODE", "Compile");

  case Mode is
     when "Compile" =>
        for Source_Dirs use (...);
     when "Analyze" =>
        for Source_Dirs use ("dir1", "dir2");
        for Source_Files use ("file1.ads", "file2.ads", "file1.adb", "file2.adb");
  end case;

end My_Project;
```

Then, GNATprove should be called by specifying the value of the MODE external variable as follows:

```
gnatprove -P my_project -XMODE=Analyze
```

4.2.3 Excluding Files From Analysis

When choosing a default value of `SPARK_Mode => On`, it may be needed to exclude some files from analysis (for example, because they contain non-SPARK code, or code that does not need to be formally analyzed).

The set of files to exclude can be identified by specifying a different value of various project attributes in the mode used for formal verification:

- `Excluded_Source_Dirs`: list of excluded source directory names
- `Excluded_Source_Files`: list of excluded source file names
- `Excluded_Source_List_File`: name of a file listing excluded source file names

For example:

```
project My_Project is
  package Builder is
     for Global_Configuration_Pragmas use "spark.adc";
  end Builder;

  type Modes is ("Compile", "Analyze");
  Mode : Modes := External ("MODE", "Compile");

  case Mode is
```

```
    when "Compile" =>
        null;
    when "Analyze" =>
        for Excluded_Source_Files use ("file1.ads", "file1.adb", "file2.adb");
  end case;

end My_Project;
```

Then, GNATprove should be called by specifying the value of the MODE external variable as follows:

```
gnatprove -P my_project -XMODE=Analyze
```

4.2.4 Using Multiple Projects

Sometimes, it is more convenient to analyze a subset of the source files with the default SPARK_Mode => On and the rest of the source files with no setting for SPARK_Mode. In that case, one can use two project files with different defaults, with each source file in one of the projects only. Files in one project can still refer to files in the other project by using a limited with clause between projects, as follows:

```
limited with "project_b"
project My_Project_A is
   package Compiler is
      for Local_Configuration_Pragmas use "spark.adc";
   end Compiler;
   for Source_Files use ("file1.ads", "file2.ads", "file1.adb", "file2.adb");
end My_Project_A;
```

```
limited with "project_a"
project My_Project_B is
   for Source_Files use ("file3.ads", "file4.ads", "file3.adb", "file4.adb");
end My_Project_B;
```

where spark.adc is a configuration file containing at least the following line:

```
pragma SPARK_Mode (On);
```

4.3 Using SPARK_Mode in Code

The pragma or aspect SPARK_Mode can be used in the code to identify precisely which parts of a program are in SPARK.

4.3.1 Basic Usage

The form of a pragma SPARK_Mode is as follows:

```
pragma SPARK_Mode [ (On | Off) ]
```

For example:

```
pragma SPARK_Mode (On);
package P is
```

The form of an aspect SPARK_Mode is as follows:

```
with SPARK_Mode => [ On | Off ]
```

For example:

```
package P with
  SPARK_Mode => On
is
```

A default argument of On is assumed for any SPARK_Mode pragma or aspect for which no argument is explicitly specified.

For example:

```
package P is
   pragma SPARK_Mode;   --  On is implicit here
```

or

```
package P with
  SPARK_Mode  --  On is implicit here
is
```

We say that a package or a subprogram is library-level if it is either top-level or defined in a library-level package. The SPARK_Mode pragma can be used in the following places in the code:

- immediately within or before a library-level package spec
- immediately within a library-level package body
- immediately following the private keyword of a library-level package spec
- immediately following the begin keyword of a library-level package body
- immediately following a library-level subprogram spec
- immediately within a library-level subprogram body
- immediately within a library-level task spec
- immediately within a library-level task body
- immediately following the private keyword of a library-level task spec
- immediately within a library-level protected spec
- immediately within a library-level protected body
- immediately following the private keyword of a library-level protected spec

The SPARK_Mode aspect can be used in the following places in the code:

- on a library-level package spec or body
- on a library-level subprogram spec or body
- on a library-level task spec or body
- on a library-level protected spec or body

If a SPARK_Mode pragma or aspect is not specified for a subprogram, package, task or protected spec/body, then its value is inherited from the current mode that is active at the point where the declaration occurs.

Note that a generic package instance is considered to be declared at its instantiation point. For example, a generic package cannot be both marked SPARK_Mode and instantiated in a subprogram body.

4.3.2 Consistency Rules

The basic rule is that you cannot turn SPARK_Mode back On, once you have explicitly turned if Off. So the following rules apply:

If a subprogram spec has SPARK_Mode Off, then the body cannot have SPARK_Mode On.

For a package, we have four parts:

1. the package public declarations

2. the package private part

3. the body of the package

4. the elaboration code after begin

For a package, the rule is that if you explicitly turn SPARK_Mode Off for any part, then all the following parts cannot have SPARK_Mode On. Note that this may require repeating a pragma SPARK_Mode (Off) in the body. For example, if we have a configuration pragma SPARK_Mode (On) that turns the mode On by default everywhere, and one particular package spec has pragma SPARK_Mode (Off), then that pragma will need to be repeated in the package body.

Task types and protected types are handled similarly. If SPARK_Mode is set to Off on one part, it cannot be set to On on the following parts, among the three parts:

1. the spec

2. the private part

3. the body

There is an exception to this rule, when SPARK_Mode occurs in the code of a generic instantiated in code where SPARK_Mode is Off. In that case, occurrences of SPARK_Mode in the generic are ignored for this instance.

4.3.3 Examples of Use

Verifying Selected Subprograms

If only a few selected subprograms are in SPARK, then it makes sense to set no default for SPARK_Mode, and instead set SPARK_Mode => On directly on the subprograms of interest. For example:

```
 1  package Selected_Subprograms is
 2
 3     procedure Critical_Action with
 4       SPARK_Mode => On;
 5
 6     procedure Sub_Action (X : out Boolean) with
 7       Post => X = True;
 8
 9     procedure Non_Critical_Action;
10
11  end Selected_Subprograms;
```

Note that, although the bodies of procedures Sub_Action and Non_Critical_Action are not analyzed, it is valid to call Sub_Action in the body of procedure Critical_Action, even without specifying SPARK_Mode => On on the spec of Sub_Action. Indeed, GNATprove checks in that case that the spec of Sub_Action is in SPARK.

```
1   package body Selected_Subprograms is
2
3      procedure Critical_Action with
4        SPARK_Mode => On
5      is
6         -- this procedure body is analyzed
7         X : Boolean;
8      begin
9         Sub_Action (X);
10        pragma Assert (X = True);
11     end Critical_Action;
12
13     procedure Sub_Action (X : out Boolean) is
14     begin
15        -- this procedure body is not analyzed
16        X := True;
17     end Sub_Action;
18
19     procedure Non_Critical_Action is
20     begin
21        -- this procedure body is not analyzed
22        null;
23     end Non_Critical_Action;
24
25  end Selected_Subprograms;
```

Verifying Selected Units

If only a few selected units are in SPARK, then it makes sense to set no default for SPARK_Mode, and instead set SPARK_Mode => On directly on the units of interest. For example:

```
1   package Selected_Units with
2     SPARK_Mode => On
3   is
4
5      procedure Critical_Action;
6
7      procedure Sub_Action (X : out Boolean) with
8        Post => X = True;
9
10     procedure Non_Critical_Action with
11       SPARK_Mode => Off;
12
13  end Selected_Units;
```

Note that procedure Sub_Action can be called inside SPARK code, because its spec is in SPARK, even though its body is marked SPARK_Mode => Off. On the contrary, procedure Non_Critical_Action whose spec is marked SPARK_Mode => Off cannot be called inside SPARK code.

```
1   package body Selected_Units with
2     SPARK_Mode => On
3   is
4
5      procedure Critical_Action is
6         -- this procedure body is analyzed
7         X : Boolean;
```

```
8     begin
9        Sub_Action (X);
10       pragma Assert (X = True);
11    end Critical_Action;
12
13    procedure Sub_Action (X : out Boolean) with
14       SPARK_Mode => Off
15    is
16    begin
17       --  this procedure body is not analyzed
18       X := True;
19    end Sub_Action;
20
21    procedure Non_Critical_Action with
22       SPARK_Mode => Off
23    is
24    begin
25       --  this procedure body is not analyzed
26       null;
27    end Non_Critical_Action;
28
29 end Selected_Units;
```

Excluding Selected Unit Bodies

If a unit spec is in SPARK, but its body is not in SPARK, the spec can be marked with SPARK_Mode => On and the body with SPARK_Mode => Off. This allows client code in SPARK to use this unit. If SPARK_Mode is On by default, then it need not be repeated on the unit spec.

```
1  package Exclude_Unit_Body with
2     SPARK_Mode => On
3  is
4
5     type T is private;
6
7     function Get_Value return Integer;
8
9     procedure Set_Value (V : Integer) with
10       Post => Get_Value = V;
11
12 private
13    pragma SPARK_Mode (Off);
14
15    --  the private part of the package spec is not analyzed
16
17    type T is access Integer;
18 end Exclude_Unit_Body;
```

Note that the private part of the spec (which is physically in the spec file, but is logically part of the implementation) can be excluded as well, by using a pragma SPARK_Mode (Off) at the start of the private part.

```
1  package body Exclude_Unit_Body with
2     SPARK_Mode => Off
3  is
4     --  this package body is not analyzed
5
```

```
6      Value : T := new Integer;
7
8      function Get_Value return Integer is
9      begin
10        return Value.all;
11     end Get_Value;
12
13     procedure Set_Value (V : Integer) is
14     begin
15        Value.all := V;
16     end Set_Value;
17
18  end Exclude_Unit_Body;
```

This scheme also works on generic units, which can then be instantiated both in code where SPARK_Mode is On, in which case only the body of the instantiated generic is excluded, or in code where SPARK_Mode is Off, in which case both the spec and the body of the instantiated generic are excluded.

```
1  generic
2     type T is private;
3  package Exclude_Generic_Unit_Body with
4     SPARK_Mode => On
5  is
6     procedure Process (X : in out T);
7  end Exclude_Generic_Unit_Body;
```

```
1  package body Exclude_Generic_Unit_Body with
2     SPARK_Mode => Off
3  is
4     --  this package body is not analyzed
5     procedure Process (X : in out T) is
6     begin
7        null;
8     end Process;
9  end Exclude_Generic_Unit_Body;
```

```
1  with Exclude_Generic_Unit_Body;
2  pragma Elaborate_All (Exclude_Generic_Unit_Body);
3
4  package Use_Generic with
5     SPARK_Mode => On
6  is
7     --  the spec of this generic instance is analyzed
8     package G1 is new Exclude_Generic_Unit_Body (Integer);
9
10    procedure Do_Nothing;
11
12 end Use_Generic;
```

```
1  package body Use_Generic with
2     SPARK_Mode => Off
3  is
4     type T is access Integer;
5
6     --  this generic instance is not analyzed
7     package G2 is new Exclude_Generic_Unit_Body (T);
8
```

```
9    procedure Do_Nothing is
10   begin
11      null;
12   end Do_Nothing;
13
14 end Use_Generic;
```

Excluding Selected Parts of a Unit

If most units are in SPARK except from some subprograms and packages, it makes sense to set the default to
SPARK_Mode (On), and set SPARK_Mode => Off on non-SPARK declarations. We assume here that a value of
SPARK_Mode => On is specified as a configuration pragma.

```
1  package Exclude_Selected_Parts is
2
3     procedure Critical_Action;
4
5     procedure Non_Critical_Action;
6
7     package Non_Critical_Data with
8       SPARK_Mode => Off
9     is
10       type T is access Integer;
11       X : T;
12       function Get_X return Integer;
13     end Non_Critical_Data;
14
15 end Exclude_Selected_Parts;
```

Note that procedure Non_Critical_Action can be called inside SPARK code, because its spec is in SPARK,
even though its body is marked SPARK_Mode => Off.

Note also that the local package Non_Critical_Data can contain any non-SPARK types, variables and subpro-
grams, as it is marked SPARK_Mode => Off. It may be convenient to define such a local package to gather non-
SPARK declarations, which allows to mark globally the unit Exclude_Selected_Parts with SPARK_Mode
=> On.

```
1  package body Exclude_Selected_Parts is
2
3     procedure Critical_Action is
4     begin
5        -- this procedure body is analyzed
6        Non_Critical_Action;
7     end Critical_Action;
8
9     procedure Non_Critical_Action with
10       SPARK_Mode => Off
11    is
12    begin
13       -- this procedure body is not analyzed
14       null;
15    end Non_Critical_Action;
16
17    package body Non_Critical_Data with
18      SPARK_Mode => Off
19    is
```

```ada
20        -- this package body is not analyzed
21        function Get_X return Integer is
22        begin
23           return X.all;
24        end Get_X;
25     end Non_Critical_Data;
26
27  end Exclude_Selected_Parts;
```

OVERVIEW OF SPARK LANGUAGE

This chapter provides an overview of the SPARK language, detailing for each feature its consequences in terms of execution and formal verification. This is not a reference manual for the SPARK language, which can be found in:

- the Ada Reference Manual (for Ada features), and
- the SPARK 2014 Reference Manual (for SPARK-specific features)

More details on how GNAT compiles SPARK code can be found in the GNAT Reference Manual.

SPARK can be seen as a large subset of Ada with additional aspects/pragmas/attributes, the latest version SPARK 2014 being a much larger subset than previous versions of SPARK. It includes in particular:

- richer types (subtypes with bounds not known statically, discriminant records, type predicates)
- more flexible features to structure programs (function and operator overloading, early returns and exits, raise statements)
- code sharing features (generics, expression functions)
- object oriented features (tagged types, dispatching)
- concurrency features (tasks, protected objects)

In the rest of this chapter, the marker [Ada 2005] (resp. [Ada 2012]) is used to denote that a feature defined in Ada 2005 (resp. Ada 2012) is supported in SPARK, and the marker [Ravenscar] is used to denote that a concurrency feature from Ada which belongs to the Ravenscar profile is supported in SPARK. The marker [SPARK] is used to denote that a feature is specific to SPARK. Both the GNAT compiler and GNATprove analyzer support all features listed here.

Some code snippets presented in this section are available in the example called gnatprove_by_example distributed with the SPARK toolset. It can be found in the share/examples/spark directory below the directory where the toolset is installed, and can be accessed from the IDE (either GPS or GNATBench) via the *Help* → *SPARK* → *Examples* menu item.

5.1 Language Restrictions

5.1.1 Excluded Ada Features

To facilitate formal verification, SPARK enforces a number of global simplifications to Ada 2012. The most notable simplifications are:

- The use of access types and allocators is not permitted. Formal verification of programs with pointers requires tracking which memory is allocated and which memory has been freed, as well as separation between different blocks of memory, which are not doable precisely without a lot of manual work. As a replacement, SPARK provides rich generic data structures in the *Formal Containers Library*.

- All expressions (including function calls) are free of side-effects. Functions with side-effects are more complex to treat logically and may lead to non-deterministic evaluation due to conflicting side-effects in sub-expressions of an enclosing expression. Functions with side-effects should be written as procedures in SPARK.

- Aliasing of names is not permitted. Aliasing may lead to unexpected interferences, in which the value denoted locally by a given name changes as the result of an update to another locally named variable. Formal verification of programs with aliasing is less precise and requires more manual work. See *Absence of Interferences*.

- The goto statement is not permitted. Gotos can be used to create loops, which require a specific treatment in formal verification, and thus should be precisely identified. See *Loop Invariants* and *Loop Variants*.

- The use of controlled types is not permitted. Controlled types lead to the insertion of implicit calls by the compiler. Formal verification of implicit calls makes it harder for users to interact with formal verification tools, as there is no source code on which information can be reported.

- Handling of exceptions is not permitted. Exception handling gives raise to numerous interprocedural control-flow paths. Formal verification of programs with exception handlers requires tracking properties along all those paths, which is not doable precisely without a lot of manual work. But raising exceptions is allowed (see *Raising Exceptions and Other Error Signaling Mechanisms*).

The features listed above are excluded from SPARK because, currently, they defy formal verification. As formal verification technology advances the list will be revisited and it may be possible to relax some of these restrictions. There are other features which are technically feasible to formally verify but which are currently not supported in SPARK, such as access-to-subprogram types.

Uses of these features in SPARK code are detected by GNATprove and reported as errors. Formal verification is not possible on subprograms using these features. But these features can be used in subprograms in Ada not identified as SPARK code, see *Identifying SPARK Code*.

5.1.2 Partially Analyzed Ada Features

SPARK reinforces the strong typing of Ada with a stricter initialization policy (see *Data Initialization Policy*), and thus provides no means currently of specifying that some input data may be invalid. As a result, the following features are allowed in SPARK, but only partially analyzed by GNATprove:

- The result of a call to `Unchecked_Conversion` is assumed to be a valid value of the resulting type.

- The evaluation of attribute `Valid` is assumed to always return True.

This is illustrated in the following example:

```
1  package Validity with
2     SPARK_Mode
3  is
4
5     procedure Convert (X : Integer; Y : out Float);
6
7  end Validity;
```

```
1  with Ada.Unchecked_Conversion;
2
3  package body Validity with
4     SPARK_Mode
5  is
6
7     function Int_To_Float is new Ada.Unchecked_Conversion (Integer, Float);
8
9     procedure Convert (X : Integer; Y : out Float) is
10    begin
```

```
11        pragma Assert (X'Valid);
12        Y := Int_To_Float (X);
13        pragma Assert (Y'Valid);
14     end Convert;
15
16  end Validity;
```

GNATprove proves both assertions, but issues warnings about its assumptions that the evaluation of attribute `Valid` on both input parameter `X` and the result of the call to `Unchecked_Conversion` return True:

```
validity.adb:11:22: info: assertion proved
validity.adb:11:22: warning: attribute Valid is assumed to return True
validity.adb:13:22: info: assertion proved
validity.adb:13:22: info: initialization of "Y" proved
validity.adb:13:22: warning: attribute Valid is assumed to return True
validity.ads:5:36: info: initialization of "Y" proved
```

5.1.3 Data Initialization Policy

Modes on parameters and data dependency contracts (see *Data Dependencies*) in SPARK have a stricter meaning than in Ada:

- Parameter mode `in` (resp. global mode `Input`) indicates that the object denoted in the parameter (resp. data dependencies) should be completely initialized before calling the subprogram. It should not be written in the subprogram.

- Parameter mode `out` (resp. global mode `Output`) indicates that the object denoted in the parameter (resp. data dependencies) should be completely initialized before returning from the subprogram. It should not be read in the program prior to initialization.

- Parameter mode `in out` (resp. global mode `In_Out`) indicates that the object denoted in the parameter (resp. data dependencies) should be completely initialized before calling the subprogram. It can be written in the subprogram.

- Global mode `Proof_In` indicates that the object denoted in the data dependencies should be completely initialized before calling the subprogram. It should not be written in the subprogram, and only read in contracts and assertions.

Hence, all inputs should be completely initialized at subprogram entry, and all outputs should be completely initialized at subprogram output. Similarly, all objects should be completely initialized when read (e.g. inside subprograms), at the exception of record subcomponents (but not array subcomponents) provided the subcomponents that are read are initialized.

A consequence of the rules above is that a parameter (resp. global variable) that is partially written in a subprogram should be marked as `in out` (resp. `In_Out`), because the input value of the parameter (resp. global variable) is *read* when returning from the subprogram.

GNATprove will issue check messages if a subprogram does not respect the aforementioned data initialization policy. For example, consider a procedure `Proc` which has a parameter and a global item of each mode:

```
1  package Data_Initialization with
2    SPARK_Mode
3  is
4    type Data is record
5       Val : Float;
6       Num : Natural;
7    end record;
```

```
8
9      G1, G2, G3 : Data;
10
11     procedure Proc
12       (P1 : in      Data;
13        P2 :     out Data;
14        P3 : in out Data)
15     with
16       Global => (Input  => G1,
17                  Output => G2,
18                  In_Out => G3);
19
20     procedure Call_Proc with
21       Global => (Output => (G1, G2, G3));
22
23  end Data_Initialization;
```

Procedure `Proc` should completely initialize its outputs `P2` and `G2`, but it only initalizes them partially. Similarly, procedure `Call_Proc` which calls `Proc` should completely initalize all of `Proc`'s inputs prior to the call, but it only initalizes `G1` completely.

```
1   package body Data_Initialization with
2     SPARK_Mode
3   is
4
5     procedure Proc
6       (P1 : in      Data;
7        P2 :     out Data;
8        P3 : in out Data) is
9     begin
10       P2.Val := 0.0;
11       G2.Num := 0;
12       -- fail to completely initialize P2 and G2 before exit
13     end Proc;
14
15    procedure Call_Proc is
16       X1, X2, X3 : Data;
17    begin
18       X1.Val := 0.0;
19       X3.Num := 0;
20       G1.Val := 0.0;
21       G1.Num := 0;
22       -- fail to completely initialize X1, X3 and G3 before call
23       Proc (X1, X2, X3);
24    end Call_Proc;
25
26  end Data_Initialization;
```

On this program, GNATprove issues 6 high check messages, corresponding to the violations of the data initialization policy:

```
data_initialization.adb:23:07: high: "G3.Num" is not an input in the Global contract
↪of subprogram "Call_Proc" at data_initialization.ads:20
data_initialization.adb:23:07: high: "G3.Num" is not initialized
data_initialization.adb:23:07: high: "G3.Val" is not an input in the Global contract
↪of subprogram "Call_Proc" at data_initialization.ads:20
data_initialization.adb:23:07: high: "G3.Val" is not initialized
data_initialization.adb:23:07: high: either make "G3.Num" an input in the Global
↪contract or initialize it before use
```

```
data_initialization.adb:23:07: high: either make "G3.Val" an input in the Global
    contract or initialize it before use
data_initialization.adb:23:07: info: initialization of "G1.Num" proved
data_initialization.adb:23:07: info: initialization of "G1.Val" proved
data_initialization.adb:23:13: high: "X1.Num" is not initialized
data_initialization.adb:23:13: info: initialization of "X1.Val" proved
data_initialization.adb:23:17: warning: unused assignment to "X2"
data_initialization.adb:23:21: high: "X3.Val" is not initialized
data_initialization.adb:23:21: info: initialization of "X3.Num" proved
data_initialization.adb:23:21: warning: unused assignment to "X3"
data_initialization.ads:12:07: warning: unused variable "P1"
data_initialization.ads:13:07: high: "P2.Num" is not initialized in "Proc"
data_initialization.ads:13:07: info: initialization of "P2.Val" proved
data_initialization.ads:14:07: warning: "P3" is not modified, could be IN
data_initialization.ads:14:07: warning: unused variable "P3"
data_initialization.ads:16:27: low: unused global "G1"
data_initialization.ads:17:27: high: "G2.Val" is not an input in the Global contract
    of subprogram "Proc" at line 11
data_initialization.ads:17:27: high: "G2.Val" is not initialized
data_initialization.ads:17:27: high: either make "G2.Val" an input in the Global
    contract or initialize it before use
data_initialization.ads:17:27: info: initialization of "G2.Num" proved
data_initialization.ads:18:27: low: unused global "G3"
data_initialization.ads:18:27: warning: "G3" is not modified, could be INPUT
data_initialization.ads:21:28: info: initialization of "G1.Num" proved
data_initialization.ads:21:28: info: initialization of "G1.Val" proved
data_initialization.ads:21:32: info: initialization of "G2.Num" proved
data_initialization.ads:21:32: info: initialization of "G2.Val" proved
data_initialization.ads:21:36: info: initialization of "G3.Num" proved
data_initialization.ads:21:36: info: initialization of "G3.Val" proved
```

While a user can justify individually such messages with pragma `Annotate` (see section *Justifying Check Messages*), it is under her responsibility to then ensure correct initialization of subcomponents that are read, as GNATprove relies during proof on the property that data is properly initialized before being read.

Note also the various warnings that GNATprove issues on unused parameters, global items and assignments, also based on the stricter SPARK interpretation of parameter and global modes.

5.1.4 Absence of Interferences

In SPARK, an assignment to a variable cannot change the value of another variable. This is enforced by forbidding the use of access types (pointers) in SPARK, and by restricting aliasing between parameters and global variables so that only benign aliasing is accepted (i.e. aliasing that does not cause interference).

The precise rules detailed in SPARK RM 6.4.2 can be summarized as follows:

- Two output parameters should never be aliased.

- An input and an output parameters should not be aliased, unless the input parameter is always passed by copy.

- An output parameter should never be aliased with a global variable referenced by the subprogram.

- An input parameter should not be aliased with a global variable referenced by the subprogram, unless the input parameter is always passed by copy.

These rules extend the existing rules in Ada RM 6.4.1 for restricting aliasing, which already make it illegal to call a procedure with problematic (non-benign) aliasing between parameters of scalar type that are *known to denote the same object* (a notion formally defined in Ada RM).

For example, in the following example:

```
1  package Aliasing with
2     SPARK_Mode
3  is
4     Glob : Integer;
5
6     procedure Whatever (In_1, In_2 : Integer; Out_1, Out_2 : out Integer) with
7       Global => Glob;
8
9  end Aliasing;
```

Procedure `Whatever` can only be called on arguments that satisfy the following constraints:

1. Arguments for `Out_1` and `Out_2` should not be aliased.

2. Variable `Glob` should not be passed in argument for `Out_1` and `Out_2`.

Note that there are no constraints on input parameters `In_1` and `In_2`, as these are always passed by copy (being of a scalar type). This would not be the case if these input parameters were of a record or array type.

For example, here are examples of correct and illegal (according to Ada and SPARK rules) calls to procedure `Whatever`:

```
1  with Aliasing; use Aliasing;
2
3  procedure Check_Param_Aliasing with
4     SPARK_Mode
5  is
6     X, Y, Z : Integer := 0;
7  begin
8     Whatever (In_1 => X, In_2 => X, Out_1 => X, Out_2 => X);  --  illegal
9     Whatever (In_1 => X, In_2 => X, Out_1 => X, Out_2 => Y);  --  correct
10    Whatever (In_1 => X, In_2 => X, Out_1 => Y, Out_2 => X);  --  correct
11    Whatever (In_1 => Y, In_2 => Z, Out_1 => X, Out_2 => X);  --  illegal
12 end Check_Param_Aliasing;
```

GNATprove (like GNAT compiler, since these are also Ada rules) correctly detects the two illegal calls and issues errors:

```
check_param_aliasing.adb:8:45: writable actual for "Out_1" overlaps with actual for
  ."Out_2"
check_param_aliasing.adb:11:45: writable actual for "Out_1" overlaps with actual for
  ."Out_2"
```

Here are other examples of correct and incorrect calls (according to SPARK rules) to procedure `Whatever`:

```
1  with Aliasing; use Aliasing;
2
3  procedure Check_Aliasing with
4     SPARK_Mode
5  is
6     X, Y, Z : Integer := 0;
7  begin
8     Whatever (In_1 => X, In_2 => X, Out_1 => X, Out_2 => Glob);     --  incorrect
9     Whatever (In_1 => X, In_2 => Y, Out_1 => Z, Out_2 => Glob);     --  incorrect
10    Whatever (In_1 => Glob, In_2 => Glob, Out_1 => X, Out_2 => Y);  --  correct
11 end Check_Aliasing;
```

GNATprove correctly detects the two incorrect calls and issues high check messages:

```
check_aliasing.adb:8:22: info: initialization of "X" proved
check_aliasing.adb:8:57: high: formal parameter "Out_2" and global "Glob" are aliased
  ↪(SPARK RM 6.4.2)
```

5.1.5 Raising Exceptions and Other Error Signaling Mechanisms

Raising an exception is allowed in SPARK to signal an error, but handling the exception raised to perform recovery or mitigation actions is outside of the SPARK subset. Typically, such exception handling code should be added to top-level subprograms in full Ada, or to a last chance handler called by the runtime when an exception is raised, none of which is analyzed by GNATprove.

GNATprove treats raising an exception specially:

- in flow analysis, the program paths that lead to a `raise_statement` are not considered when checking the contract of the subprogram, which is only concerned with executions that terminate normally; and

- in proof, a check is generated for each `raise_statement`, to prove that no such program point is reachable.

Multiple error signaling mechanisms are treated the same way:

- raising an exception

- `pragma Assert (X)` where X is an expression statically equivalent to `False`

- calling a procedure with an aspect or pragma `No_Return` that has no outputs (unless the call is itself inside such a procedure, in which case the check is only generated on the call to the enclosing error-signaling procedure)

For example, consider the artificial subprogram `Check_OK` which raises an exception when parameter OK is `False`:

```
1   package Abnormal_Terminations with
2     SPARK_Mode
3   is
4
5     G1, G2 : Integer := 0;
6
7     procedure Check_OK (OK : Boolean) with
8       Global => (Output => G1),
9       Pre    => OK;
10
11  end Abnormal_Terminations;
```

```
1   package body Abnormal_Terminations with
2     SPARK_Mode
3   is
4
5     procedure Check_OK (OK : Boolean) is
6     begin
7       if OK then
8          G1 := 1;
9       else
10         G2 := 1;
11         raise Program_Error;
12      end if;
13     end Check_OK;
14
15  end Abnormal_Terminations;
```

Note that, although G2 is assigned in Check_OK, its assignment is directly followed by a raise_statement, so G2 is never assigned on an execution of Check_OK that terminates normally. As a result, G2 is not mentioned in the data dependencies of Check_OK. During flow analysis, GNATprove verifies that the body of Check_OK implements its declared data dependencies.

During proof, GNATprove generates a check that the raise_statement on line 11 is never reached. Here, it is proved thanks to the precondition of Check_OK which states that parameter OK should always be True on entry:

```
abnormal_terminations.adb:11:10: info: raise statement proved unreachable
abnormal_terminations.ads:8:27: info: initialization of "G1" proved
```

GNATprove also checks that procedures that are marked with aspect or pragma No_Return do not return: they should either raise an exception or loop forever on any input.

5.2 Subprogram Contracts

The most important feature to specify the intended behavior of a SPARK program is the ability to attach a contract to subprograms. In this document, a *subprogram* can be a procedure, a function or a protected entry. This contract is made up of various optional parts:

- The *precondition* introduced by aspect Pre specifies constraints on callers of the subprogram.

- The *postcondition* introduced by aspect Post specifies (partly or completely) the functional behavior of the subprogram.

- The *contract cases* introduced by aspect Contract_Cases is a way to partition the behavior of a subprogram. It can replace or complement a precondition and a postcondition.

- The *data dependencies* introduced by aspect Global specify the global data read and written by the subprogram.

- The *flow dependencies* introduced by aspect Depends specify how subprogram outputs depend on subprogram inputs.

Which contracts to write for a given verification objective, and how GNATprove generates default contracts, is detailed in *How to Write Subprogram Contracts*.

The contract on a subprogram describes the behavior of successful calls. Executions that end up by signalling an error, as described in *Raising Exceptions and Other Error Signaling Mechanisms*, are not covered by the subprogram's contract. A call to a subprogram is successful if execution terminates normally, or if execution loops without errors for a subprogram marked with aspect No_Return that has some outputs (this is typically the case of a non-terminating subprogram implementing the main loop of a controller).

5.2.1 Preconditions

[Ada 2012]

The precondition of a subprogram specifies constraints on callers of the subprogram. Typically, preconditions are written as conjunctions of constraints that fall in one of the following categories:

- exclusion of forbidden values of parameter, for example X /= 0 or Y not in Active_States

- specification of allowed parameter values, for example X in 1 .. 10 or Y in Idle_States

- relations that should hold between parameter values, for example (if Y in Active_State then Z /= Null_State)

- expected values of global variables denoting the state of the computation, for example `Current_State` in `Active_States`

- invariants about the global state that should hold when calling this subprogram, for example `Is_Complete (State_Mapping)`

- relations involving the global state and input parameters that should hold when calling this subprogram, for example `X in Next_States (Global_Map, Y)`

When the program is compiled with assertions (for example with switch `-gnata` in GNAT), the precondition of a subprogram is checked at run time every time the subprogram is called. An exception is raised if the precondition fails. Not all assertions need to be enabled though. For example, a common idiom is to enable only preconditions (and not other assertions) in the production binary, by setting pragma `Assertion_Policy` as follows:

```
pragma Assertion_Policy (Pre => Check);
```

When a subprogram is analyzed with GNATprove, its precondition is used to restrict the contexts in which it may be executed, which is required in general to prove that the subprogram's implementation:

- is free from run-time errors (see *Writing Contracts for Program Integrity*); and

- ensures that the postcondition of the subprogram always holds (see *Writing Contracts for Functional Correctness*).

In particular, the default precondition of `True` used by GNATprove when no explicit one is given may not be precise enough, unless it can be analyzed in the context of its callers by GNATprove (see *Contextual Analysis of Subprograms Without Contracts*). When a caller is analyzed with GNATprove, it checks that the precondition of the called subprogram holds at the point of call. And even when the implementation of the subprogram is not analyzed with GNATprove, it may be necessary to add a precondition to the subprogram for analyzing its callers (see *Writing Contracts on Imported Subprograms*).

For example, consider the procedure `Add_To_Total` which increments global counter `Total` by the value given in parameter `Incr`. To ensure that there are no integer overflows in the implementation, `Incr` should not be too large, which a user can express with the following precondition:

```
procedure Add_To_Total (Incr : in Integer) with
  Pre => Incr >= 0 and then Total <= Integer'Last - Incr;
```

To ensure that the value of `Total` remains non-negative, one should also add the condition `Total >= 0` to the precondition:

```
procedure Add_To_Total (Incr : in Integer) with
  Pre => Incr >= 0 and then Total in 0 .. Integer'Last - Incr;
```

Finally, GNATprove also analyzes preconditions to ensure that they are free from run-time errors in all contexts. This may require writing the precondition in a special way. For example, the precondition of `Add_To_Total` above uses the shortcut boolean operator `and then` instead of `and`, so that calling the procedure in a context where `Incr` is negative does not result in an overflow when evaluating `Integer'Last - Incr`. Instead, the use of `and then` ensures that a precondition failure will occur before the expression `Integer'Last - Incr` is evaluated.

Note: It is good practice to use the shortcut boolean operator `and then` instead of `and` in preconditions. This is required in some cases by GNATprove to prove absence of run-time errors inside preconditions.

5.2.2 Postconditions

[Ada 2012]

The postcondition of a subprogram specifies partly or completely the functional behavior of the subprogram. Typically, postconditions are written as conjunctions of properties that fall in one of the following categories:

- possible values returned by a function, using the special attribute `Result` (see *Attribute Result*), for example `Get'Result in Active_States`

- possible values of output parameters, for example `Y in Active_States`

- expected relations between output parameter values, for example `if Success then Y /= Null_State`

- expected relations between input and output parameter values, possibly using the special attribute `Old` (see *Attribute Old*), for example `if Success then Y /= Y'Old`

- expected values of global variables denoting updates to the state of the computation, for example `Current_State in Active_States`

- invariants about the global state that should hold when returning from this subprogram, for example `Is_Complete (State_Mapping)`

- relations involving the global state and output parameters that should hold when returning from this subprogram, for example `X in Next_States (Global_Map, Y)`

When the program is compiled with assertions (for example with switch `-gnata` in GNAT), the postcondition of a subprogram is checked at run time every time the subprogram returns. An exception is raised if the postcondition fails. Usually, postconditions are enabled during tests, as they provide dynamically checkable oracles of the intended behavior of the program, and disabled in the production binary for efficiency.

When a subprogram is analyzed with GNATprove, it checks that the postcondition of a subprogram cannot fail. This verification is modular: GNATprove considers all calling contexts in which the precondition of the subprogram holds for the analysis of a subprogram. GNATprove also analyzes postconditions to ensure that they are free from run-time errors, like any other assertion.

For example, consider the procedure `Add_To_Total` which increments global counter `Total` with the value given in parameter `Incr`. This intended behavior can be expressed in its postcondition:

```
procedure Add_To_Total (Incr : in Integer) with
  Post => Total = Total'Old + Incr;
```

The postcondition of a subprogram is used to analyze calls to the subprograms. In particular, the default postcondition of `True` used by GNATprove when no explicit one is given may not be precise enough to prove properties of its callers, unless it analyzes the subprogam's implementation in the context of its callers (see *Contextual Analysis of Subprograms Without Contracts*).

Recursive subprograms and mutually recursive subprograms are treated in this respect exactly like non-recursive ones. Provided the execution of these subprograms always terminates (a property that is not verified by GNATprove), then GNATprove correctly checks that their postcondition is respected by using this postcondition for recursive calls.

Special care should be exercized for functions that return a boolean, as a common mistake is to write the expected boolean result as the postcondition:

```
function Total_Above_Threshold (Threshold : in Integer) return Boolean with
  Post => Total > Threshold;
```

while the correct postcondition uses *Attribute Result*:

```
function Total_Above_Threshold (Threshold : in Integer) return Boolean with
  Post => Total_Above_Threshold'Result = Total > Threshold;
```

Both GNAT compiler and GNATprove issue a warning on the semantically correct but likely functionally wrong postcondition.

5.2.3 Contract Cases

[SPARK]

When a subprogram has a fixed set of different functional behaviors, it may be more convenient to specify these behaviors as contract cases rather than a postcondition. For example, consider a variant of procedure Add_To_Total which either increments global counter Total by the given parameter value when possible, or saturates at a given threshold. Each of these behaviors can be defined in a contract case as follows:

```
procedure Add_To_Total (Incr : in Integer) with
  Contract_Cases => (Total + Incr < Threshold  => Total = Total'Old + Incr,
                     Total + Incr >= Threshold => Total = Threshold);
```

Each contract case consists in a guard and a consequence separated by the symbol =>. When the guard evaluates to True on subprogram entry, the corresponding consequence should also evaluate to True on subprogram exit. We say that this contract case was enabled for the call. Exactly one contract case should be enabled for each call, or said equivalently, the contract cases should be disjoint and complete.

For example, the contract cases of Add_To_Total express that the subprogram should be called in two distinct cases only:

- on inputs that can be added to Total to obtain a value strictly less than a given threshold, in which case Add_To_Total adds the input to Total.

- on inputs whose addition to Total exceeds the given threshold, in which case Add_To_Total sets Total to the threshold value.

When the program is compiled with assertions (for example with switch -gnata in GNAT), all guards are evaluated on entry to the subprogram, and there is a run-time check that exactly one of them is True. For this enabled contract case, there is another run-time check when returning from the subprogram that the corresponding consequence evaluates to True.

When a subprogram is analyzed with GNATprove, it checks that there is always exactly one contract case enabled, and that the consequence of the contract case enabled cannot fail. If the subprogram also has a precondition, GNATprove performs these checks only for inputs that satisfy the precondition, otherwise for all inputs.

In the simple example presented above, there are various ways to express an equivalent postcondition, in particular using *Conditional Expressions*:

```
procedure Add_To_Total (Incr : in Integer) with
  Post => (if Total'Old + Incr < Threshold  then
             Total = Total'Old + Incr
           else
             Total = Threshold);

procedure Add_To_Total (Incr : in Integer) with
  Post => Total = (if Total'Old + Incr < Threshold then Total'Old + Incr else
 Threshold);

procedure Add_To_Total (Incr : in Integer) with
  Post => Total = Integer'Min (Total'Old + Incr, Threshold);
```

In general, an equivalent postcondition may be cumbersome to write and less readable. Contract cases also provide a way to automatically verify that the input space is partitioned in the specified cases, which may not be obvious with a single expression in a postcondition when there are many cases.

The guard of the last case may be others, to denote all cases not captured by previous contract cases. For example, the contract of Add_To_Total may be written:

```
procedure Add_To_Total (Incr : in Integer) with
  Contract_Cases => (Total + Incr < Threshold => Total = Total'Old + Incr,
                     others                    => Total = Threshold);
```

When others is used as a guard, there is no need for verification (both at run-time and using GNATprove) that the set of contract cases covers all possible inputs. Only disjointness of contract cases is checked in that case.

5.2.4 Data Dependencies

[SPARK]

The data dependencies of a subprogram specify the global data that a subprogram is allowed to read and write. Together with the parameters, they completely specify the inputs and outputs of a subprogram. Like parameters, the global variables mentioned in data dependencies have a mode: Input for inputs, Output for outputs and In_Out for global variables that are both inputs and outputs. A last mode of Proof_In is defined for inputs that are only read in contracts and assertions. For example, data dependencies can be specified for procedure Add_To_Total which increments global counter Total as follows:

```
procedure Add_To_Total (Incr : in Integer) with
  Global => (In_Out => Total);
```

For protected subprograms, the protected object is considered as an implicit parameter of the subprogram:

- it is an implicit parameter of mode in of a protected function; and

- it is an implicit parameter of mode in out of a protected procedure or a protected entry.

Data dependencies have no impact on compilation and the run-time behavior of a program. When a subprogram is analyzed with GNATprove, it checks that the implementation of the subprogram:

- only reads global inputs mentioned in its data dependencies,

- only writes global outputs mentioned in its data dependencies, and

- always completely initializes global outputs that are not also inputs.

See *Data Initialization Policy* for more details on this analysis of GNATprove. During its analysis, GNATprove uses the specified data dependencies of callees to analyze callers, if present, otherwise a default data dependency contract is generated (see *Generation of Dependency Contracts*) for callees.

There are various benefits when specifying data dependencies on a subprogram, which gives various reasons for users to add such contracts:

- GNATprove verifies automatically that the subprogram implementation respects the specified accesses to global data.

- GNATprove uses the specified contract during flow analysis, to analyze the data and flow dependencies of the subprogram's callers, which may result in a more precise analysis (less false alarms) than with the generated data dependencies.

- GNATprove uses the specified contract during proof, to check absence of run-time errors and the functional contract of the subprogram's callers, which may also result in a more precise analysis (less false alarms) than with the generated data dependencies.

When data dependencies are specified on a subprogram, they should mention all global data read and written in the subprogram. When a subprogram has neither global inputs nor global outputs, it can be specified using the null data dependencies:

```
function Get (X : T) return Integer with
  Global => null;
```

When a subprogram has only global inputs but no global outputs, it can be specified either using the `Input` mode:

```
function Get_Sum return Integer with
  Global => (Input => (X, Y, Z));
```

or equivalently without any mode:

```
function Get_Sum return Integer with
  Global => (X, Y, Z);
```

Note the use of parentheses around a list of global inputs or outputs for a given mode.

Global data that is both read and written should be mentioned with the `In_Out` mode, and not as both input and output. For example, the following data dependencies on `Add_To_Total` are illegal and rejected by GNATprove:

```
procedure Add_To_Total (Incr : in Integer) with
  Global => (Input  => Total,
             Output => Total);   --  INCORRECT
```

Global data that is partially written in the subprogram should also be mentioned with the `In_Out` mode, and not as an output. See *Data Initialization Policy*.

5.2.5 Flow Dependencies

[SPARK]

The flow dependencies of a subprogram specify how its outputs (both output parameters and global outputs) depend on its inputs (both input parameters and global inputs). For example, flow dependencies can be specified for procedure `Add_To_Total` which increments global counter `Total` as follows:

```
procedure Add_To_Total (Incr : in Integer) with
  Depends => (Total => (Total, Incr));
```

The above flow dependencies can be read as "the output value of global variable `Total` depends on the input values of global variable `Total` and parameter `Incr`".

Outputs (both parameters and global variables) may have an implicit input part depending on their type:

- an unconstrained array A has implicit input bounds `A'First` and `A'Last`
- a discriminated record R has implicit input discriminants, for example `R.Discr`

Thus, an output array A and an output discriminated record R may appear in input position inside a flow-dependency contract, to denote the input value of the bounds (for the array) or the discriminants (for the record).

For protected subprograms, the protected object is considered as an implicit parameter of the subprogram which may be mentioned in the flow dependencies, under the name of the protected unit (type or object) being declared:

- as an implicit parameter of mode `in` of a protected function, it can be mentioned on the right-hand side of flow dependencies; and
- as an implicit parameter of mode `in out` of a protected procedure or a protected entry, it can be mentioned on both sides of flow dependencies.

Flow dependencies have no impact on compilation and the run-time behavior of a program. When a subprogram is analyzed with GNATprove, it checks that, in the implementation of the subprogram, outputs depend on inputs as specified in the flow dependencies. During its analysis, GNATprove uses the specified flow dependencies of callees to analyze callers, if present, otherwise a default flow dependency contract is generated for callees (see *Generation of Dependency Contracts*).

When flow dependencies are specified on a subprogram, they should mention all flows from inputs to outputs. In particular, the output value of a parameter or global variable that is partially written by a subprogram depends on its input value (see *Data Initialization Policy*).

When the output value of a parameter or global variable depends on its input value, the corresponding flow dependency can use the shorthand symbol + to denote that a variable's output value depends on the variable's input value plus any other input listed. For example, the flow dependencies of Add_To_Total above can be specified equivalently:

```
procedure Add_To_Total (Incr : in Integer) with
  Depends => (Total =>+ Incr);
```

When an output value depends on no input value, meaning that it is completely (re)initialized with constants that do not depend on variables, the corresponding flow dependency should use the null input list:

```
procedure Init_Total with
  Depends => (Total => null);
```

5.2.6 State Abstraction and Contracts

[SPARK]

The subprogram contracts mentioned so far always used directly global variables. In many cases, this is not possible because the global variables are defined in another unit and not directly visible (because they are defined in the private part of a package specification, or in a package implementation). The notion of abstract state in SPARK can be used in that case (see *State Abstraction*) to name in contracts global data that is not visible.

State Abstraction and Dependencies

Suppose the global variable Total incremented by procedure Add_To_Total is defined in the package implementation, and a procedure Cash_Tickets in a client package calls Add_To_Total. Package Account which defines Total can define an abstract state State that represents Total, as seen in *State Abstraction*, which allows using it in Cash_Tickets's data and flow dependencies:

```
procedure Cash_Tickets (Tickets : Ticket_Array) with
  Global  => (Output => Account.State),
  Depends => (Account.State => Tickets);
```

As global variable Total is not visible from clients of unit Account, it is not visible either in the visible part of Account's specification. Hence, externally visible subprograms in Account must also use abstract state State in their data and flow dependencies, for example:

```
procedure Init_Total with
  Global  => (Output => State),
  Depends => (State => null);

procedure Add_To_Total (Incr : in Integer) with
  Global  => (In_Out => State),
  Depends => (State =>+ Incr);
```

Then, the implementations of Init_Total and Add_To_Total can define refined data and flow dependencies introduced respectively by Refined_Global and Refined_Depends, which give the precise dependencies for these subprograms in terms of concrete variables:

```
procedure Init_Total with
  Refined_Global  => (Output => Total),
```

```
   Refined_Depends => (Total => null)
is
begin
   Total := 0;
end Init_Total;

procedure Add_To_Total (Incr : in Integer) with
  Refined_Global  => (In_Out => Total),
  Refined_Depends => (Total =>+ Incr)
is
begin
   Total := Total + Incr;
end Add_To_Total;
```

Here, the refined dependencies are the same as the abstract ones where `State` has been replaced by `Total`, but that's not always the case, in particular when the abstract state is refined into multiple concrete variables (see *State Abstraction*). GNATprove checks that:

- each abstract global input has at least one of its constituents mentioned by the concrete global inputs
- each abstract global in_out has at least one of its constituents mentioned with mode input and one with mode output (or at least one constituent with mode in_out)
- each abstract global output has to have all its constituents mentioned by the concrete global outputs
- the concrete flow dependencies are a subset of the abstract flow dependencies

GNATprove uses the abstract contract (data and flow dependencies) of `Init_Total` and `Add_To_Total` when analyzing calls outside package `Account` and the more precise refined contract (refined data and flow dependencies) of `Init_Total` and `Add_To_Total` when analyzing calls inside package `Account`.

Refined dependencies can be specified on both subprograms and tasks for which data and/or flow dependencies that are specified include abstract states which are refined in the current unit.

State Abstraction and Functional Contracts

If global variables are not visible for data dependencies, they are not visible either for functional contracts. For example, in the case of procedure `Add_To_Total`, if global variable `Total` is not visible, we cannot express anymore the precondition and postcondition of `Add_To_Total` as in *Preconditions* and *Postconditions*. Instead, we define accessor functions to retrieve properties of the state that we need to express, and we use these in contracts. For example here:

```
function Get_Total return Integer;

procedure Add_To_Total (Incr : in Integer) with
  Pre  => Incr >= 0 and then Get_Total in 0 .. Integer'Last - Incr,
  Post => Get_Total = Get_Total'Old + Incr;
```

Function `Get_Total` may be defined either in the private part of package `Account` or in its implementation. It may take the form of a regular function or an expression function (see *Expression Functions*), for example:

```
Total : Integer;

function Get_Total return Integer is (Total);
```

Although no refined preconditions and postconditions are required on the implementation of `Add_To_Total`, it is possible to provide a refined postcondition introduced by `Refined_Post` in that case, which specifies a more precise functional behavior of the subprogram. For example, procedure `Add_To_Total` may also increment the value of a counter `Call_Count` at each call, which can be expressed in the refined postcondition:

```
procedure Add_To_Total (Incr : in Integer) with
  Refined_Post => Total = Total'Old + Incr and Call_Count = Call_Count'Old + 1
is

  ...
end Add_To_Total;
```

A refined postcondition can be given on a subprogram implementation even when the unit does not use state abstraction, and even when the default postcondition of `True` is used implicitly on the subprogram declaration.

GNATprove uses the abstract contract (precondition and postcondition) of `Add_To_Total` when analyzing calls outside package `Account` and the more precise refined contract (precondition and refined postcondition) of `Add_To_Total` when analyzing calls inside package `Account`.

5.3 Package Contracts

Subprograms are not the only entities to bear contracts in SPARK. Package contracts are made up of various optional parts:

- The *state abstraction* specifies how global variables defined in the package are referred to abstractly where they are not visible. Aspect `Abstract_State` introduces abstract names and aspect `Refined_State` specifies the mapping between these names and global variables.

- The *package initialization* introduced by aspect `Initializes` specifies which global data (global variables and abstract state) defined in the package is initialized at package startup.

- The *package initial condition* introduced by aspect `Initial_Condition` specifies the properties holding after package startup.

Package startup (a.k.a. package *elaboration* in Ada RM) consists in the evaluation of all declarations in the package specification and implementation, in particular the evaluation of constant declarations and those variable declarations which contain an initialization expression, as well as the statements sometimes given at the end of a package body that are precisely executed at package startup.

5.3.1 State Abstraction

[SPARK]

The state abstraction of a package specifies a mapping between abstract names and concrete global variables defined in the package. State abstraction allows to define *Subprogram Contracts* at an abstract level that does not depend on a particular choice of implementation (see *State Abstraction and Contracts*), which is better both for maintenance (no need to change contracts) and scalability of analysis (contracts can be much smaller).

Basic State Abstraction

One abstract name may be mapped to more than one concrete variable, but no two abstract names can be mapped to the same concrete variable. When state abstraction is specified on a package, all non-visible global variables defined in the private part of the package specification and in its implementation should be mapped to abstract names. Thus, abstract names correspond to a partitioning of the non-visible global variables defined in the package.

The simplest use of state abstraction is to define a single abstract name (conventionally called `State`) to denote all non-visible global variables defined in the package. For example, consider package `Account` defining a global variable `Total` in its implementation, which is abstracted as `State`:

```
package Account with
  Abstract_State => State
is
   . . .
end Account;

package body Account with
  Refined_State => (State => Total)
is
   Total : Integer;
   . . .
end Account;
```

The aspect `Refined_State` maps each abstract name to a list of concrete global variables defined in the package. The list can be simply `null` to serve as placeholder for future definitions of global variables. Instead of concrete global variables, one can also use abstract names for the state of nested packages and private child packages, whose state is considered to be also defined in the parent package.

If global variable `Total` is defined in the private part of `Account`'s package specification, then the declaration of `Total` must use the special aspect `Part_Of` to declare its membership in abstract state `State`:

```
package Account with
  Abstract_State => State
is
   . . .
private
   Total : Integer with Part_Of => State;
   . . .
end Account;
```

This ensures that `Account`'s package specification can be checked by GNATprove even if its implementation is not in SPARK, or not available for analysis, or not yet developed.

A package with state abstraction must have a package body that states how abstract states are refined in aspect `Refined_State`, unless the package body is not in SPARK. If there is no other reason for the package to have a body, then one should use `pragma Elaborate_Body` in the package spec to make it legal for the package to have a body on which to express state refinement.

In general, an abstract name corresponds to multiple global variables defined in the package. For example, we can imagine adding global variables to log values passed in argument to procedure `Add_To_Total`, that are also mapped to abstract name `State`:

```
package Account with
  Abstract_State => State
is
   . . .
end Account;

package body Account with
  Refined_State => (State => (Total, Log, Log_Size))
is
   Total    : Integer;
   Log      : Integer_Array;
   Log_Size : Natural;
   . . .
end Account;
```

We can also imagine defining different abstract names for the total and the log:

```
package Account with
  Abstract_State => (State, Internal_State)
is
  ...
end Account;

package body Account with
  Refined_State => (State => Total,
                    Internal_State => (Log, Log_Size))
is
   Total    : Integer;
   Log      : Integer_Array;
   Log_Size : Natural;
   ...
end Account;
```

The abstract names defined in a package are visible everywhere the package name itself is visible:

- in the scope where the package is declared, for a locally defined package

- in units that have a clause with <package>;

- in units that have a clause limited with <package>;

The last case allows subprograms in two packages to mutually reference the abstract state of the other package in their data and flow dependencies.

Special Cases of State Abstraction

Global constants with a statically known value are not part of a package's state. On the contrary, *constant with variable inputs* are constants whose value depends on the value of either a variable or a subprogram parameter. Since they participate in the flow of information between variables, constants with variable inputs are treated like variables: they are part of a package's state, and they must be listed in its state refinement whenever they are not visible. For example, constant Total_Min is not part of the state refinement of package Account below, while constant with variable inputs Total_Max is part of it:

```
package body Account with
  Refined_State => (State => (Total, Total_Max))
is
   Total     : Integer;
   Total_Min : constant Integer := 0;
   Total_Max : constant Integer := Compute_Total_Max(...);
   ...
end Account;
```

Global variables are not always the only constituents of a package's state. For example, if a package P contains a nested package N, then N's state is part of P's state. As a consequence, if N is hidden, then its state must be listed in P's refinement. For example, we can nest Account in the body of the Account_Manager package as follows:

```
package Account_Manager with
  Abstract_State => State
is
  ...
end Account_Manager;

package body Account_Manager with
  Refined_State => (State => Account.State)
```

```
is
   package Account with
     Abstract_State => State
   is
     . . .
   end Account;
   . . .
end Account_Manager;
```

State In The Private Part

Global variables and nested packages which themselves contain state may be declared in the private part of a package.
For each such global variable and nested package state, it is mandatory to identify, using aspect Part_Of, the abstract
state of the enclosing package of which it is a constituent:

```
package Account_Manager with
  Abstract_State => (Totals, Details)
is
   . . .
private
   Total_Accounts : Integer with Part_Of => Totals;

   package Account with
     Abstract_State => (State with Part_Of => Details)
   is
      Total : Integer with Part_Of => Totals;
      . . .
   end Account;
   . . .
end Account_Manager;
```

The purpose of using Part_Of is to enforce that each constituent of an abstract state is known at the declaration of
the constituent (not having to look at the package body), which is useful for both code understanding and tool analysis
(including compilation).

As the state of a private child package is logically part of its parent package, aspect Part_Of must also be specified
in that case:

```
private package Account_Manager.Account with
  Abstract_State => (State with Part_Of => Details)
is
   Total : Integer with Part_Of => Totals;
   . . .
end Account_Manager.Account;
```

Aspect Part_Of can also be specified on a generic package instantiation inside a private part, to specify that all the
state (visible global variables and abstract states) of the package instantiation is a constituent of an abstract state of the
enclosing package:

```
package Account_Manager with
  Abstract_State => (Totals, Details)
is
   . . .
private
   package Account is new Generic_Account (Max_Total) with Part_Of => Details;
```

```
      ...
end Account_Manager;
```

5.3.2 Package Initialization

[SPARK]

The package initialization specifies which global data (global variables, constant with variable inputs, and abstract state) defined in the package is initialized at package startup. The corresponding global variables may either be initialized at declaration, or by the package body statements. Thus, package initialization can be seen as the output data dependencies of the package elaboration procedure generated by the compiler.

For example, we can specify that the state of package Account is initialized at package startup as follows:

```
package Account with
   Abstract_State => State,
   Initializes    => State
is
   ...
end Account;
```

Then, unless Account's implementation is not in SPARK, it should initialize the corresponding global variable Total either at declaration:

```
package body Account with
   Refined_State => (State => Total)
is
   Total : Integer := 0;
   ...
end Account;
```

or in the package body statements:

```
package body Account with
   Refined_State => (State => Total)
is
   Total : Integer;
   ...
begin
   Total := 0;
end Account;
```

These initializations need not correspond to direct assignments, but may be performed in a call, for example here to procedure Init_Total as seen in *State Abstraction and Dependencies*. A mix of initializations at declaration and in package body statements is also possible.

Package initializations also serve as dependency contracts for global variables' initial values. That is, if the initial value of a global variable, state abstraction, or constant with variable inputs listed in a package initialization depends on the value of a variable defined outside the package, then this dependency must be listed in the package's initialization. For example, we can initialize Total by reading the value of an external variable:

```
package Account with
   Abstract_State => State,
   Initializes    => (State => External_Variable)
is
   ...
```

```
end Account;

package body Account with
  Refined_State => (State => Total)
is
   Total : Integer := External_Variable;
   ...
end Account;
```

5.3.3 Package Initial Condition

[SPARK]

The package initial condition specifies the properties holding after package startup. Thus, package initial condition can be seen as the postcondition of the package elaboration procedure generated by the compiler. For example, we can specify that the value of Total defined in package Account's implementation is initially zero:

```
package Account with
  Abstract_State    => State,
  Initial_Condition => Get_Total = 0
is
   function Get_Total return Integer;
   ...
end Account;
```

This is ensured either by initializing Total with value zero at declaration, or by assigning the value zero to Total in the package body statements, as seen in *Package Initialization*.

When the program is compiled with assertions (for example with switch -gnata in GNAT), the initial condition of a package is checked at run time after package startup. An exception is raised if the initial condition fails.

When a package is analyzed with GNATprove, it checks that the initial condition of a package cannot fail. GNATprove also analyzes the initial condition expression to ensure that it is free from run-time errors, like any other assertion.

5.3.4 Interfaces to the Physical World

[SPARK]

Volatile Variables

Most embedded programs interact with the physical world or other programs through so-called *volatile* variables, which are identified as volatile to protect them from the usual compiler optimizations. In SPARK, volatile variables are also analyzed specially, so that possible changes to their value from outside the program are taken into account, and so that changes to their value from inside the program are also interpreted correctly (in particular for checking flow dependencies).

For example, consider package Volatile_Or_Not which defines a volatile variable V and a non-volatile variable N, and procedure Swap_Then_Zero which starts by swapping the values of V and N before zeroing them out:

```
1  package Volatile_Or_Not with
2    SPARK_Mode,
3    Initializes => V
4  is
5     V : Integer with Volatile;
```

```
6     N : Integer;
7
8     procedure Swap_Then_Zero with
9       Global  => (In_Out => (N, V)),
10      Depends => (V => N, N => null, null => V);
11
12  end Volatile_Or_Not;
```

```
1   package body Volatile_Or_Not with
2     SPARK_Mode
3   is
4     procedure Swap_Then_Zero is
5        Tmp : constant Integer := V;
6     begin
7        --  Swap values of V and N
8        V := N;
9        N := Tmp;
10       --  Zero out values of V and N
11       V := 0;
12       N := 0;
13    end Swap_Then_Zero;
14
15  end Volatile_Or_Not;
```

Compare the difference in contracts between volatile variable V and non-volatile variable N:

- The *Package Initialization* of package Volatile_Or_Not mentions V although this variable is not initialized at declaration or in the package body statements. This is because a volatile variable is assumed to be initialized.

- The *Flow Dependencies* of procedure Swap_Then_Zero are very different for V and N. If both variables were not volatile, the correct contract would state that both input values are not used with null => (V, N) and that both output values depend on no inputs with (V, N) => null. The difference lies with the special treatment of volatile variable V: as its value may be read at any time, the intermediate value N assigned to V on line 8 of volatile_or_not.adb needs to be mentioned in the flow dependencies for output V.

GNATprove checks that Volatile_Or_Not and Swap_Then_Zero implement their contract, and it issues a warning on the first assignment to N:

```
volatile_or_not.adb:9:09: warning: unused assignment
```

This warning points to a real issue, as the intermediate value of N is not used before N is zeroed out on line 12. But note that no warning is issued on the similar first assignment to V, because the intermediate value of V may be read outside the program before V is zeroed out on line 11.

Note that in real code, the memory address of the volatile variable is set through aspect Address or the corresponding representation clause, so that it can be read or written outside the program.

Flavors of Volatile Variables

Not all volatile variables are read and written outside the program, sometimes they are only read or only written outside the program. For example, the log introduced in *State Abstraction* could be implemented as an output port for the program logging the information, and as an input port for the program performing the logging. Two aspects are defined in SPARK to distinguish these different flavors of volatile variables:

- Aspect Async_Writers indicates that the value of the variable may be changed at any time (asynchronously) by hardware or software outside the program.

- Aspect `Async_Readers` indicates that the value of the variable may be read at any time (asynchronously) by hardware or software outside the program.

Aspect `Async_Writers` has an effect on GNATprove's proof: two successive reads of such a variable may return different results. Aspect `Async_Readers` has an effect on GNATprove's flow analysis: an assignment to such a variable always has a potential effect, even if the value is never read in the program, since an external reader might actually read the value assigned.

These aspects are well suited to model respectively a sensor and a display, but not an input stream or an actuator, for which the act of reading or writing has an effect that should be reflected in the flow dependencies. Two more aspects are defined in SPARK to further refine the previous flavors of volatile variables:

- Aspect `Effective_Reads` indicates that reading the value of the variable has an effect (for example, removing a value from an input stream). It can only be specified on a variable that also has `Async_Writers` set.

- Aspect `Effective_Writes` indicates that writing the value of the variable has an effect (for example, sending a command to an actuator). It can only be specified on a variable that also has `Async_Readers` set.

Both aspects `Effective_Reads` and `Effective_Writes` have an effect on GNATprove's flow analysis: reading the former or writing the latter is modelled as having an effect on the value of the variable, which needs to be reflected in flow dependencies. Because reading a variable with `Effective_Reads` set has an effect on its value, such a variable cannot be only a subprogram input, it must be also an output.

For example, the program writing in a log each value passed as argument to procedure `Add_To_Total` may model the output port `Log_Out` as a volatile variable with `Async_Readers` and `Effective_Writes` set:

```
1  package Logging_Out with
2     SPARK_Mode
3  is
4     Total    : Integer;
5     Log_Out : Integer with Volatile, Async_Readers, Effective_Writes;
6
7     procedure Add_To_Total (Incr : in Integer) with
8        Global  => (In_Out => Total, Output => Log_Out),
9        Depends => (Total =>+ Incr, Log_Out => Incr);
10
11 end Logging_Out;
```

```
1  package body Logging_Out with
2     SPARK_Mode
3  is
4     procedure Add_To_Total (Incr : in Integer) is
5     begin
6        Total := Total + Incr;
7        Log_Out := Incr;
8     end Add_To_Total;
9
10 end Logging_Out;
```

while the logging program may model the input port `Log_In` as a volatile variable with `Async_Writers` and `Effective_Reads` set:

```
1  package Logging_In with
2     SPARK_Mode
3  is
4     Log_In : Integer with Volatile, Async_Writers, Effective_Reads;
5
6     type Integer_Array is array (Positive range 1 .. 100) of Integer;
```

```
7    Log       : Integer_Array;
8    Log_Size : Natural;
9
10   procedure Get with
11     Global  => (In_Out => (Log, Log_Size, Log_In)),
12     Depends => ((Log_Size, Log_In) =>+ null, Log =>+ (Log_Size, Log_In));
13
14 end Logging_In;
```

```
1  package body Logging_In with
2    SPARK_Mode
3  is
4    procedure Get is
5    begin
6       Log_Size := Log_Size + 1;
7       Log (Log_Size) := Log_In;
8    end Get;
9
10 end Logging_In;
```

GNATprove checks the specified data and flow dependencies on both programs.

A volatile variable on which none of the four aspects `Async_Writers`, `Async_Readers`, `Effective_Reads` or `Effective_Writes` is set is assumed to have all four aspects set to `True`. A volatile variable on which some of the four aspects are set to `True` is assumed to have the remaining ones set to `False`. See SPARK RM 7.1.3 for details.

External State Abstraction

Volatile variables may be part of *State Abstraction*, in which case the volatility of the abstract name must be specified by using aspect `External` on the abstract name, as follows:

```
package Account with
  Abstract_State => (State with External)
is
  ...
end Account;
```

An external state may represent both volatile variables and non-volatile ones, for example:

```
package body Account with
  Refined_State => (State => (Total, Log, Log_Size))
is
  Total    : Integer;
  Log      : Integer_Array with Volatile;
  Log_Size : Natural with Volatile;
  ...
end Account;
```

The different *Flavors of Volatile Variables* may also be specified in the state abstraction, which is then used by GNATprove to refine the analysis. For example, the program writing in a log seen in the previous section can be rewritten to abstract global variables as follows:

```
1  package Logging_Out_Abstract with
2    SPARK_Mode,
3    Abstract_State => (State with External => (Async_Readers, Effective_Writes)),
```

```
 4    Initializes => State
 5  is
 6     procedure Add_To_Total (Incr : in Integer) with
 7        Global  => (In_Out => State),
 8        Depends => (State =>+ Incr);
 9
10  end Logging_Out_Abstract;
```

```
 1  package body Logging_Out_Abstract with
 2     SPARK_Mode,
 3     Refined_State => (State => (Log_Out, Total))
 4  is
 5     Total   : Integer := 0;
 6     Log_Out : Integer := 0 with Volatile, Async_Readers, Effective_Writes;
 7
 8     procedure Add_To_Total (Incr : in Integer) with
 9        Refined_Global  => (In_Out => Total, Output => Log_Out),
10        Refined_Depends => (Total =>+ Incr, Log_Out => Incr)
11     is
12     begin
13        Total := Total + Incr;
14        Log_Out := Incr;
15     end Add_To_Total;
16
17  end Logging_Out_Abstract;
```

while the logging program seen in the previous section may be rewritten to abstract global variables as follows:

```
 1  package Logging_In_Abstract with
 2     SPARK_Mode,
 3     Abstract_State => (State with External => (Async_Writers, Effective_Reads))
 4  is
 5     procedure Get with
 6        Global  => (In_Out => State),
 7        Depends => (State =>+ null);
 8
 9  end Logging_In_Abstract;
```

```
 1  package body Logging_In_Abstract with
 2     SPARK_Mode,
 3     Refined_State => (State => (Log_In, Log, Log_Size))
 4  is
 5     Log_In : Integer with Volatile, Async_Writers, Effective_Reads;
 6
 7     type Integer_Array is array (Positive range 1 .. 100) of Integer;
 8     Log      : Integer_Array := (others => 0);
 9     Log_Size : Natural := 0;
10
11     procedure Get with
12        Refined_Global  => (In_Out => (Log, Log_Size, Log_In)),
13        Refined_Depends => ((Log_Size, Log_In) =>+ null, Log =>+ (Log_Size, Log_In))
14     is
15     begin
16        Log_Size := Log_Size + 1;
17        Log (Log_Size) := Log_In;
18     end Get;
19
```

```
end Logging_In_Abstract;
```

GNATprove checks the specified data and flow dependencies on both programs.

An external abstract state on which none of the four aspects `Async_Writers`, `Async_Readers`, `Effective_Reads` or `Effective_Writes` is set is assumed to have all four aspects set to `True`. An external abstract state on which some of the four aspects are set to `True` is assumed to have the remaining ones set to `False`. See SPARK RM 7.1.2 for details.

5.4 Type Contracts

SPARK contains various features to constrain the values of a given type:

- A *scalar range* may be specified on a scalar type or subtype to bound its values.

- A *record discriminant* may be specified on a record type to distinguish between variants of the same record.

- A *predicate* introduced by aspect `Static_Predicate`, `Dynamic_Predicate` or `Predicate` may be specified on a type or subtype to express a property verified by objects of the type.

- A *type invariant* introduced by aspect `Type_Invariant` or `Invariant` may be specified on the completion of a private type to express a property that is only guaranteed outside of the type scope.

- A *default initial condition* introduced by aspect `Default_Initial_Condition` on a private type specifies the initialization status and possibly properties of the default initialization for a type.

Note that SPARK does not yet support aspect `Type_Invariant` from Ada 2012.

5.4.1 Scalar Ranges

[Ada 83]

Scalar types (signed integer types, modulo types, fixed-point types, floating-point types) can be given a low bound and a high bound to specify that values of the type must remain within these bounds. For example, the global counter `Total` can never be negative, which can be expressed in its type:

```
Total : Integer range 0 .. Integer'Last;
```

Any attempt to assign a negative value to variable `Total` results in raising an exception at run time. During analysis, GNATprove checks that all values assigned to `Total` are positive or null. The anonymous subtype above can also be given an explicit name:

```
subtype Nat is Integer range 0 .. Integer'Last;
Total : Nat;
```

or we can use the equivalent standard subtype `Natural`:

```
Total : Natural;
```

or `Nat` can be defined as a derived type instead of a subtype:

```
type Nat is new Integer range 0 .. Integer'Last;
Total : Nat;
```

or as a new signed integer type:

```
type Nat is range 0 .. Integer'Last;
Total : Nat;
```

All the variants above result in the same range checks both at run-time and in GNATprove. GNATprove also uses the range information for proving properties about the program (for example, the absence of overflows in computations).

5.4.2 Record Discriminants

[Ada 83]

Record types can use discriminants to:

- define multiple variants and associate each component to a specific variant

- bound the size of array components

For example, the log introduced in *State Abstraction* could be implemented as a discriminated record with a discriminant Kind selecting between two variants of the record for logging either only the minimum and maximum entries or the last entries, and a discriminant Capacity specifying the maximum number of entries logged:

```
1  package Logging_Discr with
2     SPARK_Mode
3  is
4     type Log_Kind is (Min_Max_Values, Last_Values);
5     type Integer_Array is array (Positive range <>) of Integer;
6
7     type Log_Type (Kind : Log_Kind; Capacity : Natural) is record
8        case Kind is
9           when Min_Max_Values =>
10             Min_Entry : Integer;
11             Max_Entry : Integer;
12          when Last_Values =>
13             Log_Data : Integer_Array (1 .. Capacity);
14             Log_Size : Natural;
15       end case;
16    end record;
17
18    subtype Min_Max_Log is Log_Type (Min_Max_Values, 0);
19    subtype Ten_Values_Log is Log_Type (Last_Values, 10);
20
21    function Log_Size (Log : Log_Type) return Natural;
22
23    function Last_Entry (Log : Log_Type) return Integer with
24       Pre => Log.Kind = Last_Values and then Log.Log_Size in 1 .. Log.Capacity;
25
26 end Logging_Discr;
```

Subtypes of Log_Type can specify fixed values for Kind and Capacity, like in Min_Max_Log and Ten_Values_Log. The discriminants Kind and Capacity are accessed like regular components, for example:

```
1  package body Logging_Discr with
2     SPARK_Mode
3  is
4     function Log_Size (Log : Log_Type) return Natural is
5     begin
6        case Log.Kind is
7           when Min_Max_Values =>
8              return 2;
```

```
 9          when Last_Values =>
10              return Log.Log_Size;
11        end case;
12     end Log_Size;
13
14     function Last_Entry (Log : Log_Type) return Integer is
15     begin
16        return Log.Log_Data (Log.Log_Size);
17     end Last_Entry;
18
19  end Logging_Discr;
```

Any attempt to access a component not present in a variable (because it is of a different variant), or to access an array component outside its bounds, results in raising an exception at run time. During analysis, GNATprove checks that components accessed are present, and that array components are accessed within bounds:

```
logging_discr.adb:4:13: info: range check proved
logging_discr.adb:10:23: info: discriminant check proved
logging_discr.adb:14:13: info: range check proved
logging_discr.adb:16:17: info: discriminant check proved
logging_discr.adb:16:31: info: discriminant check proved
logging_discr.adb:16:31: info: index check proved
logging_discr.ads:13:13: info: range check proved
logging_discr.ads:18:37: info: range check proved
logging_discr.ads:18:53: info: range check proved
logging_discr.ads:19:40: info: range check proved
logging_discr.ads:19:53: info: range check proved
logging_discr.ads:24:48: info: discriminant check proved
```

5.4.3 Predicates

[Ada 2012]

Predicates can be used on any type to express a property verified by objects of the type at all times. Aspects `Static_Predicate` and `Dynamic_Predicate` are defined in Ada 2012 to associate a predicate to a type. Aspect `Dynamic_Predicate` allows to express more general predicates than aspect `Static_Predicate`, at the cost of restricting the use of variables of the type. The following table summarizes the main similarities and differences between both aspects:

Feature	Static_Predicate	Dynamic_Predicate
Applicable to scalar type	Yes	Yes
Applicable to array/record type	No	Yes
Allows simple comparisons with static values	Yes	Yes
Allows conjunctions/disjunctions	Yes	Yes
Allows function calls	No	Yes
Allows general Boolean properties	No	Yes
Can be used in membership test	Yes	Yes
Can be used as range in for-loop	Yes	No
Can be used as choice in case-statement	Yes	No
Can be used as prefix with attributes First, Last or Range	No	No
Can be used as index type in array	No	No

Aspect `Predicate` is specific to GNAT and can be used instead of `Static_Predicate` or `Dynamic_Predicate`. GNAT treats it as a `Static_Predicate` whenever possible and as a

`Dynamic_Predicate` in the remaining cases, thus not restricting uses of variables of the type more than necessary.

Predicates are inherited by subtypes and derived types. If a subtype or a derived type inherits a predicate and defines its own predicate, both predicates are checked on values of the new type. Predicates are restricted in SPARK so that they cannot depend on variable input. In particular, a predicate cannot mention a global variable in SPARK, although it can mention a global constant.

GNATprove checks that all values assigned to a type with a predicate are allowed by its predicate (for all three forms of predicate: `Predicate`, `Static_Predicate` and `Dynamic_Predicate`). GNATprove generates a predicate check even in cases where there is no corresponding run-time check, for example when assigning to a component of a record with a predicate. GNATprove also uses the predicate information for proving properties about the program.

Static Predicates

A static predicate allows specifying which values are allowed or forbidden in a scalar type, when this specification cannot be expressed with *Scalar Ranges* (because it has *holes*). For example, we can express that the global counter `Total` cannot be equal to `10` or `100` with the following static predicate:

```
subtype Count is Integer with
  Static_Predicate => Count /= 10 and Count /= 100;
Total : Count;
```

or equivalently:

```
subtype Count is Integer with
  Static_Predicate => Count in Integer'First .. 9 | 11 .. 99 | 101 .. Integer'Last;
Total : Count;
```

Uses of the name of the subtype `Count` in the predicate refer to variables of this type. Scalar ranges and static predicates can also be combined, and static predicates can be specified on subtypes, derived types and new signed integer types. For example, we may define `Count` as follows:

```
type Count is new Natural with
  Static_Predicate => Count /= 10 and Count /= 100;
```

Any attempt to assign a forbidden value to variable `Total` results in raising an exception at run time. During analysis, GNATprove checks that all values assigned to `Total` are allowed.

Similarly, we can express that values of type `Normal_Float` are the *normal* 32-bits floating-point values (thus excluding *subnormal* values), assuming here that `Float` is the 32-bits floating-point type on the target:

```
subtype Normal_Float is Float with
  Static_Predicate => Normal_Float <= -2.0**(-126) or Normal_Float = 0.0 or Normal_
  Float >= 2.0**(-126);
```

Any attempt to assign a subnormal value to a variable of type `Normal_Value` results in raising an exception at run time. During analysis, GNATprove checks that only normal values are assigned to such variables.

Dynamic Predicates

A dynamic predicate allows specifying properties of scalar types that cannot be expressed as static predicates. For example, we can express that values of type `Odd` and `Even` are distributed according to their name as follows:

```
subtype Odd is Natural with
  Dynamic_Predicate => Odd mod 2 = 1;

subtype Even is Natural with
  Dynamic_Predicate => Even mod 2 = 0;
```

or that values of type `Prime` are prime numbers as follows:

```
type Prime is new Positive with
  Dynamic_Predicate => (for all Divisor in 2 .. Prime / 2 => Prime mod Divisor /= 0);
```

A dynamic predicate also allows specifying relations between components of a record. For example, we can express that the values paired together in a record are always distinct as follows:

```
type Distinct_Pair is record
  Val1, Val2 : Integer;
end record
  with Dynamic_Predicate => Distinct_Pair.Val1 /= Distinct_Pair.Val2;
```

or that a record stores pairs of values with their greatest common divisor as follows:

```
type Bundle_Values is record
  X, Y : Integer;
  GCD  : Natural;
end record
  with Dynamic_Predicate => Bundle_Values.GCD = Get_GCD (Bundle_Values.X, Bundle_
  ↪Values.Y);
```

or that the number of elements `Count` in a resizable table is always less than or equal to its maximal number of elements `Max` as follows:

```
type Resizable_Table (Max : Natural) is record
   Count : Natural;
   Data  : Data_Array(1 .. Max);
end record
  with Dynamic_Predicate => Resizable_Table.Count <= Resizable_Table.Max;
```

A dynamic predicate also allows specifying global properties over the content of an array. For example, we can express that elements of an array are stored in increasing order as follows:

```
type Ordered_Array is array (Index) of Integer
  with Dynamic_Predicate =>
    (for all I in Index => (if I < Index'Last then Ordered_Array(I) < Ordered_
  ↪Array(I+1)));
```

or that a special end marker is always present in the array as follows:

```
type Ended_Array is array (Index) of Integer
  with Dynamic_Predicate =>
    (for some I in Index => Ended_Array(I) = End_Marker);
```

Dynamic predicates are checked only at specific places at run time, as mandated by the Ada Reference Manual:

- when converting a value to the type with the predicate
- when returning from a call, for each in-out and out parameter passed by reference
- when declaring an object, except when there is no initialization expression and no subcomponent has a default expression

Thus, not all violations of the dynamic predicate are caught at run time. On the contrary, during analysis, GNATprove checks that initialized variables whose type has a predicate always contain a value allowed by the predicate.

5.4.4 Type Invariants

[Ada 2012]

In SPARK, type invariants can only be specified on completions of private types (and not directly on private types declarations). They express a property that is only quaranteed outside of the immediate scope of the type bearing the invariant. Aspect `Type_Invariant` is defined in Ada 2012 to associate an invariant to a type. Aspect `Invariant` is specific to GNAT and can be used instead of `Type_Invariant`.

GNATprove checks that, outside of the immediate scope of a type with an invariant, all values of this type are allowed by its invariant. In order to provide such a strong guarantee, GNATprove generates an invariant check even in cases where there is no corresponding run-time check, for example on global variables that are modified by a subprogram. GNATprove also uses the invariant information for proving properties about the program.

As an example, let us consider a stack, which can be queried for the maximum of the elements stored in it:

```
package P is

   type Stack is private;

   function Max (S : Stack) return Element;

private
```

In the implementation, an additional component is allocated for the maximum, which is kept up to date by the implementation of the stack. This information is a type invariant, which can be specified using a `Type_Invariant` aspect:

```
private

   type Stack is record
      Content : Element_Array := (others => 0);
      Size    : My_Length := 0;
      Max     : Element := 0;
   end record with
      Type_Invariant => Is_Valid (Stack);

   function Is_Valid (S : Stack) return Boolean is
     ((for all I in 1 .. S.Size => S.Content (I) <= S.Max)
      and (if S.Max > 0 then
              (for some I in 1 .. S.Size => S.Content (I) = S.Max)));

   function Max (S : Stack) return Element is (S.Max);

end P;
```

Like for type predicates, the name of the type can be used inside the invariant expression to refer to the current instance of the type. Here the type predicate of `Stack` expresses that the `Max` field of a valid stack is the maximum of the elements stored in the stack.

To make sure that the invariant holds for every value of type `Stack` outside of the package P, GNATprove introduces invariant checks in several places. First, at the type declaration, it will make sure that the invariant holds every time an object of type `Stack` is default initialized. Here, as the stack is empty by default and the default value of `Max` is 0, the check will succeed. It is also possible to forbid default initialization of objects of type `Stack` altogether by using a *Default Initial Condition* of `False`:

```
type Stack is private with Default_Initial_Condition => False;

type Stack is record
   Content : Element_Array;
   Size    : My_Length;
   Max     : Element;
end record with Type_Invariant => Is_Valid (Stack);
```

A check is also introduced to make sure the invariant holds for every global object declared in the scope of `Stack` after it has been initialized:

```
package body P is

   The_Stack : Stack := (Content => (others => 1),
                         Size    => 5,
                         Max     => 0);

begin

   The_Stack.Max := 1;

end P;
```

Here the global variable `The_Stack` is allowed to break its invariant during the elaboration of `P`. The invariant check will only be done at the end of the elaboration of `P`, and will succeed.

In the same way, variables and parameters of a subprogram are allowed to break their invariants in the subprogram body. Verification conditions are generated to ensure that no invariant breaking value can leak outside of `P`. More precisely, invariant checks on subprogram parameters are performed:

- when calling a subprogram visible outside of `P` from inside of `P`. Such a subprogram can be either declared in the visible part of `P` or in another unit,

- when returning from a subprogram declared in the visible part of `P`.

For example, let us consider the implementation of a procedure `Push` that pushes an element of top of a stack. It is declared in the visible part of the specification of `P`:

```
function Size (S : Stack) return My_Length;

procedure Push (S : in out Stack; E : Element) with
  Pre => Size (S) < My_Length'Last;

procedure Push_Zero (S : in out Stack) with
  Pre => Size (S) < My_Length'Last;
```

It is then implemented using an internal procedure `Push_Internal` declared in the body of `P`:

```
procedure Push_Internal (S : in out Stack; E : Element) with
  Pre  => S.Size < My_Length'Last,
  Post => S.Size = S.Size'Old + 1 and S.Content (S.Size) = E
  and S.Content (1 .. S.Size)'Old = S.Content (1 .. S.Size - 1)
  and S.Max = S.Max'Old
is
begin
   S.Size := S.Size + 1;
   S.Content (S.Size) := E;
end Push_Internal;
```

```
procedure Push (S : in out Stack; E : Element) is
begin
   Push_Internal (S, E);
   if S.Max < E then
      S.Max := E;
   end if;
end Push;

procedure Push_Zero (S : in out Stack) is
begin
   Push (S, 0);
end Push_Zero;
```

On exit of `Push_Internal`, the invariant of `Stack` is broken. It is OK since `Push_Internal` is not visible from outside of P. Invariant checks are performed when exiting `Push` and when calling it from inside `Push_Zero`. They both succeed. Note that, because of invariant checks on parameters, it is not allowed in SPARK to call a function that is visible from outside P in the invariant of `Stack` otherwise this would lead to a recursive proof. In particular, it is not allowed to make `Is_Valid` visible in the public declarations of P. In the same way, the function `Size` cannot be used in the invariant of `Stack`. We also avoid using `Size` in the contract of `Push_Internal` as it would have enforced additional invariant checks on its parameter.

Checks are also performed for global variables accessed by subprograms inside P. Even if it is allowed to break the invariant of a global variable when inside the body of a subprogram declared in P, invariant checks are performed when calling and returning from every subprogram inside P. For example, if `Push` and `Push_Internal` are accessing directly the global stack `The_Stack` instead of taking it as a parameter, there will be a failed invariant check on exit of `Push_Internal`:

```
procedure Push_Internal (E : Element) with
  Pre  => The_Stack.Size < My_Length'Last
is
begin
   The_Stack.Size := The_Stack.Size + 1;
   The_Stack.Content (The_Stack.Size) := E;
end Push_Internal;

procedure Push (E : Element) is
begin
   Push_Internal (E);
   if The_Stack.Max < E then
      The_Stack.Max := E;
   end if;
end Push;
```

In this way, users will never have to use contracts to ensure that the invariant holds on global variable `The_Stack` through local subprogram calls.

5.4.5 Default Initial Condition

[SPARK]

Private types in a package define an encapsulation mechanism that prevents client units from accessing the implementation of the type. That boundary may also be used to specify properties that hold for default initialized values of that type in client units. For example, the log introduced in *State Abstraction* could be implemented as a private type with a default initial condition specifying that the size of the log is initially zero, where uses of the name of the private type `Log_Type` in the argument refer to variables of this type:

```
 1  package Logging_Priv with
 2    SPARK_Mode
 3  is
 4    Max_Count : constant := 100;
 5
 6    type Log_Type is private with
 7      Default_Initial_Condition => Log_Size (Log_Type) = 0;
 8
 9    function Log_Size (Log : Log_Type) return Natural;
10
11    procedure Append_To_Log (Log : in out Log_Type; Incr : in Integer) with
12      Pre => Log_Size (Log) < Max_Count;
13
14  private
15
16    type Integer_Array is array (1 .. Max_Count) of Integer;
17
18    type Log_Type is record
19      Log_Data : Integer_Array;
20      Log_Size : Natural := 0;
21    end record;
22
23    function Log_Size (Log : Log_Type) return Natural is (Log.Log_Size);
24
25  end Logging_Priv;
```

This may be useful to analyze with GNATprove client code that defines a variable of type `Log_Type` with default initialization, and then proceeds to append values to this log, as procedure `Append_To_Log`'s precondition requires that the log size is not maximal:

```
The_Log : Log_Type;
...
Append_To_Log (The_Log, X);
```

GNATprove's flow analysis also uses the presence of a default initial condition as an indication that default initialized variables of that type are considered as fully initialized. So the code snippet above would pass flow analysis without messages being issued on the read of `The_Log`. If the full definition of the private type is in SPARK, GNATprove also checks that the type is indeed fully default initialized, and if not issues a message like here:

```
logging_priv.ads:18:04: medium: type "Log_Type" is not fully initialized
```

If partial default initialization of the type is intended, in general for efficiency like here, then the corresponding message can be justified with pragma `Annotate`, see section *Justifying Check Messages*.

Aspect `Default_Initial_Condition` can also be specified without argument to only indicate that default initialized variables of that type are considered as fully initialized. This is equivalent to `Default_Initial_Condition => True`:

```
type Log_Type is private with
  Default_Initial_Condition;
```

The argument can also be `null` to specify that default initialized variables of that type are *not* considered as fully initialized:

```
type Log_Type is private with
  Default_Initial_Condition => null;
```

This is different from an argument of `False` which can be used to indicate that variables of that type should always be explicitly initialized (otherwise GNATprove will not be able to prove the condition `False` on the default initialization and will issue a message during proof).

5.5 Specification Features

SPARK contains many features for specifying the intended behavior of programs. Some of these features come from Ada 2012 (*Attribute Old* and *Expression Functions* for example). Other features are specific to SPARK (*Attribute Loop_Entry* and *Ghost Code* for example). In this section, we describe these features and their impact on execution and formal verification.

5.5.1 Aspect `Constant_After_Elaboration`

Aspect `Constant_After_Elaboration` can be specified on a library level variable that has an initialization expression. When specified, the corresponding variable can only be changed during the elaboration of its enclosing package. SPARK ensures that users of the package do not change the variable. This feature can be particularly useful in tasking code since variables that are Constant_After_Elaboration are guaranteed to prevent unsynchronized modifications (see *Tasks and Data Races*).

```
package CAE is
   Var : Integer := 0 with
     Constant_After_Elaboration;

   --  The following is illegal because users of CAE could call Illegal
   --  and that would cause an update of Var after CAE has been
   --  elaborated.
   procedure Illegal with
     Global => (Output => Var);
end CAE;

package body CAE is
   procedure Illegal is
   begin
      Var := 10;
   end Illegal;

   --  The following subprogram is legal because it is declared inside
   --  the body of CAE and therefore it cannot be directly called
   --  from a user of CAE.
   procedure Legal is
   begin
      Var := Var + 2;
   end Legal;

begin
   --  The following statements are legal since they take place during
   --  the elaboration of CAE.
   Var := Var + 1;
   Legal;
end CAE;
```

5.5.2 Attribute Old

[Ada 2012]

In a Postcondition

Inside *Postconditions*, attribute Old refers to the values that expressions had at subprogram entry. For example, the postcondition of procedure Increment might specify that the value of parameter X upon returning from the procedure has been incremented:

```
procedure Increment (X : in out Integer) with
  Post => X = X'Old + 1;
```

At run time, a copy of the variable X is made when entering the subprogram. This copy is then read when evaluating the expression X'Old in the postcondition. Because it requires copying the value of X, the type of X cannot be limited.

Strictly speaking, attribute Old must apply to a *name* in Ada syntax, for example a variable, a component selection, a call, but not an addition like X + Y. For expressions that are not *names*, attribute Old can be applied to their qualified version, for example:

```
procedure Increment_One_Of (X, Y : in out Integer) with
  Post => X + Y = Integer'(X + Y)'Old + 1;
```

Because the compiler unconditionnally creates a copy of the expression to which attribute Old is applied at subprogram entry, there is a risk that this feature might confuse users in more complex postconditions. Take the example of a procedure Extract, which copies the value of array A at index J into parameter V, and zeroes out this value in the array, but only if J is in the bounds of A:

```
procedure Extract (A : in out My_Array; J : Integer; V : out Value) with
  Post => (if J in A'Range then V = A(J)'Old);   -- INCORRECT
```

Clearly, the value of A(J) at subprogram entry is only meaningful if J is in the bounds of A. If the code above was allowed, then a copy of A(J) would be made on entry to subprogram Extract, even when J is out of bounds, which would raise a run-time error. To avoid this common pitfall, use of attribute Old in expressions that are potentially unevaluated (like the then-part in an if-expression, or the right argument of a shortcut boolean expression - See Ada RM 6.1.1) is restricted to plain variables: A is allowed, but not A(J). The GNAT compiler issues the following error on the code above:

```
prefix of attribute "Old" that is potentially unevaluated must denote an entity
```

The correct way to specify the postcondition in the case above is to apply attribute Old to the entity prefix A:

```
procedure Extract (A : in out My_Array; J : Integer; V : out Value) with
  Post => (if J in A'Range then V = A'Old(J));
```

In Contract Cases

The rule for attribute Old inside *Contract Cases* is more permissive. Take for example the same contract as above for procedure Extract, expressed with contract cases:

```
procedure Extract (A : in out My_Array; J : Integer; V : out Value) with
  Contract_Cases => ((J in A'Range) => V = A(J)'Old,
                      others          => True);
```

Only the expressions used as prefixes of attribute Old in the *currently enabled case* are copied on entry to the subprogram. So if Extract is called with J out of the range of A, then the second case is enabled, so A(J) is not copied when entering procedure Extract. Hence, the above code is allowed.

It may still be the case that some contracts refer to the value of objects at subprogram entry inside potentially unevaluated expressions. For example, an incorrect variation of the above contract would be:

```
procedure Extract (A : in out My_Array; J : Integer; V : out Value) with
  Contract_Cases => (J >= A'First => (if J <= A'Last then V = A(J)'Old),  -- ⌴
  ⌴INCORRECT
                     others        => True);
```

For the same reason that such uses are forbidden by Ada RM inside postconditions, the SPARK RM forbids these uses inside contract cases (see SPARK RM 6.1.3(2)). The GNAT compiler issues the following error on the code above:

```
prefix of attribute "Old" that is potentially unevaluated must denote an entity
```

The correct way to specify the consequence expression in the case above is to apply attribute Old to the entity prefix A:

```
procedure Extract (A : in out My_Array; J : Integer; V : out Value) with
  Contract_Cases => (J >= A'First => (if J <= A'Last then V = A'Old(J)),
                     others        => True);
```

In a Potentially Unevaluated Expression

In some cases, the compiler issues the error discussed above (on attribute Old applied to a non-entity in a potentially unevaluated context) on an expression that can safely be evaluated on subprogram entry, for example:

```
procedure Extract (A : in out My_Array; J : Integer; V : out Value) with
  Post => (if J in A'Range then V = Get_If_In_Range(A,J)'Old);  -- ERROR
```

where function Get_If_In_Range returns the value A(J) when J is in the bounds of A, and a default value otherwise.

In that case, the solution is either to rewrite the postcondition using non-shortcut boolean operators, so that the expression is not *potentially evaluated* anymore, for example:

```
procedure Extract (A : in out My_Array; J : Integer; V : out Value) with
  Post => J not in A'Range or V = Get_If_In_Range(A,J)'Old;
```

or to rewrite the postcondition using an intermediate expression function, so that the expression is not *potentially evaluated* anymore, for example:

```
function Extract_Post (A : My_Array; J : Integer; V, Get_V : Value) return Boolean is
  (if J in A'Range then V = Get_V);

procedure Extract (A : in out My_Array; J : Integer; V : out Value) with
  Post => Extract_Post (A, J, V, Get_If_In_Range(A,J)'Old);
```

or to use the GNAT pragma Unevaluated_Use_Of_Old to allow such uses of attribute Old in potentially unevaluated expressions:

```
pragma Unevaluated_Use_Of_Old (Allow);

procedure Extract (A : in out My_Array; J : Integer; V : out Value) with
  Post => (if J in A'Range then V = Get_If_In_Range(A,J)'Old);
```

GNAT does not issue an error on the code above, and always evaluates the call to `Get_If_In_Range` on entry to procedure `Extract`, even if this value may not be used when executing the postcondition. Note that the formal verification tool GNATprove correctly generates all required checks to prove that this evaluation on subprogram entry does not fail a run-time check or a contract (like the precondition of `Get_If_In_Range` if any).

Pragma `Unevaluated_Use_Of_Old` applies to uses of attribute `Old` both inside postconditions and inside contract cases. See GNAT RM for a detailed description of this pragma.

5.5.3 Attribute `Result`

[Ada 2012]

Inside *Postconditions* of functions, attribute `Result` refers to the value returned by the function. For example, the postcondition of function `Increment` might specify that it returns the value of parameter X plus one:

```
function Increment (X : Integer) return Integer with
  Post => Increment'Result = X + 1;
```

Contrary to `Attribute Old`, attribute `Result` does not require copying the value, hence it can be applied to functions that return a limited type. Attribute `Result` can also be used inside consequence expressions in *Contract Cases*.

5.5.4 Attribute `Loop_Entry`

[SPARK]

It is sometimes convenient to refer to the value of variables at loop entry. In many cases, the variable has not been modified between the subprogram entry and the start of the loop, so this value is the same as the value at subprogram entry. But *Attribute Old* cannot be used in that case. Instead, we can use attribute `Loop_Entry`. For example, we can express that after J iterations of the loop, the value of parameter array X at index J is equal to its value at loop entry plus one:

```
procedure Increment_Array (X : in out Integer_Array) is
begin
   for J in X'Range loop
      X(J) := X(J) + 1;
      pragma Assert (X(J) = X'Loop_Entry(J) + 1);
   end loop
end Increment_Array;
```

At run time, a copy of the variable X is made when entering the loop. This copy is then read when evaluating the expression X'Loop_Entry. No copy is made if the loop is never entered. Because it requires copying the value of X, the type of X cannot be limited.

Attribute `Loop_Entry` can only be used in top-level *Assertion Pragmas* inside a loop. It is mostly useful for expressing complex *Loop Invariants* which relate the value of a variable at a given iteration of the loop and its value at loop entry. For example, we can express that after J iterations of the loop, the value of parameter array X at all indexes already seen is equal to its value at loop entry plus one, and that its value at all indexes not yet seen is unchanged, using *Quantified Expressions*:

```
procedure Increment_Array (X : in out Integer_Array) is
begin
   for J in X'Range loop
      X(J) := X(J) + 1;
      pragma Loop_Invariant (for all K in X'First .. J => X(J) = X'Loop_Entry(J) + 1);
      pragma Loop_Invariant (for all K in J + 1 .. X'Last => X(J) = X'Loop_Entry(J));
```

```
      end loop
end Increment_Array;
```

Attribute `Loop_Entry` may be indexed by the name of the loop to which it applies, which is useful to refer to the value of a variable on entry to an outer loop. When used without loop name, the attribute applies to the closest enclosing loop. For examples, `X'Loop_Entry` is the same as `X'Loop_Entry(Inner)` in the loop below, which is not the same as `X'Loop_Entry(Outter)` (although all three assertions are true):

```
procedure Increment_Matrix (X : in out Integer_Matrix) is
begin
   Outter: for J in X'Range(1) loop
      Inner: for K in X'Range(2) loop
         X(J,K) := X(J,K) + 1;
         pragma Assert (X(J) = X'Loop_Entry(J,K) + 1);
         pragma Assert (X(J) = X'Loop_Entry(Inner)(J,K) + 1);
         pragma Assert (X(J) = X'Loop_Entry(Outter)(J,K) + 1);
      end loop Inner;
   end loop Outter;
end Increment_Matrix;
```

By default, similar restrictions exist for the use of attribute `Loop_Entry` and the use of attribute `Old` *In a Potentially Unevaluated Expression*. The same solutions apply here, in particular the use of GNAT pragma `Unevaluated_Use_Of_Old`.

5.5.5 Attribute Update

[SPARK]

It is quite common in *Postconditions* to relate the input and output values of parameters. While this can be as easy as `X = X'Old + 1` in the case of scalar parameters, it is more complex to express for array and record parameters. Attribute `Update` is useful in that case, to denote the updated value of a composite variable. For example, we can express more clearly that procedure `Zero_Range` zeroes out the elements of its array parameter X between `From` and `To` by using attribute `Update`:

```
procedure Zero_Range (X : in out Integer_Array; From, To : Positive) with
  Post => X = X'Old'Update(From .. To => 0);
```

than with an equivalent postcondition using *Quantified Expressions* and *Conditional Expressions*:

```
procedure Zero_Range (X : in out Integer_Array; From, To : Positive) with
  Post => (for all J in X'Range =>
              (if J in From .. To then X(J) = 0 else X(J) = X'Old(J)));
```

Attribute `Update` takes in argument a list of associations between indexes (for arrays) or components (for records) and values. Components can only be mentioned once, with the semantics that all values are evaluated before any update. Array indexes may be mentioned more than once, with the semantics that updates are applied in left-to-right order. For example, the postcondition of procedure `Swap` expresses that the values at indexes J and K in array X have been swapped:

```
procedure Swap (X : in out Integer_Array; J, K : Positive) with
  Post => X = X'Old'Update(J => X'Old(K), K => X'Old(J));
```

and the postcondition of procedure `Rotate_Clockwize_Z` expresses that the point P given in parameter has been rotated 90 degrees clockwise around the Z axis (thus component Z is preserved while components X and Y are modified):

```
procedure Rotate_Clockwize_Z (P : in out Point_3D) with
   Post => P = P'Old'Update(X => P.Y'Old, Y => - P.X'Old);
```

Similarly to its use in combination with attribute `Old` in postconditions, attribute `Update` is useful in combination with *Attribute Loop_Entry* inside *Loop Invariants*. For example, we can express the property that, after iteration `J` in the main loop in procedure `Zero_Range`, the value of parameter array `X` at all indexes already seen is equal to zero:

```
procedure Zero_Range (X : in out Integer_Array; From, To : Positive) is
begin
   for J in From .. To loop
      X(J) := 0;
      pragma Loop_Invariant (X = X'Loop_Entry'Update(From .. J => 0));
   end loop;
end Zero_Range;
```

Attribute `Update` can also be used outside of assertions. It is particularly useful in expression functions. For example, the functionality in procedure `Rotate_Clockwize_Z` could be expressed equivalently as an expression function:

```
function Rotate_Clockwize_Z (P : Point_3D) return Point_3D is
   (P'Update(X => P.Y, Y => - P.X));
```

Because it requires copying the value of `P`, the type of `P` cannot be limited.

5.5.6 Conditional Expressions

[Ada 2012]

A conditional expression is a way to express alternative possibilities in an expression. It is like the ternary conditional expression `cond ? expr1 : expr2` in C or Java, except more powerful. There are two kinds of conditional expressions in Ada:

- if-expressions are the counterpart of if-statements in expressions

- case-expressions are the counterpart of case-statements in expressions

For example, consider the variant of procedure `Add_To_Total` seen in *Contract Cases*, which saturates at a given threshold. Its postcondition can be expressed with an if-expression as follows:

```
procedure Add_To_Total (Incr : in Integer) with
   Post => (if Total'Old + Incr < Threshold  then
               Total = Total'Old + Incr
            else
               Total = Threshold);
```

Each branch of an if-expression (there may be one, two or more branches when `elsif` is used) can be seen as a logical implication, which explains why the above postcondition can also be written:

```
procedure Add_To_Total (Incr : in Integer) with
   Post => (if Total'Old + Incr < Threshold then Total = Total'Old + Incr) and
           (if Total'Old + Incr >= Threshold then Total = Threshold);
```

or equivalently (as the absence of `else` branch above is implicitly the same as `else True`):

```
procedure Add_To_Total (Incr : in Integer) with
   Post => (if Total'Old + Incr < Threshold then Total = Total'Old + Incr else True)
   and
           (if Total'Old + Incr >= Threshold then Total = Threshold else True);
```

If-expressions are not necessarily of boolean type, in which case they must have an `else` branch that gives the value of the expression for cases not covered in previous conditions (as there is no implicit `else True` in such a case). For example, here is a postcondition equivalent to the above, that uses an if-expression of `Integer` type:

```
procedure Add_To_Total (Incr : in Integer) with
  Post => Total = (if Total'Old + Incr < Threshold then Total'Old + Incr else
  Threshold);
```

Although case-expressions can be used to cover cases of any scalar type, they are mostly used with enumerations, and the compiler checks that all cases are disjoint and that together they cover all possible cases. For example, consider a variant of procedure `Add_To_Total` which takes an additional `Mode` global input of enumeration value `Single`, `Double`, `Negate` or `Ignore`, with the intuitive corresponding leverage effect on the addition. The postcondition of this variant can be expressed using a case-expression as follows:

```
procedure Add_To_Total (Incr : in Integer) with
  Post => (case Mode is
             when Single => Total = Total'Old + Incr,
             when Double => Total = Total'Old + 2 * Incr,
             when Ignore => Total = Total'Old,
             when Negate => Total = Total'Old - Incr);
```

Like if-expressions, case-expressions are not necessarily of boolean type. For example, here is a postcondition equivalent to the above, that uses a case-expression of `Integer` type:

```
procedure Add_To_Total (Incr : in Integer) with
  Post => Total = Total'Old + (case Mode is
                                when Single => Incr,
                                when Double => 2 * Incr,
                                when Ignore => 0,
                                when Negate => - Incr);
```

A last case of `others` can be used to denote all cases not covered by previous conditions. If-expressions and case-expressions should always be parenthesized.

5.5.7 Quantified Expressions

[Ada 2012]

A quantified expression is a way to express a property over a collection, either an array or a container (see *Formal Containers Library*):

- a *universally quantified expression* using `for all` expresses a property that holds for all elements of a collection

- an *existentially quantified expression* using `for some` expresses a property that holds for at least one element of a collection

For example, consider the procedure `Increment_Array` that increments each element of its array parameter X by one. Its postcondition can be expressed using a universally quantified expression as follows:

```
procedure Increment_Array (X : in out Integer_Array) with
  Post => (for all J in X'Range => X(J) = X'Old(J) + 1);
```

The negation of a universal property being an existential property (the opposite is true too), the postcondition above can be expressed also using an existentially quantified expression as follows:

```
procedure Increment_Array (X : in out Integer_Array) with
  Post => not (for some J in X'Range => X(J) /= X'Old(J) + 1);
```

At run time, a quantified expression is executed like a loop, which exits as soon as the value of the expression is known: if the property does not hold (resp. holds) for a given element of a universally (resp. existentially) quantified expression, execution of the loop does not proceed with remaining elements and returns the value False (resp. True) for the expression.

When a quantified expression is analyzed with GNATprove, it uses the logical counterpart of the quantified expression. GNATprove also checks that the expression is free from run-time errors. For this checking, GNATprove checks that the enclosed expression is free from run-time errors over the *entire range* of the quantification, not only at points that would actually be reached at run time. As an example, consider the following expression:

```
(for all I in 1 .. 10 => 1 / (I - 3) > 0)
```

This quantified expression cannot raise a run-time error, because the enclosed expression 1 / (I - 3) > 0 is false for the first value of the range I = 1, so the execution of the loop exits immediately with the value False for the quantified expression. GNATprove is stricter and requires the enclosed expression 1 / (I - 3) > 0 to be free from run-time errors over the entire range I in 1 .. 10 (including I = 3) so it issues a check message for a possible division by zero in this case.

Quantified expressions should always be parenthesized.

5.5.8 Expression Functions

[Ada 2012]

An expression function is a function whose implementation is given by a single expression. For example, the function Increment can be defined as an expression function as follows:

```
function Increment (X : Integer) return Integer is (X + 1);
```

For compilation and execution, this definition is equivalent to:

```
function Increment (X : Integer) return Integer is
begin
   return X + 1;
end Increment;
```

For GNATprove, this definition as expression function is equivalent to the same function body as above, plus a post-condition:

```
function Increment (X : Integer) return Integer with
  Post => Increment'Result = X + 1
is
begin
   return X + 1;
end Increment;
```

Thus, a user does not need in general to add a postcondition to an expression function, as the implicit postcondition generated by GNATprove is the most precise one. If a user adds a postcondition to an expression function, GNATprove uses this postcondition to analyze the function's callers as well as the most precise implicit postcondition.

On the contrary, it may be useful in general to add a precondition to an expression function, to constrain the contexts in which it can be called. For example, parameter X passed to function Increment should be less than the maximal integer value, otherwise an overflow would occur. We can specify this property in Increment's precondition as follows:

```
function Increment (X : Integer) return Integer is (X + 1) with
  Pre => X < Integer'Last;
```

Note that the contract of an expression function follows its expression.

Expression functions can be defined in package declarations, hence they are well suited for factoring out common properties that are referred to in contracts. For example, consider the procedure `Increment_Array` that increments each element of its array parameter X by one. Its precondition can be expressed using expression functions as follows:

```
package Increment_Utils is

   function Not_Max (X : Integer) return Boolean is (X < Integer'Last);

   function None_Max (X : Integer_Array) return Boolean is
     (for all J in X'Range => Not_Max (X(J)));

   procedure Increment_Array (X : in out Integer_Array) with
     Pre => None_Max (X);

end Increment_Utils;
```

Expression functions can be defined over private types, and still be used in the contracts of publicly visible subprograms of the package, by declaring the function publicly and defining it in the private part. For example:

```
package Increment_Utils is

   type Integer_Array is private;

   function None_Max (X : Integer_Array) return Boolean;

   procedure Increment_Array (X : in out Integer_Array) with
     Pre => None_Max (X);

private

   type Integer_Array is array (Positive range <>) of Integer;

   function Not_Max (X : Integer) return Boolean is (X < Integer'Last);

   function None_Max (X : Integer_Array) return Boolean is
     (for all J in X'Range => Not_Max (X(J)));

end Increment_Utils;
```

If an expression function is defined in a unit spec, GNATprove can use its implicit postcondition at every call. If an expression function is defined in a unit body, GNATprove can use its implicit postcondition at every call in the same unit, but not at calls inside other units. This is true even if the expression function is declared in the unit spec and defined in the unit body.

5.5.9 Ghost Code

[SPARK]

Sometimes, the variables and functions that are present in a program are not sufficient to specify intended properties and to verify these properties with GNATprove. In such a case, it is possible in SPARK to insert in the program additional code useful for specification and verification, specially identified with the aspect `Ghost` so that it can be discarded during compilation. So-called *ghost code* in SPARK are these parts of the code that are only meant for specification and verification, and have no effect on the functional behavior of the program.

Various kinds of ghost code are useful in different situations:

- *Ghost functions* are typically used to express properties used in contracts.
- *Global ghost variables* are typically used to keep track of the current state of a program, or to maintain a log of past events of some type. This information can then be referred to in contracts.
- *Local ghost variables* are typically used to hold intermediate values during computation, which can then be referred to in assertion pragmas like loop invariants.
- *Ghost types* are those types only useful for defining ghost variables.
- *Ghost procedures* can be used to factor out common treatments on ghost variables. Ghost procedures should not have non-ghost outputs, either output parameters or global outputs.
- *Ghost packages* provide a means to encapsulate all types and operations for a specific kind of ghost code.
- *Imported ghost subprograms* are used to provide placeholders for properties that are defined in a logical language, when using manual proof.

When the program is compiled with assertions (for example with switch -gnata in GNAT), ghost code is executed like normal code. Ghost code can also be selectively enabled by setting pragma Assertion_Policy as follows:

```
pragma Assertion_Policy (Ghost => Check);
```

GNATprove checks that ghost code cannot have an effect on the behavior of the program. GNAT compiler also performs some of these checks, although not all of them. Apart from these checks, GNATprove treats ghost code like normal code during its analyses.

Ghost Functions

Ghost functions are useful to express properties only used in contracts, and to factor out common expressions used in contracts. For example, function Get_Total introduced in *State Abstraction and Functional Contracts* to retrieve the value of variable Total in the contract of Add_To_Total could be marked as a ghost function as follows:

```
function Get_Total return Integer with Ghost;
```

and still be used exactly as seen in *State Abstraction and Functional Contracts*:

```
procedure Add_To_Total (Incr : in Integer) with
   Pre  => Incr >= 0 and then Get_Total in 0 .. Integer'Last - Incr,
   Post => Get_Total = Get_Total'Old + Incr;
```

The definition of Get_Total would be also the same:

```
Total : Integer;

function Get_Total return Integer is (Total);
```

Although it is more common to define ghost functions as *Expression Functions*, a regular function might be used too:

```
function Get_Total return Integer is
begin
   return Total;
end Get_Total;
```

In that case, GNATprove uses only the contract of Get_Total (either user-specified or the default one) when analyzing its callers, like for a non-ghost regular function. (The same exception applies as for regular functions, when GNATprove can analyze a subprogram in the context of its callers, as described in *Contextual Analysis of Subprograms Without Contracts*.)

In the usual context where ghost code is not kept in the final executable, the user is given more freedom to use in ghost code constructs that are less efficient than in normal code, which may be useful to express rich properties. For example, the ghost functions defined in the *Formal Containers Library* in GNAT typically copy the entire content of the argument container, which would not be acceptable for non-ghost functions.

Ghost Variables

Ghost variables are useful to keep track of local or global information during the computation, which can then be referred to in contracts or assertion pragmas.

Case 1: Keeping Intermediate Values

Local ghost variables are commonly used to keep intermediate values. For example, we can define a local ghost variable Init_Total to hold the initial value of variable Total in procedure Add_To_Total, which allows checking the relation between the initial and final values of Total in an assertion:

```
procedure Add_To_Total (Incr : in Integer) is
   Init_Total : Integer := Total with Ghost;
begin
   Total := Total + Incr;
   pragma Assert (Total = Init_Total + Incr);
end Add_To_Total;
```

Case 2: Keeping Memory of Previous State

Global ghost variables are commonly used to memorize the value of a previous state. For example, we can define a global ghost variable Last_Incr to hold the previous value passed in argument when calling procedure Add_To_Total, which allows checking in its precondition that the sequence of values passed in argument is non-decreasing:

```
Last_Incr : Integer := Integer'First with Ghost;

procedure Add_To_Total (Incr : in Integer) with
  Pre => Incr >= Last_Incr;

procedure Add_To_Total (Incr : in Integer) is
begin
   Total := Total + Incr;
   Last_Incr := Incr;
end Add_To_Total;
```

Case 3: Logging Previous Events

Going beyond the previous case, global ghost variables can be used to store a complete log of events. For example, we can define global ghost variables Log and Log_Size to hold the sequence of values passed in argument to procedure Add_To_Total, as in *State Abstraction*:

```
Log      : Integer_Array with Ghost;
Log_Size : Natural with Ghost;

procedure Add_To_Total (Incr : in Integer) with
  Post => Log_Size = Log_Size'Old + 1 and Log = Log'Old'Update (Log_Size => Incr);

procedure Add_To_Total (Incr : in Integer) is
begin
   Total := Total + Incr;
   Log_Size := Log_Size + 1;
   Log (Log_Size) := Incr;
end Add_To_Total;
```

The postcondition of Add_To_Total above expresses that Log_Size is incremented by one at each call, and that the current value of parameter Incr is appended to Log at each call (using *Attribute Old* and *Attribute Update*).

Ghost Types

Ghost types can only be used to define ghost variables. For example, we can define ghost types Log_Type and Log_Size_Type that specialize the types Integer_Array and Natural for ghost variables:

```
subtype Log_Type is Integer_Array with Ghost;
subtype Log_Size_Type is Natural with Ghost;

Log      : Log_Type with Ghost;
Log_Size : Log_Size_Type with Ghost;
```

Ghost Procedures

Ghost procedures are useful to factor out common treatments on ghost variables. For example, we can define a ghost procedure Append_To_Log to append a value to the log as seen previously.

```
Log      : Integer_Array with Ghost;
Log_Size : Natural with Ghost;

procedure Append_To_Log (Incr : in Integer) with
  Ghost,
  Post => Log_Size = Log_Size'Old + 1 and Log = Log'Old'Update (Log_Size => Incr);

procedure Append_To_Log (Incr : in Integer) is
begin
   Log_Size := Log_Size + 1;
   Log (Log_Size) := Incr;
end Append_To_Log;
```

Then, this procedure can be called in Add_To_Total as follows:

```
procedure Add_To_Total (Incr : in Integer) is
begin
   Total := Total + Incr;
   Append_To_Log (Incr);
end Add_To_Total;
```

Ghost Packages

Ghost packages are useful to encapsulate all types and operations for a specific kind of ghost code. For example, we can define a ghost package `Logging` to deal with all logging operations on package `Account`:

```ada
package Logging with
  Ghost
is
   Log      : Integer_Array;
   Log_Size : Natural;

   procedure Append_To_Log (Incr : in Integer) with
     Post => Log_Size = Log_Size'Old + 1 and Log = Log'Old'Update (Log_Size => Incr);

   ...

end Logging;
```

The implementation of package `Logging` is the same as if it was not a ghost package. In particular, a `Ghost` aspect is implicitly added to all declarations in `Logging`, so it is not necessary to specify it explicitly. `Logging` can be defined either as a local ghost package or as a separate unit. In the latter case, unit `Account` needs to reference unit `Logging` in a with-clause like for a non-ghost unit:

```ada
with Logging;

package Account is
   ...
end Account;
```

Imported Ghost Subprograms

When using manual proof (see *GNATprove and Manual Proof*), it may be more convenient to define some properties in the logical language of the prover rather than in SPARK. In that case, ghost functions might be marked as imported, so that no implementation is needed. For example, the ghost procedure `Append_To_Log` seen previously may be defined equivalently as a ghost imported function as follows:

```ada
function Append_To_Log (Log : Log_type; Incr : in Integer) return Log_Type with
  Ghost,
  Import;
```

where `Log_Type` is an Ada type used also as placeholder for a type in the logical language of the prover. To avoid any inconsistency between the interpretations of `Log_Type` in GNATprove and in the manual prover, it is preferable in such a case to mark the definition of `Log_Type` as not in SPARK, so that GNATprove does not make any assumptions on its content. This can be achieved by defining `Log_Type` as a private type and marking the private part of the enclosing package as not in SPARK:

```ada
package Logging with
  SPARK_Mode,
  Ghost
is
   type Log_Type is private;

   function Append_To_Log (Log : Log_type; Incr : in Integer) return Log_Type with
     Import;

   ...
```

```
private
   pragma SPARK_Mode (Off);

   type Log_Type is new Integer;   -- Any definition is fine here
end Logging;
```

A ghost imported subprogram cannot be executed, so calls to `Append_To_Log` above should not be enabled during compilation, otherwise a compilation error is issued. Note also that GNATprove will not attempt proving the contract of a ghost imported subprogram, as it does not have its body.

Removal of Ghost Code

By default, GNAT completely discards ghost code during compilation, so that no ghost code is present in the object code or the executable. This ensures that, even if parts of the ghost could have side-effects when executed (writing to variables, performing system calls, raising exceptions, etc.), by default the compiler ensures that it cannot have any effect on the behavior of the program.

This is also essential in domains submitted to certification where all instructions in the object code should be traceable to source code and requirements, and where testing should ensure coverage of the object code. As ghost code is not present in the object code, there is no additional cost for maintaining its traceability and ensuring its coverage by tests.

GNAT provides an easy means to check that no ignored ghost code is present in a given object code or executable, which relies on the property that, by definition, each ghost declaration or ghost statement mentions at least one ghost entity. GNAT prefixes all names of such ignored ghost entities in the object code with the string ___ghost_ (except for names of ghost compilation units). The initial triple underscore ensures that this substring cannot appear anywhere in the name of non-ghost entities or ghost entities that are not ignored. Thus, one only needs to check that the substring ___ghost_ does not appear in the list of names from the object code or executable.

On Unix-like platforms, this can done by checking that the following command does not output anything:

```
nm <object files or executable> | grep ___ghost_
```

The same can be done to check that a ghost compilation unit called `my_unit` (whatever the capitalization) is not included at all (entities in that unit would have been detected by the previous check) in the object code or executable. For example on Unix-like platforms:

```
nm <object files or executable> | grep my_unit
```

5.6 Assertion Pragmas

SPARK contains features for directing formal verification with GNATprove. These features may also be used by other tools, in particular the GNAT compiler. Assertion pragmas are refinements of pragma `Assert` defined in Ada. For all assertion pragmas, an exception `Assertion_Error` is raised at run time when the property asserted does not hold, if the program was compiled with assertions. The real difference between assertion pragmas is how they are used by GNATprove during proof.

5.6.1 Pragma `Assert`

[Ada 2005]

Pragma `Assert` is the simplest assertion pragma. GNATprove checks that the property asserted holds, and uses the information that it holds for analyzing code that follows. For example, consider two assertions of the same property X > 0 in procedure `Assert_Twice`:

```
1   procedure Assert_Twice (X : Integer) with
2      SPARK_Mode
3   is
4   begin
5      pragma Assert (X > 0);
6      pragma Assert (X > 0);
7   end Assert_Twice;
```

As expected, the first assertion on line 5 is not provable in absence of a suitable precondition for `Assert_Twice`, but GNATprove proves that it holds the second time the property is asserted on line 6:

```
assert_twice.adb:5:19: medium: assertion might fail, cannot prove X > 0 (e.g. when X
   = 0)
assert_twice.adb:6:19: info: assertion proved
```

GNATprove considers that an execution of `Assert_Twice` with X <= 0 stops at the first assertion that fails. Thus X > 0 when execution reaches the second assertion. This is true if assertions are executed at run time, but not if assertions are discarded during compilation. In the latter case, unproved assertions should be inspected carefully to ensure that the property asserted will indeed hold at run time. This is true of all assertion pragmas, which GNATprove analyzes like pragma `Assert` in that respect.

5.6.2 Pragma `Assertion_Policy`

[Ada 2005/Ada 2012]

Assertions can be enabled either globally or locally. Here, *assertions* denote either *Assertion Pragmas* of all kinds (among which *Pragma Assert*) or functional contracts of all kinds (among which *Preconditions* and *Postconditions*).

By default, assertions are ignored in compilation, and can be enabled globally by using the compilation switch `-gnata`. They can be enabled locally by using pragma `Assertion_Policy` in the program, or globally if the pragma is put in a configuration file. They can be enabled for all kinds of assertions or specific ones only by using the version of pragma `Assertion_Policy` that takes named associations which was introduced in Ada 2012.

When used with the standard policies `Check` (for enabling assertions) or `Ignore` (for ignoring assertions) , pragma `Assertion_Policy` has no effect on GNATprove. GNATprove takes all assertions into account, whatever the assertion policy in effect at the point of the assertion. For example, consider a code with some assertions enabled and some ignored:

```
1    pragma Assertion_Policy (Pre => Check, Post => Ignore);
2
3    procedure Assert_Enabled (X : in out Integer) with
4       SPARK_Mode,
5       Pre  => X > 0,    --  executed at run time
6       Post => X > 2     --  ignored at run time
7    is
8       pragma Assertion_Policy (Assert => Check);
9       pragma Assert (X >= 0);    --  executed at run time
10
11      pragma Assertion_Policy (Assert => Ignore);
12      pragma Assert (X >= 0);    --  ignored at run time
13   begin
14      X := X - 1;
15   end Assert_Enabled;
```

Although the postcondition and the second assertion are not executed at run time, GNATprove analyzes them and issues corresponding messages:

```
assert_enabled.adb:6:11: medium: postcondition might fail, cannot prove X > 2 (e.g.
    when X = 0)
assert_enabled.adb:9:19: info: assertion proved
assert_enabled.adb:12:19: info: assertion proved
assert_enabled.adb:14:11: info: overflow check proved
```

On the contrary, when used with the GNAT-specific policy `Disable`, pragma `Assertion_Policy` causes the corresponding assertions to be skipped both during execution and analysis with GNATprove. For example, consider the same code as above where policy `Ignore` is replaced with policy `Disable`:

```ada
 1  pragma Assertion_Policy (Pre => Check, Post => Disable);
 2
 3  procedure Assert_Disabled (X : in out Integer) with
 4    SPARK_Mode,
 5    Pre  => X > 0,   --  executed at run time
 6    Post => X > 2    --  ignored at compile time and in analysis
 7  is
 8     pragma Assertion_Policy (Assert => Check);
 9     pragma Assert (X >= 0);  --  executed at run time
10
11     pragma Assertion_Policy (Assert => Disable);
12     pragma Assert (X >= 0);  --  ignored at compile time and in analysis
13  begin
14     X := X - 1;
15  end Assert_Disabled;
```

On this program, GNATprove does not analyze the postcondition and the second assertion, and it does not issue corresponding messages:

```
assert_disabled.adb:9:19: info: assertion proved
assert_disabled.adb:14:11: info: overflow check proved
```

The policy of `Disable` should thus be reserved for assertions that are not compilable, typically because a given build environment does not define the necessary entities.

5.6.3 Loop Invariants

[SPARK]

Pragma `Loop_Invariant` is a special kind of assertion used in loops. GNATprove performs two checks that ensure that the property asserted holds at each iteration of the loop:

1. *loop invariant initialization*: GNATprove checks that the property asserted holds during the first iteration of the loop.

2. *loop invariant preservation*: GNATprove checks that the property asserted holds during an arbitrary iteration of the loop, assuming that it held in the previous iteration.

Each of these properties can be independently true or false. For example, in the following loop, the loop invariant is false during the first iteration and true in all remaining iterations:

```ada
Prop := False;
for J in 1 .. 10 loop
   pragma Loop_Invariant (Prop);
   Prop := True;
end loop;
```

Thus, GNATprove checks that property 2 holds but not property 1:

```
simple_loops.adb:8:30: info: initialization of "Prop" proved
simple_loops.adb:8:30: medium: loop invariant might fail in first iteration, cannot
 prove Prop (e.g. when Prop = False)
```

Conversely, in the following loop, the loop invariant is true during the first iteration and false in all remaining iterations:

```
   Prop := True;
   for J in 1 .. 10 loop
      pragma Loop_Invariant (Prop);
      Prop := False;
   end loop;
```

Thus, GNATprove checks that property 1 holds but not property 2:

```
simple_loops.adb:14:30: info: initialization of "Prop" proved
simple_loops.adb:14:30: medium: loop invariant might fail after first iteration,
 cannot prove Prop (e.g. when Prop = False)
```

The following loop shows a case where the loop invariant holds both during the first iteration and all remaining iterations:

```
   Prop := True;
   for J in 1 .. 10 loop
      pragma Loop_Invariant (Prop);
      Prop := Prop;
   end loop;
```

GNATprove checks here that both properties 1 and 2 hold:

```
simple_loops.adb:20:30: info: initialization of "Prop" proved
simple_loops.adb:20:30: info: loop invariant initialization proved
```

In general, it is not sufficient that a loop invariant is true for GNATprove to prove it. The loop invariant should also be *inductive*: it should be precise enough that GNATprove can check loop invariant preservation by assuming *only* that the loop invariant held during the last iteration. For example, the following loop is the same as the previous one, except the loop invariant is true but not inductive:

```
   Prop := True;
   for J in 1 .. 10 loop
      pragma Loop_Invariant (if J > 1 then Prop);
      Prop := Prop;
   end loop;
```

GNATprove cannot check property 2 on that loop:

```
simple_loops.adb:26:30: info: loop invariant initialization proved
simple_loops.adb:26:44: medium: loop invariant might fail after first iteration,
 cannot prove Prop (e.g. when J = 2 and Prop = False)
```

Note that using CodePeer static analysis allows here to fully prove the loop invariant, which is possible because CodePeer generates its own sound approximation of loop invariants (see *Using CodePeer Static Analysis* for details):

```
simple_loops_cdp.adb:26:30: info: loop invariant proved
```

Note also that not using an assertion (*Pragma Assert*) instead of a loop invariant also allows here to fully prove the corresponding property, by relying on *Automatic Unrolling of Simple For-Loops*:

```
simple_loops_unroll.adb:26:22: info: assertion proved
```

Returning to the case where neither automatic loop unrolling nor CodePeer are used, the reasoning of GNATprove for checking property 2 in that case can be summarized as follows:

- Let's take iteration K of the loop, where K > 1 (not the first iteration).

- Let's assume that the loop invariant held during iteration K-1, so we know that if K-1 > 1 then Prop holds.

- The previous assumption can be rewritten: if K > 2 then Prop.

- But all we know is that K > 1, so we cannot deduce Prop.

See *How to Write Loop Invariants* for further guidelines.

Pragma `Loop_Invariant` may appear anywhere at the top level of a loop: it is usually added at the start of the loop, but it may be more convenient in some cases to add it at the end of the loop, or in the middle of the loop, in cases where this simplifies the asserted property. In all cases, GNATprove checks loop invariant preservation by reasoning on the virtual loop that starts and ends at the loop invariant.

It is possible to use multiple loop invariants, which should be grouped together without intervening statements or declarations. The resulting complete loop invariant is the conjunction of individual ones. The benefits of writing multiple loop invariants instead of a conjunction can be improved readability and better provability (because GNATprove checks each pragma `Loop_Invariant` separately).

Finally, *Attribute Loop_Entry* and *Attribute Update* can be very useful to express complex loop invariants.

Note: Users that are already familiar with the notion of loop invariant in other proof systems should be aware that loop invariants in SPARK are slightly different from the usual ones. In SPARK, a loop invariant must hold when execution reaches the corresponding pragma inside the loop. Hence, it needs not hold when the loop is never entered, or when exiting the loop.

5.6.4 Loop Variants

[SPARK]

Pragma `Loop_Variant` is a special kind of assertion used in loops. GNATprove checks that the given scalar value decreases (or increases) at each iteration of the loop. Because a scalar value is always bounded by its type in Ada, it cannot decrease (or increase) at each iteration an infinite number of times, thus one of two outcomes is possible:

1. the loop exits, or

2. a run-time error occurs.

Therefore, it is possible to prove the termination of loops in SPARK programs by proving both a loop variant for each plain-loop or while-loop (for-loops always terminate in Ada) and the absence of run-time errors.

For example, the while-loops in procedure `Terminating_Loops` compute the value of $X - X \bmod 3$ (or equivalently $X / 3 * 3$) in variable Y:

```
1  procedure Terminating_Loops (X : Natural) with
2     SPARK_Mode
3  is
4     Y : Natural;
5  begin
6     Y := 0;
7     while X - Y >= 3 loop
8        Y := Y + 3;
```

```
9        pragma Loop_Variant (Increases => Y);
10     end loop;
11
12     Y := 0;
13     while X - Y >= 3 loop
14        Y := Y + 3;
15        pragma Loop_Variant (Decreases => X - Y);
16     end loop;
17  end Terminating_Loops;
```

GNATprove is able to prove both loop variants, as well as absence of run-time errors in the subprogram, hence that loops terminate:

```
terminating_loops.adb:7:12: info: overflow check proved
terminating_loops.adb:7:14: info: initialization of "Y" proved
terminating_loops.adb:8:12: info: initialization of "Y" proved
terminating_loops.adb:8:14: info: overflow check proved
terminating_loops.adb:9:07: info: loop variant proved
terminating_loops.adb:9:41: info: initialization of "Y" proved
terminating_loops.adb:13:12: info: overflow check proved
terminating_loops.adb:13:14: info: initialization of "Y" proved
terminating_loops.adb:14:12: info: initialization of "Y" proved
terminating_loops.adb:14:14: info: overflow check proved
terminating_loops.adb:15:07: info: loop variant proved
terminating_loops.adb:15:43: info: overflow check proved
terminating_loops.adb:15:45: info: initialization of "Y" proved
```

Pragma `Loop_Variant` may appear anywhere a loop invariant appears. It is also possible to use multiple loop variants, which should be grouped together with loop invariants. A loop variant may be more complex than a single decreasing (or increasing) value, and be given instead by a list of either decreasing or increasing values (possibly a mix of both). In that case, the order of the list defines the lexicographic order of progress. See SPARK RM 5.5.3 for details.

5.6.5 Pragma `Assume`

[SPARK]

Pragma `Assume` is a variant of *Pragma Assert* that does not require GNATprove to check that the property holds. This is used to convey trustable information to GNATprove, in particular properties about external objects that GNATprove has no control upon. GNATprove uses the information that the assumed property holds for analyzing code that follows. For example, consider an assumption of the property X > 0 in procedure `Assume_Then_Assert`, followed by an assertion of the same property:

```
1  procedure Assume_Then_Assert (X : Integer) with
2    SPARK_Mode
3  is
4  begin
5    pragma Assume (X > 0);
6    pragma Assert (X > 0);
7  end Assume_Then_Assert;
```

As expected, GNATprove does not check the property on line 5, but used it to prove that the assertion holds on line 6:

```
assume_then_assert.adb:6:19: info: assertion proved
```

GNATprove considers that an execution of `Assume_Then_Assert` with `X <= 0` stops at the assumption on line 5, and it does not issue a message in that case because the user explicitly indicated that this case is not possible. Thus `X > 0` when execution reaches the assertion on line 6. This is true if assertions (of which assumptions are a special kind) are executed at run time, but not if assertions are discarded during compilation. In the latter case, assumptions should be inspected carefully to ensure that the property assumed will indeed hold at run time. This inspection may be facilitated by passing a justification string as the second argument to pragma `Assume`.

5.6.6 Pragma `Assert_And_Cut`

[SPARK]

Pragma `Assert_And_Cut` is a variant of *Pragma Assert* that allows hiding some information to GNATprove. GNATprove checks that the property asserted holds, and uses *only* the information that it holds for analyzing code that follows. For example, consider two assertions of the same property `X = 1` in procedure `Forgetful_Assert`, separated by a pragma `Assert_And_Cut`:

```
1  procedure Forgetful_Assert (X : out Integer) with
2     SPARK_Mode
3  is
4  begin
5     X := 1;
6
7     pragma Assert (X = 1);
8
9     pragma Assert_And_Cut (X > 0);
10
11     pragma Assert (X > 0);
12     pragma Assert (X = 1);
13  end Forgetful_Assert;
```

GNATprove proves that the assertion on line 7 holds, but it cannot prove that the same assertion on line 12 holds:

```
forgetful_assert.adb:1:29: info: initialization of "X" proved
forgetful_assert.adb:7:19: info: assertion proved
forgetful_assert.adb:7:19: info: initialization of "X" proved
forgetful_assert.adb:9:27: info: assertion proved
forgetful_assert.adb:9:27: info: initialization of "X" proved
forgetful_assert.adb:11:19: info: assertion proved
forgetful_assert.adb:11:19: info: initialization of "X" proved
forgetful_assert.adb:12:19: info: initialization of "X" proved
forgetful_assert.adb:12:19: medium: assertion might fail, cannot prove X = 1 (e.g.
  when X = 2)
```

GNATprove *forgets* the exact value of `X` after line 9. All it knows is the information given in pragma `Assert_And_Cut`, here that `X > 0`. And indeed GNATprove proves that such an assertion holds on line 11. But it cannot prove the assertion on line 12, and the counterexample displayed mentions a possible value of 2 for `X`, showing indeed that GNATprove forgot its value of 1.

Pragma `Assert_And_Cut` may be useful in two cases:

1. When the automatic provers are overwhelmed with information from the context, pragma `Assert_And_Cut` may be used to simplify this context, thus leading to more automatic proofs.

2. When GNATprove is proving checks for each path through the subprogram (see switch `--proof` in *Running GNATprove from the Command Line*), and the number of paths is very large, pragma `Assert_And_Cut` may be used to reduce the number of paths, thus leading to faster automatic proofs.

For example, consider procedure `P` below, where all that is needed to prove that the code using `X` is free from run-time errors is that `X` is positive. Let's assume that we are running GNATprove with switch `--proof=per_path` so that a formula is generated for each execution path. Without the pragma, GNATprove considers all execution paths through `P`, which may be many. With the pragma, GNATprove only considers the paths from the start of the procedure to the pragma, and the paths from the pragma to the end of the procedure, hence many fewer paths.

```ada
procedure P is
   X : Integer;
begin
   -- complex computation that sets X
   pragma Assert_And_Cut (X > 0);
   -- complex computation that uses X
end P;
```

5.7 Overflow Modes

Annotations such as preconditions, postconditions, assertions, loop invariants, are analyzed by GNATprove with the exact same meaning that they have during execution. In particular, evaluating the expressions in an annotation may raise a run-time error, in which case GNATprove will attempt to prove that this error cannot occur, and report a warning otherwise.

Integer overflows are a kind of run-time error that occurs when the result of an arithmetic computation does not fit in the bounds of the machine type used to hold the result. In some cases, it is convenient to express properties in annotations as they would be expressed in mathematics, where quantities are unbounded, for example:

```ada
function Add (X, Y : Integer) return Integer with
   Pre  => X + Y in Integer,
   Post => Add'Result = X + Y;
```

The precondition of `Add` states that the result of adding its two parameters should fit in type `Integer`. In the default mode, evaluating this expression will fail an overflow check, because the result of `X + Y` is stored in a temporary of type `Integer`. If the compilation switch `-gnato13` is used, then annotations are compiled specially, so that arithmetic operations use unbounded intermediate results. In this mode, GNATprove does not generate a check for the addition of `X` and `Y` in the precondition of `Add`, as there is no possible overflow here.

There are three overflow modes:

- Use base type for intermediate operations (STRICT): in this mode, all intermediate results for predefined arithmetic operators are computed using the base type, and the result must be in range of the base type.

- Most intermediate overflows avoided (MINIMIZED): in this mode, the compiler attempts to avoid intermediate overflows by using a larger integer type, typically Long_Long_Integer, as the type in which arithmetic is performed for predefined arithmetic operators.

- All intermediate overflows avoided (ELIMINATED): in this mode, the compiler avoids all intermediate overflows by using arbitrary precision arithmetic as required.

The desired mode for handling intermediate overflow can be specified using either the Overflow_Mode pragma or an equivalent compiler switch. The pragma has the form:

```ada
pragma Overflow_Mode ([General =>] MODE [, [Assertions =>] MODE]);
```

where MODE is one of

- STRICT: intermediate overflows checked (using base type)

- MINIMIZED: minimize intermediate overflows

- ELIMINATED: eliminate intermediate overflows

For example:

```
pragma Overflow_Mode (General => Strict, Assertions => Eliminated);
```

specifies that general expressions outside assertions be evaluated in the usual strict mode, and expressions within assertions be evaluated in "eliminate intermediate overflows" mode. Currently, GNATprove only supports pragma `Overflow_Mode` being specified in a configuration pragma file.

Additionally, a compiler switch `-gnato??` can be used to control the checking mode default. Here *?* is one of the digits *1* through *3*:

1. use base type for intermediate operations (STRICT)

2. minimize intermediate overflows (MINIMIZED)

3. eliminate intermediate overflows (ELIMINATED)

The switch `-gnato13`, like the `Overflow_Mode` pragma above, specifies that general expressions outside assertions be evaluated in the usual strict mode, and expressions within assertions be evaluated in "eliminate intermediate overflows" mode.

Note that these modes apply only to the evaluation of predefined arithmetic, membership, and comparison operators for signed integer arithmetic.

For further details of the meaning of these modes, and for further information about the treatment of overflows for fixed-point and floating-point arithmetic please refer to the "Overflow Check Handling in GNAT" appendix in the GNAT User's Guide.

5.8 Object Oriented Programming and Liskov Substitution Principle

SPARK supports safe Object Oriented Programming by checking behavioral subtyping between parent types and derived types, a.k.a. Liskov Substitution Principle: every overriding operation of the derived type should behave so that it can be substituted for the corresponding overridden operation of the parent type anywhere.

5.8.1 Class-Wide Subprogram Contracts

[Ada 2012]

Specific *Subprogram Contracts* are required on operations of tagged types, so that GNATprove can check Liskov Substitution Principle on every overriding operation:

- The *class-wide precondition* introduced by aspect `Pre'Class` is similar to the normal precondition.

- The *class-wide postcondition* introduced by aspect `Post'Class` is similar to the normal postcondition.

Although these contracts are defined in Ada 2012, they have a stricter meaning in SPARK for checking Liskov Substitution Principle:

- The class-wide precondition of an overriding operation should be weaker (more permissive) than the class-wide precondition of the corresponding overridden operation.

- The class-wide postcondition of an overriding operation should be stronger (more restrictive) than the class-wide postcondition of the corresponding overridden operation.

For example, suppose that the `Logging` unit introduced in *Ghost Packages* defines a tagged type `Log_Type` for logs, with corresponding operations:

```
package Logging with
   SPARK_Mode
is
   Max_Count : constant := 10_000;

   type Log_Count is range 0 .. Max_Count;

   type Log_Type is tagged private;

   function Log_Size (Log : Log_Type) return Log_Count;

   procedure Init_Log (Log : out Log_Type) with
     Post'Class => Log.Log_Size = 0;

   procedure Append_To_Log (Log : in out Log_Type; Incr : in Integer) with
     Pre'Class  => Log.Log_Size < Max_Count,
     Post'Class => Log.Log_Size = Log.Log_Size'Old + 1;

private

   subtype Log_Index is Log_Count range 1 .. Max_Count;
   type Integer_Array is array (Log_Index) of Integer;

   type Log_Type is tagged record
      Log_Data : Integer_Array;
      Log_Size : Log_Count;
   end record;

   function Log_Size (Log : Log_Type) return Log_Count is (Log.Log_Size);

end Logging;
```

and that this type is derived in `Range_Logging.Log_Type` which additionally keeps track of the minimum and maximum values in the log, so that they can be accessed in constant time:

```
with Logging; use type Logging.Log_Count;

package Range_Logging with
   SPARK_Mode
is
   type Log_Type is new Logging.Log_Type with private;

   not overriding
   function Log_Min (Log : Log_Type) return Integer;

   not overriding
   function Log_Max (Log : Log_Type) return Integer;

   overriding
   procedure Init_Log (Log : out Log_Type) with
     Post'Class => Log.Log_Size = 0 and
                   Log.Log_Min = Integer'Last and
                   Log.Log_Max = Integer'First;

   overriding
```

```
21    procedure Append_To_Log (Log : in out Log_Type; Incr : in Integer) with
22      Pre'Class  => Log.Log_Size < Logging.Max_Count,
23      Post'Class => Log.Log_Size = Log.Log_Size'Old + 1 and
24                    Log.Log_Min = Integer'Min (Log.Log_Min'Old, Incr) and
25                    Log.Log_Max = Integer'Max (Log.Log_Max'Old, Incr);
26
27  private
28
29    type Log_Type is new Logging.Log_Type with record
30      Min_Entry : Integer;
31      Max_Entry : Integer;
32    end record;
33
34    function Log_Min (Log : Log_Type) return Integer is (Log.Min_Entry);
35    function Log_Max (Log : Log_Type) return Integer is (Log.Max_Entry);
36
37  end Range_Logging;
```

GNATprove proves that the contracts on `Logging.Append_To_Log` and its overriding `Range_Logging.`
`Append_To_Log` respect the Liskov Substitution Principle:

```
range_logging.ads:16:20: info: class-wide postcondition is stronger than overridden
↪one
range_logging.ads:22:20: info: class-wide precondition is weaker than overridden one
range_logging.ads:23:20: info: class-wide postcondition is stronger than overridden
↪one
```

Units `Logging` and `Range_Logging` need not be implemented, or available, or in SPARK. It is sufficient that
the specification of `Logging` and `Range_Logging` are in SPARK for this checking. Here, the postcondition of
`Range_Logging.Append_To_Log` is strictly stronger than the postcondition of `Logging.Append_To_Log`,
as it also specifies the new expected value of the minimum and maximum values. The preconditions of both procedures
are exactly the same, which is the most common case, but in other cases it might be useful to be more permissive in
the overriding operation's precondition. For example, `Range_Logging.Append_To_Log` could allocate dynamically additional memory for storing an unbounded number of events, instead of being limited to `Max_Count` events
like `Logging.Append_To_Log`, in which case its precondition would be simply `True` (the default precondition).

A derived type may inherit both from a parent type and from one or more interfaces, which only provide abstract
operations and no components. GNATprove checks Liskov Substitution Principle on every overriding operation, both
when the overridden operation is inherited from the parent type and when it is inherited from an interface.

GNATprove separately checks that a subprogram implements its class-wide contract, like for a specific contract.

5.8.2 Mixing Class-Wide and Specific Subprogram Contracts

[Ada 2012]

It is possible to specify both a specific contract and a class-wide contract on a subprogram, in order to use a more
precise contract (the specific one) for non-dispatching calls and a contract compatible with the Liskov Substitution
Principle (the class-wide contract) for dispatching calls. In that case, GNATprove checks that:

- The specific precondition is weaker (more permissive) than the class-wide precondition.

- The specific postcondition is stronger (more restrictive) than the class-wide postcondition.

For example, `Logging.Append_To_Log` could set a boolean flag `Special_Value_Logged` when some
`Special_Value` is appended to the log, and express this property in its specific postcondition so that it is available
for analyzing non-dispatching calls to the procedure:

```
procedure Append_To_Log (Log : in out Log_Type; Incr : in Integer) with
  Pre'Class  => Log.Log_Size < Max_Count,
  Post'Class => Log.Log_Size = Log.Log_Size'Old + 1,
  Post       => Log.Log_Size = Log.Log_Size'Old + 1 and
                (if Incr = Special_Value then Special_Value_Logged = True);
```

This additional postcondition would play no role in dispatching calls, thus it is not involved in checking the Liskov Substitution Principle. Note that the absence of specific precondition on procedure `Append_To_Log` does not mean that the default precondition of `True` is used: as a class-wide precondition is specified on procedure `Append_To_Log`, it is also used as specific precondition. Similarly, if a procedure has a class-wide contract and a specific precondition, but no specific postcondition, then the class-wide postcondition is also used as specific postcondition.

When both a specific contract and a class-wide contract are specified on a subprogram, GNATprove only checks that the subprogram implements its specific (more precise) contract.

5.8.3 Dispatching Calls and Controlling Operands

[Ada 2012]

In a dispatching call, the *controlling operand* is the parameter of class-wide type whose dynamic type determinates the actual subprogram called. The dynamic type of this controlling operand may be any type derived from the specific type corresponding to the class-wide type of the parameter (the specific type is `T` when the class-wide type is `T'Class`). Thus, in general it is not possible to know in advance which subprograms may be called in a dispatching call, when separately analyzing a unit.

In SPARK, there is no need to know all possible subprograms called in order to analyze a dispatching call, which makes it possible for GNATprove to perform this analysis without knowledge of the whole program. As SPARK enforces Liskov Substitution Principle, the class-wide contract of an overriding operation is always less restrictive than the class-wide contract of the corresponding overridden operation. Thus, GNATprove uses the class-wide contract of the operation for the specific type of controlling operand to analyze a dispatching call.

For example, suppose a global variable `The_Log` of class-wide type defines the log that should be used in the program:

```
The_Log : Logging.Log_Type'Class := ...
```

The call to `Append_To_Log` in procedure `Add_To_Total` may dynamically call either `Logging.Append_To_Log` or `Range_Logging.Append_To_Log`:

```
procedure Add_To_Total (Incr : in Integer) is
begin
   Total := Total + Incr;
   The_Log.Append_To_Log (Incr);
end Add_To_Total;
```

Because GNATprove separately checks Liskov Substitution Principle for procedure `Append_To_Log`, it can use the class-wide contract of `Logging.Append_To_Log` for analyzing procedure `Add_To_Total`.

5.8.4 Dynamic Types and Invisible Components

[SPARK]

The *Data Initialization Policy* in SPARK applies specially to objects of tagged type. In general, the dynamic type of an object of tagged type may be different from its static type, hence the object may have invisible components, that are only revealed when the object is converted to a class-wide type.

For objects of tagged type, modes on parameters and data dependency contracts have a different meaning depending on the object's static type:

- For objects of a specific (not class-wide) tagged type, the constraints described in *Data Initialization Policy* apply to the visible components of the object only.

- For objects of a class-wide type, the constraints described in *Data Initialization Policy* apply to all components of the object, including invisible ones.

GNATprove checks during flow analysis that no uninitialized data is read in the program, and that the specified data dependencies and flow dependencies are respected in the implementation, based on the semantics above for objects of tagged type. For example, it detects no issues during flow analysis on procedure `Use_Logging` which initializes parameter `Log` and then updates it:

```
1  with Logging; use Logging;
2
3  procedure Use_Logging (Log : out Log_Type) with
4     SPARK_Mode
5  is
6  begin
7     Log.Init_Log;
8     Log.Append_To_Log (1);
9  end Use_Logging;
```

If parameter `Log` is of dynamic type `Logging.Log_Type`, then the call to `Init_Log` initializes all components of `Log` as expected, and the call to `Append_To_Log` can safely read those. If parameter `Log` is of dynamic type `Range_Logging.Log_Type`, then the call to `Init_Log` only initializes those components of `Log` that come from the parent type `Logging.Log_Type`, but since the call to `Append_To_Log` only read those, then there is no read of uninitialized data. This is in contrast with what occurs in procedure `Use_Logging_Classwide`:

```
1  with Logging; use Logging;
2
3  procedure Use_Logging_Classwide (Log : out Log_Type'Class) with
4     SPARK_Mode
5  is
6  begin
7     Log_Type (Log).Init_Log;
8     Log.Append_To_Log (2);
9  end Use_Logging_Classwide;
```

on which GNATprove issues an error during flow analysis:

```
use_logging_classwide.adb:3:34: info: initialization of "Log" proved
use_logging_classwide.adb:3:34: info: initialization of extension of "Log" proved
use_logging_classwide.adb:8:04: high: extension of "Log" is not initialized
use_logging_classwide.adb:8:04: info: initialization of "Log" proved
```

Indeed, the call to `Init_Log` (a non-dispatching call to `Logging.Init_Log` due to the conversion on its parameter) only initializes those components of `Log` that come from the parent type `Logging.Log_Type`, but the call to `Append_To_Log` may read other components from `Range_Logging.Log_Type` which may not be initialized.

A consequence of these rules for data initialization policy is that a parameter of a specific tagged type cannot be converted to a class-wide type, for example for a dispatching call. A special aspect `Extensions_Visible` is defined in SPARK to allow this case. When `Extensions_Visible` is specified on a subprogram, the data initialization policy for the subprogram parameters of a specific tagged type requires that the constraints described in *Data Initialization Policy* apply to all components of the object, as if the parameter was of a class-wide type. This allows converting this object to a class-wide type.

5.9 Concurrency and Ravenscar Profile

Concurrency in SPARK requires enabling the Ravenscar profile (see *Guide for the use of the Ada Ravenscar Profile in high integrity systems* by Alan Burns, Brian Dobbing, and Tullio Vardanega). This profile defines a subset of Ada's concurrency features targeted at real time systems. In particular, it is concerned with determinism, schedulability analysis and memory-boundedness. This profile is compatible with the Ravenscar Ada run-time provided with GNAT supporting task synchronization and communication, while remaining small enough to be certifiable to the highest integrity levels.

Concurrency in SPARK also requires that tasks do not start executing before the program has been completely elaborated, which is expressed by setting pragma `Partition_Elaboration_Policy` to the value `Sequential`. Together with the requirement to set the Ravenscar profile, this means that a concurrent SPARK program should define the following configuration pragmas, either in a configuration pragma file (see *Setting the Default SPARK_Mode* for an example of defining a configuration pragma file in your project file) or at the start of files:

```
pragma Profile (Ravenscar);
pragma Partition_Elaboration_Policy (Sequential);
```

While the Ravenscar profile is recommended for high-integrity concurrent applications, GNATprove also supports the GNAT Extended Ravenscar profile (see Section 4.5 "The Extended Ravenscar Profiles" in GNAT User's Guide Supplement for GNAT Pro Safety-Critical and GNAT Pro High-Security). To use the GNAT Extended Ravenscar profile simply replace `Ravenscar` with `GNAT_Extended_Ravenscar` in the pragma `Profile` in the above code.

In particular, the GNAT Extended Ravenscar profile allows the use of two forms of the delay statements depending on the type of their expression:

- If the expression is of the type Ada.Real_Time.Time then for the purposes of determining global inputs and outputs the delay statement is considered to be just like the delay statement, i.e. to reference the state abstraction Ada.Real_Time.Clock_Time as an input (see SPARK RM 9(17) for details).

- If the expression is of the type Ada.Calendar.Time then it is considered to reference the state abstraction Ada.Calendar.Clock_Time, which is defined similarly to Ada.Real_Time.Clock_Time but represents a different time base.

5.9.1 Tasks and Data Races

[Ravenscar]

Concurrent Ada programs are made of several *tasks*, that is, separate threads of control which share the same address space. In Ravenscar, only library-level, nonterminating tasks are allowed.

Task Types and Task Objects

Like ordinary objects, tasks have a type in Ada and can be stored in composite objects such as arrays and records. The definition of a task type looks like the definition of a subprogram. It is made of two parts: a declaration, usually empty as Ravenscar does not allow tasks to have entries (for task rendezvous), and a body containing the list of statements to be executed by objects of the task type. The body of nonterminating tasks (the only ones allowed in Ravenscar) usually takes the form of an infinite loop. For task objects of a given type to be parameterized, task types can have discriminants. As an example, a task type `Account_Management` can be declared as follows:

```
package Account is
   Num_Accounts : Natural := 0;

   task type Account_Management;
```

```
end Account;

package body Account is

   task body Account_Management is
   begin
      loop
         Get_Next_Account_Created;
         Num_Accounts := Num_Accounts + 1;
      end loop;
   end Account_Management;

end Account;
```

Then, tasks of type `Account_Management` can be created at library level, either as complete objects or as components of other objects:

```
package Bank is
   Special_Accounts : Account_Management;

   type Account_Type is (Regular, Premium, Selective);
   type Account_Array is array (Account_Type) of Account_Management;
   All_Accounts : Account_Array;
end Bank;
```

If only one object of a given task type is needed, then the task object can be declared directly giving a declaration and a body. An anonymous task type is then defined implicitly for the declared type object. For example, if we only need one task `Account_Management` then we can write:

```
package Account is
   Num_Accounts : Natural := 0;

   task Account_Management;
end Account;

package body Account is

   task body Account_Management is
   begin
      loop
         Get_Next_Account_Created;
         Num_Accounts := Num_Accounts + 1;
      end loop;
   end Account_Management;

end Account;
```

Preventing Data Races

In Ravenscar, communication between tasks can only be done through shared objects (tasks cannot communicate through rendezvous as task entries are not allowed in Ravenscar). In SPARK, the language is further restricted to avoid the possibility of erroneous concurrent access to shared data (a.k.a. data races). More precisely, tasks can only share *synchronized* objects, that is, objects that are protected against concurrent accesses. These include atomic objects, protected objects (see *Protected Objects and Deadlocks*), and suspension objects (see *Suspension Objects*). As an example, our previous definition of the `Account_Management` task type was not in SPARK. Indeed, data races could occur when accessing the global variable `Num_Accounts`, as detected by GNATprove:

```
bank1.ads:5:04: high: possible data race when accessing variable "account1.num_
⌄accounts"
bank1.ads:5:04: high: with task "bank1.all_accounts"
bank1.ads:5:04: high: with task "bank1.special_accounts"
```

To avoid this problem, shared variable Num_Account can be declared atomic:

```
package Account is
   Num_Accounts : Natural := 0 with Atomic;

   task type Account_Management;
end Account;
```

With this modification, GNATprove now alerts us that the increment of Num_Account is not legal, as a volatile variable (which is the case of atomic variables) cannot be read as a subexpression of a larger expression in SPARK:

```
account2.adb:15:26: volatile object cannot appear in this context (SPARK RM 7.1.3(12))
```

This can be fixed by copying the current value of Num_Account in a temporary before the increment:

```
declare
   Tmp : constant Natural := Num_Accounts;
begin
   Num_Accounts := Tmp + 1;
end;
```

But note that even with that fix, there is no guarante that Num_Accounts is incremented by one each time an account is created. Indeed, two tasks may read the same value of Num_Accounts and store this value in Tmp before both updating it to Tmp + 1. In such a case, two accounts have been created but Num_Accounts has been increased by 1 only. There is no *data race* in this program, which is confirmed by running GNATprove with no error, but there is by design a *race condition* on shared data that causes the program to malfunction. The correct way to fix this in SPARK is to use *Protected Types and Protected Objects*.

As they cannot cause data races, constants and variables that are constant after elaboration (see *Aspect Constant_After_Elaboration*) are considered as synchronized and can be accessed by multiple tasks. For example, we can declare a global constant Max_Accounts and use it inside Account_Management without risking data races:

```
package Account is
   Num_Accounts : Natural := 0 with Atomic;
   Max_Accounts : constant Natural := 100;

   task type Account_Management;
end Account;

package body Account is

   task body Account_Management is
   begin
      loop
         Get_Next_Account_Created;
         declare
            Tmp : constant Natural := Num_Accounts;
         begin
            if Tmp < Max_Accounts then
               Num_Accounts := Tmp + 1;
            end if;
         end;
```

```
      end loop;
   end Account_Management;

end Account;
```

It is possible for a task to access an unsynchronized global variable only if this variable is declared in the same package as the task and if there is a single task accessing this variable. To allow this property to be statically verified, only tasks of an anonymous task type are allowed to access unsynchronized variables and the variables accessed should be declared to belong to the task using aspect `Part_Of`. Global variables declared to belong to a task are handled just like local variables of the task, that is, they can only be referenced from inside the task body. As an example, we can state that `Num_Accounts` is only accessed by the task object `Account_Management` in the following way:

```
package Account is
   task Account_Management;

   Num_Accounts : Natural := 0 with Part_Of => Account_Management;
end Account;
```

5.9.2 Task Contracts

[SPARK]

Dependency contracts can be specified on tasks. As tasks should not terminate in SPARK, such contracts specify the dependencies between outputs and inputs of the task *updated while the task runs*:

- The *data dependencies* introduced by aspect `Global` specify the global data read and written by the task.

- The *flow dependencies* introduced by aspect `Depends` specify how task outputs depend on task inputs.

This is a difference between tasks and subprograms, for which such contracts describe the dependencies between outputs and inputs *when the subprogram returns*.

Data Dependencies

Data dependencies on tasks follow the same syntax as the ones on subprograms (see *Data Dependencies*). For example, data dependencies can be specified for task (type or object) `Account_Management` as follows:

```
package Account is
   Num_Accounts : Natural := 0 with Atomic;

   task type Account_Management with
     Global => (In_Out => Num_Accounts);
end Account;
```

Flow Dependencies

Flow dependencies on tasks follow the same syntax as the ones on subprograms (see *Flow Dependencies*). For example, flow dependencies can be specified for task (type or object) `Account_Management` as follows:

```
package Account is
   Num_Accounts : Natural := 0 with Atomic;

   task type Account_Management with
     Depends => (Account_Management => Account_Management,
```

```
                Num_Accounts          => Num_Accounts);
end Account;
```

Notice that the task unit itself is both an input and an output of the task:

- It is an input because task discriminants (if any) and task attributes may be read in the task body.

- It is an output so that the task unit may be passed as in out parameter in a subprogram call. But note that the task object cannot be modified once created.

The dependency of the task on itself can be left implicit as well, as follows:

```
package Account is
   Num_Accounts : Natural := 0 with Atomic;

   task type Account_Management with
     Depends => (Num_Accounts => Num_Accounts);
end Account;
```

5.9.3 Protected Objects and Deadlocks

[Ravenscar]

In Ada, protected objects are used to encapsulate shared data and protect it against data races (low-level unprotected concurrent access to data) and race conditions (lack of proper synchronization between reads and writes of shared data). They coordinate access to the protected data guaranteeing that read-write accesses are always exclusive while allowing concurrent read-only accesses. In Ravenscar, only library-level protected objects are allowed.

Protected Types and Protected Objects

Definitions of protected types resemble package definitions. They are made of two parts, a declaration (divided into a public part and a private part) and a body. The public part of a protected type's declaration contains the declarations of the subprograms that can be used to access the data declared in its private part. The body of these subprograms are located in the protected type's body. In Ravenscar, protected objects should be declared at library level, either as complete objects or as components of other objects. As an example, here is how a protected type can be used to coordinate concurrent accesses to the global variable Num_Accounts:

```
package Account is

   protected type Protected_Natural is
      procedure Incr;
      function Get return Natural;
   private
      The_Data : Natural := 0;
   end Protected_Natural;

   Num_Accounts : Protected_Natural;
   Max_Accounts : constant Natural := 100;

   task type Account_Management;
end Account;

package body Account is

   protected body Protected_Natural is
      procedure Incr is
```

```
      begin
         The_Data := The_Data + 1;
      end Incr;

      function Get return Natural is (The_Data);
   end Protected_Natural;

   task body Account_Management is
   begin
      loop
         Get_Next_Account_Created;
         if Num_Accounts.Get < Max_Accounts then
            Num_Accounts.Incr;
         end if;
      end loop;
   end Account_Management;

end Account;
```

Contrary to the previous version using an atomic global variable (see *Preventing Data Races*), this version prevents also any race condition when incrementing the value of Num_Accounts. But note that there is still a possible race condition between the time the value of Num_Accounts is read and checked to be less than Max_Accounts and the time it is incremented. So this version does not guarantee that Num_Accounts stays below Max_Accounts. The correct way to fix this in SPARK is to use protected entries (see *Protected Subprograms*).

Note that, in SPARK, to avoid initialization issues on protected objects, both private variables and variables belonging to a protected object must be initialized at declaration (either explicitly or through default initialization).

Just like for tasks, it is possible to directly declare a protected object if it is the only one of its type. In this case, an anonymous protected type is implicitly declared for it. For example, if Num_Account is the only Protected_Natural we need, we can directly declare:

```
package Account is

   protected Num_Accounts is
      procedure Incr;
      function Get return Natural;
   private
      The_Data : Natural := 0;
   end Num_Accounts;

end Account;

package body Account is

   protected body Num_Accounts is
      procedure Incr is
      begin
         The_Data := The_Data + 1;
      end Incr;

      function Get return Natural is (The_Data);
   end Num_Accounts;

end Account;
```

Protected Subprograms

The access mode granted by protected subprograms depends on their kind:

- Protected procedures provide exclusive read-write access to the private data of a protected object.

- Protected functions offer concurrent read-only access to the private data of a protected object.

- Protected *entries* are conceptually procedures with a *barrier*. When an entry is called, the caller waits until the condition of the barrier is true to be able to access the protected object.

So that scheduling is deterministic, Ravenscar requires that at most one entry is specified in a protected unit and at most one task is waiting on a given entry at every time. To ensure this, GNATprove checks that no two tasks can call the same protected object's entry. As an example, we could replace the procedure Incr of Protected_Natural to wait until The_Data is smaller than Max_Accounts before incrementing it. As only simple Boolean variables are allowed as entry barriers in Ravenscar, we add such a Boolean flag Not_Full as a component of the protected object:

```
package Account is

   protected type Protected_Natural is
      entry Incr;
      function Get return Natural;
   private
      The_Data : Natural := 0;
      Not_Full : Boolean := True;
   end Protected_Natural;

   Num_Accounts : Protected_Natural;
   Max_Accounts : constant Natural := 100;

   task type Account_Management;
end Account;

package body Account is

   protected body Protected_Natural is
      entry Incr when Not_Full is
      begin
         The_Data := The_Data + 1;
         if The_Data = Max_Accounts then
            Not_Full := False;
         end if;
      end Incr;

      function Get return Natural is (The_Data);
   end Protected_Natural;

   task body Account_Management is
   begin
      loop
         Get_Next_Account_Created;
         Num_Accounts.Incr;
      end loop;
   end Account_Management;

end Account;
```

This version fixes the remaining race condition on this example, thus ensuring that every new account created bumps the value of `Num_Accounts` by 1, and that `Num_Accounts` stays below `Max_Accounts`.

To avoid data races, protected subprograms should not access unsynchronized objects (see *Tasks and Data Races*). Like for tasks, it is still possible for subprograms of a protected object of an anonymous protected type to access an unsynchronized object declared in the same package as long as it is not accessed by any task or subprogram from other protected objects. In this case, the unsynchronized object should have a `Part_Of` aspect referring to the protected object. It is then handled as if it was a private variable of the protected object. This is typically done so that the address in memory of the variable can be specified, using either aspect `Address` or a corresponding representation clause. Here is how this could be done with `Num_Account`:

```ada
package Account is
   protected Protected_Num_Accounts is
      procedure Incr;
      function Get return Natural;
   end Protected_Num_Accounts;

   Num_Accounts : Natural := 0 with
     Part_Of => Protected_Num_Accounts,
     Address => ...
end Account;
```

As it can prevent access to a protected object for an unbounded amount of time, a task should not be blocked or delayed while inside a protected subprogram. Actions that can block a task are said to be *potentially blocking*. For example, calling a protected entry, explicitly waiting using a `delay_until` statement (note that `delay` statements are forbidden in Ravenscar), or suspending on a suspension object (see *Suspension Objects*) are potentially blocking actions. In Ada, it is an error to do a potentially blocking action while inside a protected subprogram. Note that a call to a function or a procedure on another protected object is not considered to be potentially blocking. Indeed, such a call cannot block a task in the absence of deadlocks (which is enforced in Ravenscar using the priority ceiling protocol, see *Avoiding Deadlocks and Priority Ceiling Protocol*).

GNATprove verifies that no potentially blocking action is performed from inside a protected subprogram in a modular way on a per subprogram basis. Thus, if a subprogram can perform a potentially blocking operation, every call to this subprogram from inside a protected subprogram will be flagged as a potential error. As an example, the procedure Incr_Num_Accounts is potentially blocking and thus should not be called, directly or indirectly, from a protected subprogram:

```ada
package Account is

   protected type Protected_Natural is
      entry Incr;
   private
      The_Data : Natural := 0;
   end Protected_Natural;

   Num_Accounts : Protected_Natural;

   procedure Incr_Num_Accounts;

end Account;

package body Account is

   procedure Incr_Num_Accounts is
   begin
      Num_Accounts.Incr;
   end Incr_Num_Accounts;

end Account;
```

Avoiding Deadlocks and Priority Ceiling Protocol

To ensure exclusivity of read-write accesses, when a procedure or an entry of a protected object is called, the protected object is locked so that no other task can access it, be it in a read-write or a read-only mode. In the same way, when a protected function is called, no other task can access the protected object in read-write mode. A *deadlock* happens when two or more tasks are unable to run because each of them is trying to access a protected object that is currently locked by another task.

To ensure absence of deadlocks on a single core, Ravenscar requires the use of the Priority Ceiling Protocol. This protocol ensures that no task can be blocked trying to access a protected object locked by another task. It relies on task's *priorities*. The priority of a task is a number encoding its urgency. On a single core, scheduling ensures that the current running task can only be preempted by another task if it has a higher priority. Using this property, the Priority Ceiling Protocol works by increasing the priorities of tasks accessing a protected object to a priority that is at least as high as the priorities of other tasks accessing this object. This ensures that, while holding a lock, the currently running task cannot be preempted by a task which could later be blocked by this lock.

To enforce this protocol, every task is associated with a *base priority*, either given at declaration using the `Priority` aspect or defaulted. This base priority is static and cannot be modified after the task's declaration. A task also has an *active priority* which is initially the task's base priority but will be increased when the task enters a protected action. For example, we can set the base priority of `Account_Management` to 5 at declaration:

```
package Account is
   task type Account_Management with Priority => 5;
end Account;
```

Likewise, each protected object is associated at declaration with a *ceiling priority* which should be equal or higher than the active priority of any task accessing it. The ceiling priority of a protected object does not need to be static, it can be set using a discriminant for example. Still, like for tasks, Ravenscar requires that it is set once and for all at the object's declaration and cannot be changed afterwards. As an example, let us attach a ceiling priority to the protected object `Num_Accounts`. As `Num_Accounts` will be used by `Account_Management`, its ceiling priority should be no lower than 5:

```
package Account is

   protected Num_Accounts with Priority => 7 is
      procedure Incr;
      function Get return Natural;
   private
      The_Data : Natural := 0;
   end Num_Accounts;

   task type Account_Management with Priority => 5;

end Account;
```

5.9.4 Suspension Objects

[Ravenscar]

The language-defined package `Ada.Synchronous_Task_Control` provides a type for semaphores called *suspension objects*. They allow lighter synchronization mechanisms than protected objects (see *Protected Objects and Deadlocks*). More precisely, a suspension object has a Boolean state which can be set atomically to True using the `Set_True` procedure. When a task suspends on a suspension object calling the `Suspend_Until_True` procedure, it is blocked until the state of the suspension object is True. At that point, the state of the suspension object is set back to False and the task is unblocked. Note that `Suspend_Until_True` is potentially blocking and therefore should not be called directly or indirectly from within *Protected Subprograms*. In the following example, the suspension object `Semaphore` is used to make sure `T1` has initialized the shared data by the time `T2` begins processing it:

```
Semaphore : Suspension_Object;
task T1;
task T2;

task body T1 is
begin
  Initialize_Shared_Data;
  Set_True (Semaphore);
  loop
    ...
  end loop;
end T1;

task body T2 is
begin
  Suspend_Until_True (Semaphore);
  loop
    ...
  end loop;
end T2;
```

In Ada, an exception is raised if a task tries to suspend on a suspension object on which another task is already waiting on that same suspension object. Like for verifying that no two tasks can be queued on a protected entry, this verification is done by GNATprove by checking that no two tasks ever suspend on the same suspension object. In the following example, the suspension objects `Semaphore1` and `Semaphore2` are used to ensure that `T1` and `T2` never call `Enter_Protected_Region` at the same time. GNATprove will successfully verify that only one task can suspend on each suspension object:

```
Semaphore1, Semaphore2 : Suspension_Object;
task T1;
task T2;

task body T1 is
begin
  loop
    Suspend_Until_True (Semaphore1);
    Enter_Protected_Region;
    Set_True (Semaphore2);
  end loop;
end T1;

task body T2 is
begin
  loop
    Suspend_Until_True (Semaphore2);
    Enter_Protected_Region;
    Set_True (Semaphore1);
  end loop;
end T2;
```

5.9.5 State Abstraction and Concurrency

[SPARK]

Protected objects, as well as suspension objects, are *effectively volatile* which means that their value as seen from a given task may change at any time due to some other task accessing the protected object or suspension object. If they are part of a state abstraction, the volatility of the abstract state must be specified by using the External aspect (see *External State Abstraction*). Note that task objects, though they can be part of a package's hidden state, are not effectively volatile and can therefore be components of normal state abstractions. For example, the package Synchronous_Abstractions defines two abstract states, one for external objects, containing the atomic variable V, the suspension object S, and the protected object P, and one for normal objects, containing the task T:

```
package Synchronous_Abstractions with
  Abstract_State => (Normal_State, (Synchronous_State with External))
is
end Synchronous_Abstractions;

package body Synchronous_Abstractions with
  Refined_State => (Synchronous_State => (P,V,S), Normal_State => T)
is
  task T;

  S : Suspension_Object;

  V : Natural := 0 with Atomic, Async_Readers, Async_Writers;

  protected P is
    function Read return Natural;
  private
    V : Natural := 0;
  end P;

  protected body P is
    function Read return Natural is (V);
  end P;

  task body T is ...
end  Synchronous_Abstractions;
```

To avoid data races, task bodies, as well as protected subprograms, should only access synchronized objects (see *Preventing Data Races*). State abstractions containing only synchronized objects can be specified to be synchronized using the Synchronous aspect. Only synchronized state abstractions can be accessed from task bodies and protected subprograms. For example, if we want the procedure Do_Something to be callable from the task Use_Synchronized_State, then the state abstraction Synchronous_State must be annotated using the Synchronous aspect:

```
package Synchronous_Abstractions with
  Abstract_State => (Normal_State,
                     (Synchronous_State with Synchronous, External))
is
  procedure Do_Something with Global => (In_Out => Synchronous_State);
end Synchronous_Abstractions;

task body Use_Synchronized_State is
begin
  loop
    Synchronous_Abstractions.Do_Something;
  end loop;
end Use_Synchronized_State;
```

5.9.6 Project-wide Tasking Analysis

Tasking-related analysis, as currently implemented in GNATprove, is subject to two limitations:

First, the analysis is always done when processing a source file with task objects or with a subprogram that can be used as a main subprogram of a partition (i.e. is at library level, has no parameters, and is either a procedure or a function returning an integer type).

In effect, you might get spurious checks when:

- a subprogram satisfies conditions for being used as a main subprogram of a partition but is not really used that way, i.e. it is not specified in the Main attribute of the GNAT project file you use to build executables, and

- it "withs" or is "withed" (directly or indirectly) from a library-level package that declares some task object, and

- both the fake "main" subprogram and the task object access the same resource in a way that violates tasking-related rules (e.g. suspends on the same suspension object).

As a workaround, either wrap the fake "main" subprogram in a library-level package or give it a dummy parameter.

Second, the analysis is only done in the context of all the units "withed" (directly and indirectly) by the currently analyzed source file.

In effect, you might miss checks when:

- building a library that declares tasks objects in unrelated source files, i.e. files that are never "withed" (directly or indirectly) from the same file, and those tasks objects access the same resource in a way that violates tasking-related rules, or

- using a library that internally declares some tasks objects, they access some tasking-sensitive resource, and your main subprogram also accesses this resource.

As a workaround, when building library projects add a dummy main subprogram that "withs" all the library-level packages of your project.

5.9.7 Interrupt Handlers

SPARK puts no restrictions on the Ada interrupt handling and GNATprove merely checks that interrupt handlers will be safely executed. In Ada interrupts handlers are defined by annotating protected procedures, for example:

```
with Ada.Interrupts.Names; use Ada.Interrupts.Names;

protected P is
   procedure Signal with Attach_Handler => SIGINT;
end P;
```

Currently GNATprove emits a check for each handler declaration saying that the corresponding interrupt might be already reserved. In particular, it might be reserved by either the system or the Ada runtime; see GNAT pragmas Interrupt_State and Unreserve_All_Interrupts for details. Once examined, those checks can be suppressed with pragma Annotate.

If pragma Priority or Interrupt_Priority is explicitly specified for a protected type, then GNATprove will check that its value is in the range of the System.Any_Priority or System.Interrupt_Priority, respectively; see Ada RM D.3(6.1/3).

For interrupt handlers whose bodies are annotated with SPARK_Mode => On, GNATprove will additionally check that:

- the interrupt handler does not call (directly or indirectly) the Ada.Task_Identification.Current_Task routine, which might cause a Program_Error runtime exception; see Ada RM C.7.1(17/3);

- all global objects read (either as an Input or a Proof_In) by the interrupt handler are initialized at elaboration;

- there are no unsynchronized objects accessed both by the interrupt handler and by some task (or by some other interrupt handler);

- there are no protected objects locked both by the interrupt handler and by some task (or by some other interrupt handler).

5.10 SPARK Libraries

5.10.1 Functional Containers Library

To model complex data structures, one often needs simpler, mathematical like containers. The mathematical containers provided in the SPARK library are unbounded and may contain indefinite elements. Furthermore, to be usable in every context, they are neither controlled nor limited. So that these containers can be used safely, we have made them functional, that is, no primitives are provided which would allow to modify an existing container. Instead, their API features functions creating new containers from existing ones. As an example, functional containers provide no `Insert` procedure but rather a function `Add` which creates a new container with one more element than its parameter:

```
function Add (C : Container; E : Element_Type) return Container;
```

As a consequence, these containers are highly inefficient. They are also memory consuming as the allocated memory is not reclaimed when the container is no longer referenced. Thus, they should in general be used in ghost code and annotations so that they can be removed from the final executable.

There are 3 functional containers, which are part of the GNAT standard library:

- `Ada.Containers.Functional_Maps`

- `Ada.Containers.Functional_Sets`

- `Ada.Containers.Functional_Vectors`

Sequences defined in `Functional_Vectors` are no more than ordered collections of elements. In an Ada like manner, the user can choose the range used to index the elements:

```
function Length (S : Sequence) return Count_Type;
function Get (S : Sequence; N : Index_Type) return Element_Type;
```

Functional sets offer standard mathematical set functionalities such as inclusion, union, and intersection. They are neither ordered nor hashed:

```
function Contains (S : Set; E : Element_Type) return Boolean;
function "<=" (Left : Set; Right : Set) return Boolean;
```

Functional maps offer a dictionary between any two types of elements:

```
function Has_Key (M : Map; K : Key_Type) return Boolean;
function Get (M : Map; K : Key_Type) return Element_Type;
```

Each functional container type supports iteration as appropriate, so that its elements can easily be quantified over.

These containers can easily be used to model user defined data structures. They were used to this end to annotate and verify a package of allocators (see *allocators* example in the *Examples in the Toolset Distribution*). In this example, an allocator featuring a free list implemented in an array is modeled by a record containing a set of allocated resources and a sequence of available resources:

```
type Status is (Available, Allocated);
type Cell is record
   Stat : Status;
   Next : Resource;
end record;
type Allocator is array (Valid_Resource) of Cell;
type Model is record
   Available : Sequence;
   Allocated : Set;
end record;
```

Note: Functional sets and maps represent elements modulo equivalence. For proof, the range of quantification over their content includes all elements that are equivalent to elements included in the container. On the other hand, for execution, the iteration is only done on elements which have actually been included in the container. This difference may make interaction between test and proof tricky when the equivalence relation is not the equality.

5.10.2 Formal Containers Library

Containers are generic data structures offering a high-level view of collections of objects, while guaranteeing fast access to their content to retrieve or modify it. The most common containers are lists, vectors, sets and maps, which are defined as generic units in the Ada Standard Library. In critical software where verification objectives severely restrict the use of pointers, containers offer an attractive alternative to pointer-intensive data structures.

The Ada Standard Library defines two kinds of containers:

- The controlled containers using dynamic allocation, for example `Ada.Containers.Vectors`. They define containers as controlled tagged types, so that memory for the container is automatic reallocated during assignment and automatically freed when the container object's scope ends.

- The bounded containers not using dynamic allocation, for example `Ada.Containers.Bounded_Vectors`. They define containers as discriminated tagged types, so that the memory for the container can be reserved at initialization.

Although bounded containers are better suited to critical software development, neither controlled containers nor bounded containers can be used in SPARK, because their API does not lend itself to adding suitable contracts (in particular preconditions) ensuring correct usage in client code.

The formal containers are a variation of the bounded containers with API changes that allow adding suitable contracts, so that GNATprove can prove that client code manipulates containers correctly. There are 7 formal containers, which are part of the GNAT standard library:

- `Ada.Containers.Formal_Vectors`
- `Ada.Containers.Formal_Indefinite_Vectors`
- `Ada.Containers.Formal_Doubly_Linked_Lists`
- `Ada.Containers.Formal_Hashed_Sets`
- `Ada.Containers.Formal_Ordered_Sets`
- `Ada.Containers.Formal_Hashed_Maps`
- `Ada.Containers.Formal_Ordered_Maps`

Lists, sets and maps are always bounded. Vectors can be bounded or unbounded depending on the value of the formal parameter `Bounded` when instantiating the generic unit. Bounded containers do not use dynamic allocation. Unbounded vectors use dynamic allocation to expand their internal block of memory.

Lists, sets and maps can only be used with definite objects (objects for which the compiler can compute the size in memory, hence not `String` nor `T'Class`). Vectors come in two flavors for definite objects (`Formal_Vectors`) and indefinite objects (`Formal_Indefinite_Vectors`).

Modified API of Formal Containers

The visible specification of formal containers is in SPARK, with suitable contracts on subprograms to ensure correct usage, while their private part and implementation is not in SPARK. Hence, GNATprove can be used to prove correct usage of formal containers in client code, but not to prove that formal containers implement their specification.

Procedures `Update_Element` or `Query_Element` that iterate over a container are not defined on formal containers. Specification and analysis of such procedures that take an access-to-procedure in parameter is beyond the capabilities of SPARK and GNATprove. See *Excluded Ada Features*.

Procedures and functions that query the content of a container take the container in parameter. For example, function `Has_Element` that queries if a container has an element at a given position is declared as follows:

```
function Has_Element (Container : T; Position : Cursor) return Boolean;
```

This is different from the API of controlled containers and bounded containers, where it is sufficient to pass a cursor to these subprograms, as the cursor holds a reference to the underlying container:

```
function Has_Element (Position : Cursor) return Boolean;
```

Cursors of formal containers do not hold a reference to a specific container, as this would otherwise introduce aliasing between container and cursor variables, which is not supported in SPARK. See *Absence of Interferences*. As a result, the same cursor can be applied to multiple container objects.

For each container type, the library provides model functions that are used to annotate subprograms from the API. The different models supply different levels of abstraction of the container's functionalities. These model functions are grouped in *Ghost Packages* named `Formal_Model`.

The higher level view of a container is usually the mathematical structure of element it represents. We use a sequence for ordered containers such as lists and vectors and a mathematical map for imperative maps. This allows us to specify the effects of a subprogram in a very high level way, not having to consider cursors nor order of elements in a map:

```
procedure Increment_All (L : in out List) with
  Post =>
    (for all N in 1 .. Length (L) =>
       Element (Model (L), N) = Element (Model (L)'Old, N) + 1);

procedure Increment_All (S : in out Map) with
  Post =>
    (for all K of Model (S)'Old => Has_Key (Model (S), K))
      and
    (for all K of Model (S) =>
       Has_Key (Model (S)'Old, K)
         and Get (Model (S), K) = Get (Model (S)'Old, K) + 1);
```

For sets and maps, there is a lower level model representing the underlying order used for iteration in the container, as well as the actual values of elements/keys. It is a sequence of elements/keys. We can use it if we want to specify in `Increment_All` on maps that the order and actual values of keys are preserved:

```
procedure Increment_All (S : in out Map) with
  Post =>
    Keys (S) = Keys (S)'Old
      and
```

```
    (for all K of Model (S) =>
       Get (Model (S), K) = Get (Model (S)'Old, K) + 1);
```

Finally, cursors are modeled using a functional map linking them to their position in the container. For example, we can state that the positions of cursors in a list are not modified by a call to Increment_All:

```
procedure Increment_All (L : in out List) with
  Post =>
    Positions (L) = Positions (L)'Old
       and
    (for all N in 1 .. Length (L) =>
       Element (Model (L), N) = Element (Model (L)'Old, N) + 1);
```

Switching between the different levels of model functions allows to express precise considerations when needed without polluting upper level specifications. For example, consider a variant of the List.Find function defined in the API of formal containers, which returns a cursor holding the value searched if there is one, and the special cursor No_Element otherwise:

```
1  with Element_Lists; use Element_Lists; use Element_Lists.Lists;
2  with Ada.Containers; use Ada.Containers; use Element_Lists.Lists.Formal_Model;
3
4  function My_Find (L : List; E : Element_Type) return Cursor with
5    SPARK_Mode,
6    Contract_Cases =>
7      (Contains (L, E)      => Has_Element (L, My_Find'Result) and then
8                               Element (L, My_Find'Result) = E,
9      not Contains (L, E) => My_Find'Result = No_Element);
```

The ghost functions mentioned above are specially useful in *Loop Invariants* to refer to cursors, and positions of elements in the containers. For example, here, ghost function Positions is used in the loop invariant to query the position of the current cursor in the list, and Model is used to specify that the value searched is not contained in the part of the container already traversed (otherwise the loop would have exited):

```
1  function My_Find (L : List; E : Element_Type) return Cursor with
2    SPARK_Mode
3  is
4     Cu : Cursor := First (L);
5
6  begin
7     while Has_Element (L, Cu) loop
8        pragma Loop_Invariant (for all I in 1 .. P.Get (Positions (L), Cu) - 1 =>
9                               Element (Model (L), I) /= E);
10
11       if Element (L, Cu) = E then
12          return Cu;
13       end if;
14
15       Next (L, Cu);
16    end loop;
17
18    return No_Element;
19  end My_Find;
```

GNATprove proves that function My_Find implements its specification:

```
my_find.adb:7:26: info: initialization of "Cu.Node" proved
my_find.adb:8:30: info: loop invariant initialization proved
```

```
my_find.adb:8:30: info: loop invariant preservation proved
my_find.adb:8:49: info: precondition proved
my_find.adb:8:70: info: initialization of "Cu.Node" proved
my_find.adb:9:33: info: precondition proved
my_find.adb:11:10: info: precondition proved
my_find.adb:11:22: info: initialization of "Cu.Node" proved
my_find.adb:12:17: info: initialization of "Cu.Node" proved
my_find.adb:15:07: info: precondition proved
my_find.adb:15:16: info: initialization of "Cu.Node" proved
my_find.ads:6:03: info: complete contract cases proved
my_find.ads:6:03: info: disjoint contract cases proved
my_find.ads:7:26: info: contract case proved
my_find.ads:8:29: info: precondition proved
my_find.ads:9:26: info: contract case proved
```

Quantification over Formal Containers

Quantified Expressions can be used over the content of a formal container to express that a property holds for all elements of a container (using `for all`) or that a property holds for at least one element of a container (using `for some`).

For example, we can express that all elements of a formal list of integers are prime as follows:

```
(for all Cu in My_List => Is_Prime (Element (My_List, Cu)))
```

On this expression, the GNAT compiler generates code that iterates over `My_List` using the functions `First`, `Has_Element` and `Next` given in the `Iterable` aspect applying to the type of formal lists, so the quantified expression above is equivalent to:

```
declare
   Cu     : Cursor_Type := First (My_List);
   Result : Boolean := True;
begin
   while Result and then Has_Element (My_List, Cu) loop
      Result := Is_Prime (Element (My_List, Cu));
      Cu     := Next (My_List, Cu);
   end loop;
end;
```

where `Result` is the value of the quantified expression. See GNAT Reference Manual for details on aspect `Iterable`.

5.10.3 SPARK Lemma Library

As part of the SPARK product, a library of lemmas is available through the project file `<spark-install>/lib/gnat/spark_lemmas.gpr`. To use this library in a program, you need to add a corresponding dependency in your project file, for example:

```
with "spark_lemmas";
project My_Project is
   ...
end My_Project;
```

You may need to update the environment variable `GPR_PROJECT_PATH` for the lemma library project to be found by GNAT compiler, as described in *Installation of GNATprove*.

You also need to set the environment variable SPARK_LEMMAS_OBJECT_DIR to the absolute path of the object directory where you want compilation and verification artefacts for the lemma library to be created. This should be an absolute path (not a relative one) otherwise these artefacts will be created inside you SPARK install.

Finally, if you instantiate in your code a generic from the lemma library, you also need to pass -gnateDSPARK_BODY_MODE=Off as a compilation switch for these generic units.

This library consists in a set of ghost null procedures with contracts (called *lemmas*). Here is an example of such a lemma:

```
procedure Lemma_Div_Is_Monotonic
  (Val1  : Int;
   Val2  : Int;
   Denom : Pos)
with
  Global => null,
  Pre  => Val1 <= Val2,
  Post => Val1 / Denom <= Val2 / Denom;
```

whose body is simply a null procedure:

```
procedure Lemma_Div_Is_Monotonic
  (Val1  : Int;
   Val2  : Int;
   Denom : Pos)
is null;
```

This procedure is ghost (as part of a ghost package), which means that the procedure body and all calls to the procedure are compiled away when producing the final executable without assertions (when switch *-gnata* is not set). On the contrary, when compiling with assertions for testing (when switch *-gnata* is set) the precondition of the procedure is executed, possibly detecting invalid uses of the lemma. However, the main purpose of such a lemma is to facilitate automatic proof, by providing the prover specific properties expressed in the postcondition. In the case of Lemma_Div_Is_Monotonic, the postcondition expresses an inequality between two expressions. You may use this lemma in your program by calling it on specific expressions, for example:

```
R1 := X1 / Y;
R2 := X2 / Y;
Lemma_Div_Is_Monotonic (X1, X2, Y);
--  at this program point, the prover knows that R1 <= R2
--  the following assertion is proved automatically:
pragma Assert (R1 <= R2);
```

Note that the lemma may have a precondition, stating in which contexts the lemma holds, which you will need to prove when calling it. For example, a precondition check is generated in the code above to show that X1 <= X2. Similarly, the types of parameters in the lemma may restrict the contexts in which the lemma holds. For example, the type Pos for parameter Denom of Lemma_Div_Is_Monotonic is the type of positive integers. Hence, a range check may be generated in the code above to show that Y is positive.

All the lemmas provided in the SPARK lemma library have been proved either automatically or using Coq interactive prover. The Why3 session file recording all proofs, as well as the individual Coq proof scripts, are available as part of the SPARK product under directory <spark-install>/lib/gnat/proof. For example, the proof of lemma Lemma_Div_Is_Monotonic is a Coq proof of the mathematical property (in Coq syntax):

```
1 subgoals
h1 : in_range val1
h2 : in_range val2
h3 : in_range1 denom
h4 : (val1 <= val2)%Z
                                                        (1/1)
(val1 ÷ denom <= val2 ÷ denom)%Z
```

Currently, the SPARK lemma library provides the following lemmas:

- Lemmas on signed integer arithmetic in file `spark-arithmetic_lemmas.ads`, that are instantiated for 32 bits signed integers (`Integer`) in file `spark-integer_arithmetic_lemmas.ads` and for 64 bits signed integers (`Long_Integer`) in file `spark-long_integer_arithmetic_lemmas.ads`.

- Lemmas on modular integer arithmetic in file `spark-mod_arithmetic_lemmas.ads`, that are instantiated for 32 bits modular integers (`Interfaces.Unsigned_32`) in file `spark-mod32_arithmetic_lemmas.ads` and for 64 bits modular integers (`Interfaces.Unsigned_64`) in file `spark-mod64_arithmetic_lemmas.ads`.

- Lemmas on floating point arithmetic in file `spark-floating_point_arithmetic_lemmas.ads`, that are instantiated for single-precision floats (`Float`) in file `spark-float_arithmetic_lemmas.ads` and for double-precision floats (`Long_Float`) in file `spark-long_float_arithmetic_lemmas.ads`.

- Lemmas on unconstrained arrays in file `spark-unconstrained_array_lemmas.ads`, that need to be instantiated by the user for her specific type of index and element, and specific ordering function between elements.

To apply lemmas to signed or modular integers of different types than the ones used in the instances provided in the library, just convert the expressions passed in arguments, as follows:

```
R1 := X1 / Y;
R2 := X2 / Y;
Lemma_Div_Is_Monotonic (Integer(X1), Integer(X2), Integer(Y));
--  at this program point, the prover knows that R1 <= R2
--  the following assertion is proved automatically:
pragma Assert (R1 <= R2);
```

SPARK TUTORIAL

This chapter describes a simple use of the SPARK toolset on a program written completely in SPARK, within the GPS integrated development environment. All the tools may also be run from the command-line, see *Command Line Invocation*.

Note: If you're using SPARK Discovery instead of SPARK Pro, some of the proofs in this tutorial may not be obtained automatically. See the section on *Alternative Provers* to install additional provers that are not present in SPARK Discovery.

6.1 Writing SPARK Programs

As a running example, we consider a naive searching algorithm for an unordered collection of elements. The algorithm returns whether the collection contains the desired value, and if so, at which index. The collection is implemented here as an array. We deliberately start with an incorrect program for package `Search`, in order to explain how the SPARK toolset can help correct these errors. The final version of the `linear_search` example is part of the *Examples in the Toolset Distribution*.

We start with creating a GNAT project file in `search.gpr`:

```
1  project Search is
2     for Source_Dirs use (".");
3
4     package Compiler is
5        for Default_Switches ("Ada") use ("-gnatwa");
6     end Compiler;
7  end Search;
```

It specifies that the source code to inspect is in the current directory, and that the code should be compiled at maximum warning level (switch -gnatwa). GNAT projects are used by most tools in the GNAT toolsuite; for in-depth documentation of this technology, consult the GNAT User's Guide. Documentation and examples for the SPARK language and tools are also available via the *Help → SPARK* menu in GPS.

The obvious specification of `Linear_Search` is given in file `linear_search.ads`, where we specify that the spec is in SPARK by using aspect `SPARK_Mode`.

```
1  package Linear_Search
2     with SPARK_Mode
3  is
4
5     type Index is range 1 .. 10;
6     type Element is new Integer;
```

```
7
8      type Arr is array (Index) of Element;
9
10     function Search
11        (A        : Arr;
12         Val      : Element;
13         At_Index : out Index) return Boolean;
14     --   Returns True if A contains value Val, in which case it also returns
15     --   in At_Index the first index with value Val. Returns False otherwise.
16   end Linear_Search;
```

The implementation of Linear_Search is given in file linear_search.adb, where we specify that the body is in **SPARK** by using aspect SPARK_Mode. It is as obvious as its specification, using a loop to go through the array parameter A and looking for the first index at which Val is found, if there is such an index.

```
1    package body Linear_Search
2      with SPARK_Mode
3    is
4
5      function Search
6         (A        : Arr;
7          Val      : Element;
8          At_Index : out Index) return Boolean
9      is
10        Pos : Index := A'First;
11     begin
12        while Pos < A'Last loop
13           if A(Pos) = Val then
14              At_Index := Pos;
15              return True;
16           end if;
17
18           Pos := Pos + 1;
19        end loop;
20
21        return False;
22     end Search;
23
24   end Linear_Search;
```

We can check that the above code is valid Ada by using the Build > Check Semantic menu, which completes without any errors or warnings:

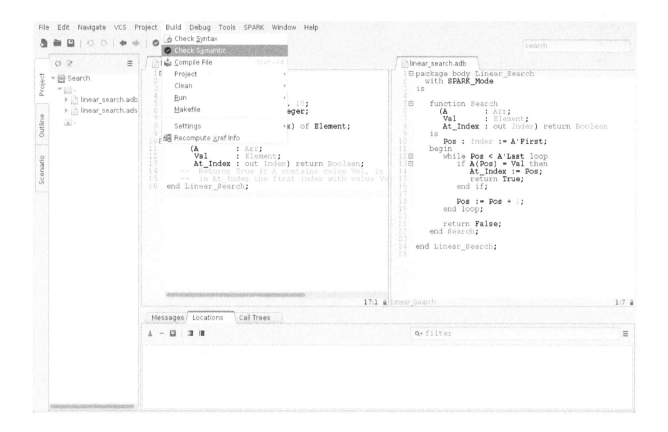

6.1.1 Checking SPARK Legality Rules

Now, let us run GNATprove on this unit, using the *SPARK → Examine File* menu, so that it issues errors on SPARK code that violates SPARK rules:

It detects here that function `Search` is not in SPARK, because it has an `out` parameter:

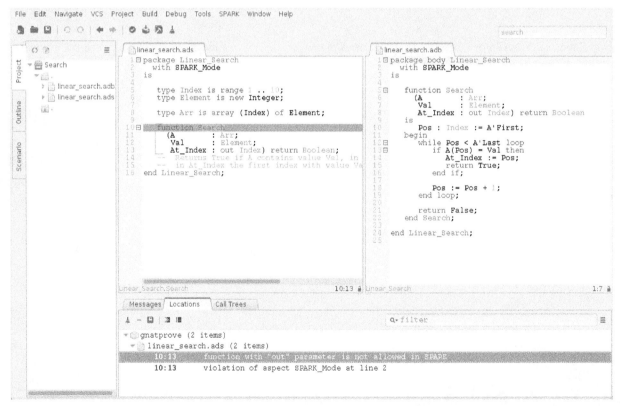

The permission in Ada 2012 to have `out` parameters to functions is not allowed in SPARK, because it causes calls to have side-effects (assigning to their `out` parameters), which means that various calls in the same expression may be conflicting, yielding different results depending on the order of evaluation of the expression.

We correct this problem by defining a record type `Search_Result` in `linear_search.ads` holding both the Boolean result and the index for cases when the value is found, and making `Search` return this type:

```
package Linear_Search
  with SPARK_Mode
is

   type Index is range 1 .. 10;
   type Element is new Integer;

   type Arr is array (Index) of Element;

   type Search_Result is record
      Found    : Boolean;
      At_Index : Index;
   end record;

   function Search
     (A   : Arr;
      Val : Element) return Search_Result;

end Linear_Search;
```

The implementation of `Search` in `linear_search.adb` is modified to use this type:

```
package body Linear_Search
  with SPARK_Mode
is

   function Search
     (A   : Arr;
      Val : Element) return Search_Result
   is
      Pos : Index := A'First;
      Res : Search_Result;
   begin
      while Pos < A'Last loop
         if A (Pos) = Val then
            Res.At_Index := Pos;
            Res.Found := True;
            return Res;
         end if;

         Pos := Pos + 1;
      end loop;

      Res.Found := False;
      return Res;
   end Search;

end Linear_Search;
```

6.1.2 Checking SPARK Initialization Policy

Re-running GNATprove on this unit, still using the *SPARK → Examine File* menu, now reports a different kind of error. This time it is the static analysis pass of GNATprove called *flow analysis* that detects an attempt of the program to return variable Res while it is not fully initialized, thus violating the initialization policy of SPARK:

Inside the GPS editor, we can click on the icon, either on the left of the message, or on line 23 in file linear_search.adb, to show the path on which Res.At_Index is not initialized:

Another click on the icon makes the path disappear.

This shows that, when the value is not found, the component `At_Index` of the value returned is indeed not initialized. Although that is allowed in Ada, SPARK requires that all inputs and outputs of subprograms are completely initialized (and the value returned by a function is such an output). As a solution, we could give a dummy value to component `At_Index` when the search fails, but we choose here to turn the type `Search_Result` in `linear_search.ads` into a discriminant record, so that the component `At_Index` is only usable when the search succeeds:

```
type Search_Result (Found : Boolean := False) is record
   case Found is
      when True =>
         At_Index : Index;
      when False =>
         null;
   end case;
end record;
```

Then, in the implementation of `Search` in `linear_search.adb`, we change the value of the discriminant depending on the success of the search:

```
function Search
   (A   : Arr;
    Val : Element) return Search_Result
is
   Pos : Index := A'First;
   Res : Search_Result;
begin
   while Pos < A'Last loop
      if A(Pos) = Val then
         Res := (Found    => True,
                 At_Index => Pos);
```

```
12          return Res;
13        end if;
14
15        Pos := Pos + 1;
16     end loop;
17
18     Res := (Found => False);
19     return Res;
20   end Search;
```

Now re-running GNATprove on this unit, using the *SPARK → Examine File* menu, shows that there are no reads of uninitialized data.

6.1.3 Writing Functional Contracts

We now have a valid SPARK program. It is not yet very interesting SPARK code though, as it does not contain any contracts, which are necessary to be able to apply formal verification modularly on each subprogram, independently of the implementation of other subprograms. The precondition constrains the value of input parameters, while the postcondition states desired properties of the result of the function. See *Preconditions* and *Postconditions* for more details. Here, we can require in the precondition of Search in linear_search.ads that callers of Search always pass a non-negative value for parameter Val, and we can state that, when the search succeeds, the index returned points to the desired value in the array:

```
1   function Search
2      (A   : Arr;
3       Val : Element) return Search_Result
4   with
5     Pre  => Val >= 0,
6     Post => (if Search'Result.Found then
7                A (Search'Result.At_Index) = Val),
```

Notice the use of an if-expression in the postcondition to express an implication: if the search succeeds it implies that the value at the returned index is the value that was being searched for. Note also the use of Search'Result to denote the value returned by the function.

This contract is still not very strong. Many faulty implementations of the search would pass this contract, for example one that always fails (thus returning with Search'Result.Found = False). We could reinforce the postcondition, but we choose here to do it through a contract by cases, which adds further constraints to the usual contract by precondition and postcondition. We want to consider here three cases:

- the desired value is found at the first index (1)

- the desired value is found at other indexes (2 to 10)

- the desired value is not found in the range 1 to 10

In the first case, we want to state that the index returned is 1. In the second case, we want to state that the search succeeds. In the third case, we want to state that the search fails. We use a helper function Value_Found_In_Range in linear_search.ads to express that a value Val is found in an array A within given bounds Low and Up:

```
1   function Value_Found_In_Range
2      (A       : Arr;
3       Val     : Element;
4       Low, Up : Index) return Boolean
5   is (for some J in Low .. Up => A(J) = Val);
6
7   function Search
```

```
 8       (A   : Arr;
 9        Val : Element) return Search_Result
10     with
11       Pre  => Val >= 0,
12       Post => (if Search'Result.Found then
13                 A (Search'Result.At_Index) = Val),
14       Contract_Cases =>
15         (A(1) = Val =>
16            Search'Result.At_Index = 1,
17          Value_Found_In_Range (A, Val, 2, 10) =>
18            Search'Result.Found,
19          (for all J in Arr'Range => A(J) /= Val) =>
20            not Search'Result.Found);
```

Note that we express `Value_Found_In_Range` as an expression function, a function whose body consists of a single expression, which can be given in a specification file.

Note also the use of quantified expressions to express properties over collections: `for some` in `Value_Found_In_Range` expresses an existential property (there exists an index in this range such that ...), `for all` in the third contract case expresses a universal property (all indexes in this range are such that ...).

Each contract case consists of a guard (on the left of the arrow symbol) evaluated on subprogram entry, and a consequence (on the right of the arrow symbol) evaluated on subprogram exit. The special expression `Search'Result` may be used in consequence expressions. The three guards here should cover all possible cases, and be disjoint. When a contract case is activated (meaning its guard holds on entry), its consequence should hold on exit.

The program obtained so far is a valid SPARK program, which GNAT analyzes semantically without errors or warnings.

6.2 Testing SPARK Programs

We can compile the above program, and test it on a set of selected inputs. The following test program in file `test_search.adb` exercises the case where the searched value is present in the array and the case where it is not:

```
 1  with Linear_Search; use Linear_Search;
 2  with Ada.Text_IO;    use Ada.Text_IO;
 3
 4  procedure Test_Search is
 5     A   : constant Arr := (1, 5, 3, 8, 8, 2, 0, 1, 0, 4);
 6     Res : Search_Result;
 7
 8  begin
 9     Res := Search (A, 1);
10     if Res.Found then
11        if Res.At_Index = 1 then
12           Put_Line ("OK: Found existing value at first index");
13        else
14           Put_Line ("not OK: Found existing value at other index");
15        end if;
16     else
17        Put_Line ("not OK: Did not find existing value");
18     end if;
19
20     Res := Search (A, 6);
21     if not Res.Found then
```

```
22        Put_Line ("OK: Did not find non-existing value");
23     else
24        Put_Line ("not OK: Found non-existing value");
25     end if;
26  end Test_Search;
```

We can check that the implementation of `Linear_Search` passes this test by compiling and running the test program:

```
$ gnatmake test_search.adb
$ test_search
> OK: Found existing value at first index
> OK: Did not find non-existing value
```

Note: We use above the command-line interface to compile and run the test program `test_search.adb`. You can do the same inside GPS by selecting the menu *Project → Properties* and inside the panel *Main* of folder *Sources*, add `test_search.adb` as a main file. Then, click *OK*. To generate the `test_search` executable, you can now select the menu *Build → Project → test_search.adb* and to run the `test_search` executable, you can select the menu *Build → Run → test_search*.

But only part of the program was really tested, as the contract was not checked during execution. To check the contract at run time, we recompile with the switch `-gnata` (a for assertions, plus switch `-f` to force recompilation of sources that have not changed):

- a check is inserted that the precondition holds on subprogram entry

- a check is inserted that the postcondition holds on subprogram exit

- a check is inserted that the guards of contract cases are disjoint on subprogram entry (no two cases are activated at the same time)

- a check is inserted that the guards of contract cases are complete on subprogram entry (one case must be activated)

- a check is inserted that the consequence of the activated contract case holds on subprogram exit

Note that the evaluation of the above assertions may also trigger other run-time check failures, like an index out of bounds. With these additional run-time checks, an error is reported when running the test program:

```
$ gnatmake -gnata -f test_search.adb
$ test_search
> raised SYSTEM.ASSERTIONS.ASSERT_FAILURE : contract cases overlap for subprogram
 ↪search
```

Note: We use above the command-line interface to add compilation switch `-gnata` and force recompilation with switch `-f`. You can do the same inside GPS by selecting the menu *Project → Properties* and inside the panel *Ada* of the subfolder *Switches* of folder *Build*, select the checkbox *Enable assertions*. Then, click *OK*. To force recompilation with the new switch, you can now select the menu *Build → Clean → Clean All* followed by recompilation with *Build → Project → test_search.adb*. Then run the `test_search` executable with *Build → Run → test_search*.

It appears that two contract cases for `Search` are activated at the same time! More information can be generated at run time if the code is compiler with the switch `-gnateE`:

```
$ gnatmake -gnata -gnateE -f test_search.adb
$ test_search
```

```
> raised SYSTEM.ASSERTIONS.ASSERT_FAILURE : contract cases overlap for subprogram
↪search
>    case guard at linear_search.ads:33 evaluates to True
>    case guard at linear_search.ads:35 evaluates to True
```

It shows here that the guards of the first and second contract cases hold at the same time. This failure in annotations can be debugged with `gdb` like a failure in the code (provided the program was compiled with appropriate switches, like `-g -O0`). The stack trace inside GPS shows that the error occurs on the first call to `Search` in the test program:

Indeed, the value 1 is present twice in the array, at indexes 1 and 8, which makes the two guards `A(1) = Val` and `Value_Found_In_Range (A, Val, 2, 10)` evaluate to `True`. We correct the contract of `Search` in `linear_search.ads` by strengthening the guard of the second contract case, so that it only applies when the value is not found at index 1:

```
1        Contract_Cases =>
2           (A(1) = Val =>
3              Search'Result.At_Index = 1,
4           A(1) /= Val and then Value_Found_In_Range (A, Val, 2, 10) =>
5              Search'Result.Found,
6           (for all J in Arr'Range => A(J) /= Val) =>
7              not Search'Result.Found);
```

With this updated contract, the test passes again, but this time with assertions checked at run time:

```
$ gnatmake -gnata test_search.adb
$ test_search
> OK: Found existing value at first index
> OK: Did not find non-existing value
```

The program obtained so far passes successfully a test campaign (of one test!) that achieves 100% coverage for all the common coverage criteria, once impossible paths have been ruled out: statement coverage, condition coverage, the MC/DC coverage used in avionics, and even the full static path coverage.

6.3 Proving SPARK Programs

Formal verification of SPARK programs is a two-step process:

1. the first step checks that flows through the program correctly implement the specified flows (if any), and that all values read are initialized.

2. the second step checks that the program correctly implement its specified contracts (if any), and that no run-time error can be raised.

Step 1 is implemented as a static analysis pass in the tool GNATprove, in `flow` mode. We have seen this flow analysis at work earlier (see *Checking SPARK Initialization Policy*). Step 2 is implemented as a deductive verification (a.k.a. *proof*) pass in the tool GNATprove, in the default `all` mode.

The difference between these two steps should be emphasized. Flow analysis in step 1 is a terminating algorithm, which typically takes 2 to 10 times as long as compilation to complete. Proof in step 2 is based on the generation of logical formulas for each check to prove, which are then passed on to automatic provers to decide whether the logical formula holds or not. The generation of logical formulas is a translation phase, which typically takes 10 times as long as compilation to complete. The automatic proof of logical formulas may take a very long time, or never terminate, hence the use of a timeout (1s at proof level 0) for each call to the automatic provers. It is this last step which takes the most time when calling GNATprove on a program, but it is also a step which can be completely parallelized (using switch `-j` to specify the number of parallel processes): each logical formula can be proved independently, so the more cores are available the faster it completes.

Note: The proof results presented in this tutorial may slightly vary from the results you obtain on your machine, as automatic provers may take more or less time to complete a proof depending on the platform and machine used.

Let us continue with our running example. This time we will see how step 2 works to prove contracts and absence of run-time errors, using the main mode `all` of GNATprove reached through the *SPARK → Prove File* menu.

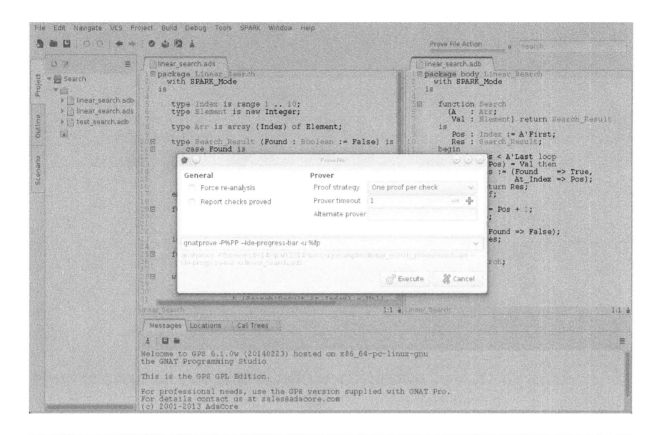

Note: The proof panels presented in this tutorial correspond to an advanced user profile. A simpler proof panel is displayed when the basic user profile is selected (the default). You can switch to the advanced user profile in menu *Edit → Preferences → SPARK*, by changing the value of *User profile* from `Basic` to `Advanced`. See *Running GNATprove from GPS* for details.

We use the default settings and click on *Execute*. It completes in a few seconds, with a message stating that some checks could not be proved:

Note that there is no such message on the postcondition of `Search`, which means that it was proved. Likewise, there are no such messages on the body of `Search`, which means that no run-time errors can be raised when executing the function.

These messages correspond to checks done when exiting from `Search`. It is expected that not much can be proved at this point, given that the body of `Search` has a loop but no loop invariant, so the formulas generated for these checks assume the worst about locations modified in the loop. A loop invariant is a special pragma `Loop_Invariant` stating an assertion in a loop, which can be both executed at run-time like a regular pragma `Assert`, and used by GNATprove to summarize the effect of successive iterations of the loop. We need to add a loop invariant in `linear_search.adb` stating enough properties about the cumulative effect of loop iterations, so that the contract cases of `Search` become provable. Here, it should state that the value searched was not previously found:

```
pragma Loop_Invariant
   (not Value_Found_In_Range (A, Val, A'First, Pos));
```

As stated above, this invariant holds exactly between the two statements in the loop in `linear_search.adb` (after the if-statement, before the increment of the index). Thus, it should be inserted at this place. With this loop invariant, two checks previously not proved are now proved, and a check previously proved becomes unproved:

The new unproved checks may seem odd, since all we did was add information in the form of a loop invariant. The reason is that we also removed information at the same time. By adding a loop invariant, we require GNATprove to prove iterations around the (virtual) loop formed by the following steps:

1. Take any context satisfying the loop invariant, which summarizes all previous iterations of the loop.

2. Execute the end of a source loop iteration (just the increment here).

3. Test whether the loop exits, and continue with values which do not exit.

4. Execute the start of a source loop iteration (just the if-statement here).

5. Check that the loop invariant still holds.

Around this virtual loop, nothing guarantees that the index `Pos` is below the maximal index at step 2 (the increment), so the range check cannot be proved. It was previously proved because, in the absence of a loop invariant, GNATprove proves iterations around the source loop, and then we get the information that, since the loop did not exit, its test `Pos < A'Last` is false, so the range check can be proved.

We solve this issue by setting the type of `Pos` in `linear_search.adb` to the base type of `Index`, which ranges past the last value of `Index`. (This may not be the simplest solution, but we use it here for the dynamics of this tutorial.)

```
      Pos : Index'Base := A'First;
```

And we add the range information for `Pos` to the loop invariant in `linear_search.adb`:

```
         pragma Loop_Invariant
            (Pos in A'Range
               and then
             not Value_Found_In_Range (A, Val, A'First, Pos));
```

This allows GNATprove to prove the range check, but not the contract:

This is actually progress! Indeed, the loop invariant should be strong enough to:

1. prove the absence of run-time errors in the loop and after the loop

2. prove that it is preserved from iteration to iteration

3. prove the postcondition and contract cases of the subprogram

So we have just achieved goal 1 above!

As we have modified the code and annotations, it is a good time to compile and run our test program, before doing any more formal verification work. This helps catch bugs early, and it's easy to do! In particular, the loop invariant will be dynamically checked at each iteration through the loop. Here, testing does not show any problems:

```
$ gnatmake -gnata test_search.adb
$ test_search
> OK: Found existing value at first index
> OK: Did not find non-existing value
```

The next easy thing to do is to increase the timeout of automatic provers. Its default of 1s is deliberately low, to facilitate interaction with GNATprove during the development of annotations, but it is not sufficient to prove the more complex checks. Let's increase it to 10s (or equivalently set the Proof level to 2 in the proof panel corresponding to a basic user profile), and rerun GNATprove:

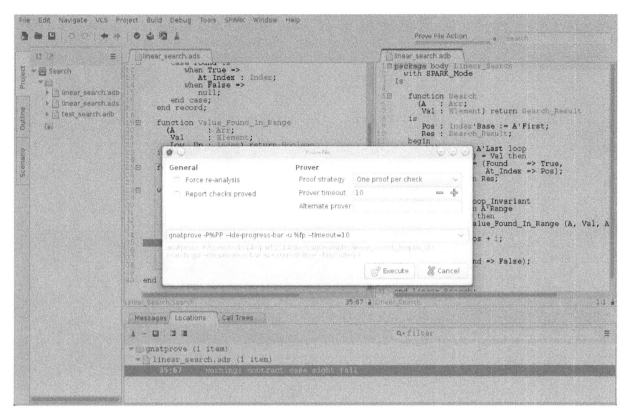

The unproved check remains in the contract cases of `Linear_Search`. The next step is to use the *SPARK → Prove Line* contextual menu available on line 35:

We select the `Progressively split` value for choice `Proof strategy` in the window raised in order to maximize proof precision (or equivalently set the `Proof level` to 3 in the proof panel corresponding to a basic user profile), and click on *Execute*:

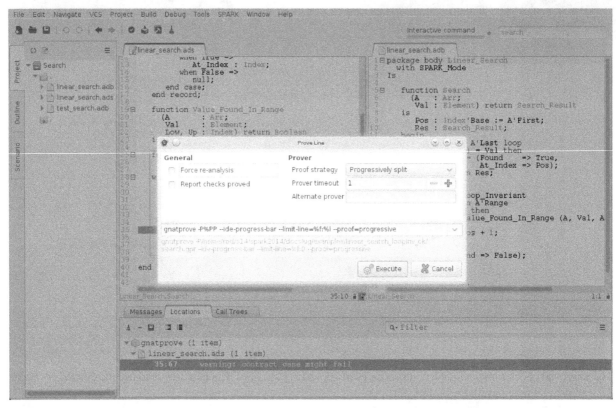

This runs GNATprove only on the checks that originate from line 35, in a special mode which considers separately individual execution paths if needed. The check is still not proved, but GPS now displays an icon, either on the left of the message, or on line 35 in file `linear_search.ads`, to show the path on which the contract case is not proved:

This corresponds to a case where the implementation of `Search` does not find the searched value, but the guard of the second contract case holds, meaning that the value is present in the range 2 to 10. Looking more closely at the path highlighted, we can see that the loop exits when `Pos = A'Last`, so the value 10 is never considered! We correct this bug by changing the loop test in `linear_search.adb` from a strict to a non-strict comparison operation:

```
    while Pos <= A'Last loop
```

On this modified code, we rerun GNATprove on line 35, checking the box `Report checks proved` to get information even when a check is proved. The reassuring green color (and the accompanying info message) show that the check was proved this time:

As usual after code changes, we rerun the test program, which shows no errors. Rerunning GNATprove on the complete file shows no more unproved checks. The `Linear_Search` unit has been fully proved. To see all the checks that were proved, we can rerun the tool with box `Report checks proved` checked, which displays the results previously computed:

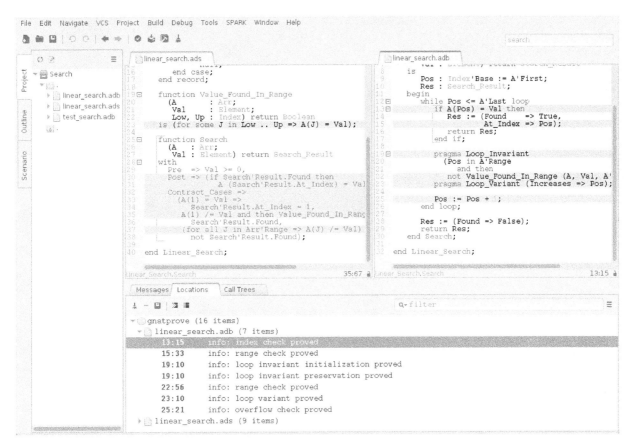

Note that one thing that was not proved is that `Search` terminates. As it contains a while-loop, it could loop forever. To prove that it is not the case, we add a loop variant, which specifies a quantity varying monotonically with each iteration. Since this quantity is bounded by its type, and we have proved absence of run-time errors in `Search`, proving this monotonicity property also shows that there cannot be an infinite number of iterations of the loop. The natural loop variant for `Search` is the index `Pos`, which increases at each loop iteration:

```
pragma Loop_Variant (Increases => Pos);
```

With this line inserted after the loop invariant in `linear_search.adb`, the test program still runs without errors (it checks dynamically that the loop variant is respected), and the program is still fully proved. Here is the final version of `Linear_Search`, with the complete annotations:

```
1   package Linear_Search
2      with SPARK_Mode
3   is
4
5      type Index is range 1 .. 10;
6      type Element is new Integer;
7
8      type Arr is array (Index) of Element;
9
10     type Search_Result (Found : Boolean := False) is record
11        case Found is
12           when True =>
13              At_Index : Index;
14           when False =>
15              null;
16        end case;
17     end record;
```

```
18
19     function Value_Found_In_Range
20        (A         : Arr;
21         Val       : Element;
22         Low, Up : Index) return Boolean
23     is (for some J in Low .. Up => A(J) = Val);
24
25     function Search
26        (A   : Arr;
27         Val : Element) return Search_Result
28     with
29       Pre  => Val >= 0,
30       Post => (if Search'Result.Found then
31                    A (Search'Result.At_Index) = Val),
32       Contract_Cases =>
33         (A(1) = Val =>
34            Search'Result.At_Index = 1,
35          A(1) /= Val and then Value_Found_In_Range (A, Val, 2, 10) =>
36            Search'Result.Found,
37          (for all J in Arr'Range => A(J) /= Val) =>
38            not Search'Result.Found);
39
40  end Linear_Search;
```

```
1   package body Linear_Search
2     with SPARK_Mode
3   is
4
5      function Search
6         (A   : Arr;
7          Val : Element) return Search_Result
8      is
9         Pos : Index'Base := A'First;
10        Res : Search_Result;
11     begin
12        while Pos <= A'Last loop
13           if A(Pos) = Val then
14              Res := (Found    => True,
15                      At_Index => Pos);
16              return Res;
17           end if;
18
19           pragma Loop_Invariant
20             (Pos in A'Range
21                and then
22              not Value_Found_In_Range (A, Val, A'First, Pos));
23           pragma Loop_Variant (Increases => Pos);
24
25           Pos := Pos + 1;
26        end loop;
27
28        Res := (Found => False);
29        return Res;
30     end Search;
31
32  end Linear_Search;
```

The final version of the linear_search example is part of the *Examples in the Toolset Distribution*. This concludes our tutorial on the SPARK toolset.

FORMAL VERIFICATION WITH GNATPROVE

The GNATprove tool is packaged as an executable called `gnatprove`. Like other tools in GNAT toolsuite, GNAT-prove is based on the structure of GNAT projects, defined in `.gpr` files.

A crucial feature of GNATprove is that it interprets annotations exactly like they are interpreted at run time during tests. In particular, their executable semantics includes the verification of run-time checks, which can be verified statically with GNATprove. GNATprove also performs additional verifications on the specification of the expected behavior itself, and its correspondence to the code.

7.1 How to Run GNATprove

7.1.1 Setting Up a Project File

Basic Project Set Up

If not already done, create a GNAT project file (*.gpr*), as documented in the GNAT User's Guide, section *GNAT Project Manager*. See also *Project Attributes* for optional project attributes to specify the proof directory and other GNATprove switches in the project file directly.

Note that you can use the project wizard from GPS to create a project file interactively, via the menu *File → New Project....* In the dialog, see in particular the default option (*Single Project*).

If you want to get started quickly, and assuming a standard naming scheme using `.ads`/ `.adb` lower case files and a single source directory, then your project file will look like:

```
project My_Project is
   for Source_Dirs use (".");
end My_Project;
```

saved in a file called `my_project.gpr`.

Having Different Switches for Compilation and Verification

In some cases, you may want to pass different compilation-level switches to GNAT and GNATprove, for example use warning switches only for compilation, in the same project file. In that case, you can use a scenario variable to specify different switches for compilation and verification:

```
project My_Project is

   type Modes is ("Compile", "Analyze");
   Mode : Modes := External ("MODE", "Compile");
```

```
   package Compiler is
      case Mode is
         when "Compile" =>
            for Switches ("Ada") use ...
         when "Analyze" =>
            for Switches ("Ada") use ...
      end case;
   end Compiler;

end My_Project;
```

With the above project, compilation is done using the `Compile` default mode:

```
gprbuild -P my_project.gpr
```

while formal verification is done using the `Analyze` mode:

```
gnatprove -P my_project.gpr -XMODE=Analyze
```

7.1.2 Running GNATprove from the Command Line

GNATprove can be run from the command line as follows:

```
gnatprove -P <project-file.gpr>
```

In the appendix, section *Command Line Invocation*, you can find an exhaustive list of switches; here we only give an overview over the most common uses. Note that GNATprove cannot be run without a project file.

There are essentially three common ways you can select the files which will be analyzed by GNATprove:

- Analyze everything:

```
gnatprove -P <project-file.gpr> -U
```

  With switch -U, all units of all projects in the project tree are analyzed. This includes units that are not used yet.

  This is usually what you want to use for an overnight analysis of a complex project.

- Analyze this project:

```
gnatprove -P <project-file.gpr>
```

  All main units in the project and all units they (recursively) depend on are analyzed. If there are no main units specified, analyze all files in the project.

  This is what you want to use for the analysis of a particular executable only, or if you want to analyze different executables within a complex project with different options.

- Analyze files:

```
gnatprove -P <project-file.gpr> [-u] FILES...
```

  If -u is specified, we only analyze the given files. If -u is not specified, we also analyze all units these files (recursively) depend on.

  This is intended for the day-to-day command-line or IDE use of GNATprove when implementing a project.

GNATprove consists of two distinct analyses: flow analysis and proof. Flow analysis checks the correctness of aspects related to data flow (Global, Depends, Abstract_State, Initializes, and refinement versions of these), and verifies the initialization of variables. Proof verifies the absence of run-time errors and the correctness of assertions such as Pre and Post aspects. Using the switch --mode=<mode>, whose possible values are check, check_all, flow, prove all, stone, bronze, silver and gold, you can choose which analysis is performed:

- In mode check, GNATprove partially checks that the program does not violate SPARK restrictions. The benefit of using this mode prior to mode check_all is that it is much faster, as it does not require the results of flow analysis.

- In mode check_all (stone is a synonym for this mode), GNATprove fully checks that the program does not violate SPARK restrictions, including checks not performed in mode check like the absence of side-effects in functions. Mode check_all includes mode check.

- In mode flow (bronze is a synonym for this mode), GNATprove checks that no uninitialized data are read in the program, and that the specified data dependencies and flow dependencies are respected in the implementation. Mode flow includes mode check_all. This phase is called *flow analysis*.

- In mode prove , GNATprove checks that the program is free from run-time errors, and that the specified functional contracts are respected in the implementation. Mode prove includes mode check_all, as well as the part of mode flow that checks that no uninitialized data are read, to guarantee soundness of the proof results. This phase is called *proof*.

- In the default mode all, GNATprove does both flow analysis and proof. The silver and gold modes are synonyms for this mode.

Using the option --limit-line= one can limit proofs to a particular file and line of an Ada file. For example, if you want to prove only line 12 of file example.adb, you can add the option --limit-line=example.adb:12 to the call to GNATprove. Using the option --limit-subp= one can limit proofs to a subprogram declared in a particular file at a particular line.

A number of options exist to influence the behavior for proof. Internally, the prover(s) specified with option --prover is/are called repeatedly for each check or assertion. Using the option --timeout, one can change the maximal time that is allocated to each prover to prove each check or assertion. Using the option --steps (default: 100), one can set the maximum number of reasoning steps that the prover is allowed to perform before giving up. The steps option should be used when predictable results are required, because the results with a timeout may differ depending on the computing power or current load of the machine. The option -j activates parallel compilation and parallel proofs. With -jnnn, at most nnn cores can be used in parallel. With the special value -j0, at most N cores can be used in parallel, when N is the number of cores on the machine.

Note: When the project has a main file, or a file is passed as starting point to gnatprove, and the dependencies in the project are very linear (unit A depends only on unit B, which depends only on unit C, etc), then even when the -j switch is used, gnatprove may only consider one file at a time. This problem can be avoided by additionally using the -U switch.

The way checks are passed to the prover can also be influenced using the option --proof. By default, the prover is invoked a single time for each check or assertion (mode per_check). This can be changed using mode per_path to invoke the prover for each *path* that leads to the check. This option usually takes much longer, because the prover is invoked much more often, but may give better proof results. Finally, in mode progressive, invoking the prover a single time on the entire check is tried, and only if the check is not proved, then other techniques that progressively consider each path in isolation are tried.

The proof mode set with --proof can be extended with a qualifier all or lazy, so that the entire switch may for example look like this: --proof=progressive:all. With this qualifier, one can select if proof should stop at the first unproved formula (to save time) for a check or should continue attempting to prove the other formulas related to the same check (typically to identify more precisely which formulas are left unproved, which can be then be handled with manual proof). The former is most suited for fully automatic proof, it is the default value, and can be explicitly selected with `lazy`. The latter is most suited for combination of automatic and manual proof and can be selected with `all`.

Instead of setting individually switches that influence the speed and power of proof, one may use the switch `--level`, which corresponds to predefined proof levels, from the faster level 0 to the more powerful level 4. More precisely, each value of `--level` is equivalent to directly setting a collection of other switches discussed above:

- `--level=0` is equivalent to `--prover=cvc4 --proof=per_check --timeout=1`

- `--level=1` is equivalent to `--prover=cvc4,z3,altergo --proof=per_check --timeout=1`

- `--level=2` is equivalent to `--prover=cvc4,z3,altergo --proof=per_check --timeout=5`

- `--level=3` is equivalent to `--prover=cvc4,z3,altergo --proof=progressive --timeout=5`

- `--level=4` is equivalent to `--prover=cvc4,z3,altergo --proof=progressive --timeout=10`

If both `--level` is set and an underlying switch is set (`--prover`, `--timeout`, or `--proof`), the value of the latter takes precedence over the value set through `--level`.

Note that using `--level` does not provide results that are reproducible accross different machines. For nightly builds or shared repositories, consider using the `--steps` or `--replay` switches instead. The number of steps required to proved an example can be accessed by running GNATprove with the option `--report=statistics`.

GNATprove also supports using the static analysis tool CodePeer as an additional source for the proof of checks, by specifying the command line option `--codepeer=on` (see *Using CodePeer Static Analysis*).

By default, GNATprove avoids reanalyzing unchanged files, on a per-unit basis. This mechanism can be disabled with the option `-f`.

When GNATprove proves a check, it stores this result in a session file, along with the required time and steps for this check to be proved. This information can be used to replay the proofs, to check that they are indeed correct. When GNATprove is invoked using the `--replay` option, it will attempt such a replay, using the same prover that was able to prove the check last time, with some slightly higher time and step limit. In this mode, the user-provided steps and time limits are ignored. If the `--prover` option is not provided, GNATprove will attempt to replay all checks, otherwise it will replay only the proofs proved by one of the specified provers. If all replays succeeded, GNATprove output will be exactly the same as a normal run of GNATprove. If a replay failed, the corresponding check will be reported as not proved. If a replay has not been attempted because the corresponding prover is not available (a third-party prover that is not configured, or the user has selected other provers using the `--prover` option), a warning will be issued that the proof could not be replayed, but the check will still be marked as proved.

By default, GNATprove stops at the first unit where it detect errors (violations of Ada or SPARK legality rules). The option `-k` can be used to get GNATprove to issue errors of the same kind for multiple units. If there are any violations of Ada legality rules, GNATprove does not attempt any analysis. If there are violations of SPARK legality rules, GNATprove stops after the checking phase and does not attempt flow analysis or proof.

When an error is detected, or when issuing check messages, GNATprove returns with a non-zero exit status. When an error is detected, GNATprove also issues a message about termination in error. Otherwise, GNATprove returns with an exit status of zero, even when warnings are issued.

7.1.3 Using the GNAT Target Runtime Directory

If you are using GNAT as your target compiler and explicitly specify a runtime and target to use in your project, for instance:

```
for Target use "arm-eabi";
for Runtime ("Ada") use "ravenscar-sfp-stm32f4";
```

GNATprove will take such setting into account and will use the GNAT runtime directory, as long as your target compiler is found in your PATH environment variable. Note that you will need to use a matching version of GNAT and SPARK (e.g. GNAT 18.2 and SPARK 18.2).

The handling of runtimes of GNATprove is in fact unified with that of the GNAT compiler. For details, see "GNAT User's Guide Supplement for Cross Platforms", Section 3. If you specify a target, note that GNATprove requires additional configuration, see the section *Specifying the Target Architecture and Implementation-Defined Behavior*.

7.1.4 Specifying the Target Architecture and Implementation-Defined Behavior

A SPARK program is guaranteed to be unambiguous, so that formal verification of properties is possible. However, some behaviors (for example some representation attribute values like the `Size` attribute) may depend on the compiler used. By default, GNATprove adopts the same choices as the GNAT compiler. GNATprove also supports other compilers by providing special switches:

- `-gnateT` for specifying the target configuration
- `--pedantic` for warnings about possible implementation-defined behavior

Note that, even with switch `--pedantic`, GNATprove only detects some implementation-defined behaviors. For more details, see the dedicated section on how to *Ensure Portability of Programs*.

Note that GNATprove will always choose the smallest multiple of 8 bits for the base type, which is a safe and conservative choice for any Ada compiler.

Target Parameterization

By default, GNATprove assumes that the compilation target is the same as the host on which it is run, for setting target dependent values, such as endianness or sizes and alignments of standard types. If your target is not the same as the host on which you run GNATprove, you have to tell GNATprove the specificities of your target.

Note that specifying the `Target` attribute of project files is not enough for GNATprove. In addition, you need to add the following to your project file, under a scenario variable as seen in *Having Different Switches for Compilation and Verification*:

```
project My_Project is
   [...]
   package Builder is
      case Mode is
         when "Compile" =>
            ...
         when "Analyze" =>
            for Global_Compilation_Switches ("Ada") use ("-gnateT=" & My_Project
 ↪'Project_Dir & "/target.atp");
      end case;
   end Builder;
end My_Project;
```

where `target.atp` is a file stored here in the same directory as the project file `my_project.gpr`, which contains the target parametrization. The format of this file is described in the GNAT User's Guide as part of the `-gnateT` switch description.

Target parameterization can be used:

- to specify a target different than the host on which GNATprove is run, when cross-compilation is used. If GNAT is the cross compiler, the configuration file can be generated by calling the compiler for your target with the switch -gnatet=target.atp. Otherwise, the target file should be generated manually.

- to specify the parameters for a different compiler than GNAT, even when the host and target are the same. In that case, the target file should be generated manually.

Here is an example of a configuration file for a bare board PowerPC 750 processor configured as big-endian:

```
Bits_BE                      1
Bits_Per_Unit                8
Bits_Per_Word               32
Bytes_BE                     1
Char_Size                    8
Double_Float_Alignment       0
Double_Scalar_Alignment      0
Double_Size                 64
Float_Size                  32
Float_Words_BE               1
Int_Size                    32
Long_Double_Size            64
Long_Long_Size              64
Long_Size                   32
Maximum_Alignment           16
Max_Unaligned_Field         64
Pointer_Size                32
Short_Enums                  0
Short_Size                  16
Strict_Alignment             1
System_Allocator_Alignment   8
Wchar_T_Size                32
Words_BE                     1

float          6   I   32   32
double        15   I   64   64
long double   15   I   64   64
```

Parenthesized Arithmetic Operations

In Ada, non-parenthesized arithmetic operations could be re-ordered by the compiler, which may result in a failing computation (due to overflow checking) becoming a successful one, and vice-versa. By default, GNATprove evaluates all expressions left-to-right, like GNAT. When the switch --pedantic is used, a warning is emitted for every operation that could be re-ordered:

- any operand of a binary adding operation (+,-) that is itself a binary adding operation;

- any operand of a binary multiplying operation (*,/,mod,rem) that is itself a binary multiplying operation.

7.1.5 Using CodePeer Static Analysis

Note: CodePeer is only available as part of SPARK Pro 17 and beyond, but is not included in SPARK Discovery.

CodePeer is a static analysis tool developed and commercialized by AdaCore (see http://www.adacore.com/codepeer). GNATprove supports using CodePeer as an additional source for the proof of checks, by specifying the command line option `--codepeer=on`. CodePeer will be run before automatic provers. If it proves a check, GNATprove will not attempt to run another prover on this check.

When run by GNATprove, CodePeer does not attempt to generate preconditions, and relies instead on user-provided preconditions for its analysis. CodePeer analysis inside GNATprove is sound, in that it does not allow to prove a check that could fail. CodePeer analysis may allow to prove more properties than the strict contract-based reasoning performed in SPARK allow in general:

1. CodePeer generates a sound approximation of data dependencies for subprograms based on the implementation of subprograms and the call-graph relating subprograms. Hence CodePeer may be able to prove properties which cannot be deduced otherwise based on too coarse user-provided data dependencies.

2. CodePeer generates a sound approximation of loop invariants for loops. Hence CodePeer may be able to prove properties which cannot be deduced otherwise based on imprecise loop invariants, or in absence of a loop invariant.

In addition, CodePeer is using the same choice as GNAT compiler for the rounding of fixed-point multiplication and division. This makes it more precise for the analysis of code compiled with GNAT. If some code using fixed-point arithmetic is compiled with another compiler than GNAT, and the code uses fixed-point multiplication or division, the choice of rounding made in CodePeer may not be suitable, in which case `--codepeer=on` should not be used.

CodePeer analysis is particularly interesting when analyzing code using floating-point computations, as CodePeer is both fast and precise for proving bounds of floating-point operations.

7.1.6 Running GNATprove from GPS

GNATprove can be run from GPS. When GNATprove is installed and found on your PATH, a *SPARK* menu is available with the following entries:

Submenu	Action
Examine All	This runs GNATprove in flow analysis mode on all mains and the units they depend on in the project.
Examine All Sources	This runs GNATprove in flow analysis mode on all files in the project.
Examine File	This runs GNATprove in flow analysis mode on the current unit, its body and any subunits.
Prove All	This runs GNATprove on all mains and the units they depend on in the project.
Prove All Sources	This runs GNATprove on all files in the project.
Prove File	This runs GNATprove on the current unit, its body and any subunits.
Show Report	This displays the report file generated by GNATprove.
Clean Proofs	This removes all files generated by GNATprove.

The three "Prove..." entries run GNATprove in the mode given by the project file, or in the default mode "all" if no mode is specified.

The menus *SPARK → Examine/Prove All* run GNATprove on all main files in the project, and all files they depend on (recursively). Both main files in the root project and in projects that are included in the root project are considered. The menus *SPARK → Examine/Prove All Sources* run GNATprove on all files in all projects. On a project that has neither main files nor includes other projects, menus *SPARK → Examine/Prove All* and *SPARK → Examine/Prove All Sources* are equivalent.

Keyboard shortcuts for these menu items can be set using the *Edit → Preferences* dialog in GPS, and opening the *General → Key Shortcuts* section.

Note: The changes made by users in the panels raised by these submenus are persistent from one session to the other. Be sure to check that the selected checkboxes and additional switches that were previously added are still appropriate.

When editing an Ada file, GNATprove can also be run from a *SPARK* contextual menu, which can be obtained by a right click:

Submenu	Action
Examine File	This runs GNATprove in flow analysis mode on the current unit, its body and any subunits.
Examine Subprogram	This runs GNATprove in flow analysis mode on the current subprogram.
Prove File	This runs GNATprove on the current unit, its body and any subunits.
Prove Subprogram	This runs GNATprove on the current subprogram.
Prove Line	This runs GNATprove on the current line.
Prove Check	This runs GNATprove on the current failing condition. GNATprove must have been run at least once for this option to be available in order to know which conditions are failing.

Except from *Examine File* and *Prove File*, all other submenus are also applicable to code inside generic units, in which case the corresponding action is applied to all instances of the generic unit in the project. For example, if a generic unit is instantiated twice, selecting *Prove Subprogram* on a subprogram inside the generic unit will apply proof to the two corresponding subprograms in instances of the generic unit.

The menus *SPARK → Examine ...* open a panel which allows setting various switches for GNATprove's analysis. The main choice offered in this panel is to select the mode of analysis, among modes check, check_all and flow (the default).

The menus *SPARK → Prove ...* open a panel which allows setting various switches for GNATprove's analysis. By default, this panel offers a few simple choices, like the proof level (see description of switch --level in *Running GNATprove from the Command Line*). If the user changes its User profile for SPARK (in the SPARK section of the Preferences dialog - menu *Edit → Preferences*) from Basic to Advanced, then a more complex panel is displayed for proof, with more detailed switches.

GNATprove project switches can be edited from the panel GNATprove (menu *Edit → Project Properties*, in the *Build → Switches* section of the dialog).

When proving a check fails on a specific path through a subprogram (for both checks verified in flow analysis and in proof), GNATprove may generate path information for the user to see. The user can display this path in GPS by clicking on the icon to the left of the failed proof message, or to the left of the corresponding line in the editor. The path is hidden again when re-clicking on the same icon.

For checks verified in proof, GNATprove may also generate counterexample information for the user to see (see *Understanding Counterexamples*). The user can display this counterexample in GPS by clicking on the icon to the left of the failed proof message, or to the left of the corresponding line in the editor. The counterexample is hidden again when re-clicking on the same icon.

A monospace font with ligature like Fira Code (https://github.com/tonsky/FiraCode) or Hasklig (https://github.com/i-tu/Hasklig) can be separately installed and selected to make contracts more readable inside GPS or GNATbench. See the following screenshot which shows how symbols like => (arrow) or >= (greater than or equal) are displayed in such a font:

```
10  function LCP (A : Text; X, Y : Integer) return Natural with
11     SPARK_Mode,
12     Pre  ⇒ X in A'Range and then Y in A'Range,
13     Post ⇒
14       (for all K in 0 .. LCP'Result - 1 ⇒ A (X + K) = A (Y + K))
15         and then (X + LCP'Result = A'Last + 1
16                      or else Y + LCP'Result = A'Last + 1
17                      or else A (X + LCP'Result) /= A (Y + LCP'Result)),
18     Contract_Cases ⇒
19       (A (X) /= A (Y) ⇒ LCP'Result = 0,
20        X = Y           ⇒ LCP'Result = A'Last - X + 1,
21        others          ⇒ LCP'Result ≥ 0);
```

7.1.7 Running GNATprove from GNATbench

GNATprove can be run from GNATbench. When GNATprove is installed and found on your PATH, a *SPARK* menu is available with the following entries:

Submenu	Action
Examine All	This runs GNATprove in flow analysis mode on all mains and the units they depend on in the project.
Examine All Sources	This runs GNATprove in flow analysis mode on all files in the project.
Examine File	This runs GNATprove in flow analysis mode on the current unit, its body and any subunits.
Prove All	This runs GNATprove on all mains and the units they depend on in the project.
Prove All Sources	This runs GNATprove on all files in the project.
Prove File	This runs GNATprove on the current unit, its body and any subunits.
Show Report	This displays the report file generated by GNATprove.
Clean Proofs	This removes all files generated by GNATprove.

The three "Prove..." entries run GNATprove in the mode given by the project file, or in the default mode "all" if no mode is specified.

The menus *SPARK → Examine/Prove All* run GNATprove on all main files in the project, and all files they depend on (recursively). Both main files in the root project and in projects that are included in the root project are considered. The menus *SPARK → Examine/Prove All Sources* run GNATprove on all files in all projects. On a project that has neither main files nor includes other projects, menus *SPARK → Examine/Prove All* and *SPARK → Examine/Prove All Sources* are equivalent.

Note: The changes made by users in the panels raised by these submenus are persistent from one session to the other. Be sure to check that the selected checkboxes and additional switches that were previously added are still appropriate.

When editing an Ada file, GNATprove can also be run from a *SPARK* contextual menu, which can be obtained by a right click:

Submenu	Action
Examine File	This runs GNATprove in flow analysis mode on the current unit, its body and any subunits.
Examine Subprogram	This runs GNATprove in flow analysis mode on the current subprogram.
Prove File	This runs GNATprove on the current unit, its body and any subunits.
Prove Subprogram	This runs GNATprove on the current subprogram.
Prove Line	This runs GNATprove on the current line.

7.1.8 GNATprove and Manual Proof

When automated provers fail to prove some condition that is valid, the validity may be proved using manual proof inside GPS or an external interactive prover.

In the appendix, section *Alternative Provers*, is explained how to use different provers than the one GNATprove uses as default.

Calling an Interactive Prover From the Command Line

When the prover used by GNATprove is configured as interactive, for each analysed condition, either:

- It is the first time the prover is used on the condition then a file (containing the condition as input to the specified prover) is created in the project's proof directory (see *Project Attributes*). GNATprove outputs a message concerning this condition indicating the file that was created. The created file should be edited by the user in order to prove the condition.

- The prover has already been used on this condition and the editable file exists. The prover is run on the file and the success or failure of the proof is reported in the same way it is done with the default prover.

Note: Once a manual proof file is created and has been edited by the user, in order to run the prover on the file, the same prover must be once again specified to GNATprove. Once the condition is proved, the result will be saved in the why3 session so GNATprove won't need to be specified the prover again to know that the condition is valid.

Analysis with GNATprove can be limited to a single condition with the `--limit-line` option:

```
gnatprove -P <project-file.gpr> --prover=<prover> --limit-line=<file>:<line>:<column>:
 <check-kind>
```

Where `check-kind` can be deduced from the message associated to the failing condition reported by GNATprove:

Warning	Check kind
run-time checks	
divide by zero might fail	VC_DIVISION_CHECK
array index check might fail	VC_INDEX_CHECK
overflow check might fail	VC_OVERFLOW_CHECK
float overflow check might fail	VC_FP_OVERFLOW_CHECK
range check might fail	VC_RANGE_CHECK
predicate check might fail	VC_PREDICATE_CHECK
predicate check might fail on default value	VC_PREDICATE_CHECK_ON_DEFAULT_VAL
invariant check might fail	VC_INVARIANT_CHECK
invariant check might fail on default value	VC_INVARIANT_CHECK_ON_DEFAULT_VAL
length check might fail	VC_LENGTH_CHECK
	Continued on next pa

Table 7.1 – continued from previous page

Warning	Check kind
discriminant check might fail	VC_DISCRIMINANT_CHECK
tag check might fail	VC_TAG_CHECK
ceiling priority might not be in Interrupt_Priority	VC_CEILING_INTERRUPT
interrupt might be reserved	VC_INTERRUPT_RESERRED
ceiling priority protocol might not be respected	VC_CEILING_PRIORITY_PROTOCOL
task might terminate	VC_TASK_TERMINATION
assertions	
initial condition might fail	VC_INITIAL_CONDITION
default initial condition might fail	VC_DEFAULT_INITIAL_CONDITION
call to nonreturning subprogram might be executed	VC_PRECONDITION
precondition might fail	VC_PRECONDITION
precondition of main program might fail	VC_PRECONDITION_MAIN
postcondition might fail	VC_POSTCONDITION
refined postcondition might fail	VC_REFINED_POST
contract case might fail	VC_CONTRACT_CASE
contract cases might not be disjoint	VC_DISJOINT_CONTRACT_CASES
contract cases might not be complete	VC_COMPLETE_CONTRACT_CASES
loop invariant might fail in first iteration	VC_LOOP_INVARIANT_INIT
loop invariant might fail after first iteration	VC_LOOP_INVARIANT_PRESERV
loop variant might fail	VC_LOOP_VARIANT
assertion might fail	VC_ASSERT
exception might be raised	VC_RAISE
Liskov Substitution Principle	
precondition might be stronger than class-wide precondition	VC_WEAKER_PRE
precondition is stronger than the default class-wide precondition of True	VC_TRIVIAL_WEAKER_PRE
postcondition might be weaker than class-wide postcondition	VC_STRONGER_POST
class-wide precondition might be stronger than overridden one	VC_WEAKER_CLASSWIDE_PRE
class-wide postcondition might be weaker than overridden one	VC_STRONGER_CLASSWIDE_POST

Calling an Interactive Prover From GPS

After running GNATprove with proof mode, the menu *SPARK → Prove Check* is available by right-clicking on a check message in the location tab or by right-clicking on a line that fails because of a single condition (i.e. there is only one check in the output of GNATprove concerning this line).

In the dialog box, the field "Alternate prover" can be filled to use another prover than Alt-Ergo. If the alternative prover is configured as "interactive", after the execution of *SPARK → Prove Check*, GPS opens the manual proof file with the editor corresponding to the prover under the condition that an editor is specified in the configuration of the alternative prover.

Once the editor is closed, GPS re-executes *SPARK → Prove Check*. The user should verify the same alternative prover as before is still specified. After execution, GPS will offer to re-edit the file if the proof fails.

Manual Proof Within GPS

After running GNATprove with proof mode, the menu *SPARK → Start Manual Proof* is available by right-clicking on a check message in the location tab.

The manual proof interface immediately starts. It will change the GPS window by adding a Manual Proof console, a Proof Tree and the current Verification Condition being dealt with. This is an experimental system that allows the user to directly visualize the condition given to the prover. We provide safe transformations that can be used to help the prover. For example, you can directly provide a value to an existential in the goal, perform an induction on an integer or instantiate hypothesis with values that should be used by the prover.

At first, you can type `help` in the Manual Proof console. This will return the available commands. The most useful commands to the beginner are `list-provers` and `list-transforms`. `list-provers` returns the list of provers available on your machine. You can use any of them on your goal by typing its name in the console. For example, one can type `z3` to launch `z3` on the current Verification Condition. `list-transforms` returns a list of transformations that can be used on the Verification Condition. You can then try transformations like `assert (0 = 0)`. It will add two subgoals in the Proof Tree, one asking you to prove $0 = 0$ and one assuming $0 = 0$ to prove the current condition. The first one is easy, `CVC4` should be able to solve it. The corresponding part of the Proof Tree switched to green because `CVC4` proved the subgoal.

Once the goal is completely proved, you will get a popup window asking you if you want to save the session and exit. Answer yes and run GNATprove again on your file. The condition that was failing before should now be reported as checked. If you want to exit manual proof, you can select *SPARK → Exit Manual Proof* in the menu. It is recommended to close it using the menu because it makes sure to close everything related to manual proof.

More details on how to use it are available in *Manual Proof Using GPS*.

7.1.9 GNATprove and Network File Systems or Shared Folders

On Linux and Mac-OS, GNATprove needs to create a Unix domain socket file. This might be a problem if GNATprove attempts to create such a file in a directory that is a shared folder or on a network file system like NFS, which does not support such folders. To minimize changes for this to occur, GNATprove determines the folder to create that special file as follows:

- if the environment variable `TMPDIR` is set, and the corresponding directory exists and is writeable, use that; otherwise,

- if `/tmp` exists and is writable, use that; otherwise,

- use the `gnatprove` subfolder of the object directory of the root project.

7.2 How to View GNATprove Output

GNATprove produces two kinds of outputs: the one which is echoed to standard output or displayed in your IDE (GPS or GNATbench), and the one which is produced in a file `gnatprove.out`, which lies in the `gnatprove` subdirectory of the object directory of your project.

When switch `--output-header` is used, this file starts with a header containing extra information about the run including:

- The date and time of GNATprove run

- The GNATprove version that has generated this report

- The host for which GNATprove is configured (e.g. Windows 32 bits)

- The full command-line of the GNATprove invocation, including project file

- The GNATprove switches specified in the project file

7.2.1 The Analysis Results Summary Table

A summary table at the start of file `gnatprove.out` provides an overview of the verification results for all checks in the project. The table may look like this:

```
------------------------------------------------------------------------------------

,------------------------------------

SPARK Analysis Results       Total        Flow    Interval                      ⌴
⌴Provers   Justified   Unproved
------------------------------------------------------------------------------------

,---------------------------------

Data Dependencies                  .            .          .                       ⌴
⌴.         .
Flow Dependencies                  .            .          .                       ⌴
.         .
Initialization               2100         2079          .                       ⌴
.         .         21                                                            .
Non-Aliasing                       .            .          .                       ⌴
.  .              .
Run-time Checks              596             .          .    480 (altergo  31%, CVC4 ⌴
⌴69%)          .    116
Assertions                    3             .          .      3 (altergo  33%, CVC4 ⌴
⌴67%)          .        .
Functional Contracts        323             .          .    168 (altergo  24%, CVC4 ⌴
⌴76%)          .    155
LSP Verification                   .            .          .                       ⌴
⌴.        .         .

------------------------------------------------------------------------------------

,------------------------------

Total                       3022   2079 (69%)            .                     651⌴
⌴(22%)         .    292 (9%)
------------------------------------------------------------------------------------
```

The following table explains the lines of the summary table:

Line Description	Explanation
Data Dependencies	Verification of *Data Dependencies* and parameter modes
Flow Dependencies	Verification of *Flow Dependencies*
Initialization	Verification of *Data Initialization Policy*
Non-Aliasing	Verification of *Absence of Interferences*
Run-time Checks	Verification of absence of run-time errors (AoRTE) (except those raising `Storage_Error`)
Assertions	Verification of *Assertion Pragmas*
Functional Contracts	Verification of functional contracts (includes *Subprogram Contracts*, *Package Contracts* and *Type Contracts*)
LSP Verification	Verification related to *Object Oriented Programming and Liskov Substitution Principle*

We now explain the columns of the table.

- The `Total` column describes the total number of checks in this category.

- The `Flow` column describes the number of checks proved by flow analysis.

- The `Interval` column describes the number of checks (overflow and range checks) proved by a simple static analysis of bounds for floating-point expressions based on type bounds of sub-expressions.

- The `Provers` column describes the number of checks proved by automatic or manual provers. The column also gives information on the provers used, and the percentage of checks proved by each prover. Note that sometimes a check is proved by a combination of provers, hence the use of percentage instead of an absolute count. Also note that generally the prover which is run first (as determined by the `--prover` command line switch) proves the most checks, because each prover is called only on those checks that were not previously proved. The prover percentages are provided in alphabetical order.

- The `Justified` column contains the number of checks for which the user has provided a *Direct Justification with Pragma Annotate*.

- Finally, the column `Unproved` counts the checks which have neither been proved nor justified.

7.2.2 Categories of Messages

GNATprove issues four different kinds of messages: errors, warnings, check messages and information messages.

- Errors are issued for SPARK violations or other language legality problems, or any other problem which does not allow to proceed to analysis. Errors cannot be suppressed and must be fixed to proceed with analysis.

- Warnings are issued for any suspicious situation like unused values of variables, useless assignements, etc. Warnings are prefixed with the text `"warning:   "` and can be suppressed with `pragma Warnings`, see section *Suppressing Warnings*.

- Check messages are issued for any potential problem in the code which could affect the correctness of the program, such as missing initialization, possible failing run-time checks or unproved assertions. Checks come with a severity, and depending on the severity the message text is prefixed with `"low:   "`, `"medium:   "` or `"high:   "`. Check messages cannot be suppressed like warnings, but they can be individually justified with pragma `Annotate`, see section *Justifying Check Messages*.

- Information messages are issued to notify the user of limitations of GNATprove on some constructs, or to prevent possible confusion in understanding the output of GNATprove. They are also issued to report proved checks in some modes of GNATprove.

7.2.3 Effect of Mode on Output

GNATprove can be run in four different modes, as selected with the switch `--mode=<mode>`, whose possible values are `check`, `check_all`, `flow`, `prove` and `all` (see *Running GNATprove from the Command Line*). The output depends on the selected mode.

In modes `check` and `check_all`, GNATprove prints on the standard output a list of error messages for violations of SPARK restrictions on all the code for which `SPARK_Mode` is `On`.

In modes `flow` and `prove`, this checking is done as a first phase.

In mode `flow`, GNATprove prints on the standard output messages for possible reads of uninitialized data, mismatches between the specified data dependencies and flow dependencies and the implementation, and suspicious situations such as unused assignments and missing return statements. These messages are all based on flow analysis.

In mode `prove`, GNATprove prints on the standard output messages for possible reads of uninitialized data (using flow analysis), possible run-time errors and mismatches between the specified functional contracts and the implementation (using proof).

In mode `all`, GNATprove prints on the standard output both messages for mode `flow` and for mode `prove`.

If switch `--report=all`, `--report=provers` or `--report=statistics` is specified, GNATprove additionally prints on the standard output information messages for proved checks.

GNATprove generates global project statistics in file `gnatprove.out`, which can be displayed in GPS using the menu *SPARK → Show Report*. The statistics describe:

- which units were analyzed (with flow analysis, proof, or both)

- which subprograms in these units were analyzed (with flow analysis, proof, or both)

- the results of this analysis

7.2.4 Description of Messages

This section lists the different messages which GNATprove may output. Each message points to a very specific place in the source code. For example, if a source file `file.adb` contains a division as follows:

```
if X / Y > Z then ...
```

GNATprove may output a message such as:

```
file.adb:12:37: medium: divide by zero might fail
```

where the division sign / is precisely on line 12, column 37. Looking at the explanation in the first table below, which states that a division check verifies that the divisor is different from zero, it is clear that the message is about Y, and that GNATprove was unable to prove that Y cannot be zero. The explanations in the table below should be read with the context that is given by the source location.

When switch `--cwe` is used, a corresponding CWE id is included in the message when relevant. For example, on the example above, GNATprove will output a message such as:

```
file.adb:12:37: medium: divide by zero might fail [CWE 369]
```

Note that CWE ids are only included in check messages and warnings, never in information messages about proved checks. For more information on CWE, see the MITRE Corporation's Common Weakness Enumeration (CWE) Compatibility and Effectiveness Program (http://cwe.mitre.org/).

The following table shows the kinds of check messages issued by proof.

Message Kind	CWE	Explanation
run-time checks		
divide by zero	CWE 369	Check that the second operand of the division, mod or rem operation is different from zero.
index check	CWE 120	Check that the given index is within the bounds of the array.
overflow check	CWE 190	Check that the result of the given integer arithmetic operation is within the bounds of the base type.
fp_overflow check	CWE 739	Check that the result of the given floating point operation is within the bounds of the base type.
range check	CWE 682	Check that the given value is within the bounds of the expected scalar subtype.
predicate check	CWE 682	Check that the given value respects the applicable type predicate.
predicate check on default value	CWE 682	Check that the default value for the type respects the applicable type predicate.
invariant check		Check that the given value respects the applicable type invariant.
invariant check on default value		Check that the default value for the type respects the applicable type invariant.
length check		Check that the given array is of the length of the expected array subtype.

Continued on next page

Table 7.2 – continued from previous page

Message Kind	CWE	Explanation
discriminant check	CWE 136	Check that the discriminant of the given discrimina record has the expected value. For variant records, can happen for a simple access to a record field. there are other cases where a fixed value of the criminant is required.
tag check	CWE 136	Check that the tag of the given tagged object has expected value.
ceiling priority in Interrupt_Priority		Check that the ceiling priority specified for a tected object containing a procedure with an aspect tach_Handler is in Interrupt_Priority
interrupt is reserved		Check that the interrupt specified by Attach_Han is not reserved
ceiling priority protocol		Check that the ceiling priority protocol is respec i.e., when a task calls a protected operation, the ac priority of the task is not higher than the priority of protected object (ARM Annex D.3)
task termination		Check that the task does not terminate, as required Ravenscar
assertions		
initial condition		Check that the initial condition of a package is after elaboration.
default initial condition		Check that the default initial condition of a type is after default initialization of an object of the type.
precondition		Check that the precondition aspect of the given evaluates to True.
call to nonreturning subprogram		Check that the call to a subprogram called in case error is unreachable.
precondition of main		Check that the precondition aspect of the given m procedure evaluates to True after elaboration.
postcondition		Check that the postcondition aspect of the subprog evaluates to True.
refined postcondition		Check that the refined postcondition aspect of the s program evaluates to True.
contract case		Check that all cases of the contract case evaluate true at the end of the subprogram.
disjoint contract cases		Check that the cases of the contract cases aspect are mutually disjoint.
complete contract cases		Check that the cases of the contract cases aspect co the state space that is allowed by the precondition pect.
loop invariant in first iteration		Check that the loop invariant evaluates to True on first iteration of the loop.
loop invariant after first iteration		Check that the loop invariant evaluates to True at e further iteration of the loop.
loop variant	CWE 835	Check that the given loop variant decreases/increa as specified during each iteration of the loop. This plies termination of the loop.
assertion		Check that the given assertion evaluates to True.
raised exception		Check that the raise statement can never be reache

Continued on next pa

Table 7.2 – continued from previous page

Message Kind	CWE	Explanation
Liskov Substitution Principle		
precondition weaker than class-wide precondition		Check that the precondition aspect of the subprogram is weaker than its class-wide precondition.
precondition not True while class-wide precondition is True		Check that the precondition aspect of the subprogram is True if its class-wide precondition is True.
postcondition stronger than class-wide postcondition		Check that the postcondition aspect of the subprogram is stronger than its class-wide postcondition.
class-wide precondition weaker than overridden one		Check that the class-wide precondition aspect of the subprogram is weaker than its overridden class-wide precondition.
class-wide postcondition stronger than overridden one		Check that the class-wide postcondition aspect of the subprogram is stronger than its overridden class-wide postcondition.

The following table shows all flow analysis messages, (E)rrors, (W)arnings and (C)hecks.

Message Kind	Class	CWE	Explanation
aliasing	E		Two formal or global parameter are aliased.
function with side effects	E		A function with side effects has been detected.
cannot depend on variable	E		Certain expressions (for example: discriminant specifications and component declarations) need to be variable free.
missing global	E		Flow analysis has detected a global that was not mentioned on the Global or Initializes aspects
must be a global output	E		Flow analysis has detected an update of an in mode global.
pragma Elaborate_All needed	E		A remote state abstraction is used during the package's elaboration. Elaborate_All required for the remote package.
export must not depend on Proof_In	E		Flow analysis has detected an output of a subprogram that depends on a constant which is marked Proof_In.
class-wide mode must also be a class-wide mode of overridden subprogram	E		Miss-match between Global contracts of overridding and overridden subprograms.
class-wide dependency is not class-wide dependency of overridden subprogram	E		Miss-match between Depends contracts of overridding and overridden subprograms.
volatile function	E		A nonvolatile function may not have a volatile global.
tasking exclusivity	E		No two tasks may suspend on the same protected object or the same suspension object.
tasking exclusivity	E		No two tasks may read and write from the same unsynchronized object.
missing dependency	C		A dependency is missing from the dependency relation.
dependency relation	C		An out parameter or global is missing from the dependency relation.
missing null dependency	C		A variable is missing from the null dependency.

Continued on next page

Table 7.3 – continued from previous page

Message Kind	Class	CWE	Explanation
incorrect dependency	C		A stated dependency is not fulfilled.
not initialized	C	CWE 457	Flow analysis has detected the use of an unini variable.
initialization must not depend on something	C		Wrong Initializes aspect detected.
type is not fully initialized	C	CWE 457	A type promised to be default initialized but is
needs to be a constituent of some state abstraction	C		Flow analysis detected a constituent that has to posed through some state abstraction.
constant after elaboration	C		An object which is constant after elaboration n be changed after elaboration and as such canno output of any subprogram.
is not modified	W		The variable is declared with mode in out, but i modified, so could be declared with mode in.
unused assignment	W	CWE 563	Flow analysis has detected an assignment to a v which is not read after the assignment.
initialization has no effect	W	CWE 563	Flow analysis has detected an object which is ized, but never read.
this statement is never reached	W	CWE 561	This statement will never be executed (dead co
statement has no effect	W		Flow analysis has detected a statement which effect.
unused initial value	W	CWE 563	An in or in out parameter or global has beer which does not have any effect on any out or parameter or global.
unused	W	CWE 563	A global or locally declared variable is never u
missing return	W		A return statement seems to be missing from th tion.
no procedure exists that can initialize abstract state	W		Flow analysis detected a state abstraction that possible to initialize.
subprogram has no effect	W		A subprogram that has no exports has been det
volatile function	E		A volatile function that has no volatile globals d have to be a volatile function.

Note: Certain messages emitted by flow analysis are classified as errors and consequently cannot be suppressed or justified.

7.2.5 Understanding Counterexamples

When a check cannot be proved, GNATprove may generate a counterexample. A counterexample consists in two parts:

- a path (or set of paths) through the subprogram
- an assignment of values to variables that appear on that path

The best way to look at a counterexample is to display it in GPS by clicking on the icon to the left of the failed proof message, or to the left of the corresponding line in the editor (see *Running GNATprove from GPS*). GNATprove then displays the path in one color, and the values of variables on the path by inserting lines in the editor only (not in the file) which display these values. For example, consider procedure Counterex:

```
1   procedure Counterex (Cond : Boolean; In1, In2 : Integer; R : out Integer) with
2      SPARK_Mode,
3      Pre => In1 <= 25 and In2 <= 25
4   is
5   begin
6      R := 0;
7      if Cond then
8         R := R + In1;
9         if In1 < In2 then
10            R := R + In2;
11            pragma Assert (R < 42);
12         end if;
13      end if;
14   end Counterex;
```

The assertion on line 11 may fail when input parameter Cond is True and input parameters I1 and I2 are too big. The counterexample generated by GNATprove is displayed as follows in GPS, where each line highlighted in the path is followed by a line showing the value of variables from the previous line:

counterex.adb

```
1 ⌄ procedure Counterex (Cond : Boolean; In1, In2 : Integer; R : out Integ
     --   Cond = True and In1 = 17 and In2 = 25 and R = 0
2      SPARK_Mode,
3      Pre => In1 <= 25 and In2 <= 25
4   is
5   begin
6      R := 0;
        --   R = 0
7 ⌄   if Cond then
8         R := R + In1;
           --   R = 17
9 ⌄      if In1 < In2 then
10            R := R + In2;
               --   R = 42
11 ▣          pragma Assert (R < 42);
               --   R = 42
12         end if;
13      end if;
14   end Counterex;|
```

GNATprove also completes the message for the failed proof with an explanation giving the values of variables from the checked expression for the counterexample. Here, the message issued by GNATprove on line 11 gives the value of output parameter R:

```
counterex.adb:11:25: medium: assertion might fail, cannot prove R < 42 (e.g. when R =␣
↪42)
```

The counterexample generated by GNATprove does not always correspond to a feasible execution of the program:

1. When some contracts or loop invariants are missing, thus causing the property to become unprovable (see details in section on *Investigating Unprovable Properties*), the counterexample may help point to the missing contract or loop invariant. For example, the postcondition of procedure Double_In_Call is not provable

because the postcondition of the function `Double` that it calls is too weak, and the postcondition of procedure `Double_In_Loop` is not provable because its loop does not have a loop invariant:

```ada
package Counterex_Unprovable with
   SPARK_Mode
is

   type Int is new Integer range -100 .. 100;

   function Double (X : Int) return Int with
      Pre  => abs X <= 10,
      Post => abs Double'Result <= 20;

   procedure Double_In_Call (X : in out Int) with
      Pre  => abs X <= 10,
      Post => X = 2 * X'Old;

   procedure Double_In_Loop (X : in out Int) with
      Pre  => abs X <= 10,
      Post => X = 2 * X'Old;

end Counterex_Unprovable;
```

```ada
package body Counterex_Unprovable with
   SPARK_Mode
is

   function Double (X : Int) return Int is
   begin
      return 2 * X;
   end Double;

   procedure Double_In_Call (X : in out Int) is
   begin
      X := Double (X);
   end Double_In_Call;

   procedure Double_In_Loop (X : in out Int) is
      Result : Int := 0;
   begin
      for J in 1 .. 2 loop
         Result := Result + X;
      end loop;
      X := Result;
   end Double_In_Loop;

end Counterex_Unprovable;
```

The counterexample generated by GNATprove in both cases shows that the prover could deduce wrongly that X on ouput is -3 when its value is 1 on input, due to a missing contract in the function called or a missing loop invariant the loop executed:

```
counterex_unprovable.adb:7:16: info: overflow check proved
counterex_unprovable.adb:7:16: info: range check proved
counterex_unprovable.adb:12:12: info: precondition proved
counterex_unprovable.adb:19:20: info: initialization of "Result" proved
counterex_unprovable.adb:19:27: info: range check proved
counterex_unprovable.adb:21:12: info: initialization of "Result" proved
```

```
counterex_unprovable.ads:8:14: info: overflow check proved
counterex_unprovable.ads:9:14: info: overflow check proved
counterex_unprovable.ads:9:14: info: postcondition proved
counterex_unprovable.ads:12:14: info: overflow check proved
counterex_unprovable.ads:13:14: medium: postcondition might fail, cannot prove X
  = 2 * X'old (e.g. when X = -3 and X'Old = -1)
counterex_unprovable.ads:13:20: info: overflow check proved
counterex_unprovable.ads:16:14: info: overflow check proved
counterex_unprovable.ads:17:14: info: postcondition proved
counterex_unprovable.ads:17:20: info: overflow check proved
```

2. When some property cannot be proved due to prover shortcomings (see details in section on *Investigating Prover Shortcomings*), the counterexample may explain why the prover cannot prove the property. However, note that since the counterexample is always generated only using CVC4 prover, it can just explain why this prover cannot prove the property. Also note that if CVC4 is not selected and generating of a counterexample is not disabled by --no-counterexample switch, a counterexample is still attempted to be generated using CVC4, but the proof result of CVC4 is not taken into account in this case.

3. When using a short value of timeout or steps, the prover may hit the resource bound before it has produced a full counterexample. In such a case, the counterexample produced may not correspond to a feasible execution.

4. When the value of --proof switch is per_check (the default value), then the counterexample gives values to variables on all paths through the subprogram, not only the path which corresponds to the feasible execution. One can rerun GNATprove with value progressive or per_path to separate possible execution paths in the counterexample.

7.3 How to Use GNATprove in a Team

The most common use of GNATprove is as part of a regular quality control or quality assurance activity inside a team. Usually, GNATprove is run every night on the current codebase, and during the day by developers either on their computer or on servers. For both nightly and daily runs, GNATprove results need to be shared between team members, either for viewing results or to compare new results with the shared results. These various processes are supported by specific ways to run GNATprove and share its results.

In all cases, the source code should not be shared directly (say, on a shared drive) between developers, as this is bound to cause problems with file access rights and concurrent accesses. Rather, the typical usage is for each user to do a check out of the sources/environment, and use therefore her own version/copy of sources and project files, instead of physically sharing sources across all users.

The project file should also always specify a local, non shared, user writable directory as object directory (whether explicitly or implicitly, as the absence of an explicit object directory means the project file directory is used as object directory).

7.3.1 Possible Workflows

Multiple workflows allow to use GNATprove in a team:

1. GNATprove is run on a server or locally, and no warnings or check messages should be issued. Typically this is achieved by suppressing spurious warnings and justifying unproved check messages.

2. GNATprove is run on a server or locally, and textual results are shared in Configuration Management.

3. GNATprove is run on a server, and textual results are sent to a third-party qualimetry tool (like GNATdashboard, SonarQube, SQUORE, etc.)

4. GNATprove is run on a server or locally, and the GNATprove session files are shared in Configuration Management.

In all workflows (but critically for the first workflow), messages can be suppressed or justified. Indeed, like every sound and complete verification tool, GNATprove may issue false alarms. A first step is to identify the type of message:

- warnings can be suppressed, see *Suppressing Warnings*

- check messages can be justified, see *Justifying Check Messages*

Check messages from proof may also correspond to provable checks, which require interacting with GNATprove to find the correct contracts and/or analysis switches, see *How to Investigate Unproved Checks*.

The textual output in workflow 3 corresponds to the compiler-like output generated by GNATprove and controlled with switches `--report` and `--warnings` (see *Running GNATprove from the Command Line*). By default messages are issued only for unproved checks and warnings.

The textual output in workflow 2 comprises this compiler-like output, and possibly additional output generated by GNATprove in file `gnatprove.out` (see *Effect of Mode on Output* and *Managing Assumptions*).

Workflow 4 requires sharing session files used by GNATprove to record the state of formal verification on each source package. This is achieved by specifying in the *Project Attributes* the `Proof_Dir` proof directory, and sharing this directory under Configuration Management. To avoid conflicts, it is recommended that developers do not push their local changes to this directory in Configuration Management, but instead periodically retrieve an updated version of the directory. For example, a nightly run on a server, or a dedicated team member, can be responsible for updating the proof directory with the latest version generated by GNATprove.

A benefit of workflow 4 compared to other workflows is that it avoids reproving locally properties that were previously proved, as the shared session files keep track of which checks were proved.

7.3.2 Suppressing Warnings

GNATprove issues two kinds of warnings, which are controlled separately:

- Compiler warnings are controlled with the usual GNAT compilation switches:

    - `-gnatws` suppresses all warnings

    - `-gnatwa` enables all optional warnings

    - `-gnatw?` enables a specific warning denoted by the last character

    See the GNAT User's Guide for more details. These should passed through the compilation switches specified in the project file.

- GNATprove specific warnings are controlled with switch `--warnings`:

    - `--warnings=off` suppresses all warnings

    - `--warnings=error` treats warnings as errors

    - `--warnings=continue` issues warnings but does not stop analysis (default)

    The default is that GNATprove issues warnings but does not stop.

Both types of warnings can be suppressed selectively by the use of pragma `Warnings` in the source code. For example, GNATprove issues three warnings on procedure `Warn`, which are suppressed by the three pragma `Warnings` in the source code:

```
1  pragma Warnings (Off, "unused initial value of ""X""",
2                   Reason => "Parameter mode is mandated by API");
3
4  procedure Warn (X : in out Integer) with
```

```
5      SPARK_Mode
6    is
7       pragma Warnings (Off, "initialization has no effect",
8                        Reason => "Coding standard requires initialization");
9       Y : Integer := 0;
10      pragma Warnings (On, "initialization has no effect");
11
12   begin
13      pragma Warnings (Off, "unused assignment",
14                       Reason => "Test program requires double assignment");
15      X := Y;
16      pragma Warnings (On, "unused assignment");
17      X := Y;
18   end Warn;
```

Warnings with the specified message are suppressed in the region starting at pragma `Warnings Off` and ending at the matching pragma `Warnings On` or at the end of the enclosing scope. The `Reason` argument string is optional. A regular expression can be given instead of a specific message in order to suppress all warnings of a given form. Pragma `Warnings Off` can be added in a configuration file to suppress the corresponding warnings across all units in the project. Pragma `Warnings Off` can be specified for an entity to suppress all warnings related to this entity.

Pragma `Warnings` can also take a first argument of `GNAT` or `GNATprove` to specify that it applies only to GNAT compiler or GNATprove. For example, the previous example can be modified to use these refined pragma `Warnings`:

```
1    pragma Warnings (GNATprove, Off, "unused initial value of ""X""",
2                     Reason => "Parameter mode is mandated by API");
3
4    procedure Warn2 (X : in out Integer) with
5      SPARK_Mode
6    is
7       pragma Warnings (GNATprove, Off, "initialization has no effect",
8                        Reason => "Coding standard requires initialization");
9       Y : Integer := 0;
10      pragma Warnings (GNATprove, On, "initialization has no effect");
11
12   begin
13      pragma Warnings (GNATprove, Off, "unused assignment",
14                       Reason => "Test program requires double assignment");
15      X := Y;
16      pragma Warnings (GNATprove, On, "unused assignment");
17      X := Y;
18   end Warn2;
```

Besides the documentation benefit of using this refined version of pragma `Warnings`, it makes it possible to detect useless pragma `Warnings`, that do not suppress any warning, with switch `-gnatw.w`. Indeed, this switch can then be used both during compilation with GNAT and formal verification with GNATprove, as pragma `Warnings` that apply to only one tool can be identified as such.

See the GNAT Reference Manual for more details.

7.3.3 Suppressing Information Messages

Information messages can be suppressed by the use of pragma `Warnings` in the source code, like for warnings.

7.3.4 Justifying Check Messages

Direct Justification with Pragma Annotate

Check messages generated by GNATprove's flow analysis or proof can be selectively justified by adding a pragma `Annotate` in the source code. For example, the check message about a possible division by zero in the return expression below can be justified as follows:

```
return (X + Y) / (X - Y);
pragma Annotate (GNATprove, False_Positive,
                 "divide by zero", "reviewed by John Smith");
```

The pragma has the following form:

```
pragma Annotate (GNATprove, Category, Pattern, Reason);
```

where the following table explains the different entries:

Item	Explanation
GNATprove	is a fixed identifier
Category	is one of `False_Positive` or `Intentional`
Pattern	is a string literal describing the pattern of the check messages which shall be justified
Reason	is a string literal providing a justification for reviews

All arguments should be provided.

The *Category* currently has no impact on the behavior of the tool but serves a documentation purpose:

- `False_Positive` indicates that the check cannot fail, although GNATprove was unable to prove it.
- `Intentional` indicates that the check can fail but that it is not considered to be a bug.

Pattern should be a substring of the check message to justify.

Reason is a string provided by the user as a justification for reviews. This reason may be present in a GNATprove report.

Placement rules are as follows: in a statement list or declaration list, pragma `Annotate` applies to the preceding item in the list, ignoring other pragma `Annotate`. If there is no preceding item, the pragma applies to the enclosing construct. For example, if the pragma is the first element of the then-branch of an if-statement, it will apply to condition in the if-statement.

If the preceding or enclosing construct is a subprogram body, the pragma applies to both the subprogram body and the spec including its contract. This allows to place a justification for a check message issued by GNATprove either on the spec when it is relevant for callers. Note that this placement of a justification is ineffective on subprograms analyzed only in the context of their calls (see details in *Contextual Analysis of Subprograms Without Contracts*).

As a point of caution, the following placements of pragma Annotate will apply the pragma to a possibly large range of source lines:

- when the pragma appears in a statement list after a block, it will apply to the entire block (e.g. an if statement including all branches, or a loop including the loop body).
- when the pragma appears directly after a subprogram body, it will apply to the entire body and the spec of the subprogram.

Users should take care to not justify checks which were not intended to be justified, when placing pragma Annotate in such places.

```
procedure Do_Something_1 (X, Y : in out Integer) with
  Depends => ((X, Y) => (X, Y));
```

```
pragma Annotate (GNATprove, Intentional, "incorrect dependency """Y => X""",
                 "Dependency is kept for compatibility reasons");
```

or on the body when it is an implementation choice that need not be visible to users of the unit:

```
procedure Do_Something_2 (X, Y : in out Integer) with
  Depends => ((X, Y) => (X, Y));
```

```
procedure Do_Something_2 (X, Y : in out Integer) is
begin
   X := X + Y;
   Y := Y + 1;
end Do_Something_2;
pragma Annotate (GNATprove, Intentional, "incorrect dependency """Y => X""",
                 "Currently Y does not depend on X, but may change later");
```

Pragmas Annotate of the form above that do not justify any check message are useless and result in a warning by GNATprove. Like other warnings emitted by GNATprove, this warning is treated like an error if the switch --warnings=error is set.

Indirect Justification with Pragma Assume

Check messages generated by GNATprove's proof can alternatively be justified indirectly by adding a *Pragma Assume* in the source code, which allows the check to be proved. For example, the check message about a possible integer overflow in the assignment statement below can be justified as follows:

```
procedure Next_Tick is
begin
   pragma Assume (Clock_Ticks < Natural'Last,
                  "Device uptime is short enough that Clock_Ticks is less than 1_
↪000 always");
   Clock_Ticks := Clock_Ticks + 1;
end Next_Tick;
```

Using pragma Assume is more powerful than using pragma Annotate, as the property assumed may be used to prove more than one check. Thus, one should in general use pragma Annotate rather than pragma Assume to justify simple runtime checks. There are some cases though where using a pragma Assume may be preferred. In particular:

- To keep assumptions local:

```
pragma Assume (<External_Call's precondition>,
               "because for these internal reasons I know it holds");
External_Call;
```

  If the precondition of External_Call changes, it may not be valid anymore to assume it here, though the assumption will stay True for the same reasons it used to be. Incompatible changes in the precondition of External_Call will lead to a failure in the proof of External_Call's precondition.

- To sum up what is expected from the outside world so that it can be reviewed easily:

```
External_Find (A, E, X);
pragma Assume (X = 0 or (X in A'Range and A (X) = E),
               "because of the documentation of External_Find");
```

Maintenance and review is easier with a single pragma Assume than if it is spread out into various pragmas Annotate. If the information is required at several places, the pragma Assume can be factorized into a procedure:

```
function External_Find_Assumption (A : Array, E : Element, X : Index) return
 →Boolean
is (X = 0 or (X in A'Range and A (X) = E))
with Ghost;

procedure Assume_External_Find_Assumption (A : Array, E : Element, X : Index) with
 Ghost,
 Post => External_Find_Assumption (A, E, X)
is
    pragma Assume (External_Find_Assumption (A, E, X),
                   "because of the documentation of External_Find");
end Assume_External_Find_Assumption;

External_Find (A, E, X);
Assume_External_Find_Assumption (A, E, X);
```

In general, assumptions should be kept as small as possible (only assume what is needed for the code to work). Indirect justifications with pragma Assume should be carefully inspected as they can easily introduce errors in the verification process.

7.3.5 Sharing Proof Results Via a Memcached Server

GNATprove can cache and share results between distinct runs of the tool, even across several computers, via a Memcached server. To use this feature, you need to setup a memcached server (see https://memcached.org/) on your network or on your local machine. Then, if you add the option --memcached-server=hostname:portnumber to your invocation of gnatprove (or use the Switches Attribute of the Prove Package of your project file), then caching will be used, and speedups should be observed in many cases.

7.3.6 Managing Assumptions

Because GNATprove analyzes separately subprograms and packages, its results depend on assumptions about other subprograms and packages. For example, the verification that a subprogram is free from run-time errors depends on the property that all the subprograms it calls implement their specified contract. If a program is completely analyzed with GNATprove, GNATprove will report messages on those other subprograms, if they might not implement their contract correctly. But in general, a program is partly in SPARK and partly in other languages, mostly Ada, C and assembly languages. Thus, assumptions on parts of the program that cannot be analyzed with GNATprove need to be recorded for verification by other means, like testing, manual analysis or reviews.

When switch --assumptions is used, GNATprove generates information about remaining assumptions in its result file gnatprove.out. These remaining assumptions need to be justified to ensure that the desired verification objectives are met. An assumption on a subprogram may be generated in various cases:

- the subprogram was not analyzed (for example because it is marked SPARK_Mode => Off)

- the subprogram was not completely verified by GNATprove (that is, some unproved checks remain)

Note that currently, only assumptions on called subprograms are output, and not assumptions on calling subprograms.

The following table explains the meaning of assumptions and claims which gnatprove may output:

Assumption	Explanation
effects on parameters and global variables	The subprogram does not read or write any other parameters or global variables than what is described in its spec (signature + data dependencies).
absence of run-time errors	The subprogram is free from run-time errors.
the postcondition	The postconditon of the subprogram holds after each call of the subprogram.

7.4 How to Write Subprogram Contracts

GNATprove relies on contracts to perform its analysis. User-specified subprogram contracts are assumed to analyze a subprogram's callers, and verified when the body of the subprogram is analyzed.

By default, no contracts are compulsory in GNATprove. In the absence of user-provided contracts, GNATprove internally generates default contracts, which may or not be suitable depending on the verification objective:

- data dependencies (`Global`)

  See *Generation of Dependency Contracts*. The generated contract may be exact when completed from user-specified flow dependencies (Depends), or precise when generated from a body in SPARK, or coarse when generated from a body in full Ada.

- flow dependencies (`Depends`)

  See *Generation of Dependency Contracts*. The contract is generated from the user-specified or generated data dependencies, by considering that all outputs depend on all inputs.

- precondition (`Pre`)

  A default precondition of `True` is used in absence of a user-specified precondition.

- postcondition (`Post`)

  A default postcondition of `True` is used in absence of a user-specified postcondition, except for expression functions. For the latter, the body of the expression function is used to generate a matching postcondition. See *Expression Functions*.

Knowing which contracts to write depends on the specific verification objectives to achieve.

7.4.1 Generation of Dependency Contracts

By default, GNATprove does not require the user to write data dependencies (introduced with aspect `Global`) and flow dependencies (introduced with aspect `Depends`), as it can automatically generate them from the program.

This behavior can be disabled using the `--no-global-generation` switch, which means a missing data dependency is the same as `Global => null`. Note that this option also forces `--no-inlining` (see *Contextual Analysis of Subprograms Without Contracts*).

Note: GNATprove does not generate warning or check messages when the body of a subprogram does not respect a generated contract. Indeed, the generated contract is a safe over-approximation of the real contract, hence it is unlikely that the subprogram body respects it. The generated contract is used instead to verify proper initialization and respect of dependency contracts in the callers of the subprogram.

Note: Intrinsic subprograms such as arithmetic operations, and shift/rotate functions without user-provided functional contracts (precondition, postcondition or contract cases) are handled specially by GNATprove.

Auto Completion for Incomplete Contracts

When only the data dependencies (resp. only the flow dependencies) are given on a subprogram, GNATprove completes automatically the subprogram contract with the matching flow dependencies (resp. data dependencies).

Writing Only the Data Dependencies

When only the data dependencies are given on a subprogram, GNATprove completes them with flow dependencies that have all outputs depending on all inputs. This is a safe over-approximation of the real contract of the subprogram, which allows to detect all possible errors of initialization and contract violation in the subprogram and its callers, but which may also lead to false alarms because it is imprecise.

Take for example procedures `Add` and `Swap` for which data dependencies are given, but no flow dependencies:

```
 1   package Only_Data_Dependencies with
 2      SPARK_Mode
 3   is
 4      V : Integer;
 5
 6      procedure Add (X : Integer) with
 7         Global => (In_Out => V);
 8
 9      procedure Swap (X : in out Integer) with
10         Global => (In_Out => V);
11
12      procedure Call_Add (X, Y : Integer) with
13         Global  => (In_Out => V),
14         Depends => (V =>+ (X, Y));
15
16      procedure Call_Swap (X, Y : in out Integer) with
17         Global  => (In_Out => V),
18         Depends => (X => Y, Y => X, V => V);
19
20   end Only_Data_Dependencies;
```

GNATprove completes the contract of `Add` and `Swap` with flow dependencies that are equivalent to:

```
procedure Add (X : Integer) with
   Global  => (In_Out => V),
   Depends => (V =>+ X);

procedure Swap (X : in out Integer) with
   Global  => (In_Out => V),
   Depends => ((X, V) => (X, V));
```

Other flow dependencies with fewer dependencies between inputs and outputs would be compatible with the given data dependencies of `Add` and `Swap`. GNATprove chooses the contracts with the most dependencies. Here, this corresponds to the actual contract for `Add`, but to an imprecise contract for `Swap`:

```
1   package body Only_Data_Dependencies with
2      SPARK_Mode
3   is
4      procedure Add (X : Integer) is
5      begin
6         V := V + X;
7      end Add;
8
9      procedure Swap (X : in out Integer) is
10        Tmp : constant Integer := V;
11     begin
12        V := X;
13        X := Tmp;
14     end Swap;
15
16     procedure Call_Add (X, Y : Integer) is
17     begin
18        Add (X);
19        Add (Y);
20     end Call_Add;
21
22     procedure Call_Swap (X, Y : in out Integer) is
23     begin
24        Swap (X);
25        Swap (Y);
26        Swap (X);
27     end Call_Swap;
28
29   end Only_Data_Dependencies;
```

This results in false alarms when GNATprove verifies the dependency contract of procedure Call_Swap which calls Swap, while it succeeds in verifying the dependency contract of Call_Add which calls Add:

```
only_data_dependencies.ads:18:18: medium: missing dependency "X => V"
only_data_dependencies.ads:18:18: medium: missing dependency "X => X"
only_data_dependencies.ads:18:26: medium: missing dependency "Y => V"
only_data_dependencies.ads:18:26: medium: missing dependency "Y => Y"
only_data_dependencies.ads:18:34: medium: missing dependency "V => X"
only_data_dependencies.ads:18:34: medium: missing dependency "V => Y"
```

The most precise dependency contract for Swap would be:

```
procedure Swap (X : in out Integer) with
  Global  => (In_Out => V),
  Depends => (V => X, X => V);
```

If you add this precise contract in the program, then GNATprove can also verify the dependency contract of Call_Swap.

Note that the generated dependency contracts are used in the analysis of callers, but GNATprove generates no warnings or check messages if the body of Add or Swap have fewer flow dependencies, as seen above. That's a difference between these contracts being present in the code or auto completed.

Writing Only the Flow Dependencies

When only the flow dependencies are given on a subprogram, GNATprove completes it with the only compatible data dependencies.

Take for example procedures Add and Swap as previously, expect now flow dependencies are given, but no data dependencies:

```
1   package Only_Flow_Dependencies with
2     SPARK_Mode
3   is
4     V : Integer;
5
6     procedure Add (X : Integer) with
7       Depends => (V =>+ X);
8
9     procedure Swap (X : in out Integer) with
10      Depends => (V => X, X => V);
11
12    procedure Call_Add (X, Y : Integer) with
13      Global  => (In_Out => V),
14      Depends => (V =>+ (X, Y));
15
16    procedure Call_Swap (X, Y : in out Integer) with
17      Global  => (In_Out => V),
18      Depends => (X => Y, Y => X, V => V);
19
20  end Only_Flow_Dependencies;
```

The body of the unit is the same as before:

```
1   package body Only_Flow_Dependencies with
2     SPARK_Mode
3   is
4     procedure Add (X : Integer) is
5     begin
6        V := V + X;
7     end Add;
8
9     procedure Swap (X : in out Integer) is
10       Tmp : constant Integer := V;
11    begin
12       V := X;
13       X := Tmp;
14    end Swap;
15
16    procedure Call_Add (X, Y : Integer) is
17    begin
18       Add (X);
19       Add (Y);
20    end Call_Add;
21
22    procedure Call_Swap (X, Y : in out Integer) is
23    begin
24       Swap (X);
25       Swap (Y);
26       Swap (X);
27    end Call_Swap;
28
29  end Only_Flow_Dependencies;
```

GNATprove verifies the data and flow dependencies of all subprograms, including Call_Add and Call_Swap, based on the completed contracts for Add and Swap.

Precise Generation for SPARK Subprograms

When no data or flow dependencies are given on a SPARK subprogram, GNATprove generates precise data and flow dependencies by using path-sensitive flow analysis to track data flows in the subprogram body:

- if a variable is written completely on all paths in a subprogram body, it is considered an output of the subprogram; and

- other variables that are written in a subprogram body are considered both inputs and outputs of the subprogram (even if they are not read explicitly, their output value may depend on their input value); and

- if a variable is only read in a subprogram body, it is considered an input of the subprogram; and

- all outputs are considered to potentially depend on all inputs.

Case 1: No State Abstraction

Take for example a procedure `Set_Global` without contract which initializes a global variable `V` and is called in a number of contexts:

```
1  package Gen_Global with
2     SPARK_Mode
3  is
4     procedure Set_Global;
5
6     procedure Do_Nothing;
7
8     procedure Set_Global_Twice;
9
10 end Gen_Global;
```

```
1  package body Gen_Global with
2     SPARK_Mode
3  is
4     V : Boolean;
5
6     procedure Set_Global is
7     begin
8        V := True;
9     end Set_Global;
10
11    procedure Do_Nothing is
12    begin
13       null;
14    end Do_Nothing;
15
16    procedure Set_Global_Twice is
17    begin
18       Set_Global;
19       Set_Global;
20    end Set_Global_Twice;
21
22    procedure Set_Global_Conditionally (X : Boolean) with
23      Global  => (Output => V),
24      Depends => (V => X)
25    is
26    begin
27       if X then
```

```
28          Set_Global;
29        else
30           V := False;
31        end if;
32     end Set_Global_Conditionally;
33
34 end Gen_Global;
```

GNATprove generates data and flow dependencies for procedure `Set_Global` that are equivalent to:

```
procedure Set_Global with
  Global  => (Output => V),
  Depends => (V => null);
```

Note that the above contract would be illegal as given, because it refers to global variable V which is not visible at the point where `Set_Global` is declared in `gen_global.ads`. Instead, a user who would like to write this contract on `Set_Global` would have to use abstract state.

That generated contract for `Set_Global` allows GNATprove to both detect possible errors when calling `Set_Global` and to verify contracts given by the user on callers of `Set_Global`. For example, procedure `Set_Global_Twice` calls `Set_Global` twice in a row, which makes the first call useless as the value written in V is immediately overwritten by the second call. This is detected by GNATprove, which issues two warnings on line 18:

```
gen_global.adb:18:07: warning: statement has no effect
gen_global.adb:18:07: warning: unused assignment to "V"
gen_global.adb:23:28: info: initialization of "V" proved
gen_global.ads:4:14: info: initialization of "V" proved
gen_global.ads:6:14: warning: subprogram "Do_Nothing" has no effect
gen_global.ads:8:14: info: initialization of "V" proved
```

Note that GNATprove also issues a warning on subprogram `Do_Nothing` which has no effect, while it correctly analyzes that `Set_Global` has an effect, even if it has the same signature with no contract as `Do_Nothing`.

GNATprove also uses the generated contract for `Set_Global` to analyze procedure `Set_Global_Conditionally`, which allows it to verify the contract given by the user for `Set_Global_Conditionally`:

```
procedure Set_Global_Conditionally (X : Boolean) with
  Global  => (Output => V),
  Depends => (V => X);
```

Case 2: State Abstraction Without Dependencies

If an abstract state (see *State Abstraction*) is declared by the user but no dependencies are specified on subprogram declarations, then GNATprove generates data and flow dependencies which take abstract state into account.

For example, take unit `Gen_Global` previously seen, where an abstract state `State` is defined for package `Gen_Abstract_Global`, and refined into global variable V in the body of the package:

```
1 package Gen_Abstract_Global with
2   SPARK_Mode,
3   Abstract_State => State
4 is
5    procedure Set_Global;
6
```

```
7    procedure Set_Global_Twice;
8
9    procedure Set_Global_Conditionally (X : Boolean) with
10     Global  => (Output => State),
11     Depends => (State => X);
12
13 end Gen_Abstract_Global;
```

```
1  package body Gen_Abstract_Global with
2    SPARK_Mode,
3    Refined_State => (State => V)
4  is
5    V : Boolean;
6
7    procedure Set_Global is
8    begin
9       V := True;
10   end Set_Global;
11
12   procedure Set_Global_Twice is
13   begin
14      Set_Global;
15      Set_Global;
16   end Set_Global_Twice;
17
18   procedure Set_Global_Conditionally (X : Boolean) with
19     Refined_Global  => (Output => V),
20     Refined_Depends => (V => X)
21   is
22   begin
23      if X then
24         Set_Global;
25      else
26         V := False;
27      end if;
28   end Set_Global_Conditionally;
29
30 end Gen_Abstract_Global;
```

We have chosen here to declare procedure Set_Global_Conditionally in gen_abstract_global.ads, and so to express its user contract abstractly. We could also have kept it local to the unit.

GNATprove gives the same results on this unit as before: it issues warnings for the possible error in Set_Global_Twice and it verifies the contract given by the user for Set_Global_Conditionally:

```
gen_abstract_global.adb:14:07: warning: statement has no effect
gen_abstract_global.adb:14:07: warning: unused assignment to "V" constituent of "State
  ↵"
gen_abstract_global.adb:19:36: info: initialization of "V" constituent of "State"↵
  ↵proved
gen_abstract_global.ads:5:14: info: initialization of "V" constituent of "State"↵
  ↵proved
gen_abstract_global.ads:7:14: info: initialization of "V" constituent of "State"↵
  ↵proved
```

Case 3: State Abstraction Without Refined Dependencies

If abstract state is declared by the user and abstract dependencies are specified on subprogram declarations, but no refined dependencies are specified on subprogram implementations (as described *State Abstraction and Dependencies*), then GNATprove generates refined data and flow dependencies for subprogram implementations.

For example, take unit `Gen_Abstract_Global` previously seen, where only abstract data and flow dependencies are specified:

```
1   package Gen_Refined_Global with
2     SPARK_Mode,
3     Abstract_State => State
4   is
5      procedure Set_Global with
6        Global => (Output => State);
7
8      procedure Set_Global_Twice with
9        Global => (Output => State);
10
11     procedure Set_Global_Conditionally (X : Boolean) with
12       Global  => (Output => State),
13       Depends => (State => X);
14
15  end Gen_Refined_Global;
```

```
1   package body Gen_Refined_Global with
2     SPARK_Mode,
3     Refined_State => (State => V)
4   is
5      V : Boolean;
6
7      procedure Set_Global is
8      begin
9         V := True;
10     end Set_Global;
11
12     procedure Set_Global_Twice is
13     begin
14        Set_Global;
15        Set_Global;
16     end Set_Global_Twice;
17
18     procedure Set_Global_Conditionally (X : Boolean) is
19     begin
20        if X then
21           Set_Global;
22        else
23           Set_Global;
24        end if;
25     end Set_Global_Conditionally;
26
27  end Gen_Refined_Global;
```

GNATprove gives the same results on this unit as before: it issues warnings for the possible error in `Set_Global_Twice` and it verifies the contract given by the user for `Set_Global_Conditionally`:

```
gen_refined_global.adb:14:07: warning: statement has no effect
gen_refined_global.adb:14:07: warning: unused assignment to "V" constituent of "State"
```

```
gen_refined_global.ads:5:14: info: initialization of "V" constituent of "State" proved
gen_refined_global.ads:8:14: info: initialization of "V" constituent of "State" proved
gen_refined_global.ads:11:14: info: initialization of "V" constituent of "State"
  ↪proved
```

Note that although abstract and refined dependencies are the same here, this is not always the case, and GNATprove will use the more precise generated dependencies to analyze calls to subprograms inside the unit.

Coarse Generation for non-SPARK Subprograms

When no data or flow dependencies are given on a non-SPARK subprogram, GNATprove generates coarser data and flow dependencies based on the reads and writes to variables in the subprogram body:

- if a variable is written in a subprogram body, it is considered both an input and an output of the subprogram; and

- if a variable is only read in a subprogram body, it is considered an input of the subprogram; and

- all outputs are considered to potentially depend on all inputs.

For example, take unit `Gen_Global` previously seen, where the body of `Set_Global` is marked with `SPARK_Mode => Off`:

```
1  package Gen_Ada_Global with
2    SPARK_Mode
3  is
4    procedure Set_Global;
5
6    procedure Set_Global_Twice;
7
8  end Gen_Ada_Global;
```

```
1   package body Gen_Ada_Global with
2     SPARK_Mode
3   is
4     V : Boolean;
5
6     procedure Set_Global with
7       SPARK_Mode => Off
8     is
9     begin
10       V := True;
11     end Set_Global;
12
13     procedure Set_Global_Twice is
14     begin
15       Set_Global;
16       Set_Global;
17     end Set_Global_Twice;
18
19     procedure Set_Global_Conditionally (X : Boolean) with
20       Global  => (Output => V),
21       Depends => (V => X)
22     is
23     begin
24       if X then
25          Set_Global;
26       else
27          V := False;
```

```
28        end if;
29     end Set_Global_Conditionally;
30
31  end Gen_Ada_Global;
```

GNATprove generates a data and flow dependencies for procedure `Set_Global` that are equivalent to:

```
procedure Set_Global with
  Global  => (In_Out => V),
  Depends => (V => V);
```

This is a safe over-approximation of the real contract for `Set_Global`, which allows to detect all possible errors of initialization and contract violation in `Set_Global` callers, but which may also lead to false alarms because it is imprecise. Here, GNATprove generates a wrong high message that the call to `Set_Global` on line 25 reads an uninitialized value for `V`:

```
gen_ada_global.adb:20:28: info: initialization of "V" proved
gen_ada_global.adb:25:10: high: "V" is not an input in the Global contract of
 ⌐subprogram "Set_Global_Conditionally" at line 19
gen_ada_global.adb:25:10: high: "V" is not initialized
gen_ada_global.adb:25:10: high: either make "V" an input in the Global contract or
 ⌐initialize it before use
```

This is because the generated contract for `Set_Global` is not precise enough, and considers `V` as an input of the procedure. Even if the body of `Set_Global` is not in SPARK, the user can easily provide the precise information to GNATprove by adding a suitable contract to `Set_Global`, which requires to define an abstract state `State` like in the previous section:

```
procedure Set_Global with
  Global  => (Output => State),
  Depends => (State => null);
```

With such a user contract on `Set_Global`, GNATprove can verify the contract of `Set_Global_Conditionally` without false alarms.

Writing Dependency Contracts

Since GNATprove generates data and flow dependencies, you don't need in general to add such contracts if you don't want to.

The main reason to add such contracts is when you want GNATprove to verify that the implementation respects specified data dependencies and flow dependencies. For those projects submitted to certification, verification of data coupling and input/output relations may be a required verification objective, which can be achieved automatically with GNATprove provided the specifications are written as contracts.

Even if you write dependency contracts for the publicly visible subprograms, which describe the services offered by the unit, there is no need to write similar contracts on internal subprograms defined in the unit body. GNATprove can generate data and flow dependencies on these.

Also, as seen in the previous section, the data and flow dependencies generated by GNATprove may be imprecise, in which case it is necessary to add manual contracts to avoid false alarms.

7.4.2 Writing Contracts for Program Integrity

The most common use of contracts is to ensure program integrity, that is, the program keeps running within safe boundaries. For example, this includes the fact that the control flow of the program cannot be circumvented (e.g.

through a buffer overflow vulnerability) and that data is not corrupted (e.g. data invariants are preserved).

Preconditions can be written to ensure program integrity, and in particular they ensure:

- absence of run-time errors (AoRTE): no violations of language rules which would lead to raising an exception at run time (preconditions added to all subprograms which may raise a run-time error); and

- defensive programming: no execution of a subprogram from an unexpected state (preconditions added to subprograms in the public API, to guard against possible misuse by client units); and

- support of maintenance: prevent decrease in integrity (regressions, code rot) introduced during program evolution (preconditions added to internal subprograms, to guard against violations of the conditions to call these subprograms inside the unit itself); and

- invariant checking: ensure key data invariants are maintained throughout execution (preconditions added to all subprograms which may break the invariant).

For example, unit `Integrity` contains examples of all four kinds of preconditions:

- Precondition `X >= 0` on procedure `Seen_One` ensures AoRTE, as otherwise a negative value for `X` would cause the call to `Update` to fail a range check, as `Update` expects a non-negative value for its parameter.

- Precondition `X < Y` on procedure `Seen_Two` ensures defensive programming, as the logic of the procedure is only correctly updating global variables `Max` and `Snd` to the two maximal values seen if parameters `X` and `Y` are given in strictly increasing order.

- Precondition `X > Snd` on procedure `Update` ensures support of maintenance, as this internal procedure relies on this condition on its parameter to operate properly.

- Precondition `Invariant` on procedure `Update` ensures invariant checking, as the property that `Snd` is less than `Max` expressed in `Invariant` should be always respected.

```
1   pragma Assertion_Policy (Pre => Check);
2
3   package Integrity with
4      SPARK_Mode
5   is
6      procedure Seen_One (X : Integer) with
7         Pre => X >= 0;    --  AoRTE
8
9      procedure Seen_Two (X, Y : Natural) with
10        Pre => X < Y;  --  defensive programming
11
12  end Integrity;
```

```
1   package body Integrity with
2      SPARK_Mode
3   is
4      Max : Natural := 0;   --  max value seen
5      Snd : Natural := 0;   --  second max value seen
6
7      function Invariant return Boolean is
8         (Snd <= Max);
9
10     procedure Update (X : Natural) with
11       Pre => X > Snd and then   --  support of maintenance
12              Invariant          --  invariant checking
13     is
14     begin
15        if X > Max then
16           Snd := Max;
```

```
17        Max := X;
18     elsif X < Max then
19        Snd := X;
20     end if;
21  end Update;
22
23  procedure Seen_One (X : Integer) is
24  begin
25     if X > Snd then
26        Update (X);
27     end if;
28  end Seen_One;
29
30  procedure Seen_Two (X, Y : Natural) is
31  begin
32     if X > Max then
33        Max := Y;
34        Snd := X;
35     elsif X > Snd then
36        Update (Y);
37        Seen_One (X);
38     else
39        Seen_One (Y);
40     end if;
41  end Seen_Two;
42
43  end Integrity;
```

Note that `pragma Assertion_Policy (Pre => Check)` in `integrity.ads` ensures that the preconditions on the public procedures `Seen_One` and `Seen_Two` are always enabled at run time, while the precondition on internal subprogram `Update` is only enabled at run time if compiled with switch `-gnata` (typically set only for debugging or testing). GNATprove always takes contracts into account, whatever value of `Assertion_Policy`.

GNATprove cannot verify that all preconditions on `Integrity` are respected. Namely, it cannot verify that the call to `Update` inside `Seen_One` respects its precondition, as it is not known from the calling context that `Invariant` holds:

```
integrity.adb:26:10: medium: precondition might fail
integrity.adb:26:18: info: range check proved
integrity.adb:36:10: info: precondition proved
integrity.adb:37:10: info: precondition proved
integrity.adb:39:10: info: precondition proved
```

Note that, although `Invariant` is not required to hold either on entry to `Seen_Two`, the tests performed in if-statements in the body of `Seen_Two` ensure that `Invariant` holds when calling `Update` inside `Seen_Two`.

To prove completely the integrity of unit `Integrity`, it is sufficient to add `Invariant` as a precondition and postcondition on every subprogram which modifies the value of global variables `Max` and `Snd`:

```
1  pragma Assertion_Policy (Pre => Check);
2
3  package Integrity_Proved with
4     SPARK_Mode
5  is
6     procedure Seen_One (X : Integer) with
7        Pre  => X >= 0 and then     --  AoRTE
8                Invariant,          --  invariant checking
9        Post => Invariant;          --  invariant checking
```

```
10
11     procedure Seen_Two (X, Y : Natural) with
12        Pre  => X < Y and then     --  defensive programming
13                    Invariant,        --  invariant checking
14        Post => Invariant;            --  invariant checking
15
16     function Invariant return Boolean;
17
18  end Integrity_Proved;
```

```
1   package body Integrity_Proved with
2      SPARK_Mode
3   is
4      Max : Natural := 0;  --  max value seen
5      Snd : Natural := 0;  --  second max value seen
6
7      function Invariant return Boolean is (Snd <= Max);
8
9      procedure Update (X : Natural) with
10        Pre  => X > Snd and then  --  support of maintenance
11                    Invariant,       --  invariant checking
12        Post => Invariant            --  invariant checking
13     is
14     begin
15        if X > Max then
16           Snd := Max;
17           Max := X;
18        elsif X < Max then
19           Snd := X;
20        end if;
21     end Update;
22
23     procedure Seen_One (X : Integer) is
24     begin
25        if X > Snd then
26           Update (X);
27        end if;
28     end Seen_One;
29
30     procedure Seen_Two (X, Y : Natural) is
31     begin
32        if X > Max then
33           Max := Y;
34           Snd := X;
35        elsif X > Snd then
36           Update (Y);
37           Seen_One (X);
38        else
39           Seen_One (Y);
40        end if;
41     end Seen_Two;
42
43  end Integrity_Proved;
```

Here is the result of running GNATprove:

```
integrity_proved.adb:12:14: info: postcondition proved
integrity_proved.adb:26:10: info: precondition proved
integrity_proved.adb:26:18: info: range check proved
integrity_proved.adb:36:10: info: precondition proved
integrity_proved.adb:37:10: info: precondition proved
integrity_proved.adb:39:10: info: precondition proved
integrity_proved.ads:9:14: info: postcondition proved
integrity_proved.ads:14:14: info: postcondition proved
```

7.4.3 Writing Contracts for Functional Correctness

Going beyond program integrity, it is possible to express functional properties of the program as subprogram contracts. Such a contract can express either partially or completely the behavior of the subprogram. Typical simple functional properties express the range/constraints for parameters on entry and exit of subprograms (encoding their *type-state*), and the state of the module/program on entry and exit of subprograms (encoding a safety or security automaton). For those projects submitted to certification, expressing a subprogram requirement or specification as a complete functional contract allows GNATprove to verify automatically the implementation against the requirement/specification.

For example, unit `Functional` is the same as `Integrity_Proved` seen previously, with additional functional contracts:

- The postcondition on procedure `Update` (expressed as a `Post` aspect) is a complete functional description of the behavior of the subprogram. Note the use of an if-expression.

- The postcondition on procedure `Seen_Two` (expressed as a `Post` aspect) is a partial functional description of the behavior of the subprogram.

- The postcondition on procedure `Seen_One` (expressed as a `Contract_Cases` aspect) is a complete functional description of the behavior of the subprogram. There are three cases which correspond to different possible behaviors depending on the values of parameter X and global variables `Max` and `Snd`. The benefit of expressing the postcondition as contract cases is both the gain in readability (no need to use `'Old` for the guards, as in the postcondition of `Update`) and the automatic verification that the cases are disjoint and complete.

Note that global variables `Max` and `Snd` are referred to through public accessor functions `Max_Value_Seen` and `Second_Max_Value_Seen`. These accessor functions can be declared after the contracts in which they appear, as contracts are semantically analyzed only at the end of package declaration.

```
1   pragma Assertion_Policy (Pre => Check);
2
3   package Functional with
4     SPARK_Mode
5   is
6     procedure Seen_One (X : Integer) with
7       Pre  => X >= 0 and then    -- AoRTE
8               Invariant,          -- invariant checking
9       Post => Invariant,          -- invariant checking
10      Contract_Cases =>           -- full functional
11        (X > Max_Value_Seen =>
12           -- max value updated
13           Max_Value_Seen = X and
14           Second_Max_Value_Seen = Max_Value_Seen'Old,
15         X > Second_Max_Value_Seen and
16         X < Max_Value_Seen =>
17           -- second max value updated
18           Max_Value_Seen = Max_Value_Seen'Old and
19           Second_Max_Value_Seen = X,
20         X = Max_Value_Seen or
```

```
21          X <= Second_Max_Value_Seen =>
22            -- no value updated
23            Max_Value_Seen = Max_Value_Seen'Old and
24            Second_Max_Value_Seen = Second_Max_Value_Seen'Old);
25
26   procedure Seen_Two (X, Y : Natural) with
27     Pre  => X < Y and then            -- defensive programming
28            Invariant,                 -- invariant checking
29     Post => Invariant and then        -- invariant checking
30            Max_Value_Seen > 0 and then -- partial functional
31            Max_Value_Seen /= Second_Max_Value_Seen;
32
33   function Invariant return Boolean;
34
35   function Max_Value_Seen return Integer;
36
37   function Second_Max_Value_Seen return Integer;
38
39 end Functional;
```

```
1  package body Functional with
2    SPARK_Mode
3  is
4    Max : Natural := 0;  -- max value seen
5    Snd : Natural := 0;  -- second max value seen
6
7    function Invariant return Boolean is (Snd <= Max);
8
9    function Max_Value_Seen return Integer is (Max);
10
11   function Second_Max_Value_Seen return Integer is (Snd);
12
13   procedure Update (X : Natural) with
14     Pre  => X > Snd and then        -- support of maintenance
15            Invariant,               -- invariant checking
16     Post => Invariant and then      -- invariant checking
17            (if X > Max'Old then      -- complete functional
18               Snd = Max'Old and Max = X
19             elsif X < Max'Old then
20               Snd = X and Max = Max'Old
21             else
22               Snd = Snd'Old and Max = Max'Old)
23   is
24   begin
25      if X > Max then
26         Snd := Max;
27         Max := X;
28      elsif X < Max then
29         Snd := X;
30      end if;
31   end Update;
32
33   procedure Seen_One (X : Integer) is
34   begin
35      if X > Snd then
36         Update (X);
37      end if;
38   end Seen_One;
```

```
39
40     procedure Seen_Two (X, Y : Natural) is
41     begin
42        if X > Max then
43           Max := Y;
44           Snd := X;
45        elsif X > Snd then
46           Update (Y);
47           Seen_One (X);
48        else
49           Seen_One (Y);
50        end if;
51     end Seen_Two;
52
53  end Functional;
```

GNATprove manages to prove automatically almost all of these functional contracts, except for the postcondition of Seen_Two (note in particular the proof that the contract cases for Seen_One on line 10 are disjoint and complete):

```
functional.adb:16:14: info: postcondition proved
functional.adb:36:10: info: precondition proved
functional.adb:36:18: info: range check proved
functional.adb:46:10: info: precondition proved
functional.adb:47:10: info: precondition proved
functional.adb:49:10: info: precondition proved
functional.ads:9:14: info: postcondition proved
functional.ads:10:06: info: complete contract cases proved
functional.ads:10:06: info: disjoint contract cases proved
functional.ads:11:28: info: contract case proved
functional.ads:16:28: info: contract case proved
functional.ads:21:36: info: contract case proved
functional.ads:31:14: medium: postcondition might fail, cannot prove Max_Value_Seen /
↪= (Second_Max_Value_Seen) (e.g. when Max = 2147483647 and Snd = 2147483647)
```

The counterexample displayed for the postcondition not proved corresponds to a case where Max = Snd = 2 on entry to procedure Seen_Two. By highlighting the path for the counterexample in GPS (see *Running GNATprove from GPS*), the values of parameters for this counterexample are also displayed, here X = 0 and Y = 1. With these values, Max and Snd would still be equal to 2 on exit, thus violating the part of the postcondition stating that Max_Value_Seen /= Second_Max_Value_Seen.

Another way to see it is to run GNATprove in mode per_path (see *Running GNATprove from the Command Line* or *Running GNATprove from GPS*), and highlight the path on which the postcondition is not proved, which shows that when the last branch of the if-statement is taken, the following property is not proved:

```
functional.ads:31:14: medium: postcondition might fail, cannot prove Max_Value_Seen /
↪= (Second_Max_Value_Seen)
```

The missing piece of information here is that Max and Snd are never equal, except when they are both zero (the initial value). This can be added to function Invariant as follows:

```
function Invariant return Boolean is
   (if Max = 0 then Snd = 0 else Snd < Max);
```

With this more precise definition for Invariant, all contracts are now proved by GNATprove:

```
functional_proved.adb:17:14: info: postcondition proved
functional_proved.adb:37:10: info: precondition proved
```

```
functional_proved.adb:37:18: info: range check proved
functional_proved.adb:47:10: info: precondition proved
functional_proved.adb:48:10: info: precondition proved
functional_proved.adb:50:10: info: precondition proved
functional_proved.ads:9:14: info: postcondition proved
functional_proved.ads:10:06: info: complete contract cases proved
functional_proved.ads:10:06: info: disjoint contract cases proved
functional_proved.ads:11:28: info: contract case proved
functional_proved.ads:16:28: info: contract case proved
functional_proved.ads:21:36: info: contract case proved
functional_proved.ads:29:14: info: postcondition proved
```

In general, it may be needed to further refine the preconditions of subprograms to be able to prove their functional postconditions, to express either specific constraints on their calling context, or invariants maintained throughout the execution.

7.4.4 Writing Contracts on Imported Subprograms

Contracts are particularly useful to specify the behavior of imported subprograms, which cannot be analyzed by GNATprove. It is compulsory to specify in data dependencies the global variables these imported subprograms may read and/or write, otherwise GNATprove assumes `null` data dependencies (no global variable read or written).

Note: A subprogram whose implementation is not available to GNATprove, either because the corresponding unit body has not been developed yet, or because the unit body is not part of the files analyzed by GNATprove (see *Specifying Files To Analyze* and *Excluding Files From Analysis*), is treated by GNATprove like an imported subprogram.

Note: Intrinsic subprograms such as arithmetic operations and shift/rotate functions are handled specially by GNATprove. Except for shift/rotate operations with a user-provided functional contract (precondition, postcondition or contract cases) which are treated like regular functions.

For example, unit `Gen_Imported_Global` is a modified version of the `Gen_Abstract_Global` unit seen previously in *Generation of Dependency Contracts*, where procedure `Set_Global` is imported from C:

```
1   package Gen_Imported_Global with
2     SPARK_Mode,
3     Abstract_State => State
4   is
5     procedure Set_Global with
6       Import,
7       Convention => C,
8       Global => (Output => State);
9
10    procedure Set_Global_Twice;
11
12    procedure Set_Global_Conditionally (X : Boolean) with
13      Global   => (Output => State),
14      Depends  => (State => X);
15
16  end Gen_Imported_Global;
```

Note that we added data dependencies to procedure `Set_Global`, which can be used to analyze its callers. We did not add flow dependencies, as they are the same as the auto completed ones (see *Auto Completion for Incomplete Contracts*).

```
1  with System.Storage_Elements;
2
3  package body Gen_Imported_Global with
4     SPARK_Mode,
5     Refined_State => (State => V)
6  is
7     V : Boolean with
8        Address => System.Storage_Elements.To_Address (16#8000_0000#);
9
10    procedure Set_Global_Twice is
11    begin
12       Set_Global;
13       Set_Global;
14    end Set_Global_Twice;
15
16    procedure Set_Global_Conditionally (X : Boolean) with
17       Refined_Global  => (Output => V),
18       Refined_Depends => (V => X)
19    is
20    begin
21       if X then
22          Set_Global;
23       else
24          V := False;
25       end if;
26    end Set_Global_Conditionally;
27
28  end Gen_Imported_Global;
```

Note that we added an Address aspect to global variable V, so that it can be read/written from a C file.

GNATprove gives the same results on this unit as before: it issues warnings for the possible error in Set_Global_Twice and it verifies the contract given by the user for Set_Global_Conditionally:

```
gen_imported_global.adb:12:07: warning: statement has no effect
gen_imported_global.adb:12:07: warning: unused assignment to "V" constituent of "State
  ↵"
gen_imported_global.adb:17:36: info: initialization of "V" constituent of "State"␣
  ↵proved
gen_imported_global.ads:10:14: info: initialization of "V" constituent of "State"␣
  ↵proved
```

It is also possible to add functional contracts on imported subprograms, which GNATprove uses to prove properties of their callers. It is compulsory to specify in a precondition the conditions for calling these imported subprograms without errors, otherwise GNATprove assumes a default precondition of True (no constraints on the calling context). One benefit of these contracts is that they are verified at run time when the corresponding assertion is enabled in Ada (either with pragma Assertion_Policy or compilation switch -gnata).

Note: A subprogram whose implementation is not in SPARK is treated by GNATprove almost like an imported subprogram, except that coarse data and flow dependencies are generated (see *Coarse Generation for non-SPARK Subprograms*). In particular, unless the user adds a precondition to such a subprogram, GNATprove assumes a default precondition of True.

For example, unit Functional_Imported is a modified version of the Functional_Proved unit seen previously in *Writing Contracts for Functional Correctness*, where procedures Update and Seen_One are imported from C:

```
1   pragma Assertion_Policy (Pre => Check);
2
3   package Functional_Imported with
4      SPARK_Mode,
5      Abstract_State => Max_And_Snd,
6      Initializes => Max_And_Snd
7   is
8      procedure Seen_One (X : Integer) with
9         Import,
10        Convention => C,
11        Global => (In_Out => Max_And_Snd),
12        Pre  => X >= 0 and then      -- AoRTE
13                Invariant,           -- invariant checking
14        Post => Invariant,           -- invariant checking
15        Contract_Cases =>            -- full functional
16           (X > Max_Value_Seen =>
17              -- max value updated
18              Max_Value_Seen = X and
19              Second_Max_Value_Seen = Max_Value_Seen'Old,
20           X > Second_Max_Value_Seen and
21           X < Max_Value_Seen =>
22              -- second max value updated
23              Max_Value_Seen = Max_Value_Seen'Old and
24              Second_Max_Value_Seen = X,
25           X = Max_Value_Seen or
26           X <= Second_Max_Value_Seen =>
27              -- no value updated
28              Max_Value_Seen = Max_Value_Seen'Old and
29              Second_Max_Value_Seen = Second_Max_Value_Seen'Old);
30
31     procedure Seen_Two (X, Y : Natural) with
32        Pre  => X < Y and then              -- defensive programming
33                Invariant,                  -- invariant checking
34        Post => Invariant and then          -- invariant checking
35                Max_Value_Seen > 0 and then -- partial functional
36                Max_Value_Seen /= Second_Max_Value_Seen;
37
38     function Invariant return Boolean;
39
40     function Max_Value_Seen return Integer;
41
42     function Second_Max_Value_Seen return Integer;
43
44  end Functional_Imported;
```

```
1   with System.Storage_Elements;
2
3   package body Functional_Imported with
4      SPARK_Mode,
5      Refined_State => (Max_And_Snd => (Max, Snd))
6   is
7      Max : Natural := 0;  -- max value seen
8      for Max'Address use System.Storage_Elements.To_Address (16#8000_0000#);
9
10     Snd : Natural := 0;  -- second max value seen
11     for Snd'Address use System.Storage_Elements.To_Address (16#8000_0004#);
12
13     function Invariant return Boolean is
```

```
14        (if Max = 0 then Snd = 0 else Snd < Max);
15
16     function Max_Value_Seen return Integer is (Max);
17
18     function Second_Max_Value_Seen return Integer is (Snd);
19
20     procedure Update (X : Natural) with
21        Import,
22        Convention => C,
23        Global => (In_Out => (Max, Snd)),
24        Pre  => X > Snd and then      -- support of maintenance
25                 Invariant,            -- invariant checking
26        Post => Invariant and then    -- invariant checking
27                 (if X > Max'Old then  -- complete functional
28                     Snd = Max'Old and Max = X
29                  elsif X < Max'Old then
30                     Snd = X and Max = Max'Old
31                  else
32                     Snd = Snd'Old and Max = Max'Old);
33
34     procedure Seen_Two (X, Y : Natural) is
35     begin
36        if X > Max then
37           Max := Y;
38           Snd := X;
39        elsif X > Snd then
40           Update (Y);
41           Seen_One (X);
42        else
43           Seen_One (Y);
44        end if;
45     end Seen_Two;
46
47  end Functional_Imported;
```

Note that we added data dependencies to the imported procedures, as GNATprove would assume otherwise incorrectly `null` data dependencies.

As before, all contracts are proved by GNATprove:

```
functional_imported.adb:7:04: info: initialization of "Max" constituent of "Max_And_
↪Snd" proved
functional_imported.adb:10:04: info: initialization of "Snd" constituent of "Max_And_
↪Snd" proved
functional_imported.adb:40:10: info: precondition proved
functional_imported.adb:41:10: info: precondition proved
functional_imported.adb:43:10: info: precondition proved
functional_imported.ads:15:06: info: complete contract cases proved
functional_imported.ads:15:06: info: disjoint contract cases proved
functional_imported.ads:34:14: info: postcondition proved
```

7.4.5 Contextual Analysis of Subprograms Without Contracts

It may be convenient to create local subprograms without necessarily specifying a contract for these. GNATprove attempts to perform a contextual analysis of these local subprograms without contract, at each call site, as if the code of the subprograms was inlined. Thus, the analysis proceeds in that case as if it had the most precise contract for the local subprogram, in the context of its calls.

Let's consider as previously a subprogram which adds two to its integer input:

```
package Arith_With_Local_Subp
  with SPARK_Mode
is
   procedure Add_Two (X : in out Integer) with
     Pre  => X <= Integer'Last - 2,
     Post => X = X'Old + 2;

end Arith_With_Local_Subp;
```

And let's implement it by calling two local subprograms without contracts (which may or not have a separate declaration), which each increment the input by one:

```
package body Arith_With_Local_Subp
  with SPARK_Mode
is
   -- Local procedure without external visibility
   procedure Increment_In_Body (X : in out Integer) is
   begin
      X := X + 1;
   end Increment_In_Body;

   procedure Add_Two (X : in out Integer) is

      -- Local procedure defined inside Add_Two
      procedure Increment_Nested (X : in out Integer) is
      begin
         X := X + 1;
      end Increment_Nested;

   begin
      Increment_In_Body (X);
      Increment_Nested (X);
   end Add_Two;

end Arith_With_Local_Subp;
```

GNATprove would not be able to prove that the addition in `Increment_In_Body` or `Increment_Nested` cannot overflow in any context. If it was using only the default contract for these subprograms, it also would not prove that the contract of `Add_Two` is respected. But since it analyzes these subprograms in the context of their calls only, it proves here that no overflow is possible, and that the two increments correctly implement the contract of `Add_Two`:

```
arith_with_local_subp.adb:7:14: info: overflow check proved, in call inlined at arith_
   ↪with_local_subp.adb:19
arith_with_local_subp.adb:15:17: info: overflow check proved, in call inlined at
   ↪arith_with_local_subp.adb:20
arith_with_local_subp.ads:6:14: info: postcondition proved
arith_with_local_subp.ads:6:24: info: overflow check proved
```

This contextual analysis is available only for regular functions (not expression functions) or procedures that are not externally visible (not declared in the public part of the unit), without contracts (any of Global, Depends, Pre, Post, Contract_Cases), and respect the following conditions:

- does not contain nested subprogram or package declarations or instantiations

- not recursive

- not a generic instance

- not defined in a generic instance

- has a single point of return at the end of the subprogram

- not called in an assertion or a contract

- not called in a potentially unevaluated context

- not called before its body is seen

If any of the above conditions is violated, GNATprove issues a warning to explain why the subprogram could not be analyzed in the context of its calls, and then proceeds to analyze it normally, using the default contract. Otherwise, both flow analysis and proof are done for the subprogram in the context of its calls.

Note that it is very simple to prevent contextual analysis of a local subprogram, by adding a contract to it, for example a simple `Pre => True` or `Global => null`. To prevent contextual analysis of all subprograms, pass the switch `--no-inlining` to GNATprove. This may be convenient during development if the ultimate goal is to add contracts to subprograms to analyze them separately, as contextual analysis may cause the analysis to take much more time and memory.

7.4.6 Subprogram Termination

GNATprove is only concerned with partial correctness of subprograms, that is, it only checks that the contract of a subprogram holds when it terminates normally. What is more, GNATprove will enforce that no exception will be raised at runtime. Together, these two points ensure that every SPARK subprogram formally verified using GNATprove will always return normally in a state that respects its postcondition, as long as it terminates.

In general, GNATprove does not attempt to verify termination of subprograms. It can be instructed to do so using a GNATprove specific Annotate pragma. On the following example, we instruct GNATprove that the five F functions should terminate:

```
1   package Terminating_Annotations with SPARK_Mode is
2
3      function F_Rec (X : Natural) return Natural;
4      pragma Annotate (GNATprove, Terminating, F_Rec);
5
6      function F_While (X : Natural) return Natural;
7      pragma Annotate (GNATprove, Terminating, F_While);
8
9      function F_Not_SPARK (X : Natural) return Natural;
10     pragma Annotate (GNATprove, Terminating, F_Not_SPARK);
11
12     procedure Not_SPARK (X : Natural);
13     function F_Call (X : Natural) return Natural;
14     pragma Annotate (GNATprove, Terminating, F_Call);
15
16     function F_Term (X : Natural) return Natural;
17     pragma Annotate (GNATprove, Terminating, F_Term);
18  end Terminating_Annotations;
```

If every subprogram in a package is terminating, the package itself can be annotated with the terminating annotation. If the annotation is located on a generic package, then it should be valid for every instance of the package.

If a subprogram in SPARK is explicitly annotated as terminating, flow analysis will attempt to make sure that all the paths through the subprogram effectively return. In effect, it will look for while loops with no loop variants, recursive calls and calls to subprograms which are not known to be terminating. If GNATprove cannot make sure that the annotated subprogram is always terminating, it will then emit a failed check. As an example, let us consider the following implementation of the five F functions:

```ada
package body Terminating_Annotations with SPARK_Mode is

   function F_Rec (X : Natural) return Natural is
   begin
      if X = 0 then
         return 0;
      else
         return F_Rec (X - 1);
      end if;
   end F_Rec;

   function F_While (X : Natural) return Natural is
      Y : Natural := X;
   begin
      while Y > 0 loop
         Y := Y - 1;
      end loop;
      return Y;
   end F_While;

   function F_Not_SPARK (X : Natural) return Natural with SPARK_Mode => Off is
      Y : Natural := X;
   begin
      while Y > 0 loop
         Y := Y - 1;
      end loop;
      return Y;
   end F_Not_SPARK;

   procedure Not_SPARK (X : Natural) with SPARK_Mode => Off is
   begin
      null;
   end Not_SPARK;

   function F_Call (X : Natural) return Natural is
   begin
      Not_SPARK (X);
      return 0;
   end F_Call;

   function F_Term (X : Natural) return Natural is
      Y : Natural := X;
   begin
      Y := F_Rec (Y);
      Y := F_While (Y);
      Y := F_Not_SPARK (Y);
      Y := F_Call (Y);

      while Y > 0 loop
         pragma Loop_Variant (Decreases => Y);
         Y := Y - 1;
      end loop;
      return Y;
   end F_Term;
end Terminating_Annotations;
```

As can be easily verified by review, all these functions terminate, and all return 0. As can be seen below, GNATprove will fail to verify that `F_Rec`, `F_While`, and `F_Call` terminate.

```
1   terminating_annotations.adb:15:13: info: initialization of "Y" proved
2   terminating_annotations.adb:16:15: info: initialization of "Y" proved
3   terminating_annotations.adb:18:14: info: initialization of "Y" proved
4   terminating_annotations.adb:44:19: info: initialization of "Y" proved
5   terminating_annotations.adb:45:21: info: initialization of "Y" proved
6   terminating_annotations.adb:46:25: info: initialization of "Y" proved
7   terminating_annotations.adb:47:20: info: initialization of "Y" proved
8   terminating_annotations.adb:49:13: info: initialization of "Y" proved
9   terminating_annotations.adb:50:44: info: initialization of "Y" proved
10  terminating_annotations.adb:51:15: info: initialization of "Y" proved
11  terminating_annotations.adb:53:14: info: initialization of "Y" proved
12  terminating_annotations.ads:3:13: medium: subprogram "F_Rec" might not terminate,
    ↪terminating annotation could be incorrect
13  terminating_annotations.ads:6:13: medium: subprogram "F_While" might not terminate,
    ↪terminating annotation could be incorrect
14  terminating_annotations.ads:13:13: medium: subprogram "F_Call" might not terminate,
    ↪terminating annotation could be incorrect
15  terminating_annotations.ads:16:13: info: subprogram "F_Term" will terminate,
    ↪terminating annotation has been proved
```

Let us look at each function to understand what happens. The function `F_Rec` is recursive, and the function `F_While` contains a while loop. Both cases can theoretically lead to an infinite path in the subprogram, which is why GNATprove cannot verify them. GNATprove does not complain about not being able to verify the termination of `F_Not_SPARK`. Clearly, it is not because it could verify it, as it contains exactly the same loop as `F_While`. It is because, as the body of `F_Not_SPARK` has been excluded from analysis using `SPARK_Mode => Off`, GNATprove does not attempt to prove that it terminates. When looking at the body of `F_Call`, we can see that it calls a procedure `Not_SPARK`. Clearly, this procedure is terminating, as it does not do anything. But, as the body of `No_SPARK` has been hidden from analysis using `SPARK_Mode => Off`, GNATprove cannot deduce that it terminates. As a result, it stays in the safe side, and assumes that `Not_SPARK` could loop, which causes the verification of `F_Call` to fail. Finally, GNATprove is able to verify that `F_Term` terminates, though it contains a while loop. Indeed, the number of possible iterations of the loop has been bounded using a `Loop_Variant`. Also note that, though it was not able to prove termination of `F_Rec`, `F_While`, and `F_Call`, GNATprove will still trust the annotation and consider them as terminating when verifying `F_Term`.

Note: Possible nontermination of a subprogram may influence GNATprove proof capabilities. Indeed, to avoid soundness issues due to nontermination in logical formulas, GNATprove will not be able to see the contract of nonterminating functions if they are called from definitions of constants, from contracts, or from assertions. In such a case, an information message will be emitted, stating that (implicit) contracts of the function are not available for proof. This message won't appear if a `Terminating` annotation is supplied for the function as explained above.

7.5 How to Write Object Oriented Contracts

Object Oriented Programming (OOP) may require the use of special *Class-Wide Subprogram Contracts* for dispatching subprograms, so that GNATprove can check Liskov Substitution Principle on every overriding subprogram.

7.5.1 Object Oriented Code Without Dispatching

In the special case where OOP is used without dispatching, it is possible to use the regular *Subprogram Contracts* instead of the special *Class-Wide Subprogram Contracts*.

For example, consider a variant of the `Logging` and `Range_Logging` units presented in *Class-Wide Subprogram Contracts*, where no dispatching is allowed. Then, it is possible to use regular preconditions and postconditions as contracts, provided `Log_Type` is publicly declared as an untagged private type in both units:

```ada
package Logging_No_Dispatch with
   SPARK_Mode
is
   Max_Count : constant := 10_000;

   type Log_Count is range 0 .. Max_Count;

   type Log_Type is private;

   function Log_Size (Log : Log_Type) return Log_Count;

   procedure Init_Log (Log : out Log_Type) with
     Post => Log_Size (Log) = 0;

   procedure Append_To_Log (Log : in out Log_Type; Incr : in Integer) with
     Pre  => Log_Size (Log) < Max_Count,
     Post => Log_Size (Log) = Log_Size (Log)'Old + 1;

private

   subtype Log_Index is Log_Count range 1 .. Max_Count;
   type Integer_Array is array (Log_Index) of Integer;

   type Log_Type is tagged record
      Log_Data : Integer_Array;
      Log_Size : Log_Count;
   end record;

   function Log_Size (Log : Log_Type) return Log_Count is (Log.Log_Size);

end Logging_No_Dispatch;
```

```ada
with Logging_No_Dispatch; use Logging_No_Dispatch;

package Range_Logging_No_Dispatch with
   SPARK_Mode
is
   type Log_Type is private;

   function Log_Size (Log : Log_Type) return Log_Count;

   function Log_Min (Log : Log_Type) return Integer;

   function Log_Max (Log : Log_Type) return Integer;

   procedure Init_Log (Log : out Log_Type) with
     Post => Log_Size (Log) = 0 and
             Log_Min (Log) = Integer'Last and
             Log_Max (Log) = Integer'First;

   procedure Append_To_Log (Log : in out Log_Type; Incr : in Integer) with
     Pre  => Log_Size (Log) < Logging_No_Dispatch.Max_Count,
     Post => Log_Size (Log) = Log_Size (Log)'Old + 1 and
             Log_Min (Log) = Integer'Min (Log_Min (Log)'Old, Incr) and
```

```
23            Log_Max (Log) = Integer'Max (Log_Max (Log)'Old, Incr);
24
25  private
26
27     type Log_Type is tagged record
28       Log : Logging_No_Dispatch.Log_Type;
29       Min_Entry : Integer;
30       Max_Entry : Integer;
31     end record;
32
33     function Log_Size (Log : Log_Type) return Log_Count is (Log_Size (Log.Log));
34
35     function Log_Min (Log : Log_Type) return Integer is (Log.Min_Entry);
36     function Log_Max (Log : Log_Type) return Integer is (Log.Max_Entry);
37
38  end Range_Logging_No_Dispatch;
```

7.5.2 Writing Contracts on Dispatching Subprograms

Whenever dispatching is used, the contract that applies in proof to a dispatching call is the class-wide contract, defined as the first one present in the following list:

1. the class-wide precondition (resp. postcondition) attached to the subprogram

2. or otherwise the class-wide precondition (resp. postcondition) being inherited by the subprogram from the subprogram it overrides

3. or otherwise the default class-wide precondition (resp. postcondition) of True.

For abstract subprograms (on interfaces or regular tagged types), only a class-wide contract can be specified. For other dispatching subprograms, it is possible to specify both a regular contract and a class-wide contract. In such a case, GNATprove uses the regular contract to analyze static calls to the subprogram and the class-wide contract to analyze dispatching calls to the subprogram, and it checks that the specific contract is a refinement of the class-wide contract, as explained in *Mixing Class-Wide and Specific Subprogram Contracts*.

Let's consider the various cases that may occur when overridding a subprogram:

```
1  package Geometry with
2    SPARK_Mode
3  is
4     type Shape is tagged record
5        Pos_X, Pos_Y : Float;
6     end record;
7
8     function Valid (S : Shape) return Boolean is
9        (S.Pos_X in -100.0 .. 100.0 and S.Pos_Y in -100.0 .. 100.0);
10
11     procedure Operate (S : in out Shape) with
12       Pre'Class => Valid (S);
13
14     procedure Set_Default (S : in out Shape) with
15       Post'Class => Valid (S);
16
17     procedure Set_Default_Repeat (S : in out Shape) with
18       Post'Class => Valid (S);
19
20     procedure Set_Default_No_Post (S : in out Shape);
21
```

```
22    type Rectangle is new Shape with record
23       Len_X, Len_Y : Float;
24    end record;
25
26    function Valid (S : Rectangle) return Boolean is
27       (Valid (Shape (S)) and S.Len_X in 0.0 .. 10.0 and S.Len_Y in 0.0 .. 10.0);
28
29    procedure Operate (S : in out Rectangle);
30
31    procedure Set_Default (S : in out Rectangle);
32
33    procedure Set_Default_Repeat (S : in out Rectangle) with
34       Post'Class => Valid (S);
35
36    procedure Set_Default_No_Post (S : in out Rectangle) with
37       Post'Class => Valid (S);
38
39 end Geometry;
```

In package `Geometry`, a type `Shape` is derived in a type `Rectangle`. A function `Shape.Valid` defines what it is to be a valid shape. It is overridden by `Rectangle.Valid` which defines what it is to be a valid rectangle. Here, a valid rectangle is also a valid shape, but that need not be the case. Procedure `Set_Default` and its variants demonstrate the various configurations that can be found in practice:

1. The overridden subprogram `Shape.Set_Default` defines a class-wide contract (here only a postcondition), which is inherited in the overriding subprogram `Rectangle.Set_Default`. By the semantics of Ada, the postcondition of `Shape.Set_Default` calls `Shape.Valid`, while the inherited postcondition of `Rectangle.Set_Default` calls `Rectangle.Valid`.

2. Both the overridden subprogram `Shape.Set_Default_Repeat` and the overriding subprogram `Rectangle.Set_Default_Repeat` define a class-wide contract (here only a postcondition). Here, since the contract is simply repeated, this is equivalent to case 1 above of inheriting the contract: the postcondition of `Shape.Set_Default_Repeat` calls `Shape.Valid`, while the postcondition of `Rectangle.Set_Default_Repeat` calls `Rectangle.Valid`.

3. Only the overriding subprogram `Rectangle.Set_Default_No_Post` defines a class-wide contract (here only a postcondition). The default class-wide postcondition of `True` is used for the overridden `Shape.Set_Default_No_Post`.

In case 1, the overriding subprogram satisfies Liskov Substitution Principle by construction, so GNATprove emits no check in that case. Note that this is not the same as saying that `Shape.Set_Default` and `Rectangle.Set_Default` have the same contract: here the two postconditions differ, as one calls `Shape.Valid`, while the other calls `Rectangle.Valid`.

In case 2, GNATprove checks that Liskov Substitution Principle is verified between the contracts of the overridden and the overriding subprograms. Here, it checks that the postcondition of `Rectangle.Set_Default_Repeat` is stronger than the postcondition of `Shape.Set_Default_Repeat`.

In case 3, GNATprove also checks that Liskov Substitution Principle is verified between the default contract of the overridden subprogram and the specified contract of the overriding subprograms. Here, only a postcondition is specified for `Rectangle.Set_Default_No_Post`, so it is indeed stronger than the default postcondition of `Shape.Set_Default_No_Post`.

Hence the results of GNATprove's analysis on this program:

```
geometry.ads:34:20: info: class-wide postcondition is stronger than overridden one
geometry.ads:37:20: info: class-wide postcondition is stronger than overridden one
```

Let's consider now calls to these subprograms in procedure `Use_Geometry`:

```
1   with Geometry; use Geometry;
2
3   procedure Use_Geometry (S : in out Shape'Class) with
4     SPARK_Mode
5   is
6   begin
7      S.Set_Default;
8      S.Operate;
9
10     S.Set_Default_Repeat;
11     S.Operate;
12
13     S.Set_Default_No_Post;
14     S.Operate;
15  end Use_Geometry;
```

Here are the results of GNATprove's analysis on this program:

```
use_geometry.adb:8:05: info: precondition proved
use_geometry.adb:11:05: info: precondition proved
use_geometry.adb:14:05: medium: precondition might fail
```

Parameter S is of class-wide type Shape'Class, so it can be dynamically of both types Shape or Rectangle. All calls on S are dispatching. In this program, GNATprove needs to check that the precondition of the calls to Operate is satisfied. As procedures Shape.Set_Default and Shape.Set_Default_Repeat state precisely this condition in postcondition, the precondition to the calls to Operate that follow can be proved. As procedure Shape.Set_Default_No_Post has no postcondition, the precondition to the last call to Operate cannot be proved. Note that these proofs take into account both possible types of S, for example:

- If S is dynamically a shape, then the call to Shape.Set_Default on line 7 ensures that Shape.Valid holds, which ensures that the precondition to the call to Shape.Operate is satisfied on line 8.

- If S is dynamically a rectangle, then the call to Rectangle.Set_Default on line 7 ensures that Rectangle.Valid holds, which ensures that the precondition to the call to Rectangle.Operate is satisfied on line 8.

7.5.3 Writing Contracts on Subprograms with Class-wide Parameters

Subprograms with class-wide parameters are not in general dispatching subprograms, hence they are specified through regular *Subprogram Contracts*, not *Class-Wide Subprogram Contracts*. Inside the regular contract, calls on primitive subprograms of the class-wide parameters are dispatching though, like in the code. For example, consider procedure More_Use_Geometry which takes four class-wide parameters of type Shape'Class, which can all be dynamically of both types Shape or Rectangle:

```
1   with Geometry; use Geometry;
2
3   procedure More_Use_Geometry (S1, S2, S3, S4 : in out Shape'Class) with
4     SPARK_Mode,
5     Pre => S1.Valid
6   is
7   begin
8      S1.Operate;
9
10     if S2.Valid then
11        S2.Operate;
12     end if;
```

```
13
14      S3.Set_Default;
15      S3.Operate;
16
17      S4.Operate;
18   end More_Use_Geometry;
```

The precondition of More_Use_Geometry specifies that S1.Valid holds, which takes into account both possible types of S1:

- If S1 is dynamically a shape, then the precondition specifies that Shape.Valid holds, which ensures that the precondition to the call to Shape.Operate is satisfied on line 8.

- If S1 is dynamically a rectangle, then the precondition specifies that Rectangle.Valid holds, which ensures that the precondition to the call to Rectangle.Operate is satisfied on line 8.

Similarly, the test on S2.Valid on line 10 ensures that the precondition to the call to S2.Operate on line 11 is satisfied, and the call to S3.Set_Default on line 14 ensures through its postcondition that the precondition to the call to S3.Operate on line 15 is satisfied. But no precondition or test or call ensures that the precondition to the call to S4.Operate on line 17 is satisfied. Hence the results of GNATprove's analysis on this program:

```
more_use_geometry.adb:8:06: info: precondition proved
more_use_geometry.adb:11:09: info: precondition proved
more_use_geometry.adb:15:06: info: precondition proved
more_use_geometry.adb:17:06: medium: precondition might fail
```

7.6 How to Write Package Contracts

Like for subprogram contracts, GNATprove can generate default package contracts when not specified by a user. By default, GNATprove does not require the user to write any package contracts.

The default state abstraction generated by GNATprove maps every internal global variable to a different internal abstract state (which is not really *abstract* as a result).

The default package initialization generated by GNATprove lists all variables initialized either at declaration or in the package body statements. The generated Initializes aspect is an over-approximation of the actual Initializes aspect. All outputs are considered to be initialized from all inputs. For example, consider package Init_Data which initializes all its global variables during elaboration, from either constants or variables:

```
1   package External_Data with
2      SPARK_Mode
3   is
4      Val : Integer with Import;
5   end External_Data;
```

```
1   with External_Data;
2   pragma Elaborate_All(External_Data);
3
4   package Init_Data with
5      SPARK_Mode
6   is
7      pragma Elaborate_Body;
8      Start_From_Zero     : Integer := 0;
9      Start_From_Val      : Integer := External_Data.Val;
10     Start_From_Zero_Bis : Integer;
```

```
11      Start_From_Val_Bis   : Integer;
12   end Init_Data;
```

```
1    package body Init_Data with
2      SPARK_Mode
3    is
4    begin
5      Start_From_Zero_Bis := 0;
6      Start_From_Val_Bis   := External_Data.Val;
7    end Init_Data;
```

GNATprove generates a package initialization contract on package `Init_Data` which is equivalent to:

```
Initializes => (Start_From_Zero     => External_Data.Val,
                Start_From_Zero_Bis => External_Data.Val,
                Start_From_Val      => External_Data.Val,
                Start_From_Val_Bis  => External_Data.Val)
```

As a result, GNATprove can check that global variables are properly initialized when calling the main procedure `Main_Proc`, and it does not issue any message when analyzing this code:

```
1    with Init_Data;
2    procedure Main_Proc with
3      SPARK_Mode
4    is
5      Tmp : Integer;
6    begin
7      Tmp := Init_Data.Start_From_Zero;
8      Tmp := Init_Data.Start_From_Val;
9      Tmp := Init_Data.Start_From_Zero_Bis;
10     Tmp := Init_Data.Start_From_Val_Bis;
11   end Main_Proc;
```

The user may specify explicitly package contracts to:

- name explicitly the parts of state abstraction that can be used in subprogram dependency contracts, in order to *Address Data and Control Coupling*; or

- improve scalability and running time of GNATprove's analysis, as a single explicit abstract state may be mapped to hundreds of concrete global variables, which would otherwise be considered separately in the analysis; or

- check that initialization of global data at elaboration is as specified in the specified package initialization contracts.

7.7 How to Write Loop Invariants

As described in *Loop Invariants*, proving properties of subprograms that contain loops may require the addition of explicit loop invariant contracts. This section describes a systematic approach for writing loop invariants.

7.7.1 Automatic Unrolling of Simple For-Loops

GNATprove automatically unrolls simple for-loops, defined as:

- for-loops over a range known at compile time,

- with a number of iterations smaller than 20,

- without *Loop Invariants* or *Loop Variants*,

- that declare no local variables, or only variables of scalar type.

As a result, GNATprove conveys the exact meaning of the loop to provers, without requiring a loop invariant. While this is quite powerful, it is best applied to loops where the body of the loop is small, otherwise the unrolling may lead to complex formulas that provers cannot prove.

For example, consider the subprograms Init and Sum below:

```
package Loop_Unrolling with
   SPARK_Mode
is
   subtype Index is Integer range 1 .. 10;
   type Arr is array (Index) of Integer;

   procedure Init (A : out Arr) with
     Post => (for all J in Index => A(J) = J);

   function Sum (A : Arr) return Integer with
     Pre  => (for all J in Index => A(J) = J),
     Post => Sum'Result = (A'First + A'Last) * A'Length / 2;

end Loop_Unrolling;
```

```
package body Loop_Unrolling with
   SPARK_Mode
is
   procedure Init (A : out Arr) is
   begin
      for J in Index loop
         A (J) := J;
      end loop;
   end Init;

   function Sum (A : Arr) return Integer is
      Result : Integer := 0;
   begin
      for J in Index loop
         Result := Result + A (J);
      end loop;
      return Result;
   end Sum;

end Loop_Unrolling;
```

As the loops in both subprograms are simple for-loops, GNATprove unrolls them and manages to prove the postconditions of Init and Sum without requiring a loop invariant:

```
loop_unrolling.adb:7:16: info: initialization of "A" proved
loop_unrolling.adb:15:20: info: initialization of "Result" proved
loop_unrolling.adb:15:27: info: overflow check proved
loop_unrolling.adb:17:14: info: initialization of "Result" proved
loop_unrolling.ads:7:20: info: initialization of "A" proved
loop_unrolling.ads:8:14: info: postcondition proved
loop_unrolling.ads:8:37: info: initialization of "A" proved
loop_unrolling.ads:12:14: info: postcondition proved
```

Automatic loop unrolling can be disabled locally by explicitly adding a default loop invariant at the start of the loop:

```
for X in A .. B loop
   pragma Loop_Invariant (True);
   ...
end loop;
```

It can also be disabled globally by using the switch `--no-loop-unrolling`.

7.7.2 Automatically Generated Loop Invariants

In general, GNATprove relies on the user to manually supply the necessary information about variables modified by loop statements in the loop invariant. Though variables which are not modified in the loop need not be mentioned in the invariant, it is usually necessary to state explicitly the preservation of unmodified object parts, such as record or array components. In particular, when a loop modifies a collection, which can be either an array or a container (see *Formal Containers Library*), it may be necessary to state in the loop invariant those parts of the collection that have not been modified up to the current iteration. This property called *frame condition* in the scientific literature is essential for GNATprove, which otherwise must assume that all elements in the collection may have been modified. Special care should be taken to write adequate frame conditions, as they usually look obvious to programmers, and so it is very common to forget to write them and not being able to realize what's the problem afterwards.

To alleviate this problem, the GNATprove tool generates automatically frame conditions in some cases. As examples of use of such generated frame conditions, consider the code of procedures `Update_Arr` and `Update_Rec` below:

```
 1  package Frame_Condition with
 2     SPARK_Mode
 3  is
 4     type Index is range 1 .. 100;
 5     type Arr is array (Index) of Integer;
 6
 7     procedure Update_Arr (A : in out Arr; Idx : Index) with
 8       Post => A(Idx + 1 .. A'Last) = A(Idx + 1 .. A'Last)'Old;
 9
10     type Rec is record
11        A : Arr;
12        X : Integer;
13     end record;
14
15     procedure Update_Rec (R : in out Rec) with
16       Post => R.X = R.X'Old;
17
18  end Frame_Condition;
```

```
 1  package body Frame_Condition with
 2     SPARK_Mode
 3  is
 4     procedure Update_Arr (A : in out Arr; Idx : Index) is
 5     begin
 6        for J in A'First .. Idx loop
 7           A(J) := Integer(J);
 8        end loop;
 9     end Update_Arr;
10
11     procedure Update_Rec (R : in out Rec) is
12     begin
13        for J in R.A'Range loop
```

```
14          R.A(J)  :=  Integer(J);
15       end loop;
16    end Update_Rec;
17
18 end Frame_Condition;
```

Without this feature, GNATprove would not be able to prove the postconditions of either procedure because:

- To prove the postcondition of `Update_Arr`, one needs to know that only the indexes up to `Idx` have been updated in the loop.

- To prove the postcondition of `Update_Rec`, one needs to know that only the component `A` of record `R` has been updated in the loop.

Thanks to this feature, GNATprove automatically proves the postconditions of both procedures, without the need for loop invariants:

```
1 frame_condition.ads:8:14: info: postcondition proved
2 frame_condition.ads:8:14: info: range check proved
3 frame_condition.ads:8:37: info: range check proved
4 frame_condition.ads:16:14: info: postcondition proved
```

In particular, it is able to infer the preservation of unmodified components of record variables. It also handles unmodified components of array variables as long as they are preserved at every index in the array. As an example, consider the following loop which only updates some record component of a nested data structure:

```
1  procedure Preserved_Fields with SPARK_Mode is
2     type R is record
3        F1 : Integer := 0;
4        F2 : Integer := 0;
5     end record;
6
7     type R_Array is array (1 .. 100) of R;
8
9     type R_Array_Record is record
10       F3 : R_Array;
11       F4 : R_Array;
12    end record;
13
14    D : R_Array_Record;
15
16 begin
17    for I in 1 .. 100 loop
18       D.F3 (I).F1 := 0;
19       pragma Assert (for all J in 1 .. 100 =>
20                        D.F3 (J).F2 = D.F3'Loop_Entry (J).F2);
21       pragma Assert (D.F4 = D.F4'Loop_Entry);
22    end loop;
23
24 end Preserved_Fields;
```

Despite the absence of a loop invariant in the above code, GNATprove is able to prove that the assertions on lines 19-21 about variable `D` which is modified in the loop are proved, thanks to the generated loop invariants:

```
1 preserved_fields.adb:18:19: info: initialization of "D.F3" proved
2 preserved_fields.adb:19:22: info: assertion proved
3 preserved_fields.adb:20:24: info: initialization of "D.F3" proved
4 preserved_fields.adb:20:38: info: initialization of "D.F3" proved
```

```
5   preserved_fields.adb:21:22: info: assertion proved
6   preserved_fields.adb:21:22: info: initialization of "D.F4" proved
7   preserved_fields.adb:21:29: info: initialization of "D.F4" proved
```

Note that GNATprove will not generate a frame condition for a record component if the record variable is modified as a whole either through an assignment or through a procedure call, et cetera, even if the component happens to be preserved by the modification.

GNATprove can also infer preservation of unmodified array components for arrays that are only updated at constant indexes or at indexes equal to the loop index. As an example, consider the following loops, only updating some cells of a matrix of arrays:

```
1    procedure Preserved_Components with SPARK_Mode is
2
3       type A is array (1 .. 100) of Natural with Default_Component_Value => 1;
4
5       type A_Matrix is array (1 .. 100, 1 .. 100) of A;
6
7       M : A_Matrix;
8
9    begin
10      L1: for I in 1 .. 100 loop
11         M (I, 1) (1 .. 50) := (others => 0);
12         pragma Assert
13            (for all K1 in 1 .. 100 =>
14               (for all K2 in 1 .. 100 =>
15                  (for all K3 in 1 .. 100 =>
16                     (if K1 > I or else K2 /= 1 or else K3 > 50 then
17                           M (K1, K2) (K3) = M'Loop_Entry (K1, K2) (K3)))));
18      end loop L1;
19
20      L2: for I in 1 .. 99 loop
21         M (I + 1, I) (I .. 100) := (others => 0);
22         pragma Assert
23            (for all K1 in 1 .. 100 =>
24               (for all K2 in 1 .. 100 =>
25                  (for all K3 in 1 .. 100 =>
26                     (if K1 > I + 1 then
27                           M (K1, K2) (K3) = M'Loop_Entry (K1, K2) (K3)))));
28         pragma Assert
29            (for all K1 in 1 .. 100 =>
30               (for all K2 in 1 .. 100 =>
31                  (for all K3 in 1 .. 100 =>
32                     (if K3 < K2 then
33                           M (K1, K2) (K3) = M'Loop_Entry (K1, K2) (K3)))));
34      end loop L2;
35
36   end Preserved_Components;
```

Despite the absence of a loop invariant in the above code, GNATprove can succesfully verify the assertion on line 13 thanks to the generated loop invariant. Note that loop invariant generation for preserved array components is based on heuristics, and that it is therefore far from complete. In particular, it does not handle updates to variable indexes different from the loop index, as can be seen by the failed attempt to verify the assertion on line 22. GNATprove does not either handle dependences between indexes in an update, resulting in the failed attempt to verify the assertion on line 33:

```
1  preserved_components.adb:11:26: info: initialization of "M" proved
2  preserved_components.adb:13:10: info: assertion proved
3  preserved_components.adb:17:30: info: initialization of "M" proved
4  preserved_components.adb:17:48: info: initialization of "M" proved
5  preserved_components.adb:21:07: info: range check proved
6  preserved_components.adb:21:31: info: initialization of "M" proved
7  preserved_components.adb:21:31: info: length check proved
8  preserved_components.adb:21:34: info: length check proved
9  preserved_components.adb:27:30: info: initialization of "M" proved
10 preserved_components.adb:27:30: medium: assertion might fail, cannot prove M (K1, K2)
     (K3) = M'Loop_Entry (K1, K2) (K3) (e.g. when I = 0 and K1 = 0 and K2 = 0 and K3 = 0)
11 preserved_components.adb:27:48: info: initialization of "M" proved
12 preserved_components.adb:33:30: info: initialization of "M" proved
13 preserved_components.adb:33:30: medium: assertion might fail, cannot prove M (K1, K2)
     (K3) = M'Loop_Entry (K1, K2) (K3) (e.g. when K1 = 0 and K2 = 0 and K3 = 0)
14 preserved_components.adb:33:48: info: initialization of "M" proved
```

7.7.3 The Four Properties of a Good Loop Invariant

A loop invariant can describe more or less precisely the behavior of a loop. What matters is that the loop invariant allows proving absence of run-time errors in the subprogram, that the subprogram respects its contract, and that the loop invariant itself holds at each iteration of the loop. There are four properties that a good loop invariant should fulfill:

1. [INIT] It should be provable in the first iteration of the loop.

2. [INSIDE] It should allow proving absence of run-time errors and local assertions inside the loop.

3. [AFTER] It should allow proving absence of run-time errors, local assertions and the subprogram postcondition after the loop.

4. [PRESERVE] It should be provable after the first iteration of the loop.

As a first example, here is a variant of the search algorithm described in *SPARK Tutorial*, which returns whether a collection contains a desired value, and if so, at which index. The collection is implemented as an array.

The specification of Linear_Search is given in file linear_search.ads. The postcondition of Search expresses that, either the search returns a result within the array bounds, in which case it is the desired index, otherwise the array does not contain the value searched.

```
1  package Linear_Search
2    with SPARK_Mode
3  is
4     type Opt_Index is new Natural;
5
6     subtype Index is Opt_Index range 1 .. Opt_Index'Last - 1;
7
8     No_Index : constant Opt_Index := 0;
9
10    type Ar is array (Index range <>) of Integer;
11
12    function Search (A : Ar; I : Integer) return Opt_Index with
13      Post => (if Search'Result in A'Range then A (Search'Result) = I
14               else (for all K in A'Range => A (K) /= I));
15
16 end Linear_Search;
```

The implementation of `Linear_Search` is given in file `linear_search.adb`. The loop invariant of `Search` expresses that, at the end of each iteration, if the loop has not been exited before, then the value searched is not in the range of indexes between the start of the array `A'First` and the current index `Pos`.

```
1   package body Linear_Search
2     with SPARK_Mode
3   is
4
5      function Search (A : Ar; I : Integer) return Opt_Index is
6      begin
7         for Pos in A'Range loop
8            if A (Pos) = I then
9               return Pos;
10           end if;
11
12           pragma Loop_Invariant (for all K in A'First .. Pos => A (K) /= I);
13        end loop;
14
15        return No_Index;
16     end Search;
17
18  end Linear_Search;
```

With this loop invariant, GNATprove is able to prove all checks in `Linear_Search`, both those related to absence of run-time errors and those related to verification of contracts:

```
1   linear_search.adb:9:20: info: range check proved
2   linear_search.adb:12:33: info: loop invariant initialization proved
3   linear_search.adb:12:33: info: loop invariant preservation proved
4   linear_search.adb:12:67: info: index check proved
5   linear_search.ads:13:14: info: postcondition proved
6   linear_search.ads:13:57: info: index check proved
7   linear_search.ads:14:48: info: index check proved
```

In particular, the loop invariant fulfills all four properties that we listed above:

1. [INIT] It is proved in the first iteration (message on line 2).

2. [INSIDE] It allows proving absence of run-time errors inside the loop (messages on lines 1 and 4).

3. [AFTER] It allows proving absence of run-time errors after the loop (messages on lines 6 and 7) and the subprogram postcondition (message on line 5).

4. [PRESERVE] It is proved after the first iteration (message on line 3).

Note that the loop invariant closely resembles the second line in the postcondition of the subprogram, except with a different range of values in the quantification: instead of stating a property for all indexes in the array `A`, the loop invariant states the same property for all indexes up to the current loop index `Pos`. In fact, if we equate `Pos` to `A'Last` for the last iteration of the loop, the two properties are equal. This explains here how the loop invariant allows proving the subprogram postcondition when the value searched is not found.

Note also that we chose to put the loop invariant at the end of the loop. We could as easily put it at the start of the loop. In that case, the range of values in the quantification should be modified to state that, at the start of each iteration, if the loop has not been exited before, then the value searched is not in the range of indexes between the start of the array `A'First` and the current index `Pos` *excluded*:

```
pragma Loop_Invariant (for all K in A'First .. Pos - 1 => A (K) /= I);
```

Indeed, the test for the value at index `Pos` is done after the loop invariant in that case.

We will now demonstrate techniques to complete a loop invariant so that it fulfills all four properties [INIT], [INSIDE], [AFTER] and [PRESERVE], on a more complex algorithm searching in an ordered collection of elements. Like the naive search algorithm just described, this algorithm returns whether the collection contains the desired value, and if so, at which index. The collection is also implemented as an array.

The specification of this `Binary_Search` is given in file `binary_search.ads`:

```ada
package Binary_Search
  with SPARK_Mode
is
   type Opt_Index is new Natural;

   subtype Index is Opt_Index range 1 .. Opt_Index'Last - 1;

   No_Index : constant Opt_Index := 0;

   type Ar is array (Index range <>) of Integer;

   function Empty (A : Ar) return Boolean is (A'First > A'Last);

   function Sorted (A : Ar) return Boolean is
     (for all I1 in A'Range =>
        (for all I2 in I1 .. A'Last => A (I1) <= A (I2)));

   function Search (A : Ar; I : Integer) return Opt_Index with
     Pre  => Sorted (A),
     Post => (if Search'Result in A'Range then A (Search'Result) = I
              else (for all Index in A'Range => A (Index) /= I));

end Binary_Search;
```

The implementation of `Binary_Search` is given in file `binary_search.adb`:

```ada
package body Binary_Search
  with SPARK_Mode
is

   function Search (A : Ar; I : Integer) return Opt_Index is
      Left  : Index;
      Right : Index;
      Med   : Index;
   begin
      if Empty (A) then
         return No_Index;
      end if;

      Left  := A'First;
      Right := A'Last;

      if Left = Right and A (Left) = I then
         return Left;
      elsif A (Left) > I or A (Right) < I then
         return No_Index;
      end if;

      while Left <= Right loop
         Med := Left + (Right - Left) / 2;

         if A (Med) < I then
```

```
27          Left := Med + 1;
28       elsif A (Med) > I then
29          Right := Med - 1;
30       else
31          return Med;
32       end if;
33    end loop;
34
35    return No_Index;
36    end Search;
37
38 end Binary_Search;
```

Note that, although function `Search` has a loop, we have not given an explicit loop invariant yet, so the default loop invariant of `True` will be used by GNATprove. We are running GNATprove with a prover timeout of 60 seconds (switch `--timeout=60`) to get the results presented in the rest of this section.

7.7.4 Proving a Loop Invariant in the First Iteration

Property [INIT] is the easiest one to prove. This is equivalent to proving a pragma Assert in the sequence of statements obtained by unrolling the loop once. In particular, if the loop invariant is at the start of the loop, this is equivalent to proving a pragma Assert just before the loop. Therefore, the usual techniques for investigating unproved checks apply, see *How to Investigate Unproved Checks*.

7.7.5 Completing a Loop Invariant to Prove Checks Inside the Loop

Let's start by running GNATprove on program `Binary_Search` without loop invariant. It generates two medium messages, one corresponding to a possible run-time check failure, and one corresponding to a possible failure of the postcondition:

```
binary_search.adb:26:16: medium: array index check might fail (e.g. when A = (4 => 0,
 ↪others => -1) and A'First = 3 and A'Last = 4 and Med = 2)
binary_search.ads:21:49: medium: postcondition might fail, cannot prove A (Index) /=
 ↪I (e.g. when A = (1 => -1, others => 0) and A'First = 1 and A'Last = 3 and I = 0
 ↪and Index = 2 and Search'Result = 0)
```

We will focus here on the message inside the loop, which corresponds to property [INSIDE]. The problem is that variable `Med` varies in the loop, so GNATprove only knows that its value is in the range of its type `Index` at the start of an iteration (line 23), and that it is then assigned the value of `Left + (Right - Left) / 2` (line 24) before being used as an index into array `A` (lines 26 and 28) and inside expressions assigned to `Left` and `Right` (lines 27 and 29).

As `Left` and `Right` also vary in the loop, GNATprove cannot use the assignment on line 24 to compute a more precise range for variable `Med`, hence the message on index check.

What is needed here is a loop invariant that states that the values of `Left` and `Right` stay within the bounds of `A` inside the loop:

```
while Left <= Right loop
   pragma Loop_Invariant (Left in A'Range and Right in A'Range);

   Med := Left + (Right - Left) / 2;
```

With this simple loop invariant, GNATprove now reports that the check on line 26 is proved. GNATprove computes that the value assigned to `Med` in the loop is also within the bounds of `A`.

7.7.6 Completing a Loop Invariant to Prove Checks After the Loop

With the simple loop invariant given before, GNATprove still reports that the postcondition of Search may fail, which corresponds to property [AFTER]. By instructing GNATprove to prove checks progressively, as seens in *Proving SPARK Programs*, we even get a precise message pointing to the part of the postcondition that could not be proved:

```
binary_search.ads:21:49: medium: postcondition might fail, cannot prove A (Index) /=
  I (e.g. when A = (1 => -1, others => 0) and A'First = 1 and A'Last = 2 and I = 0
  and Index = 2 and Search'Result = 0)
```

Here, the message shows that the second line of the postcondition could not be proved. This line expresses that, in the case where Search returns No_Index after the loop, the array A should not contain the value searched I.

One can very easily check that, if GNATprove can prove this property, it can also prove the postcondition. Simply insert a pragma Assert after the loop stating this property:

```
      end loop;
      pragma Assert (for all Index in A'Range => A (Index) /= I);

      return No_Index;
```

GNATprove now succeeds in proving the postcondition, but it fails to prove the assertion:

```
binary_search.adb:36:50: medium: assertion might fail, cannot prove A (Index) /= I (e.
  g. when A = (0 => 0, 2 => 0, others => -1) and A'First = 1 and A'Last = 2 and I = 0
  and Index = 2)
```

The problem is that GNATprove only knows what the user specified about A in the precondition, namely that it is sorted in ascending order. Nowhere it is said that A does not contain the value I. Note that adding this assertion is not compulsory. It simply helps identifying what is needed to achieve property [AFTER], but it can be removed afterwards.

What is needed here is a loop invariant stating that, if A contains the value I, it must be at an index in the range Left..Right, so when the loop exits because Left > Right (so the loop test becomes false), A cannot contain the value I.

One way to express this property is to state that the value of A at index Left - 1 is less than I, while the value of A at index Right + 1 is greater than I. Taking into account the possibility that there are no such indexes in A if either Left or Right are at the boundaries of the array, we can express it as follows:

```
      while Left <= Right loop
         pragma Loop_Invariant (Left in A'Range and Right in A'Range);
         pragma Loop_Invariant (Left = A'First or else A (Left - 1) < I);
         pragma Loop_Invariant (Right = A'Last or else I < A (Right + 1));

         Med := Left + (Right - Left) / 2;
```

GNATprove manages to prove these additional loop invariants, but it still cannot prove the assertion after the loop. The reason is both simple and far-reaching. Although the above loop invariant together with the property that the array is sorted imply the property we want to express, it still requires additional work for the prover to reach the same conclusion, which may prevent automatic proof in the allocated time. In that case, it is better to express the equivalent but more explicit property directly, as follows:

```
      while Left <= Right loop
         pragma Loop_Invariant (Left in A'Range and Right in A'Range);
         pragma Loop_Invariant
           (for all Index in A'First .. Left - 1 => A (Index) < I);
         pragma Loop_Invariant
```

```
        (for all Index in A'Range =>
            (if Index > Right then I < A (Index)));

    Med := Left + (Right - Left) / 2;
```

GNATprove now proves the assertion after the loop. In general, it is simpler to understand the relationship between the loop invariant and the checks that follow the loop when the loop invariant is directly followed by the exit statement that controls loop termination. In a "for" or "while" loop, this can mean it is easier to place the Loop_Invariant pragmas at the *end* of the loop body, where they precede the (implicit) exit statement. In such cases, the loop invariant is more likely to resemble the postcondition.

7.7.7 Proving a Loop Invariant After the First Iteration

With the loop invariant given before, GNATprove also proves that the loop invariant of `Search` holds after the first iteration, which corresponds to property [PRESERVE]. In fact, we have now arrived at a loop invariant which allows GNATprove to prove all checks for subprogram `Search`.

This is not always the case. In general, when the loop invariant is not proved after the first iteration, the problem is that the loop invariant is not precise enough. The only information that GNATprove knows about the value of variables that are modified in the loop, at each loop iteration, is the information provided in the loop invariant. If the loop invariant is missing some crucial information about these variables, which is needed to prove the loop invariant after N iterations, GNATprove won't be able to prove that the loop invariant holds at each iteration.

In loops that modify variables of composite types (records and arrays), it is usually necessary at this stage to add in the loop invariant some information about those parts of the modified variables which are not modified by the loop, or which are not modified in the first N iterations of the loop. Otherwise, GNATprove assumes that these parts may also be modified, which can prevent it from proving the preservation of the loop invariant. See *Loop Invariants* for an example where this is needed.

In other cases, it may be necessary to guide the prover with intermediate assertions. A rule of thumb for deciding which properties to assert, and where to assert them, is to try to locate at which program point the prover does not success in proving the property of interest, and to restate other properties that are useful for the proof.

In yet other cases, where the difficulty is related to the size of the loop rather than the complexity of the properties, it may be useful to factor the loop into into local subprograms so that the subprograms' preconditions and postconditions provide the intermediate assertions that are needed to prove the loop invariant.

7.8 How to Investigate Unproved Checks

One of the most challenging aspects of formal verification is the analysis of failed proofs. If GNATprove fails to prove automatically that a run-time check or an assertion holds, there might be various reasons:

- [CODE] The check or assertion does not hold, because the code is wrong.

- [ASSERT] The assertion does not hold, because it is incorrect.

- [SPEC] The check or assertion cannot be proved, because of some missing assertions about the behavior of the program.

- [MODEL] The check or assertion is not proved because of current limitations in the model used by GNATprove.

- [TIMEOUT] The check or assertion is not proved because the prover timeouts.

- [PROVER] The check or assertion is not proved because the prover is not smart enough.

7.8.1 Investigating Incorrect Code or Assertion

The first step is to check whether the code is incorrect [CODE] or the assertion is incorrect [ASSERT], or both. Since run-time checks and assertions can be executed at run time, one way to increase confidence in the correction of the code and assertions is to test the program on representative inputs. The following GNAT switches can be used:

- `-gnato`: enable run-time checking of intermediate overflows
- `-gnat-p`: reenable run-time checking even if `-gnatp` was used to suppress all checks
- `-gnata`: enable run-time checking of assertions

7.8.2 Investigating Unprovable Properties

The second step is to consider whether the property is provable [SPEC]. A check or assertion might be unprovable because a necessary annotation is missing:

- the precondition of the enclosing subprogram might be too weak; or
- the postcondition of a subprogram called might be too weak; or
- a loop invariant for an enclosing loop might be too weak; or
- a loop invariant for a loop before the check or assertion might be too weak.

In particular, GNATprove does not look into subprogram bodies, so all the necessary information for calls should be explicit in the subprogram contracts. A focused manual review of the code and assertions can efficiently diagnose many cases of missing annotations. Even when an assertion is quite large, GNATprove precisely locates the part that it cannot prove, which can help figuring out the problem. It may useful to simplify the code during this investigation, for example by adding a simpler assertion and trying to prove it.

GNATprove provides path information that might help the code review. You can display inside the editor the path on which the proof failed, as described in *Running GNATprove from GPS*. In some cases, a counterexample is also generated on the path, with values of variables which exhibit the problem (see *Understanding Counterexamples*). In many cases, this is sufficient to spot a missing assertion.

A property can also be conceptually provable, but the model used by GNATprove can currently not reason about it [MODEL]. (See *GNATprove Limitations* for a list of the current limitations in GNATprove.) In particular using the following features of the language may yield checks that should be true, but cannot be proved:

- Floating point arithmetic (although using CodePeer integration may help here)
- The specific value of dispatching calls when the tag is known

To use CodePeer integration, pass the switch `--codepeer=on` to GNATprove. In those cases where no prover, including CodePeer, can prove the check, the missing information can usually be added using `pragma Assume`.

It may be difficult sometimes to distinguish between unprovable properties and prover shortcomings (the next section). The most generally useful action to narrow down the issue to its core is to insert assertions in the code that *test* whether the property (or part of it) can be proved at some specific point in the program. For example, if a postcondition states a property (P or Q), and the implementation contains many branches and paths, try adding assertions that P holds or Q holds where they are expected to hold. This can help distinguish between the two cases:

- In the case of an unprovable property, this may point to a specific path in the program, and a specific part of the property, which cause the issue.
- In the case of a prover shortcoming, this may also help provers to manage to prove both the assertion and the property. Then, it is good practice to keep in the code only those assertions that help getting automatic proof, and to remove other assertions that were inserted during interaction.

7.8.3 Investigating Prover Shortcomings

The last step is to investigate if the prover would find a proof given enough time [TIMEOUT] or if another prover can find a proof [PROVER]. To that end, GNATprove provides switch `--level`, usable either from the command-line (see *Running GNATprove from the Command Line*), inside GPS (see *Running GNATprove from GPS*) or inside GNATbench (see *Running GNATprove from GNATbench*). The level of 0 is only adequate for simple proofs. In general, one should increase the level of proof (up to level 4) until no more automatic proofs can be obtained.

As described in the section about *Running GNATprove from the Command Line*, switch `--level` is equivalent to setting directly various lower level switches like `--timeout`, `--prover`, and `--proof`. Hence, one can also set more powerful (and thus leading to longer proof time) values for the individual switches rather than using the predefined combinations set through `--level`.

Note that for the above experiments, it is quite convenient to use the *SPARK → Prove Line* or *SPARK → Prove Subprogram* menus in GPS, as described in *Running GNATprove from GPS* and *Running GNATprove from GNATbench*, to get faster results for the desired line or subprogram.

A current limitation of automatic provers is that they don't handle floating-point arithmetic very precisely, in particular when there are either a lot of operations, or some non-linear operations (multiplication, division, exponentiation). In that case, it may be profitable to use CodePeer integration, which is activated with the switch `--codepeer=on`, as CodePeer is both fast and precise for proving bounds of floating-point operations.

Another common limitation of automatic provers is that they don't handle non-linear arithmetic well. For example, they might fail to prove simple checks involving multiplication, division, modulo or exponentiation.

In that case, a user may either:

- add in the code a call to a lemma from the SPARK lemma library (see details in *Manual Proof Using SPARK Lemma Library*), or
- add in the code a call to a user lemma (see details in *Manual Proof Using User Lemmas*), or
- add an assumption in the code (see details in *Indirect Justification with Pragma Assume*), or
- add a justification in the code (see details in *Direct Justification with Pragma Annotate*), or
- manually review the unproved checks and record that they can be trusted (for example by storing the result of GNATprove under version control).

In the future, GNATprove may provide a *user view* of the formula passed to the prover, for advanced users to inspect. This view would express in an Ada-like syntax the actual formula whose proof failed, to make it easier for users to interpret it. This format is yet to be defined.

For advanced users, in particular those who would like to do manual proof, we will provide a description of the format of the proof files generated by GNATprove, so that users can understand the actual files passed to the prover. Each individual file is stored under the sub-directory `gnatprove` of the project object directory (default is the project directory). The file name follows the convention:

```
<file>_<line>_<column>_<check>_<num>.<ext>
```

where:

- `file` is the name of the Ada source file for the check
- `line` is the line where the check appears
- `column` is the column
- `check` is an identifier for the check
- `num` is an optional number and identifies different paths through the program, between the start of the subprogram and the location of the check

- `ext` is the extension corresponding to the file format chosen. The format of the file depends on the prover used. For example, files for Alt-Ergo are are in Why3 format, and files for CVC4 are in SMTLIB2 format.

For example, the proof files generated for prover Alt-Ergo for a range check at line 160, column 42, of the file `f.adb` are stored in:

```
f.adb_160_42_range_check.why
f.adb_160_42_range_check_2.why
f.adb_160_42_range_check_3.why
...
```

Corresponding proof files generated for prover CVC4 are stored in:

```
f.adb_160_42_range_check.smt2
f.adb_160_42_range_check_2.smt2
f.adb_160_42_range_check_3.smt2
...
```

To be able to inspect these files, you should instruct GNATprove to keep them around by adding the switch `-d` to GNATprove's command line. You can also use the switch `-v` to get a detailed log of which proof files GNATprove is producing and attempting to prove.

7.8.4 Looking at Machine-Parsable GNATprove Output

GNATprove generates files which contain the results of SPARK analysis in machine-parsable form. These files are located in the `gnatprove` subdirectory of the project object directory, and have the suffix `.spark`. The structure of these files exposes internal details such as the exact way some checks are proved, therefore the structure of these files may change. Still, we provide here the structure of these files for convenience.

At various places in these files, we refer to entities. These are Ada entities, either subprograms or packages. Entities are defined by their name and their source location (file and line). In JSON this translates to the following dictionary for entities:

```
{ "name" : string,
  "file" : string,
  "line" : int }
```

A `.spark` file is of this form:

```
{ "spark" : list spark_result,
  "flow"  : list flow_result,
  "proof" : list proof_result }
```

Each entry is mapped to a list of entries whose format is described below.

The `spark_result` entry is simply an entity, with an extra field for spark status, so that the entire dictionary looks like this:

```
spark_result = { "name"  : string,
                 "file"  : string,
                 "line"  : int,
                 "spark" : string }
```

Field "spark" takes value in "spec", "all" or "no" to denote respectively that only the spec is in SPARK, both spec/body are in SPARK (or spec is in SPARK for a package without body), or the spec is not in SPARK.

Entries for proof are of the following form:

```
proof_result =
  { "file"      : string,
    "line"      : int,
    "col"       : int,
    "suppressed" : string,
    "rule"      : string,
    "severity"  : string,
    "tracefile" : string,
    "check_tree" : list goal,
    "msg_id"    : int,
    "how_proved" : string,
    "entity"    : entity }
```

- ("file", "line", "col") describe the source location of the message.

- "rule" describes the kind of check.

- "severity" describes the kind status of the message, possible values used by gnatwhy3 are "info", "low", "medium", "high" and "error".

- "tracefile" contains the name of a trace file, if any.

- "entity" contains the entity dictionary for the entity that this check belongs to.

- "msg_id" - if present indicates that this entry corresponds to a message issued on the commandline, with the exact same msg_id in brackets: "[#12]"

- "suppressed" - if present, the message is in fact suppressed by a pragma Annotate, and this field contains the justification message.

- "how_proved" - if present, indicates how the check has been proved (i.e. which prover). Special values are "interval" and "codepeer", which designate the special interval analysis, done in the frontend, and the CodePeer analysis, respectively. Both have their own column in the summary table.

- "check_tree" basically contains a copy of the session tree in JSON format. It's a tree structure whose nodes are goals, transformations and proof attempts:

```
goal = { "transformations" : list trans,
         "pa"              : proof_attempt }

trans = { [transname : goal] }

proof_attempt = { [prover : infos] }

infos = { "time"   : float,
          "steps"  : integer,
          "result" : string }
```

Flow entries are of the same form as for proof. Differences are in the possible values for "rule", which can only be the ones for flow messages. Also "how_proved" field is never set.

7.8.5 Understanding Proof Strategies

We now explain in more detail how the provers are run on the logical formula(s) generated for a given check, a.k.a. Verification Conditions or VCs.

- In `per_check` mode, a single VC is generated for each check at the source level (e.g. an assertion, run-time check, or postcondition); in some cases two VCs can appear. Before attempting proof, this VC is then split into the conjuncts, that is, the parts that are combined with `and` or `and then`. All provers are tried on the VCs obtained in this way until one of them proves the VC or no more provers are left.

- In `per_path` mode, a VC is generated not only for each check at the source level, but for each path to the check. For example, for an assertion that appears after an if-statement, at least two VCs will be generated - one for each path trough the if-statement. For each such VC, all provers are attempted. Unproved VCs are then further split into their conjuncts, and proof is again attempted.

- In `progressive` mode, first the actions described for `per_check` are tried. For all unproved VCs, the VC is then split into the paths that lead to the check, like for `per_path`. Each part is then attempted to be proved independently.

7.9 GNATprove by Example

GNATprove is based on advanced technology for modular static analysis and deductive verification. It is very different both from compilers, which do very little analysis of the code, and static analyzers, which execute symbolically the program. GNATprove does a very powerful local analysis of the program, but it generally does not cross subprogram boundaries. Instead, it uses the *Subprogram Contracts* provided by users to analyze calls. GNATprove also requires sometimes that users direct the analysis with *Assertion Pragmas*. Thus, it is essential to understand how GNATprove uses contracts and assertion pragmas. This section aims at providing a deeper insight into how GNATprove's flow analysis and proof work, through a step-by-step exploration of small code examples.

All the examples presented in this section, as well as some code snippets presented in the *Overview of SPARK Language*, are available in the example called `gnatprove_by_example` distributed with the SPARK toolset. It can be found in the `share/examples/spark` directory below the directory where the toolset is installed, and can be accessed from the IDE (either GPS or GNATBench) via the *Help → SPARK → Examples* menu item.

7.9.1 Basic Examples

The examples in this section have no loops, and do not use more complex features of SPARK like *Ghost Code*, *Interfaces to the Physical World*, or *Object Oriented Programming and Liskov Substitution Principle*.

Increment

Consider a simple procedure that increments its integer parameter X:

```
1  procedure Increment (X : in out Integer) with
2     SPARK_Mode
3  is
4  begin
5     X := X + 1;
6  end Increment;
```

As this procedure does not have a contract yet, GNATprove only checks that there are no possible reads of uninitialized data and no possible run-time errors in the procedure. Here, it issues a message about a possible overflow check failure on `X + 1`:

```
increment.adb:5:11: medium: overflow check might fail (e.g. when X = 2147483647)
```

The counterexample displayed tells us that `Increment` could be called on value `Integer'Last` for parameter X, which would cause the increment to raise a run-time error. One way to eliminate this vulnerability is to add a precondition to `Increment` specifying that X should be less than `Integer'Last` when calling the procedure:

```
1  procedure Increment_Guarded (X : in out Integer) with
2     SPARK_Mode,
3     Pre => X < Integer'Last
4  is
5  begin
6     X := X + 1;
7  end Increment_Guarded;
```

As this procedure has a contract now, GNATprove checks like before that there are no possible reads of uninitialized data and no possible run-time errors in the procedure, including in its contrat, and that the procedure implements its contract. As expected, GNATprove now proves that there is no possible overflow check failure on X + 1:

```
increment_guarded.adb:6:11: info: overflow check proved
```

The precondition is usually the first contract added to a subprogram, but there are other *Subprogram Contracts*. Here is a version of Increment with:

- global dependencies (aspect Global) stating that the procedure reads and writes no global variables

- flow dependencies (aspect Depends) stating that the final value of parameter X only depends on its input value

- a precondition (aspect Pre) stating that parameter X should be less than Integer'Last on entry

- a postcondition (aspect Post) stating that parameter X should have been incremented by the procedure on exit

```
1  procedure Increment_Full (X : in out Integer) with
2     SPARK_Mode,
3     Global  => null,
4     Depends => (X => X),
5     Pre     => X < Integer'Last,
6     Post    => X = X'Old + 1
7  is
8  begin
9     X := X + 1;
10 end Increment_Full;
```

GNATprove checks that Increment_Full implements its contract, and that it cannot raise run-time errors or read uninitialized data. By default, GNATprove's output is empty in such a case, but we can request that it prints one line per check proved by using switch --report=all, which we do here:

```
increment_full.adb:6:14: info: postcondition proved
increment_full.adb:6:24: info: overflow check proved
increment_full.adb:9:11: info: overflow check proved
```

As subprogram contracts are used to analyze callers of a subprogram, let's consider a procedure Increment_Calls that calls the different versions of Increment presented so far:

```
1  with Increment;
2  with Increment_Guarded;
3  with Increment_Full;
4
5  procedure Increment_Calls with
6     SPARK_Mode
7  is
8     X : Integer;
9  begin
10    X := 0;
11    Increment (X);
12    Increment (X);
```

```
13
14      X := 0;
15      Increment_Guarded (X);
16      Increment_Guarded (X);
17
18      X := 0;
19      Increment_Full (X);
20      Increment_Full (X);
21   end Increment_Calls;
```

GNATprove proves all preconditions expect the one on the second call to `Increment_Guarded`:

```
increment_calls.adb:11:15: info: initialization of "X" proved
increment_calls.adb:12:15: info: initialization of "X" proved
increment_calls.adb:15:04: info: precondition proved
increment_calls.adb:15:23: info: initialization of "X" proved
increment_calls.adb:16:04: medium: precondition might fail (e.g. when X = 2147483647)
increment_calls.adb:16:23: info: initialization of "X" proved
increment_calls.adb:19:04: info: precondition proved
increment_calls.adb:19:20: info: initialization of "X" proved
increment_calls.adb:20:04: info: precondition proved
increment_calls.adb:20:20: info: initialization of "X" proved
```

`Increment` has no precondition, so there is nothing to check here except the initialization of X when calling `Increment` on lines 11 and 12. But remember that GNATprove did issue a message about a true vulnaribility on `Increment`'s implementation.

This vulnerability was corrected by adding a precondition to `Increment_Guarded`. This has the effect of pushing the constraint on callers, here procedure `Increment_Calls`. As expected, GNATprove proves that the first call to `Increment_Guarded` on line 15 satisfies its precondition. But it does not prove the same for the second call to `Increment_Guarded` on line 16, because the value of X on line 16 was set by the call to `Increment_Guarded` on line 15, and the contract of `Increment_Guarded` does not say anything about the possible values of X on exit.

Thus, a postcondition like the one on `Increment_Full` is needed so that GNATprove can check the second call to increment X. As expected, GNATprove proves that both calls to `Increment_Full` on lines 19 and 20 satisfy their precondition.

In some cases, the user is not interested in specifying and verifying a complete contract like the one on `Increment_Full`, typically for helper subprograms defined locally in a subprogram or package body. GNATprove allows performing *Contextual Analysis of Subprograms Without Contracts* for these local subprograms. For example, consider a local definition of `Increment` inside procedure `Increment_Local`:

```
1    procedure Increment_Local with
2      SPARK_Mode
3    is
4      procedure Increment (X : in out Integer) is
5      begin
6         X := X + 1;
7      end Increment;
8
9      X : Integer;
10
11   begin
12      X := 0;
13      Increment (X);
14      Increment (X);
15      pragma Assert (X = 2);
16   end Increment_Local;
```

Although `Increment` has no contract (like the previous non-local version), GNATprove proves that this program is free from run-time errors, and that the assertion on line 15 holds:

```
increment_local.adb:6:12: info: initialization of "X" proved, in call inlined at
  increment_local.adb:13
increment_local.adb:6:12: info: initialization of "X" proved, in call inlined at
  increment_local.adb:14
increment_local.adb:6:14: info: overflow check proved, in call inlined at increment_
  local.adb:13
increment_local.adb:6:14: info: overflow check proved, in call inlined at increment_
  local.adb:14
increment_local.adb:15:19: info: assertion proved
increment_local.adb:15:19: info: initialization of "X" proved
```

Swap

Consider a simple procedure that swaps its integer parameters `X` and `Y`, whose simple-minded implementation is wrong:

```
1  procedure Swap_Bad (X, Y : in out Integer) with
2    SPARK_Mode
3  is
4  begin
5    X := Y;
6    Y := X;
7  end Swap_Bad;
```

As this procedure does not have a contract yet, GNATprove only checks that there are no possible reads of uninitialized data and no possible run-time errors in the procedure. Here, it simply issues a warning:

```
swap_bad.adb:1:21: warning: unused initial value of "X"
```

But we know the procedure is wrong, so we'd like to get an error of some sort! We could not detect it with GNATprove because the error is functional, and GNATprove cannot guess the intended functionality of `Swap_Bad`. Fortunately, we can give this information to GNATprove by adding a contract to `Swap_Bad`.

One such contract is the flow dependencies introduced by aspect `Depends`. Here it specifies that the final value of `X` (resp. `Y`) should depend on the initial value of `Y` (resp. `X`):

```
1  procedure Swap_Bad_Depends (X, Y : in out Integer) with
2    SPARK_Mode,
3    Depends => (X => Y, Y => X)
4  is
5  begin
6    X := Y;
7    Y := X;
8  end Swap_Bad_Depends;
```

GNATprove issues 3 check messages on `Swap_Bad_Depends`:

```
swap_bad_depends.adb:1:29: warning: unused initial value of "X"
swap_bad_depends.adb:3:03: medium: missing dependency "null => X"
swap_bad_depends.adb:3:23: medium: missing dependency "Y => Y"
swap_bad_depends.adb:3:28: medium: incorrect dependency "Y => X"
```

The last message informs us that the dependency `Y => X` stated in `Swap_Bad_Depends`'s contract is incorrect for the given implementation. That might be either an error in the code or an error in the contract. Here this is an error in the code. The two other messages are consequences of this error.

Another possible contract is the postcondition introduced by aspect Post. Here it specifies that the final value of X (resp. Y) is equal to the initial value of Y (resp. X):

```
1  procedure Swap_Bad_Post (X, Y : in out Integer) with
2     SPARK_Mode,
3     Post => X = Y'Old and Y = X'Old
4  is
5  begin
6     X := Y;
7     Y := X;
8  end Swap_Bad_Post;
```

GNATprove issues one check message on the unproved postcondition of Swap_Bad_Post, with a counterexample giving concrete values of a wrong execution:

```
swap_bad_post.adb:3:25: medium: postcondition might fail, cannot prove Y = X'old (e.g.
 ↪ when X'Old = 1 and Y = 0)
```

Both the check messages on Swap_Bad_Depends and on Swap_Bad_Post inform us that the intended functionality as expressed in the contracts is not implemented in the procedure. And looking again at the warning issued by GNATprove on Swap_Bad, this was already pointing at the same issue: swapping the values of X and Y should obviously lead to reading the initial value of X; the fact that this value is not used is a clear sign that there is an error in the implementation. The correct version of Swap uses a temporary value to hold the value of X:

```
1   procedure Swap (X, Y : in out Integer) with
2      SPARK_Mode,
3      Depends => (X => Y, Y => X),
4      Post    => X = Y'Old and Y = X'Old
5   is
6      Tmp : constant Integer := X;
7   begin
8      X := Y;
9      Y := Tmp;
10  end Swap;
```

GNATprove proves both contracts on Swap and it informs us that the postcondition was proved:

```
swap.adb:4:14: info: postcondition proved
```

Let's now consider a well-known *in place* implementation of Swap that avoids introducing a temporary variable by using bitwise operations:

```
1   with Interfaces; use Interfaces;
2
3   procedure Swap_Modulo (X, Y : in out Unsigned_32) with
4      SPARK_Mode,
5      Post => X = Y'Old and Y = X'Old
6   is
7   begin
8      X := X xor Y;
9      Y := X xor Y;
10     X := X xor Y;
11  end Swap_Modulo;
```

GNATprove understands the bitwise operations on values of modular types, and it proves here that the postcondition of Swap_Modulo is proved:

```
swap_modulo.adb:5:11: info: postcondition proved
```

GNATprove's flow analysis issues warnings like the one on Swap_Bad whenever it detects that some variables or statements are not used in the computation, which is likely uncovering an error. For example, consider procedure Swap_Warn which assigns X and Tmp_Y out of order:

```
1   procedure Swap_Warn (X, Y : in out Integer) with
2      SPARK_Mode
3   is
4      Tmp_X : Integer;
5      Tmp_Y : Integer;
6   begin
7      Tmp_X := X;
8      X := Tmp_Y;
9      Tmp_Y := Y;
10     Y := Tmp_X;
11  end Swap_Warn;
```

On this wrong implementation, GNATprove issues a high check message for the certain read of an uninitialized variable, and two warnings that point to unused constructs:

```
swap_warn.adb:1:25: warning: unused initial value of "Y"
swap_warn.adb:8:09: high: "Tmp_Y" is not initialized
swap_warn.adb:8:09: warning: "Tmp_Y" may be referenced before it has a value
swap_warn.adb:9:10: warning: unused assignment
swap_warn.adb:10:09: info: initialization of "Tmp_X" proved
```

In general, warnings issued by GNATprove's flow analysis should be carefully reviewed, as they may lead to the discovery of errors in the program.

Addition

Consider a simple function Addition that returns the sum of its integer parameters X and Y. As in *Increment*, we add a suitable precondition and postcondition for this function:

```
1   function Addition (X, Y : Integer) return Integer with
2      SPARK_Mode,
3      Depends => (Addition'Result => (X, Y)),
4      Pre     => X + Y in Integer,
5      Post    => Addition'Result = X + Y
6   is
7   begin
8      return X + Y;
9   end Addition;
```

We also added flow dependencies to Addition for illustration purposes, but they are the same as the default generated ones (the result of the function depends on all its inputs), so are not in general given explicitly.

GNATprove issues a check message about a possible overflow in the precondition of Addition:

```
addition.adb:4:16: medium: overflow check might fail (e.g. when X = -2147483648 and Y
   = -1)
addition.adb:5:14: info: postcondition proved
addition.adb:5:34: info: overflow check proved
addition.adb:8:13: info: overflow check proved
```

Indeed, if we call for example `Addition` on values `Integer'Last` for X and 1 for Y, the expression `X + Y` evaluated in the precondition does not fit in a machine integer and raises an exception at run time. In this specific case, some people may consider that it does not really matter that an exception is raised due to overflow as the failure of the precondition should also raise a run-time exception. But in general the precondition should not fail (just consider the precondition `X + Y not in Integer` for example), and even here, the different exceptions raised may be treated differently (`Constraint_Error` in the case of an overflow, `Assertion_Error` in the case of a failing precondition).

One way to avoid this vulnerability is to rewrite the precondition so that no overflow can occur:

```
1  function Addition_Rewrite (X, Y : Integer) return Integer with
2    SPARK_Mode,
3    Depends => (Addition_Rewrite'Result => (X, Y)),
4    Pre     => (X >= 0 and then Y <= Integer'Last - X) or else (X < 0 and then Y >=
     Integer'First - X),
5    Post    => Addition_Rewrite'Result = X + Y
6  is
7  begin
8     return X + Y;
9  end Addition_Rewrite;
```

Although GNATprove proves that `Addition_Rewrite` implements its contract and is free from run-time errors, the rewritten precondition is not so readable anymore:

```
addition_rewrite.adb:4:49: info: overflow check proved
addition_rewrite.adb:4:97: info: overflow check proved
addition_rewrite.adb:5:14: info: postcondition proved
addition_rewrite.adb:5:42: info: overflow check proved
addition_rewrite.adb:8:13: info: overflow check proved
```

A better way to achieve the same goal without losing in readability is to execute and analyze contracts in a special mode where overflows cannot occur, as explained in *Overflow Modes*. In that case, GNATprove proves that there are no run-time errors in function `Addition`, and that it implements its contract.

Finally, we can choose to expand the range of applicability of the function, by accepting any values of inputs X and Y, and saturating when the addition would overflow the bounds of machine integers. That's what function `Addition_Saturated` does, and its saturating behavior is expressed in *Contract Cases*:

```
1  function Addition_Saturated (X, Y : Integer) return Integer with
2    SPARK_Mode,
3    Contract_Cases => ((X + Y in Integer)     => Addition_Saturated'Result = X + Y,
4                        X + Y < Integer'First => Addition_Saturated'Result = Integer
     'First,
5                        X + Y > Integer'Last  => Addition_Saturated'Result = Integer
     'Last)
6  is
7  begin
8     if X < 0 and Y < 0 then -- both negative
9        if X < Integer'First - Y then
10          return Integer'First;
11       else
12          return X + Y;
13       end if;
14
15    elsif X > 0 and Y > 0 then -- both positive
16       if X > Integer'Last - Y then
17          return Integer'Last;
18       else
```

```
19          return X + Y;
20       end if;
21
22    else -- one positive or null, one negative or null, adding them is safe
23       return X + Y;
24    end if;
25 end Addition_Saturated;
```

GNATprove proves that `Addition_Saturated` implements its contract and is free from run-time errors:

```
addition_saturated.adb:3:03: info: complete contract cases proved
addition_saturated.adb:3:03: info: disjoint contract cases proved
addition_saturated.adb:3:44: info: contract case proved
addition_saturated.adb:4:44: info: contract case proved
addition_saturated.adb:5:44: info: contract case proved
addition_saturated.adb:9:28: info: overflow check proved
addition_saturated.adb:12:19: info: overflow check proved
addition_saturated.adb:16:27: info: overflow check proved
addition_saturated.adb:19:19: info: overflow check proved
addition_saturated.adb:23:16: info: overflow check proved
```

Note that we analyzed this function in ELIMINATED overflow mode, using the switch `-gnato13`, otherwise there would be possible overflows in the guard expressions of the contract cases.

7.9.2 Loop Examples

The examples in this section contain loops, and thus require in general that users write suitable *Loop Invariants*. We start by explaining the need for a loop invariant, and we continue with a description of the most common patterns of loops and their loop invariant. We summarize each pattern in a table of the following form:

Loop Pattern	Loop Over Data Structure
Proof Objective	Establish property P.
Loop Behavior	Loops over the data structure and establishes P.
Loop Invariant	Property P is established for the part of the data structure looped over so far.

The examples in this section use the types defined in package `Loop_Types`:

```
1  with Ada.Containers.Formal_Doubly_Linked_Lists;
2  with Ada.Containers.Formal_Vectors;
3
4  package Loop_Types
5    with SPARK_Mode
6  is
7     subtype Index_T is Positive range 1 .. 1000;
8     subtype Opt_Index_T is Natural range 0 .. 1000;
9     subtype Component_T is Natural;
10
11    type Arr_T is array (Index_T) of Component_T;
12
13    package Vectors is new Ada.Containers.Formal_Vectors (Index_T, Component_T);
14    subtype Vec_T is Vectors.Vector;
15
16    package Lists is new Ada.Containers.Formal_Doubly_Linked_Lists (Component_T);
17    subtype List_T is Lists.List;
18
19 end Loop_Types;
```

The Need for a Loop Invariant

Consider a simple procedure that increments its integer parameter X a number N of times:

```
procedure Increment_Loop (X : in out Integer; N : Natural) with
   SPARK_Mode,
   Pre  => X <= Integer'Last - N,
   Post => X = X'Old + N
is
begin
   for I in 1 .. N loop
      X := X + 1;
   end loop;
end Increment_Loop;
```

The precondition of Increment_Loop ensures that there is no overflow when incrementing X in the loop, and its postcondition states that X has been incremented N times. This contract is a generalization of the contract given for a single increment in *Increment*. GNATprove does not manage to prove either the absence of overflow or the postcondition of Increment_Loop:

```
increment_loop.adb:3:29: info: overflow check proved
increment_loop.adb:4:11: medium: postcondition might fail, cannot prove X = X'Old + N
  (e.g. when N = 1 and X = 1 and X'Old = 1)
increment_loop.adb:4:21: info: overflow check proved
increment_loop.adb:8:14: medium: overflow check might fail (e.g. when X = 2147483647)
```

As described in *How to Write Loop Invariants*, this is because variable X is modified in the loop, hence GNATprove knows nothing about it unless it is stated in a loop invariant. If we add such a loop invariant that describes precisely the value of X in each iteration of the loop:

```
procedure Increment_Loop_Inv (X : in out Integer; N : Natural) with
   SPARK_Mode,
   Pre  => X <= Integer'Last - N,
   Post => X = X'Old + N
is
begin
   for I in 1 .. N loop
      X := X + 1;
      pragma Loop_Invariant (X = X'Loop_Entry + I);
   end loop;
end Increment_Loop_Inv;
```

then GNATprove proves both the absence of overflow and the postcondition of Increment_Loop_Inv:

```
increment_loop_inv.adb:3:29: info: overflow check proved
increment_loop_inv.adb:4:11: info: postcondition proved
increment_loop_inv.adb:4:21: info: overflow check proved
increment_loop_inv.adb:8:14: info: overflow check proved
increment_loop_inv.adb:9:30: info: loop invariant initialization proved
increment_loop_inv.adb:9:30: info: loop invariant preservation proved
increment_loop_inv.adb:9:47: info: overflow check proved
```

Fortunately, many loops fall into some broad categories for which the loop invariant is known. In the following sections, we describe these common patterns of loops and their loop invariant, which involve in general iterating over the content of a collection (either an array or a container from the *Formal Containers Library*).

Initialization Loops

This kind of loops iterates over a collection to initialize every element of the collection to a given value:

Loop Pattern	Separate Initialization of Each Element
Proof Objective	Every element of the collection has a specific value.
Loop Behavior	Loops over the collection and initializes every element of the collection.
Loop Invariant	Every element initialized so far has its specific value.

In the simplest case, every element is assigned the same value. For example, in procedure `Init_Arr_Zero` below, value zero is assigned to every element of array `A`:

```
1  with Loop_Types; use Loop_Types;
2
3  procedure Init_Arr_Zero (A : out Arr_T) with
4     SPARK_Mode,
5     Post => (for all J in A'Range => A(J) = 0)
6  is
7  begin
8     for J in A'Range loop
9        A(J) := 0;
10       pragma Loop_Invariant (for all K in A'First .. J => A(K) = 0);
11       pragma Annotate (GNATprove, False_Positive, """A"" might not be initialized",
12                    "Part of array up to index J is initialized at this point");
13    end loop;
14 end Init_Arr_Zero;
```

The loop invariant expresses that all elements up to the current loop index `J` have the value zero. With this loop invariant, GNATprove is able to prove the postcondition of `Init_Arr_Zero`, namely that all elements of the array have value zero:

```
init_arr_zero.adb:3:26: info: initialization of "A" proved
init_arr_zero.adb:5:11: info: postcondition proved
init_arr_zero.adb:5:36: info: initialization of "A" proved
init_arr_zero.adb:10:30: info: loop invariant initialization proved
init_arr_zero.adb:10:30: info: loop invariant preservation proved
init_arr_zero.adb:10:59: info: initialization of "A" proved
init_arr_zero.adb:10:61: info: index check proved
```

Note: Pragma Annotate is used in `Init_Arr_Zero` to justify a message issued by flow analysis, about the possible read of uninitialized value `A(K)` in the loop invariant. Indeed, flow analysis is not currently able to infer that all elements up to the loop index `J` have been initialized, hence it issues a message that `"A" might not be initialized`. For more details, see section on *Justifying Check Messages*.

Consider now a variant of the same initialization loop over a vector:

```
1  with Loop_Types; use Loop_Types; use Loop_Types.Vectors;
2
3  procedure Init_Vec_Zero (V : in out Vec_T) with
4     SPARK_Mode,
5     Post => (for all J in First_Index (V) .. Last_Index (V) => Element (V, J) = 0)
6  is
7  begin
8     for J in First_Index (V) .. Last_Index (V) loop
9        Replace_Element (V, J, 0);
10       pragma Loop_Invariant (Last_Index (V) = Last_Index (V)'Loop_Entry);
```

```
11       pragma Loop_Invariant (for all K in First_Index (V) .. J => Element (V, K) = 0);
12    end loop;
13 end Init_Vec_Zero;
```

Like before, the loop invariant expresses that all elements up to the current loop index J have the value zero. Another loop invariant is needed here to express that the length of the vector does not change in the loop: as variable V is modified in the loop, GNATprove does not know its length stays the same (for example, calling procedure Append or Delete_Last would change this length) unless the user says so in the loop invariant. This is different from arrays whose length cannot change. With this loop invariant, GNATprove is able to prove the postcondition of Init_Vec_Zero, namely that all elements of the vector have value zero:

```
init_vec_zero.adb:5:11: info: postcondition proved
init_vec_zero.adb:5:62: info: precondition proved
init_vec_zero.adb:5:74: info: range check proved
init_vec_zero.adb:9:07: info: precondition proved
init_vec_zero.adb:9:27: info: range check proved
init_vec_zero.adb:10:30: info: loop invariant initialization proved
init_vec_zero.adb:10:30: info: loop invariant preservation proved
init_vec_zero.adb:11:30: info: loop invariant initialization proved
init_vec_zero.adb:11:30: info: loop invariant preservation proved
init_vec_zero.adb:11:67: info: precondition proved
init_vec_zero.adb:11:79: info: range check proved
```

Similarly, consider a variant of the same initialization loop over a list:

```
1  with Loop_Types; use Loop_Types; use Loop_Types.Lists;
2  with Ada.Containers; use Ada.Containers; use Loop_Types.Lists.Formal_Model;
3
4  procedure Init_List_Zero (L : in out List_T) with
5     SPARK_Mode,
6     Post => (for all E of L => E = 0)
7  is
8     Cu : Cursor := First (L);
9  begin
10    while Has_Element (L, Cu) loop
11       pragma Loop_Invariant (for all I in 1 .. P.Get (Positions (L), Cu) - 1 =>
12                                 Element (Model (L), I) = 0);
13       Replace_Element (L, Cu, 0);
14       Next (L, Cu);
15    end loop;
16 end Init_List_Zero;
```

Contrary to arrays and vectors, lists are not indexed. Instead, a cursor can be defined to iterate over the list. The loop invariant expresses that all elements up to the current cursor Cu have the value zero. To access the element stored at a given position in a list, we use the function Model which computes the mathematical sequence of the elements stored in the list. The position of a cursor in this sequence is retrieved using the Positions function. Contrary to the case of vectors, no loop invariant is needed to express that the length of the list does not change in the loop, because the postcondition remains provable here even if the length of the list changes. With this loop invariant, GNATprove is able to prove the postcondition of Init_List_Zero, namely that all elements of the list have value zero:

```
init_list_zero.adb:6:11: info: postcondition proved
init_list_zero.adb:6:12: info: precondition proved
init_list_zero.adb:10:26: info: initialization of "Cu.Node" proved
init_list_zero.adb:11:30: info: loop invariant initialization proved
init_list_zero.adb:11:30: info: loop invariant preservation proved
init_list_zero.adb:11:49: info: precondition proved
init_list_zero.adb:11:70: info: initialization of "Cu.Node" proved
```

```
init_list_zero.adb:12:32: info: precondition proved
init_list_zero.adb:13:07: info: precondition proved
init_list_zero.adb:13:27: info: initialization of "Cu.Node" proved
init_list_zero.adb:14:07: info: precondition proved
init_list_zero.adb:14:16: info: initialization of "Cu.Node" proved
```

The case of sets and maps is similar to the case of lists.

Note: The parameter of `Init_Vec_Zero` and `Init_List_Zero` is an in out parameter. This is because some components of the vector/list parameter are preserved by the initialization procedure (in particular the component corresponding to its length). This is different from `Init_Arr_Zero` which takes an out parameter, as all components of the array are initialized by the procedure (the bounds of an array are not modifiable, hence considered separately from the parameter mode).

Consider now a case where the value assigned to each element is not the same. For example, in procedure `Init_Arr_Index` below, each element of array A is assigned the value of its index:

```
1  with Loop_Types; use Loop_Types;
2
3  procedure Init_Arr_Index (A : out Arr_T) with
4    SPARK_Mode,
5    Post => (for all J in A'Range => A(J) = J)
6  is
7  begin
8     for J in A'Range loop
9        A(J) := J;
10       pragma Loop_Invariant (for all K in A'First .. J => A(K) = K);
11       pragma Annotate (GNATprove, False_Positive, """A"" might not be initialized",
12                        "Part of array up to index J is initialized at this point");
13    end loop;
14 end Init_Arr_Index;
```

The loop invariant expresses that all elements up to the current loop index J have the value of their index. With this loop invariant, GNATprove is able to prove the postcondition of `Init_Arr_Index`, namely that all elements of the array have the value of their index:

```
init_arr_index.adb:3:27: info: initialization of "A" proved
init_arr_index.adb:5:11: info: postcondition proved
init_arr_index.adb:5:36: info: initialization of "A" proved
init_arr_index.adb:10:30: info: loop invariant initialization proved
init_arr_index.adb:10:30: info: loop invariant preservation proved
init_arr_index.adb:10:59: info: initialization of "A" proved
init_arr_index.adb:10:61: info: index check proved
```

Similarly, variants of `Init_Vec_Zero` and `Init_List_Zero` that assign a different value to each element of the collection would be proved by GNATprove.

Mapping Loops

This kind of loops iterates over a collection to map every element of the collection to a new value:

Loop Pattern	Separate Modification of Each Element
Proof Objective	Every element of the collection has an updated value.
Loop Behavior	Loops over the collection and updates every element of the collection.
Loop Invariant	Every element updated so far has its specific value.

In the simplest case, every element is assigned a new value based only on its initial value. For example, in procedure `Map_Arr_Incr` below, every element of array `A` is incremented by one:

```
1   with Loop_Types; use Loop_Types;
2
3   procedure Map_Arr_Incr (A : in out Arr_T) with
4     SPARK_Mode,
5     Pre  => (for all J in A'Range => A(J) /= Component_T'Last),
6     Post => (for all J in A'Range => A(J) = A'Old(J) + 1)
7   is
8   begin
9      for J in A'Range loop
10        A(J) := A(J) + 1;
11        pragma Loop_Invariant (for all K in A'First .. J => A(K) = A'Loop_Entry(K) + 1);
12        --  The following loop invariant is generated automatically by GNATprove:
13        --  pragma Loop_Invariant (for all K in J + 1 .. A'Last => A(K) = A'Loop_
   ↪Entry(K));
14     end loop;
15  end Map_Arr_Incr;
```

The loop invariant expresses that all elements up to the current loop index `J` have been incremented (using *Attribute Loop_Entry*). With this loop invariant, GNATprove is able to prove the postcondition of `Map_Arr_Incr`, namely that all elements of the array have been incremented:

```
map_arr_incr.adb:6:11: info: postcondition proved
map_arr_incr.adb:6:52: info: overflow check proved
map_arr_incr.adb:10:20: info: overflow check proved
map_arr_incr.adb:11:30: info: loop invariant initialization proved
map_arr_incr.adb:11:30: info: loop invariant preservation proved
map_arr_incr.adb:11:61: info: index check proved
map_arr_incr.adb:11:79: info: index check proved
map_arr_incr.adb:11:82: info: overflow check proved
```

Note that the commented loop invariant expressing that other elements have not been modified is not needed, as it is an example of *Automatically Generated Loop Invariants*.

Consider now a variant of the same initialization loop over a vector:

```
1   pragma Unevaluated_Use_Of_Old (Allow);
2   with Loop_Types; use Loop_Types; use Loop_Types.Vectors;
3   use Loop_Types.Vectors.Formal_Model;
4
5   procedure Map_Vec_Incr (V : in out Vec_T) with
6     SPARK_Mode,
7     Pre  => (for all I in 1 .. Last_Index (V) =>
8                  Element (V, I) /= Component_T'Last),
9     Post => Last_Index (V) = Last_Index (V)'Old
10    and then (for all I in 1 .. Last_Index (V) =>
11                 Element (V, I) = Element (Model (V)'Old, I) + 1)
12  is
13  begin
14     for J in 1 .. Last_Index (V) loop
15        pragma Loop_Invariant (Last_Index (V) = Last_Index (V)'Loop_Entry);
16        pragma Loop_Invariant
17           (for all I in 1 .. J - 1 =>
18              Element (V, I) = Element (Model (V)'Loop_Entry, I) + 1);
19        pragma Loop_Invariant
20           (for all I in J .. Last_Index (V) =>
21              Element (V, I) = Element (Model (V)'Loop_Entry, I));
```

```
22        Replace_Element (V, J, Element (V, J) + 1);
23     end loop;
24  end Map_Vec_Incr;
```

Like before, we need an additionnal loop invariant to state that the length of the vector is not modified by the loop. The other two invariants are direct translations of those used for the loop over arrays: the first one expresses that all elements up to the current loop index J have been incremented, and the second one expresses that other elements have not been modified. Note that, as formal vectors are limited, we need to use the `Model` function of vectors to express the set of elements contained in the vector before the loop (using attributes `Loop_Entry` and `Old`). With this loop invariant, GNATprove is able to prove the postcondition of `Map_Vec_Incr`, namely that all elements of the vector have been incremented:

```
map_vec_incr.adb:8:16: info: precondition proved
map_vec_incr.adb:8:28: info: range check proved
map_vec_incr.adb:9:11: info: postcondition proved
map_vec_incr.adb:11:18: info: precondition proved
map_vec_incr.adb:11:30: info: range check proved
map_vec_incr.adb:11:35: info: precondition proved
map_vec_incr.adb:11:59: info: range check proved
map_vec_incr.adb:11:62: info: overflow check proved
map_vec_incr.adb:15:30: info: loop invariant initialization proved
map_vec_incr.adb:15:30: info: loop invariant preservation proved
map_vec_incr.adb:17:10: info: loop invariant initialization proved
map_vec_incr.adb:17:10: info: loop invariant preservation proved
map_vec_incr.adb:18:12: info: precondition proved
map_vec_incr.adb:18:24: info: range check proved
map_vec_incr.adb:18:29: info: precondition proved
map_vec_incr.adb:18:60: info: range check proved
map_vec_incr.adb:18:63: info: overflow check proved
map_vec_incr.adb:20:10: info: loop invariant initialization proved
map_vec_incr.adb:20:10: info: loop invariant preservation proved
map_vec_incr.adb:21:12: info: precondition proved
map_vec_incr.adb:21:24: info: range check proved
map_vec_incr.adb:21:29: info: precondition proved
map_vec_incr.adb:21:60: info: range check proved
map_vec_incr.adb:22:07: info: precondition proved
map_vec_incr.adb:22:27: info: range check proved
map_vec_incr.adb:22:30: info: precondition proved
map_vec_incr.adb:22:42: info: range check proved
map_vec_incr.adb:22:45: info: overflow check proved
```

Similarly, consider a variant of the same initialization loop over a list:

```
1   with Loop_Types; use Loop_Types; use Loop_Types.Lists;
2   with Ada.Containers; use Ada.Containers; use Loop_Types.Lists.Formal_Model;
3
4   procedure Map_List_Incr (L : in out List_T) with
5     SPARK_Mode,
6     Pre  => (for all E of L => E /= Component_T'Last),
7     Post => Length (L) = Length (L)'Old
8     and then (for all I in 1 .. Length (L) =>
9                   Element (Model (L), I) = Element (Model (L'Old), I) + 1)
10  is
11     Cu : Cursor := First (L);
12  begin
13     while Has_Element (L, Cu) loop
14        pragma Loop_Invariant (Length (L) = Length (L)'Loop_Entry);
```

```
15    pragma Loop_Invariant
16       (for all I in 1 .. P.Get (Positions (L), Cu) - 1 =>
17         Element (Model (L), I) = Element (Model (L'Loop_Entry), I) + 1);
18    pragma Loop_Invariant
19       (for all I in P.Get (Positions (L), Cu) .. Length (L) =>
20         Element (Model (L), I) = Element (Model (L'Loop_Entry), I));
21    Replace_Element (L, Cu, Element (L, Cu) + 1);
22    Next (L, Cu);
23  end loop;
24 end Map_List_Incr;
```

Like before, we need to use a cursor to iterate over the list. The loop invariants express that all elements up to the current loop index J have been incremented and that other elements have not been modified. Note that it is necessary to state here that the length of the list is not modified during the loop. It is because the length is used to bound the quantification over the elements of the list both in the invariant and in the postcondition. With this loop invariant, GNATprove is able to prove the postcondition of Map_List_Incr, namely that all elements of the list have been incremented:

```
map_list_incr.adb:6:12: info: precondition proved
map_list_incr.adb:7:11: info: postcondition proved
map_list_incr.adb:9:18: info: precondition proved
map_list_incr.adb:9:43: info: precondition proved
map_list_incr.adb:9:70: info: overflow check proved
map_list_incr.adb:13:26: info: initialization of "Cu.Node" proved
map_list_incr.adb:14:30: info: loop invariant initialization proved
map_list_incr.adb:14:30: info: loop invariant preservation proved
map_list_incr.adb:16:10: info: loop invariant initialization proved
map_list_incr.adb:16:10: info: loop invariant preservation proved
map_list_incr.adb:16:29: info: precondition proved
map_list_incr.adb:16:50: info: initialization of "Cu.Node" proved
map_list_incr.adb:17:12: info: precondition proved
map_list_incr.adb:17:37: info: precondition proved
map_list_incr.adb:17:71: info: overflow check proved
map_list_incr.adb:19:10: info: loop invariant initialization proved
map_list_incr.adb:19:10: info: loop invariant preservation proved
map_list_incr.adb:19:24: info: precondition proved
map_list_incr.adb:19:45: info: initialization of "Cu.Node" proved
map_list_incr.adb:20:12: info: precondition proved
map_list_incr.adb:20:32: info: range check proved
map_list_incr.adb:20:37: info: precondition proved
map_list_incr.adb:20:68: info: range check proved
map_list_incr.adb:21:07: info: precondition proved
map_list_incr.adb:21:27: info: initialization of "Cu.Node" proved
map_list_incr.adb:21:31: info: precondition proved
map_list_incr.adb:21:43: info: initialization of "Cu.Node" proved
map_list_incr.adb:21:47: info: overflow check proved
map_list_incr.adb:22:07: info: precondition proved
map_list_incr.adb:22:16: info: initialization of "Cu.Node" proved
```

Validation Loops

This kind of loops iterates over a collection to validate that every element of the collection has a valid value. The most common pattern is to exit or return from the loop if an invalid value if encountered:

Loop Pattern	Sequence Validation with Early Exit
Proof Objective	Determine (flag) if there are any invalid elements in a given collection.
Loop Behavior	Loops over the collection and exits/returns if an invalid element is encountered.
Loop Invariant	Every element encountered so far is valid.

Consider a procedure `Validate_Arr_Zero` that checks that all elements of an array `A` have value zero:

```
with Loop_Types; use Loop_Types;

procedure Validate_Arr_Zero (A : Arr_T; Success : out Boolean) with
   SPARK_Mode,
   Post => Success = (for all J in A'Range => A(J) = 0)
is
begin
   for J in A'Range loop
      if A(J) /= 0 then
         Success := False;
         return;
      end if;
      pragma Loop_Invariant (for all K in A'First .. J => A(K) = 0);
   end loop;

   Success := True;
end Validate_Arr_Zero;
```

The loop invariant expresses that all elements up to the current loop index `J` have value zero. With this loop invariant, GNATprove is able to prove the postcondition of `Validate_Arr_Zero`, namely that output parameter `Success` is True if-and-only-if all elements of the array have value zero:

```
validate_arr_zero.adb:3:41: info: initialization of "Success" proved
validate_arr_zero.adb:5:11: info: initialization of "Success" proved
validate_arr_zero.adb:5:11: info: postcondition proved
validate_arr_zero.adb:13:30: info: loop invariant initialization proved
validate_arr_zero.adb:13:30: info: loop invariant preservation proved
validate_arr_zero.adb:13:61: info: index check proved
```

Consider now a variant of the same validation loop over a vector:

```
with Loop_Types; use Loop_Types; use Loop_Types.Vectors;

procedure Validate_Vec_Zero (V : Vec_T; Success : out Boolean) with
   SPARK_Mode,
   Post => Success = (for all J in First_Index (V) .. Last_Index (V) => Element (V, J)
      = 0)
is
begin
   for J in First_Index (V) .. Last_Index (V) loop
      if Element (V, J) /= 0 then
         Success := False;
         return;
      end if;
      pragma Loop_Invariant (for all K in First_Index (V) .. J => Element (V, K) = 0);
   end loop;

   Success := True;
end Validate_Vec_Zero;
```

Like before, the loop invariant expresses that all elements up to the current loop index `J` have the value zero. Since variable `V` is not modified in the loop, no additional loop invariant is needed here for GNATprove to know that its length stays the same (this is different from the case of `Init_Vec_Zero` seen previously). With this loop invariant, GNATprove is able to prove the postcondition of `Validate_Vec_Zero`, namely that output parameter `Success` is True if-and-only-if all elements of the vector have value zero:

```
validate_vec_zero.adb:3:41: info: initialization of "Success" proved
validate_vec_zero.adb:5:11: info: initialization of "Success" proved
validate_vec_zero.adb:5:11: info: postcondition proved
validate_vec_zero.adb:5:72: info: precondition proved
validate_vec_zero.adb:5:84: info: range check proved
validate_vec_zero.adb:9:10: info: precondition proved
validate_vec_zero.adb:9:22: info: range check proved
validate_vec_zero.adb:13:30: info: loop invariant initialization proved
validate_vec_zero.adb:13:30: info: loop invariant preservation proved
validate_vec_zero.adb:13:67: info: precondition proved
validate_vec_zero.adb:13:79: info: range check proved
```

Similarly, consider a variant of the same validation loop over a list:

```
1  with Loop_Types; use Loop_Types; use Loop_Types.Lists;
2  with Ada.Containers; use Ada.Containers; use Loop_Types.Lists.Formal_Model;
3
4  procedure Validate_List_Zero (L : List_T; Success : out Boolean) with
5    SPARK_Mode,
6    Post => Success = (for all E of L => E = 0)
7  is
8    Cu : Cursor := First (L);
9  begin
10    while Has_Element (L, Cu) loop
11      pragma Loop_Invariant (for all I in 1 .. P.Get (Positions (L), Cu) - 1 =>
12                               Element (Model (L), I) = 0);
13      if Element (L, Cu) /= 0 then
14        Success := False;
15        return;
16      end if;
17      Next (L, Cu);
18    end loop;
19
20    Success := True;
21  end Validate_List_Zero;
```

Like in the case of `Init_List_Zero` seen previously, we need to define a cursor here to iterate over the list. The loop invariant expresses that all elements up to the current cursor `Cu` have the value zero. With this loop invariant, GNATprove is able to prove the postcondition of `Validate_List_Zero`, namely that output parameter `Success` is True if-and-only-if all elements of the list have value zero:

```
validate_list_zero.adb:4:43: info: initialization of "Success" proved
validate_list_zero.adb:6:11: info: initialization of "Success" proved
validate_list_zero.adb:6:11: info: postcondition proved
validate_list_zero.adb:6:22: info: precondition proved
validate_list_zero.adb:10:26: info: initialization of "Cu.Node" proved
validate_list_zero.adb:11:30: info: loop invariant initialization proved
validate_list_zero.adb:11:30: info: loop invariant preservation proved
validate_list_zero.adb:11:49: info: precondition proved
validate_list_zero.adb:11:70: info: initialization of "Cu.Node" proved
validate_list_zero.adb:12:32: info: precondition proved
validate_list_zero.adb:13:10: info: precondition proved
validate_list_zero.adb:13:22: info: initialization of "Cu.Node" proved
validate_list_zero.adb:17:07: info: precondition proved
```

```
validate_list_zero.adb:17:16: info: initialization of "Cu.Node" proved
```

The case of sets and maps is similar to the case of lists.

A variant of the previous validation pattern is to continue validating elements even after an invalid value has been encountered, which allows for example logging all invalid values:

Loop Pattern	Sequence Validation that Validates Entire Collection
Proof Objective	Determine (flag) if there are any invalid elements in a given collection.
Loop Behavior	Loops over the collection. If an invalid element is encountered, flag this, but keep validating (typically logging every invalidity) for the entire collection.
Loop Invariant	If invalidity is not flagged, every element encountered so far is valid.

Consider a variant of `Validate_Arr_Zero` that keeps validating elements of the array after a non-zero element has been encountered:

```
1   with Loop_Types; use Loop_Types;
2
3   procedure Validate_Full_Arr_Zero (A : Arr_T; Success : out Boolean) with
4     SPARK_Mode,
5     Post => Success = (for all J in A'Range => A(J) = 0)
6   is
7   begin
8      Success := True;
9
10     for J in A'Range loop
11        if A(J) /= 0 then
12           Success := False;
13           -- perform some logging here instead of returning
14        end if;
15        pragma Loop_Invariant (Success = (for all K in A'First .. J => A(K) = 0));
16     end loop;
17  end Validate_Full_Arr_Zero;
```

The loop invariant has been modified to state that all elements up to the current loop index J have value zero if-and-only-if the output parameter Success is True. This in turn requires to move the assignment of Success before the loop. With this loop invariant, GNATprove is able to prove the postcondition of Validate_Full_Arr_Zero, which is the same as the postcondition of Validate_Arr_Zero, namely that output parameter Success is True if-and-only-if all elements of the array have value zero:

```
validate_full_arr_zero.adb:3:46: info: initialization of "Success" proved
validate_full_arr_zero.adb:5:11: info: initialization of "Success" proved
validate_full_arr_zero.adb:5:11: info: postcondition proved
validate_full_arr_zero.adb:15:30: info: initialization of "Success" proved
validate_full_arr_zero.adb:15:30: info: loop invariant initialization proved
validate_full_arr_zero.adb:15:30: info: loop invariant preservation proved
validate_full_arr_zero.adb:15:72: info: index check proved
```

Similarly, variants of `Validate_Vec_Zero` and `Validate_List_Zero` that keep validating elements of the collection after a non-zero element has been encountered would be proved by GNATprove.

Counting Loops

This kind of loops iterates over a collection to count the number of elements of the collection that satisfy a given criterion:

Loop Pattern	Count Elements Satisfying Criterion
Proof Objective	Count elements that satisfy a given criterion.
Loop Behavior	Loops over the collection. Increments a counter each time the value of an element satisfies the criterion.
Loop Invariant	The value of the counter is either 0 when no element encountered so far satisfies the criterion, or a positive number bounded by the current iteration of the loop otherwise.

Consider a procedure `Count_Arr_Zero` that counts elements with value zero in array `A`:

```
with Loop_Types; use Loop_Types;

procedure Count_Arr_Zero (A : Arr_T; Counter : out Natural) with
   SPARK_Mode,
   Post => (Counter in 0 .. A'Length) and then
           ((Counter = 0) = (for all K in A'Range => A(K) /= 0))
is
begin
   Counter := 0;

   for J in A'Range loop
      if A(J) = 0 then
         Counter := Counter + 1;
      end if;
      pragma Loop_Invariant (Counter in 0 .. J);
      pragma Loop_Invariant ((Counter = 0) = (for all K in A'First .. J => A(K) /=
      0));
   end loop;
end Count_Arr_Zero;
```

The loop invariant expresses that the value of `Counter` is a natural number bounded by the current loop index `J`, and that `Counter` is equal to zero exactly when all elements up to the current loop index have a non-zero value. With this loop invariant, GNATprove is able to prove the postcondition of `Count_Arr_Zero`, namely that output parameter `Counter` is a natural number bounded by the length of the array `A`, and that `Counter` is equal to zero exactly when all elements in `A` have a non-zero value:

```
count_arr_zero.adb:3:38: info: initialization of "Counter" proved
count_arr_zero.adb:5:11: info: postcondition proved
count_arr_zero.adb:5:12: info: initialization of "Counter" proved
count_arr_zero.adb:6:13: info: initialization of "Counter" proved
count_arr_zero.adb:13:21: info: initialization of "Counter" proved
count_arr_zero.adb:13:29: info: overflow check proved
count_arr_zero.adb:15:30: info: initialization of "Counter" proved
count_arr_zero.adb:15:30: info: loop invariant initialization proved
count_arr_zero.adb:15:30: info: loop invariant preservation proved
count_arr_zero.adb:16:30: info: loop invariant initialization proved
count_arr_zero.adb:16:30: info: loop invariant preservation proved
count_arr_zero.adb:16:31: info: initialization of "Counter" proved
count_arr_zero.adb:16:78: info: index check proved
```

Consider now a variant of the same counting loop over a vector:

```
with Loop_Types; use Loop_Types; use Loop_Types.Vectors;

procedure Count_Vec_Zero (V : Vec_T; Counter : out Natural) with
   SPARK_Mode,
   Post => (Counter in 0 .. Natural (Length (V))) and then
           ((Counter = 0) = (for all K in First_Index (V) .. Last_Index (V) => Element
   (V, K) /= 0))
is
begin
   Counter := 0;

   for J in First_Index (V) .. Last_Index (V) loop
      if Element (V, J) = 0 then
         Counter := Counter + 1;
      end if;
      pragma Loop_Invariant (Counter in 0 .. J);
      pragma Loop_Invariant ((Counter = 0) = (for all K in First_Index (V) .. J =>
   Element (V, K) /= 0));
   end loop;
end Count_Vec_Zero;
```

Like before, the loop invariant expresses that the value of Counter is a natural number bounded by the current loop index J, and that Counter is equal to zero exactly when all elements up to the current loop index have a non-zero value. With this loop invariant, GNATprove is able to prove the postcondition of Count_Vec_Zero, namely that output parameter Counter is a natural number bounded by the length of the vector V, and that Counter is equal to zero exactly when all elements in V have a non-zero value:

```
count_vec_zero.adb:3:38: info: initialization of "Counter" proved
count_vec_zero.adb:5:11: info: postcondition proved
count_vec_zero.adb:5:12: info: initialization of "Counter" proved
count_vec_zero.adb:6:13: info: initialization of "Counter" proved
count_vec_zero.adb:6:79: info: precondition proved
count_vec_zero.adb:6:91: info: range check proved
count_vec_zero.adb:12:10: info: precondition proved
count_vec_zero.adb:12:22: info: range check proved
count_vec_zero.adb:13:21: info: initialization of "Counter" proved
count_vec_zero.adb:13:29: info: overflow check proved
count_vec_zero.adb:15:30: info: initialization of "Counter" proved
count_vec_zero.adb:15:30: info: loop invariant initialization proved
count_vec_zero.adb:15:30: info: loop invariant preservation proved
count_vec_zero.adb:16:30: info: loop invariant initialization proved
count_vec_zero.adb:16:30: info: loop invariant preservation proved
count_vec_zero.adb:16:31: info: initialization of "Counter" proved
count_vec_zero.adb:16:84: info: precondition proved
count_vec_zero.adb:16:96: info: range check proved
```

Search Loops

This kind of loops iterates over a collection to search an element of the collection that meets a given search criterion:

Loop Pattern	Search with Early Exit
Proof Objective	Find an element or position that meets a search criterion.
Loop Behavior	Loops over the collection. Exits when an element that meets the search criterion is found.
Loop Invariant	Every element encountered so far does not meet the search criterion.

Consider a procedure `Search_Arr_Zero` that searches an element with value zero in array `A`:

```
with Loop_Types; use Loop_Types;

procedure Search_Arr_Zero (A : Arr_T; Pos : out Opt_Index_T; Success : out Boolean)
  with
  SPARK_Mode,
  Post => Success = (for some J in A'Range => A(J) = 0) and then
          (if Success then A (Pos) = 0)
is
begin
  for J in A'Range loop
     if A(J) = 0 then
        Success := True;
        Pos := J;
        return;
     end if;
     pragma Loop_Invariant (for all K in A'First .. J => A(K) /= 0);
  end loop;

  Success := False;
  Pos := 0;
end Search_Arr_Zero;
```

The loop invariant expresses that all elements up to the current loop index `J` have a non-zero value. With this loop invariant, GNATprove is able to prove the postcondition of `Search_Arr_Zero`, namely that output parameter `Success` is True if-and-only-if there is an element of the array that has value zero, and that `Pos` is the index of such an element:

```
search_arr_zero.adb:3:39: info: initialization of "Pos" proved
search_arr_zero.adb:3:62: info: initialization of "Success" proved
search_arr_zero.adb:5:11: info: initialization of "Success" proved
search_arr_zero.adb:5:11: info: postcondition proved
search_arr_zero.adb:6:15: info: initialization of "Success" proved
search_arr_zero.adb:6:31: info: index check proved
search_arr_zero.adb:6:31: info: initialization of "Pos" proved
search_arr_zero.adb:15:30: info: loop invariant initialization proved
search_arr_zero.adb:15:30: info: loop invariant preservation proved
search_arr_zero.adb:15:61: info: index check proved
```

Consider now a variant of the same search loop over a vector:

```
with Loop_Types; use Loop_Types; use Loop_Types.Vectors;

procedure Search_Vec_Zero (V : Vec_T; Pos : out Opt_Index_T; Success : out Boolean)
  with
  SPARK_Mode,
  Post => Success = (for some J in First_Index (V) .. Last_Index (V) => Element (V,
    J) = 0) and then
          (if Success then Element (V, Pos) = 0)
is
```

```
8   begin
9      for J in First_Index (V) .. Last_Index (V) loop
10        if Element (V, J) = 0 then
11           Success := True;
12           Pos := J;
13           return;
14        end if;
15        pragma Loop_Invariant (for all K in First_Index (V) .. J => Element (V, K) /=␣
    ↪0);
16     end loop;
17
18     Success := False;
19     Pos := 0;
20  end Search_Vec_Zero;
```

Like before, the loop invariant expresses that all elements up to the current loop index J have a non-zero value. With this loop invariant, GNATprove is able to prove the postcondition of Search_Vec_Zero, namely that output parameter Success is True if-and-only-if there is an element of the vector that has value zero, and that Pos is the index of such an element:

```
search_vec_zero.adb:3:39: info: initialization of "Pos" proved
search_vec_zero.adb:3:62: info: initialization of "Success" proved
search_vec_zero.adb:5:11: info: initialization of "Success" proved
search_vec_zero.adb:5:11: info: postcondition proved
search_vec_zero.adb:5:73: info: precondition proved
search_vec_zero.adb:5:85: info: range check proved
search_vec_zero.adb:6:15: info: initialization of "Success" proved
search_vec_zero.adb:6:28: info: precondition proved
search_vec_zero.adb:6:40: info: initialization of "Pos" proved
search_vec_zero.adb:6:40: info: range check proved
search_vec_zero.adb:10:10: info: precondition proved
search_vec_zero.adb:10:22: info: range check proved
search_vec_zero.adb:12:17: info: range check proved
search_vec_zero.adb:15:30: info: loop invariant initialization proved
search_vec_zero.adb:15:30: info: loop invariant preservation proved
search_vec_zero.adb:15:67: info: precondition proved
search_vec_zero.adb:15:79: info: range check proved
```

Similarly, consider a variant of the same search loop over a list:

```
1   with Loop_Types; use Loop_Types; use Loop_Types.Lists;
2   with Ada.Containers; use Ada.Containers; use Loop_Types.Lists.Formal_Model;
3
4   procedure Search_List_Zero (L : List_T; Pos : out Cursor; Success : out Boolean) with
5      SPARK_Mode,
6      Post => Success = (for some E of L => E = 0) and then
7              (if Success then Element (L, Pos) = 0)
8   is
9      Cu : Cursor := First (L);
10  begin
11     while Has_Element (L, Cu) loop
12        pragma Loop_Invariant (for all I in 1 .. P.Get (Positions (L), Cu) - 1 =>
13                                 Element (Model (L), I) /= 0);
14        if Element (L, Cu) = 0 then
15           Success := True;
16           Pos := Cu;
17           return;
18        end if;
```

```
19          Next (L, Cu);
20      end loop;
21
22      Success := False;
23      Pos := No_Element;
24  end Search_List_Zero;
```

The loop invariant expresses that all elements up to the current cursor `Cu` have a non-zero value. With this loop invariant, GNATprove is able to prove the postcondition of `Search_List_Zero`, namely that output parameter `Success` is True if-and-only-if there is an element of the list that has value zero, and that `Pos` is the cursor of such an element:

```
search_list_zero.adb:4:41: info: initialization of "Pos.Node" proved
search_list_zero.adb:4:59: info: initialization of "Success" proved
search_list_zero.adb:6:11: info: initialization of "Success" proved
search_list_zero.adb:6:11: info: postcondition proved
search_list_zero.adb:6:22: info: precondition proved
search_list_zero.adb:7:15: info: initialization of "Success" proved
search_list_zero.adb:7:28: info: precondition proved
search_list_zero.adb:7:40: info: initialization of "Pos.Node" proved
search_list_zero.adb:11:26: info: initialization of "Cu.Node" proved
search_list_zero.adb:12:30: info: loop invariant initialization proved
search_list_zero.adb:12:30: info: loop invariant preservation proved
search_list_zero.adb:12:49: info: precondition proved
search_list_zero.adb:12:70: info: initialization of "Cu.Node" proved
search_list_zero.adb:13:32: info: precondition proved
search_list_zero.adb:14:10: info: precondition proved
search_list_zero.adb:14:22: info: initialization of "Cu.Node" proved
search_list_zero.adb:16:17: info: initialization of "Cu.Node" proved
search_list_zero.adb:19:07: info: precondition proved
search_list_zero.adb:19:16: info: initialization of "Cu.Node" proved
```

The case of sets and maps is similar to the case of lists. For more complex examples of search loops, see the *SPARK Tutorial* as well as the section on *How to Write Loop Invariants*.

Maximize Loops

This kind of loops iterates over a collection to search an element of the collection that maximizes a given optimality criterion:

Loop Pattern	Search Optimum to Criterion
Proof Objective	Find an element or position that maximizes an optimality criterion.
Loop Behavior	Loops over the collection. Records maximum value of criterion so far and possibly index that maximizes this criterion.
Loop Invariant	Exactly one element encountered so far corresponds to the recorded maximum over other elements encountered so far.

Consider a procedure `Search_Arr_Max` that searches an element maximum value in array A:

```
1  with Loop_Types; use Loop_Types;
2
3  procedure Search_Arr_Max (A : Arr_T; Pos : out Index_T; Max : out Component_T) with
4    SPARK_Mode,
5    Post => (for all J in A'Range => A(J) <= Max) and then
6            (for some J in A'Range => A(J) = Max) and then
```

```
7              A(Pos) = Max
8  is
9  begin
10    Max := 0;
11    Pos := A'First;
12
13    for J in A'Range loop
14       if A(J) > Max then
15          Max := A(J);
16          Pos := J;
17       end if;
18       pragma Loop_Invariant (for all K in A'First .. J => A(K) <= Max);
19       pragma Loop_Invariant (for some K in A'First .. J => A(K) = Max);
20       pragma Loop_Invariant (A(Pos) = Max);
21    end loop;
22  end Search_Arr_Max;
```

The loop invariant expresses that all elements up to the current loop index J have a value less than Max, and that Max is the value of one of these elements. The last loop invariant gives in fact this element, it is A(Pos), but this part of the loop invariant may not be present if the position Pos for the optimum is not recorded. With this loop invariant, GNATprove is able to prove the postcondition of Search_Arr_Max, namely that output parameter Max is the maximum of the elements in the array, and that Pos is the index of such an element:

```
search_arr_max.adb:3:38: info: initialization of "Pos" proved
search_arr_max.adb:3:57: info: initialization of "Max" proved
search_arr_max.adb:5:11: info: postcondition proved
search_arr_max.adb:5:44: info: initialization of "Max" proved
search_arr_max.adb:6:44: info: initialization of "Max" proved
search_arr_max.adb:7:13: info: initialization of "Pos" proved
search_arr_max.adb:7:20: info: initialization of "Max" proved
search_arr_max.adb:14:17: info: initialization of "Max" proved
search_arr_max.adb:18:30: info: loop invariant initialization proved
search_arr_max.adb:18:30: info: loop invariant preservation proved
search_arr_max.adb:18:61: info: index check proved
search_arr_max.adb:18:67: info: initialization of "Max" proved
search_arr_max.adb:19:30: info: loop invariant initialization proved
search_arr_max.adb:19:30: info: loop invariant preservation proved
search_arr_max.adb:19:62: info: index check proved
search_arr_max.adb:19:67: info: initialization of "Max" proved
search_arr_max.adb:20:30: info: loop invariant initialization proved
search_arr_max.adb:20:30: info: loop invariant preservation proved
search_arr_max.adb:20:32: info: initialization of "Pos" proved
search_arr_max.adb:20:39: info: initialization of "Max" proved
```

Consider now a variant of the same search loop over a vector:

```
1  with Loop_Types; use Loop_Types; use Loop_Types.Vectors;
2
3  procedure Search_Vec_Max (V : Vec_T; Pos : out Index_T; Max : out Component_T) with
4    SPARK_Mode,
5    Pre  => not Is_Empty (V),
6    Post => (for all J in First_Index (V) .. Last_Index (V) => Element (V, J) <= Max)
    and then
7             (for some J in First_Index (V) .. Last_Index (V) => Element (V, J) = Max)
    and then
8             Pos in First_Index (V) .. Last_Index (V) and then
9             Element (V, Pos) = Max
10 is
```

```
11  begin
12     Max := 0;
13     Pos := First_Index (V);
14
15     for J in First_Index (V) .. Last_Index (V) loop
16        if Element (V, J) > Max then
17           Max := Element (V, J);
18           Pos := J;
19        end if;
20        pragma Loop_Invariant (for all K in First_Index (V) .. J => Element (V, K) <=
    ↪Max);
21        pragma Loop_Invariant (for some K in First_Index (V) .. J => Element (V, K) =
    ↪Max);
22        pragma Loop_Invariant (Pos in First_Index (V) .. J);
23        pragma Loop_Invariant (Element (V, Pos) = Max);
24     end loop;
25  end Search_Vec_Max;
```

Like before, the loop invariant expresses that all elements up to the current loop index J have a value less than Max, and that Max is the value of one of these elements, most precisely the value of Element (V, Pos) if the position Pos for the optimum is recorded. An additional loop invariant is needed here compared to the case of arrays to state that Pos remains within the bounds of the vector. With this loop invariant, GNATprove is able to prove the postcondition of Search_Vec_Max, namely that output parameter Max is the maximum of the elements in the vector, and that Pos is the index of such an element:

```
search_vec_max.adb:3:38: info: initialization of "Pos" proved
search_vec_max.adb:3:57: info: initialization of "Max" proved
search_vec_max.adb:6:11: info: postcondition proved
search_vec_max.adb:6:62: info: precondition proved
search_vec_max.adb:6:74: info: range check proved
search_vec_max.adb:6:80: info: initialization of "Max" proved
search_vec_max.adb:7:63: info: precondition proved
search_vec_max.adb:7:75: info: range check proved
search_vec_max.adb:7:80: info: initialization of "Max" proved
search_vec_max.adb:8:11: info: initialization of "Pos" proved
search_vec_max.adb:9:11: info: precondition proved
search_vec_max.adb:9:23: info: initialization of "Pos" proved
search_vec_max.adb:9:30: info: initialization of "Max" proved
search_vec_max.adb:16:10: info: precondition proved
search_vec_max.adb:16:22: info: range check proved
search_vec_max.adb:16:27: info: initialization of "Max" proved
search_vec_max.adb:17:17: info: precondition proved
search_vec_max.adb:17:29: info: range check proved
search_vec_max.adb:18:17: info: range check proved
search_vec_max.adb:20:30: info: loop invariant initialization proved
search_vec_max.adb:20:30: info: loop invariant preservation proved
search_vec_max.adb:20:67: info: precondition proved
search_vec_max.adb:20:79: info: range check proved
search_vec_max.adb:20:85: info: initialization of "Max" proved
search_vec_max.adb:21:30: info: loop invariant initialization proved
search_vec_max.adb:21:30: info: loop invariant preservation proved
search_vec_max.adb:21:68: info: precondition proved
search_vec_max.adb:21:80: info: range check proved
search_vec_max.adb:21:85: info: initialization of "Max" proved
search_vec_max.adb:22:30: info: initialization of "Pos" proved
search_vec_max.adb:22:30: info: loop invariant initialization proved
search_vec_max.adb:22:30: info: loop invariant preservation proved
```

```
search_vec_max.adb:23:30: info: loop invariant initialization proved
search_vec_max.adb:23:30: info: loop invariant preservation proved
search_vec_max.adb:23:30: info: precondition proved
search_vec_max.adb:23:42: info: initialization of "Pos" proved
search_vec_max.adb:23:49: info: initialization of "Max" proved
```

Similarly, consider a variant of the same search loop over a list:

```
1   with Loop_Types; use Loop_Types; use Loop_Types.Lists;
2   with Ada.Containers; use Ada.Containers; use Loop_Types.Lists.Formal_Model;
3
4   procedure Search_List_Max (L : List_T; Pos : out Cursor; Max : out Component_T) with
5      SPARK_Mode,
6      Pre  => not Is_Empty (L),
7      Post => (for all E of L => E <= Max) and then
8               (for some E of L => E = Max) and then
9               Has_Element (L, Pos) and then
10              Element (L, Pos) = Max
11  is
12     Cu : Cursor := First (L);
13  begin
14     Max := 0;
15     Pos := Cu;
16
17     while Has_Element (L, Cu) loop
18        pragma Loop_Invariant (for all I in 1 .. P.Get (Positions (L), Cu) - 1 =>
19                                 Element (Model (L), I) <= Max);
20        pragma Loop_Invariant (Has_Element (L, Pos));
21        pragma Loop_Invariant (Max = 0 or else Element (L, Pos) = Max);
22
23        if Element (L, Cu) > Max then
24           Max := Element (L, Cu);
25           Pos := Cu;
26        end if;
27        Next (L, Cu);
28     end loop;
29  end Search_List_Max;
```

The loop invariant expresses that all elements up to the current cursor Cu have a value less than Max, and that Max is the value of one of these elements, most precisely the value of Element (L, Pos) if the cursor Pos for the optimum is recorded. Like for vectors, an additional loop invariant is needed here compared to the case of arrays to state that cursor Pos is a valid cursor of the list. A minor difference is that a loop invariant now starts with Max = 0 or else .. because the loop invariant is stated at the start of the loop (for convenience with the use of First_To_Previous) which requires this modification. With this loop invariant, GNATprove is able to prove the postcondition of Search_List_Max, namely that output parameter Max is the maximum of the elements in the list, and that Pos is the cursor of such an element:

```
search_list_max.adb:4:40: info: initialization of "Pos.Node" proved
search_list_max.adb:4:58: info: initialization of "Max" proved
search_list_max.adb:7:11: info: postcondition proved
search_list_max.adb:7:12: info: precondition proved
search_list_max.adb:7:35: info: initialization of "Max" proved
search_list_max.adb:8:12: info: precondition proved
search_list_max.adb:8:35: info: initialization of "Max" proved
search_list_max.adb:9:27: info: initialization of "Pos.Node" proved
search_list_max.adb:10:11: info: precondition proved
search_list_max.adb:10:23: info: initialization of "Pos.Node" proved
```

```
search_list_max.adb:10:30: info: initialization of "Max" proved
search_list_max.adb:15:11: info: initialization of "Cu.Node" proved
search_list_max.adb:17:26: info: initialization of "Cu.Node" proved
search_list_max.adb:18:30: info: loop invariant initialization proved
search_list_max.adb:18:30: info: loop invariant preservation proved
search_list_max.adb:18:49: info: precondition proved
search_list_max.adb:18:70: info: initialization of "Cu.Node" proved
search_list_max.adb:19:32: info: precondition proved
search_list_max.adb:19:58: info: initialization of "Max" proved
search_list_max.adb:20:30: info: loop invariant initialization proved
search_list_max.adb:20:30: info: loop invariant preservation proved
search_list_max.adb:20:46: info: initialization of "Pos.Node" proved
search_list_max.adb:21:30: info: initialization of "Max" proved
search_list_max.adb:21:30: info: loop invariant initialization proved
search_list_max.adb:21:30: info: loop invariant preservation proved
search_list_max.adb:21:46: info: precondition proved
search_list_max.adb:21:58: info: initialization of "Pos.Node" proved
search_list_max.adb:23:10: info: precondition proved
search_list_max.adb:23:22: info: initialization of "Cu.Node" proved
search_list_max.adb:23:28: info: initialization of "Max" proved
search_list_max.adb:24:17: info: precondition proved
search_list_max.adb:24:29: info: initialization of "Cu.Node" proved
search_list_max.adb:25:17: info: initialization of "Cu.Node" proved
search_list_max.adb:27:07: info: precondition proved
search_list_max.adb:27:16: info: initialization of "Cu.Node" proved
```

The case of sets and maps is similar to the case of lists. For more complex examples of search loops, see the *SPARK Tutorial* as well as the section on *How to Write Loop Invariants*.

Update Loops

This kind of loops iterates over a collection to update individual elements based either on their value or on their position. The first pattern we consider is the one that updates elements based on their value:

Loop Pattern	Modification of Elements Based on Value
Proof Objective	Elements of the collection are updated based on their value.
Loop Behavior	Loops over a collection and assigns the elements whose value satisfies a given modification criterion.
Loop Invariant	Every element encountered so far has been assigned according to its value.

Consider a procedure `Update_Arr_Zero` that sets to zero all elements in array A that have a value smaller than a given `Threshold`:

```
1  with Loop_Types; use Loop_Types;
2
3  procedure Update_Arr_Zero (A : in out Arr_T; Threshold : Component_T) with
4     SPARK_Mode,
5     Post => (for all J in A'Range => A(J) = (if A'Old(J) <= Threshold then 0 else A
    →'Old(J)))
6  is
7  begin
8     for J in A'Range loop
9        if A(J) <= Threshold then
10          A(J) := 0;
```

```
11        end if;
12        pragma Loop_Invariant (for all K in A'First .. J => A(K) = (if A'Loop_Entry(K)
   ↪<= Threshold then 0 else A'Loop_Entry(K)));
13        --  The following loop invariant is generated automatically by GNATprove:
14        --  pragma Loop_Invariant (for all K in J + 1 .. A'Last => A(K) = A'Loop_
   ↪Entry(K));
15      end loop;
16  end Update_Arr_Zero;
```

The loop invariant expresses that all elements up to the current loop index J have been zeroed out if initially smaller than Threshold (using *Attribute Loop_Entry*). With this loop invariant, GNATprove is able to prove the postcondition of Update_Arr_Zero, namely that all elements initially smaller than Threshold have been zeroed out, and that other elements have not been modified:

```
update_arr_zero.adb:5:11: info: postcondition proved
update_arr_zero.adb:12:30: info: loop invariant initialization proved
update_arr_zero.adb:12:30: info: loop invariant preservation proved
update_arr_zero.adb:12:61: info: index check proved
update_arr_zero.adb:12:83: info: index check proved
update_arr_zero.adb:12:124: info: index check proved
```

Note that the commented loop invariant expressing that other elements have not been modified is not needed, as it is an example of *Automatically Generated Loop Invariants*.

Consider now a variant of the same update loop over a vector:

```
1  pragma Unevaluated_Use_Of_Old (Allow);
2  with Loop_Types; use Loop_Types; use Loop_Types.Vectors;
3  use Loop_Types.Vectors.Formal_Model;
4
5  procedure Update_Vec_Zero (V : in out Vec_T; Threshold : Component_T) with
6    SPARK_Mode,
7    Post => Last_Index (V) = Last_Index (V)'Old
8    and (for all I in 1 .. Last_Index (V) =>
9            Element (V, I) =
10              (if Element (Model (V)'Old, I) <= Threshold then 0
11               else Element (Model (V)'Old, I)))
12  is
13  begin
14    for J in First_Index (V) .. Last_Index (V) loop
15       pragma Loop_Invariant (Last_Index (V) = Last_Index (V)'Loop_Entry);
16       pragma Loop_Invariant
17         (for all I in 1 .. J - 1 =>
18             Element (V, I) =
19               (if Element (Model (V)'Loop_Entry, I) <= Threshold then 0
20                else Element (Model (V)'Loop_Entry, I)));
21       pragma Loop_Invariant
22         (for all I in J .. Last_Index (V) =>
23             Element (V, I) = Element (Model (V)'Loop_Entry, I));
24       if Element (V, J) <= Threshold then
25          Replace_Element (V, J, 0);
26       end if;
27    end loop;
28  end Update_Vec_Zero;
```

Like for Map_Vec_Incr, we need to use the Model function over arrays to access elements of the vector before the loop as the vector type is limited. The loop invariant expresses that all elements up to the current loop index J have been zeroed out if initially smaller than Threshold, that elements that follow the current loop index have not been modified, and that the length of V is not modified (like in Init_Vec_Zero). With this loop invariant, GNATprove is able to prove the postcondition of Update_Vec_Zero:

```
update_vec_zero.adb:7:11: info: postcondition proved
update_vec_zero.adb:9:13: info: precondition proved
update_vec_zero.adb:9:25: info: range check proved
update_vec_zero.adb:10:18: info: precondition proved
update_vec_zero.adb:10:42: info: range check proved
update_vec_zero.adb:11:20: info: precondition proved
update_vec_zero.adb:11:44: info: range check proved
update_vec_zero.adb:15:30: info: loop invariant initialization proved
update_vec_zero.adb:15:30: info: loop invariant preservation proved
update_vec_zero.adb:17:10: info: loop invariant initialization proved
update_vec_zero.adb:17:10: info: loop invariant preservation proved
update_vec_zero.adb:17:30: info: overflow check proved
update_vec_zero.adb:18:14: info: precondition proved
update_vec_zero.adb:18:26: info: range check proved
update_vec_zero.adb:19:19: info: precondition proved
update_vec_zero.adb:19:50: info: range check proved
update_vec_zero.adb:20:21: info: precondition proved
update_vec_zero.adb:20:52: info: range check proved
update_vec_zero.adb:22:10: info: loop invariant initialization proved
update_vec_zero.adb:22:10: info: loop invariant preservation proved
update_vec_zero.adb:23:14: info: precondition proved
update_vec_zero.adb:23:26: info: range check proved
update_vec_zero.adb:23:31: info: precondition proved
update_vec_zero.adb:23:62: info: range check proved
update_vec_zero.adb:24:10: info: precondition proved
update_vec_zero.adb:24:22: info: range check proved
update_vec_zero.adb:25:10: info: precondition proved
update_vec_zero.adb:25:30: info: range check proved
```

Similarly, consider a variant of the same update loop over a list:

```
1   with Loop_Types; use Loop_Types; use Loop_Types.Lists;
2   with Ada.Containers; use Ada.Containers; use Loop_Types.Lists.Formal_Model;
3
4   procedure Update_List_Zero (L : in out List_T; Threshold : Component_T) with
5     SPARK_Mode,
6     Post => Length (L) = Length (L)'Old
7     and (for all I in 1 .. Length (L) =>
8             Element (Model (L), I) =
9               (if Element (Model (L'Old), I) <= Threshold then 0
10              else Element (Model (L'Old), I)))
11  is
12    Cu : Cursor := First (L);
13  begin
14    while Has_Element (L, Cu) loop
15       pragma Loop_Invariant (Length (L) = Length (L)'Loop_Entry);
16       pragma Loop_Invariant
17         (for all I in 1 .. P.Get (Positions (L), Cu) - 1 =>
18             Element (Model (L), I) =
19               (if Element (Model (L'Loop_Entry), I) <= Threshold then 0
20              else Element (Model (L'Loop_Entry), I)));
21       pragma Loop_Invariant
22         (for all I in P.Get (Positions (L), Cu) .. Length (L) =>
23             Element (Model (L), I) = Element (Model (L'Loop_Entry), I));
24       if Element (L, Cu) <= Threshold then
25          Replace_Element (L, Cu, 0);
```

```
26        end if;
27        Next (L, Cu);
28     end loop;
29  end Update_List_Zero;
```

The loop invariant expresses that all elements up to the current cursor Cu have been zeroed out if initially smaller than Threshold (using function Model to access the element stored at a given position in the list and function Positions to query the position of the current cursor), and that elements that follow the current loop index have not been modified. Note that it is necessary to state here that the length of the list is not modified during the loop. It is because the length is used to bound the quantification over the elements of the list both in the invariant and in the postcondition.

With this loop invariant, GNATprove is able to prove the postcondition of Update_List_Zero, namely that all elements initially smaller than Threshold have been zeroed out, and that other elements have not been modified:

```
update_list_zero.adb:6:11: info: postcondition proved
update_list_zero.adb:8:13: info: precondition proved
update_list_zero.adb:9:18: info: precondition proved
update_list_zero.adb:10:20: info: precondition proved
update_list_zero.adb:14:26: info: initialization of "Cu.Node" proved
update_list_zero.adb:15:30: info: loop invariant initialization proved
update_list_zero.adb:15:30: info: loop invariant preservation proved
update_list_zero.adb:17:10: info: loop invariant initialization proved
update_list_zero.adb:17:10: info: loop invariant preservation proved
update_list_zero.adb:17:29: info: precondition proved
update_list_zero.adb:17:50: info: initialization of "Cu.Node" proved
update_list_zero.adb:18:13: info: precondition proved
update_list_zero.adb:19:18: info: precondition proved
update_list_zero.adb:20:20: info: precondition proved
update_list_zero.adb:22:10: info: loop invariant initialization proved
update_list_zero.adb:22:10: info: loop invariant preservation proved
update_list_zero.adb:22:24: info: precondition proved
update_list_zero.adb:22:45: info: initialization of "Cu.Node" proved
update_list_zero.adb:23:13: info: precondition proved
update_list_zero.adb:23:33: info: range check proved
update_list_zero.adb:23:38: info: precondition proved
update_list_zero.adb:23:69: info: range check proved
update_list_zero.adb:24:10: info: precondition proved
update_list_zero.adb:24:22: info: initialization of "Cu.Node" proved
update_list_zero.adb:25:10: info: precondition proved
update_list_zero.adb:25:30: info: initialization of "Cu.Node" proved
update_list_zero.adb:27:07: info: precondition proved
update_list_zero.adb:27:16: info: initialization of "Cu.Node" proved
```

The case of sets and maps is similar to the case of lists.

The second pattern of update loops that we consider now is the one that updates elements based on their position:

Loop Pattern	Modification of Elements Based on Position
Proof Objective	Elements of the collection are updated based on their position.
Loop Behavior	Loops over a collection and assigns the elements whose position satisfies a given modification criterion.
Loop Invariant	Every element encountered so far has been assigned according to its position.

Consider a procedure Update_Range_Arr_Zero that sets to zero all elements in array A between indexes First and `Last`:

```
1   with Loop_Types; use Loop_Types;
2
3   procedure Update_Range_Arr_Zero (A : in out Arr_T; First, Last : Index_T) with
4     SPARK_Mode,
5     Post => A = A'Old'Update (First .. Last => 0)
6   is
7   begin
8     for J in First .. Last loop
9       A(J) := 0;
10      pragma Loop_Invariant (A = A'Loop_Entry'Update (First .. J => 0));
11    end loop;
12  end Update_Range_Arr_Zero;
```

The loop invariant expresses that all elements between `First` and the current loop index `J` have been zeroed out, and that other elements have not been modified (using a combination of *Attribute Loop_Entry* and *Attribute Update* to express this concisely). With this loop invariant, GNATprove is able to prove the postcondition of `Update_Range_Arr_Zero`, namely that all elements between `First` and `Last` have been zeroed out, and that other elements have not been modified:

```
update_range_arr_zero.adb:5:11: info: postcondition proved
update_range_arr_zero.adb:10:30: info: loop invariant initialization proved
update_range_arr_zero.adb:10:30: info: loop invariant preservation proved
update_range_arr_zero.adb:10:64: info: range check proved
```

Consider now a variant of the same update loop over a vector:

```
1   pragma Unevaluated_Use_Of_Old (Allow);
2   with Loop_Types; use Loop_Types; use Loop_Types.Vectors;
3   use Loop_Types.Vectors.Formal_Model;
4
5   procedure Update_Range_Vec_Zero (V : in out Vec_T; First, Last : Index_T) with
6     SPARK_Mode,
7     Pre  => Last <= Last_Index (V),
8     Post => (for all J in 1 .. Last_Index (V) =>
9                 (if J in First .. Last then Element (V, J) = 0
10                  else Element (V, J) = Element (Model (V)'Old, J)))
11  is
12  begin
13    for J in First .. Last loop
14      Replace_Element (V, J, 0);
15      pragma Loop_Invariant (Last_Index (V) = Last_Index (V)'Loop_Entry);
16      pragma Loop_Invariant
17        (for all I in 1 .. Last_Index (V) =>
18           (if I in First .. J then Element (V, I) = 0
19            else Element (V, I) = Element (Model (V)'Loop_Entry, I)));
20    end loop;
21  end Update_Range_Vec_Zero;
```

Like for `Map_Vec_Incr`, we need to use the `Model` function over arrays to access elements of the vector before the loop as the vector type is limited. The loop invariant expresses that all elements between `First` and current loop index `J` have been zeroed, and that other elements have not been modified. With this loop invariant, GNATprove is able to prove the postcondition of `Update_Range_Vec_Zero`:

```
update_range_vec_zero.adb:8:11: info: postcondition proved
update_range_vec_zero.adb:9:44: info: precondition proved
update_range_vec_zero.adb:9:56: info: range check proved
```

```
update_range_vec_zero.adb:10:22: info: precondition proved
update_range_vec_zero.adb:10:34: info: range check proved
update_range_vec_zero.adb:10:39: info: precondition proved
update_range_vec_zero.adb:10:63: info: range check proved
update_range_vec_zero.adb:14:07: info: precondition proved
update_range_vec_zero.adb:15:30: info: loop invariant initialization proved
update_range_vec_zero.adb:15:30: info: loop invariant preservation proved
update_range_vec_zero.adb:17:10: info: loop invariant initialization proved
update_range_vec_zero.adb:17:10: info: loop invariant preservation proved
update_range_vec_zero.adb:18:41: info: precondition proved
update_range_vec_zero.adb:18:53: info: range check proved
update_range_vec_zero.adb:19:22: info: precondition proved
update_range_vec_zero.adb:19:34: info: range check proved
update_range_vec_zero.adb:19:39: info: precondition proved
update_range_vec_zero.adb:19:70: info: range check proved
```

Similarly, consider a variant of the same update loop over a list:

```ada
1   with Loop_Types; use Loop_Types; use Loop_Types.Lists;
2   with Ada.Containers; use Ada.Containers; use Loop_Types.Lists.Formal_Model;
3
4   procedure Update_Range_List_Zero (L : in out List_T; First, Last : Cursor) with
5     SPARK_Mode,
6     Pre  => Has_Element (L, First) and then Has_Element (L, Last)
7     and then P.Get (Positions (L), First) <= P.Get (Positions (L), Last),
8     Post => Length (L) = Length (L)'Old
9     and Positions (L) = Positions (L)'Old
10    and (for all I in 1 .. Length (L) =>
11              (if I in P.Get (Positions (L), First) .. P.Get (Positions (L), Last) then
12                 Element (Model (L), I) = 0
13               else Element (Model (L), I) = Element (Model (L'Old), I)))
14  is
15     Cu : Cursor := First;
16  begin
17     loop
18        pragma Loop_Invariant (Has_Element (L, Cu));
19        pragma Loop_Invariant (P.Get (Positions (L), Cu) in P.Get (Positions (L),
    ↪First) .. P.Get (Positions (L), Last));
20        pragma Loop_Invariant (Length (L) = Length (L)'Loop_Entry);
21        pragma Loop_Invariant (Positions (L) = Positions (L)'Loop_Entry);
22        pragma Loop_Invariant (for all I in 1 .. Length (L) =>
23                                   (if I in P.Get (Positions (L), First) .. P.Get
    ↪(Positions (L), Cu) - 1 then
24                                       Element (Model (L), I) = 0
25                                    else Element (Model (L), I) = Element (Model (L'Loop_
    ↪Entry), I)));
26        Replace_Element (L, Cu, 0);
27        exit when Cu = Last;
28        Next (L, Cu);
29     end loop;
30  end Update_Range_List_Zero;
```

Compared to the vector example, it requires three additional invariants. As the loop is done via a cursor, the first two loop invariants are necessary to know that the current cursor Cu stays between First and Last in the list. The fourth loop invariant states that the position of cursors in L is not modified during the loop. It is necessary to know that the two cursors First and Last keep designating the same range after the loop. With this loop invariant, GNATprove is able to prove the postcondition of Update_Range_List_Zero, namely that all elements between First and Last have been zeroed out, and that other elements have not been modified:

```
update_range_list_zero.adb:7:13: info: precondition proved
update_range_list_zero.adb:7:45: info: precondition proved
update_range_list_zero.adb:8:11: info: postcondition proved
update_range_list_zero.adb:11:23: info: precondition proved
update_range_list_zero.adb:11:55: info: precondition proved
update_range_list_zero.adb:12:16: info: precondition proved
update_range_list_zero.adb:13:19: info: precondition proved
update_range_list_zero.adb:13:44: info: precondition proved
update_range_list_zero.adb:18:30: info: loop invariant initialization proved
update_range_list_zero.adb:18:30: info: loop invariant preservation proved
update_range_list_zero.adb:18:46: info: initialization of "Cu.Node" proved
update_range_list_zero.adb:19:30: info: loop invariant initialization proved
update_range_list_zero.adb:19:30: info: loop invariant preservation proved
update_range_list_zero.adb:19:31: info: precondition proved
update_range_list_zero.adb:19:52: info: initialization of "Cu.Node" proved
update_range_list_zero.adb:19:60: info: precondition proved
update_range_list_zero.adb:19:92: info: precondition proved
update_range_list_zero.adb:20:30: info: loop invariant initialization proved
update_range_list_zero.adb:20:30: info: loop invariant preservation proved
update_range_list_zero.adb:21:30: info: loop invariant initialization proved
update_range_list_zero.adb:21:30: info: loop invariant preservation proved
update_range_list_zero.adb:22:30: info: loop invariant initialization proved
update_range_list_zero.adb:22:30: info: loop invariant preservation proved
update_range_list_zero.adb:23:42: info: precondition proved
update_range_list_zero.adb:23:74: info: precondition proved
update_range_list_zero.adb:23:95: info: initialization of "Cu.Node" proved
update_range_list_zero.adb:24:36: info: precondition proved
update_range_list_zero.adb:25:38: info: precondition proved
update_range_list_zero.adb:25:63: info: precondition proved
update_range_list_zero.adb:26:07: info: precondition proved
update_range_list_zero.adb:26:27: info: initialization of "Cu.Node" proved
update_range_list_zero.adb:27:17: info: initialization of "Cu.Node" proved
update_range_list_zero.adb:28:07: info: precondition proved
update_range_list_zero.adb:28:16: info: initialization of "Cu.Node" proved
```

7.9.3 Manual Proof Examples

The examples in this section contain properties that are difficult to prove automatically and thus require more user interaction to prove completely. The degre of interaction required depends on the difficuly of the proof:

- simple addition of calls to ghost lemmas for arithmetic properties involving multiplication, division and modulo operations, as decribed in *Manual Proof Using SPARK Lemma Library*

- more involved addition of ghost code for universally or existentially quantified properties on data structures and containers, as described in *Manual Proof Using Ghost Code*

- interaction at the level of Verification Condition formulas in the syntax of an interactive prover for arbitrary complex properties, as described in *Manual Proof Using Coq*

- interaction at the level of Verification Condition formulas in the syntax of Why3 for arbitrary complex properties, as described in *Manual Proof Using GPS*

Manual Proof Using SPARK Lemma Library

If the property to prove is part of the *SPARK Lemma Library*, then manual proof simply consists in calling the appropriate lemma in your code. For example, consider the following assertion to prove, where X1, X2 and Y may be signed or modular positive integers:

```
R1 := X1 / Y;
R2 := X2 / Y;
pragma Assert (R1 <= R2);
```

The property here is the monotonicity of division on positive values. There is a corresponding lemma for both signed and modular integers, for both 32 bits and 64 bits integers:

- for signed 32 bits integers, use SPARK.Integer_Arithmetic_Lemmas. Lemma_Div_Is_Monotonic

- for signed 64 bits integers, use SPARK.Long_Integer_Arithmetic_Lemmas. Lemma_Div_Is_Monotonic

- for modular 32 bits integers, use SPARK.Mod32_Arithmetic_Lemmas.Lemma_Div_Is_Monotonic

- for modular 64 bits integers, use SPARK.Mod64_Arithmetic_Lemmas.Lemma_Div_Is_Monotonic

For example, the lemma for signed integers has the following signature:

```
procedure Lemma_Div_Is_Monotonic
  (Val1  : Int;
   Val2  : Int;
   Denom : Pos)
with
  Global => null,
  Pre  => Val1 <= Val2,
  Post => Val1 / Denom <= Val2 / Denom;
```

Assuming the appropriate library unit is with'ed and used in your code (see *SPARK Lemma Library* for details), using the lemma is simply a call to the ghost procedure Lemma_Div_Is_Monotonic:

```
R1 := X1 / Y;
R2 := X2 / Y;
Lemma_Div_Is_Monotonic (X1, X2, Y);
--  at this program point, the prover knows that R1 <= R2
--  the following assertion is proved automatically:
pragma Assert (R1 <= R2);
```

Note that the lemma may have a precondition, stating in which contexts the lemma holds, which you will need to prove when calling it. For example, a precondition check is generated in the code above to show that X1 <= X2. Similarly, the types of parameters in the lemma may restrict the contexts in which the lemma holds. For example, the type Pos for parameter Denom of Lemma_Div_Is_Monotonic is the type of positive integers. Hence, a range check may be generated in the code above to show that Y is positive.

To apply lemmas to signed or modular integers of different types than the ones used in the instances provided in the library, just convert the expressions passed in arguments, as follows:

```
R1 := X1 / Y;
R2 := X2 / Y;
Lemma_Div_Is_Monotonic (Integer(X1), Integer(X2), Integer(Y));
--  at this program point, the prover knows that R1 <= R2
--  the following assertion is proved automatically:
pragma Assert (R1 <= R2);
```

Manual Proof Using User Lemmas

If the property to prove is not part of the *SPARK Lemma Library*, then a user can easily add it as a separate lemma in her program. For example, suppose you need to have a proof that a fix list of numbers are prime numbers. This can be expressed easily in a lemma as follows:

```
function Is_Prime (N : Positive) return Boolean is
  (for all J in Positive range 2 .. N - 1 => N mod J /= 0);

procedure Number_Is_Prime (N : Positive)
with
  Ghost,
  Global => null,
  Pre  => N in 15486209 | 15487001 | 15487469,
  Post => Is_Prime (N);
```

Using the lemma is simply a call to the ghost procedure `Number_Is_Prime`:

```
Number_Is_Prime (15486209);
--  at this program point, the prover knows that 15486209 is prime, so
--  the following assertion is proved automatically:
pragma Assert (Is_Prime (15486209));
```

Note that the lemma here has a precondition, which you will need to prove when calling it. For example, the following incorrect call to the lemma will be detected as a precondition check failure:

```
Number_Is_Prime (10);  --  check message issued here
```

Then, the lemma procedure can be either implemented as a null procedure, in which case GNATprove will issue a check message about the unproved postcondition, which can be justified (see *Justifying Check Messages*) or proved with Coq (see *Manual Proof Using Coq*):

```
procedure Number_Is_Prime (N : Positive) is null;
```

Or it can be implemented as a normal procedure body with a single assumption:

```
procedure Number_Is_Prime (N : Positive) is
begin
   pragma Assume (Is_Prime (N));
end Number_Is_Prime;
```

Or it can be implemented in some cases as a normal procedure body with ghost code to achieve fully automatic proof, see *Manual Proof Using Ghost Code*.

Manual Proof Using Ghost Code

Guiding automatic solvers by adding intermediate assertions is a commonly used technique. More generally, whole pieces of ghost code, that is, code that do not affect the program's output, can be added to enhance automated reasoning. This section presents an example on which complex proofs involving in particular inductive reasoning can be verified automatically using ghost code.

This example focuses on proving the correctness of a sorting procedure on arrays implementing a selection sort, and, more precisely, that it always returns a permutation of the original array.

A common way to define permutations is to use the number of occurrences of elements in the array, defined inductively over the size of its array parameter:

```
1  package Sort_Types with SPARK_Mode is
2     subtype Index is Integer range 1 .. 100;
3     type Nat_Array is array (Index range <>) of Natural;
4  end Sort_Types;
```

```
1  with Sort_Types; use Sort_Types;
2
3  package Perm with SPARK_Mode, Ghost is
4     subtype Nb_Occ is Integer range 0 .. 100;
5
6     function Remove_Last (A : Nat_Array) return Nat_Array is
7       (A (A'First .. A'Last - 1))
8     with Pre  => A'Length > 0;
9
10    function Occ_Def (A : Nat_Array; E : Natural) return Nb_Occ is
11      (if A'Length = 0 then 0
12       elsif A (A'Last) = E then Occ_Def (Remove_Last (A), E) + 1
13       else Occ_Def (Remove_Last (A), E))
14    with
15      Post => Occ_Def'Result <= A'Length;
16    pragma Annotate (GNATprove, Terminating, Occ_Def);
17
18    function Occ (A : Nat_Array; E : Natural) return Nb_Occ is (Occ_Def (A, E))
19    with
20      Post => Occ'Result <= A'Length;
21
22    function Is_Perm (A, B : Nat_Array) return Boolean is
23      (for all E in Natural => Occ (A, E) = Occ (B, E));
24
25  end Perm;
```

Note that Occ was introduced as a wrapper around the recursive definition of Occ_Def. This is to work around a current limitation of the tool that only introduces axioms for postconditions of non-recursive functions (to avoid possibly introducing unsound axioms that would not be detected by the tool).

The only property of the function Occ required to prove that swapping two elements of an array is in fact a permutation, is the way Occ is modified when updating a value of the array.

There is no native construction for axioms in SPARK 2014. As a workaround, a ghost subprogram, named "lemma subprogram", can be introduced with the desired property as a postcondition. An instance of the axiom will then be available whenever the subprogram is called. Notice that an explicit call to the lemma subprogram with the proper arguments is required whenever an instance of the axiom is needed, like in manual proofs in an interactive theorem prover. Here is how a lemma subprogram can be defined for the desired property of Occ:

```
package Perm.Lemma_Subprograms with SPARK_Mode, Ghost is

   function Is_Set (A : Nat_Array; I : Index; V : Natural; R : Nat_Array)
                    return Boolean
   is (R'First = A'First and then R'Last = A'Last
       and then R (I) = V
       and then (for all J in A'Range =>
                    (if I /= J then R (J) = A (J)))) with
     Pre  => I in A'Range;

   procedure Occ_Set (A : Nat_Array; I : Index; V, E : Natural; R : Nat_Array)
   with
     Pre      => I in A'Range and then Is_Set (A, I, V, R),
     Post     =>
```

```
        (if V = A (I) then Occ (R, E) = Occ (A, E)
         elsif V = E then Occ (R, E) = Occ (A, E) + 1
         elsif A (I) = E then Occ (R, E) = Occ (A, E) - 1
         else Occ (R, E) = Occ (A, E));

end Perm.Lemma_Subprograms;
```

This "axiom" can then be used to prove an implementation of the selection sort algorithm. Lemma subprograms need to be explicitly called for every natural. To achieve that, a loop is introduced. The inductive proof necessary to demonstrate the universally quantified formula is then achieved thanks to the loop invariant, playing the role of an induction hypothesis:

```
with Perm.Lemma_Subprograms; use Perm.Lemma_Subprograms;
package body Sort
   with SPARK_Mode
is

   ------------------------------------------------------------------------

   procedure Swap (Values : in out Nat_Array;
                   X       : in      Positive;
                   Y       : in      Positive)
     with
       Pre  => (X in Values'Range and then
                Y in Values'Range and then
                  X /= Y),

       Post => Is_Perm (Values'Old, Values)
     and Values (X) = Values'Old (Y)
     and Values (Y) = Values'Old (X)
     and (for all Z in Values'Range =>
           (if Z /= X and Z /= Y then Values (Z) = Values'Old (Z)))
   is
      Temp : Integer;

      --  Ghost variables
      Init   : constant Nat_Array (Values'Range) := Values with Ghost;
      Interm : Nat_Array (Values'Range) with Ghost;

      --  Ghost procedure
      procedure Prove_Perm with Ghost,
        Pre  => X in Values'Range and then Y in Values'Range and then
        Is_Set (Init, X, Init (Y), Interm)
        and then Is_Set (Interm, Y, Init (X), Values),
        Post => Is_Perm (Init, Values)
      is
      begin
         for E in Natural loop
            Occ_Set (Init, X, Init (Y), E, Interm);
            Occ_Set (Interm, Y, Init (X), E, Values);
            pragma Loop_Invariant
              (for all F in Natural'First .. E =>
                 Occ (Values, F) = Occ (Init, F));
         end loop;
      end Prove_Perm;

   begin
      Temp          := Values (X);
```

```
      Values (X) := Values (Y);

      --  Ghost code
      pragma Assert (Is_Set (Init, X, Init (Y), Values));
      Interm := Values;

      Values (Y) := Temp;

      --  Ghost code
      pragma Assert (Is_Set (Interm, Y, Init (X), Values));
      Prove_Perm;
   end Swap;

-- Finds the index of the smallest element in the array
function Index_Of_Minimum (Values : in Nat_Array)
                              return Positive
   with
     Pre  => Values'Length > 0,
     Post => Index_Of_Minimum'Result in Values'Range and then
      (for all I in Values'Range =>
         Values (Index_Of_Minimum'Result) <= Values (I))
is
   Min : Positive;
begin
   Min := Values'First;
   for Index in Values'Range loop
      if Values (Index) < Values (Min) then
         Min := Index;
      end if;
      pragma Loop_Invariant
        (Min in Values'Range and then
           (for all I in Values'First .. Index =>
               Values (Min) <= Values (I)));
   end loop;
   return Min;
end Index_Of_Minimum;

procedure Selection_Sort (Values : in out Nat_Array) is
   Smallest : Positive;  -- Index of the smallest value in the unsorted part
begin
   if Values'Length = 0 then
      return;
   end if;

   for Current in Values'First .. Values'Last - 1 loop
      Smallest := Index_Of_Minimum (Values (Current .. Values'Last));

      if Smallest /= Current then
         Swap (Values => Values,
               X       => Current,
               Y       => Smallest);
      end if;

      pragma Loop_Invariant
        (for all I in Values'First .. Current =>
           (for all J in I + 1 .. Values'Last =>
               Values (I) <= Values (J)));
      pragma Loop_Invariant (Is_Perm (Values'Loop_Entry, Values));
```

```
      end loop;

   end Selection_Sort;

end Sort;
```

```
with Sort_Types; use Sort_Types;
with Perm; use Perm;

package Sort with SPARK_Mode is

   -- Sorts the elements in the array Values in ascending order
   procedure Selection_Sort (Values : in out Nat_Array)
     with
       Post => Is_Perm (Values'Old, Values) and then
       (if Values'Length > 0 then
          (for all I in Values'First .. Values'Last - 1 =>
             Values (I) <= Values (I + 1)));
end Sort;
```

The procedure Selection_Sort can be verified using GNATprove, with the default prover CVC4, in less than 1s per verification condition.

```
sort.adb:16:16: info: postcondition proved
sort.adb:17:18: info: index check proved
sort.adb:17:35: info: index check proved
sort.adb:18:18: info: index check proved
sort.adb:18:35: info: index check proved
sort.adb:20:48: info: index check proved
sort.adb:20:65: info: index check proved
sort.adb:25:07: info: range check proved
sort.adb:25:53: info: length check proved
sort.adb:26:07: info: range check proved
sort.adb:31:09: info: precondition proved
sort.adb:31:23: info: range check proved
sort.adb:31:32: info: index check proved
sort.adb:32:18: info: precondition proved
sort.adb:32:34: info: range check proved
sort.adb:32:43: info: index check proved
sort.adb:33:17: info: postcondition proved
sort.adb:37:13: info: precondition proved
sort.adb:37:28: info: range check proved
sort.adb:37:37: info: index check proved
sort.adb:38:13: info: precondition proved
sort.adb:38:30: info: range check proved
sort.adb:38:39: info: index check proved
sort.adb:40:16: info: loop invariant initialization proved
sort.adb:40:16: info: loop invariant preservation proved
sort.adb:46:29: info: index check proved
sort.adb:47:15: info: index check proved
sort.adb:47:29: info: index check proved
sort.adb:50:22: info: assertion proved
sort.adb:50:22: info: precondition proved
sort.adb:50:36: info: range check proved
sort.adb:50:45: info: index check proved
sort.adb:51:14: info: length check proved
sort.adb:51:17: info: length check proved
```

```
sort.adb:53:15: info: index check proved
sort.adb:53:21: info: initialization of "Temp" proved
sort.adb:53:21: info: range check proved
sort.adb:56:22: info: assertion proved
sort.adb:56:22: info: precondition proved
sort.adb:56:30: info: initialization of "Interm" proved
sort.adb:56:38: info: range check proved
sort.adb:56:47: info: index check proved
sort.adb:57:07: info: initialization of "Interm" proved
sort.adb:57:07: info: precondition proved
sort.adb:65:16: info: postcondition proved
sort.adb:67:35: info: index check proved
sort.adb:67:55: info: index check proved
sort.adb:71:20: info: range check proved
sort.adb:73:38: info: index check proved
sort.adb:73:38: info: initialization of "Min" proved
sort.adb:74:20: info: range check proved
sort.adb:77:13: info: initialization of "Min" proved
sort.adb:77:13: info: loop invariant initialization proved
sort.adb:77:13: info: loop invariant preservation proved
sort.adb:79:28: info: index check proved
sort.adb:79:44: info: index check proved
sort.adb:81:14: info: initialization of "Min" proved
sort.adb:91:50: info: overflow check proved
sort.adb:92:22: info: precondition proved
sort.adb:92:40: info: range check proved
sort.adb:94:13: info: initialization of "Smallest" proved
sort.adb:95:13: info: precondition proved
sort.adb:96:29: info: range check proved
sort.adb:97:29: info: initialization of "Smallest" proved
sort.adb:101:13: info: loop invariant initialization proved
sort.adb:101:13: info: loop invariant preservation proved
sort.adb:102:31: info: overflow check proved
sort.adb:103:28: info: index check proved
sort.adb:103:42: info: index check proved
sort.adb:104:33: info: loop invariant initialization proved
sort.adb:104:33: info: loop invariant preservation proved
sort.ads:9:16: info: postcondition proved
sort.ads:11:51: info: overflow check proved
sort.ads:12:22: info: index check proved
sort.ads:12:38: info: index check proved
sort.ads:12:38: info: overflow check proved
```

To complete the verification of our selection sort, the only remaining issue is the correctness of the axiom for Occ. It can be discharged using the definition of Occ. Since this definition is recursive, the proof requires induction, which is not normally in the reach of an automated prover. For GNATprove to verify it, it must be implemented using recursive calls on itself to assert the induction hypothesis. Note that the proof of the lemma is then conditioned to the termination of the lemma functions, which currently cannot be verified by GNATprove.

```
package body Perm.Lemma_Subprograms with SPARK_Mode is

   procedure Occ_Eq (A, B : Nat_Array; E : Natural) with
     Pre  => A = B,
     Post => Occ (A, E) = Occ (B, E);

   procedure Occ_Eq (A, B : Nat_Array; E : Natural) is
      begin
      if A'Length = 0 then
```

```
         return;
      end if;

      if A (A'Last) = E then
         pragma Assert (B (B'Last) = E);
      else
         pragma Assert (B (B'Last) /= E);
      end if;

      Occ_Eq (Remove_Last (A), Remove_Last (B), E);
   end Occ_Eq;


   procedure Occ_Set (A : Nat_Array; I : Index; V, E : Natural; R : Nat_Array)
   is
      B : Nat_Array:= Remove_Last (A);
   begin
      if A'Length = 0 then
         return;
      end if;

      if I = A'Last then
         Occ_Eq (B, Remove_Last (R), E);
      else
         B (I) := V;
         Occ_Eq (Remove_Last (R), B, E);
         Occ_Set (Remove_Last (A), I, V, E, B);
      end if;
   end Occ_Set;

end Perm.Lemma_Subprograms;
```

GNATprove proves automatically all checks on the final program, with a small timeout of 1s for the default automatic prover CVC4.

```
perm-lemma_subprograms.adb:5:14: info: postcondition proved
perm-lemma_subprograms.adb:13:14: info: index check proved
perm-lemma_subprograms.adb:14:25: info: assertion proved
perm-lemma_subprograms.adb:14:29: info: index check proved
perm-lemma_subprograms.adb:16:25: info: assertion proved
perm-lemma_subprograms.adb:16:29: info: index check proved
perm-lemma_subprograms.adb:19:07: info: precondition proved
perm-lemma_subprograms.adb:19:15: info: precondition proved
perm-lemma_subprograms.adb:19:32: info: precondition proved
perm-lemma_subprograms.adb:25:23: info: precondition proved
perm-lemma_subprograms.adb:32:10: info: precondition proved
perm-lemma_subprograms.adb:32:18: info: initialization of "B" proved
perm-lemma_subprograms.adb:32:21: info: precondition proved
perm-lemma_subprograms.adb:34:13: info: index check proved
perm-lemma_subprograms.adb:34:16: info: initialization of "B" proved
perm-lemma_subprograms.adb:35:10: info: precondition proved
perm-lemma_subprograms.adb:35:18: info: precondition proved
perm-lemma_subprograms.adb:35:35: info: initialization of "B" proved
perm-lemma_subprograms.adb:36:10: info: precondition proved
perm-lemma_subprograms.adb:36:19: info: precondition proved
perm-lemma_subprograms.adb:36:45: info: initialization of "B" proved
perm-lemma_subprograms.ads:6:20: info: index check proved
perm-lemma_subprograms.ads:8:39: info: index check proved
```

```
perm-lemma_subprograms.ads:8:47: info: index check proved
perm-lemma_subprograms.ads:13:39: info: precondition proved
perm-lemma_subprograms.ads:15:08: info: postcondition proved
perm-lemma_subprograms.ads:15:19: info: index check proved
perm-lemma_subprograms.ads:17:18: info: index check proved
```

Manual Proof Using Coq

This section presents a simple example of how to prove interactively a check with an interactive prover like Coq when GNATprove fails to prove it automatically (for installation of Coq, see also: *Coq*). Here is a simple SPARK procedure:

```
1  procedure Nonlinear (X, Y, Z : Positive; R1, R2 : out Natural) with
2    SPARK_Mode,
3    Pre  => Y > Z,
4    Post => R1 <= R2
5  is
6  begin
7    R1 := X / Y;
8    R2 := X / Z;
9  end Nonlinear;
```

When only the Alt-Ergo prover is used, GNATprove does not prove automatically the postcondition of the procedure, even when increasing the value of the timeout:

```
nonlinear.adb:1:42: info: initialization of "R1" proved
nonlinear.adb:1:46: info: initialization of "R2" proved
nonlinear.adb:4:11: info: initialization of "R1" proved
nonlinear.adb:4:11: medium: postcondition might fail, cannot prove R1 <= R2
nonlinear.adb:4:17: info: initialization of "R2" proved
nonlinear.adb:7:12: info: division check proved
nonlinear.adb:7:12: info: range check proved
nonlinear.adb:8:12: info: division check proved
nonlinear.adb:8:12: info: range check proved
```

This is expected, as the automatic prover Alt-Ergo has only a simple support for non-linear integer arithmetic. More generally, it is a known difficulty for all automatic provers, although, in the case above, using prover CVC4 is enough to prove automatically the postcondition of procedure Nonlinear. We will use this case to demonstrate the use of a manual prover, as an example of what can be done when automatic provers fail to prove a check. We will use Coq here.

The Coq input file associated to this postcondition can be produced by either selecting *SPARK → Prove Check* and specifying Coq as alternate prover in GPS or by executing on the command-line:

```
gnatprove -P <prj_file>.gpr --limit-line=nonlinear.
adb:4:11:VC_POSTCONDITION --prover=Coq
```

The generated file contains many definitions and axioms that can be used in the proof, in addition to the ones in Coq standard library. The property we want to prove is at the end of the file:

```
Theorem WP_parameter_def :
  forall (r1:Z) (r2:Z) (o:Z) (o1:Z) (result:Z)
         (r11:Z) (result1:Z) (r21:Z) (r12:Z) (r22:Z)
         (r13:Z) (r23:Z),
    ((in_range1 x)
    /\ ((in_range1 y)
    /\ ((in_range1 z)
    /\ (((0%Z <= 2147483647%Z)%Z -> (in_range r1))
```

```
    /\ (((0%Z <= 2147483647%Z)%Z -> (in_range r2))
    /\ ((z < y)%Z
    /\ (((((o = (ZArith.BinInt.Z.quot x y))
    /\ (in_range (ZArith.BinInt.Z.quot x y)))
    /\ (((mk_int__ref result) = (mk_int__ref r1))
    /\ (r11 = o)))
    /\ (((o1 = (ZArith.BinInt.Z.quot x z))
    /\ (in_range (ZArith.BinInt.Z.quot x z)))
    /\ ((result1 = r2)
    /\ (r21 = o1))))
    /\ (((r21 = r22)
    /\ (r11 = r12))
    /\ ((r23 = r21)
    /\ (r13 = r11))))))))))) ->
    (r12 <= r22)%Z.

  intros r1 r2 o o1 result r11 result1 r21 r12 r22 r13 r23
  (h1,(h2,(h3,(h4,(h5,(h6,((((h7,h8),(h9,h10)),((h11,h12),
  (h13,h14))),((h15,h16),(h17,h18))))))))))).

Qed.
```

From the `forall` to the first `.` we can see the expression of what must be proved, also called the goal. The proof starts right after the dot and ends with the `Qed` keyword. Proofs in Coq are done with the help of different tactics which will change the state of the current goal. The first tactic (automatically added) here is `intros`, which allows to "extract" variables and hypotheses from the current goal and add them to the current environment. Each parameter to the `intros` tactic is the name that the extracted element will have in the new environment. The `intros` tactic here puts all universally quantified variables and all hypotheses in the environment. The goal is reduced to a simple inequality, with all potentially useful information in the environment.

Here is the state of the proof as displayed in a suitable IDE for Coq:

```
1 subgoal

  r1, r2, o, o1, result, r11, result1, r21, r12, r22, r13, r23 : int
  h1 : in_range1 x
  h2 : in_range1 y
  h3 : in_range1 z
  h4 : (0 <= 2147483647)%Z -> in_range r1
  h5 : (0 <= 2147483647)%Z -> in_range r2
  h6 : (z < y)%Z
  h7 : o = (x ÷ y)%Z
  h8 : in_range (x ÷ y)
  h9 : mk_int__ref result = mk_int__ref r1
  h10 : r11 = o
  h11 : o1 = (x ÷ z)%Z
  h12 : in_range (x ÷ z)
  h13 : result1 = r2
  h14 : r21 = o1
  h15 : r21 = r22
  h16 : r11 = r12
  h17 : r23 = r21
  h18 : r13 = r11
_____(1/1)
  (r12 <= r22)%Z
```

Some expresions are enclosed in `()%Z`, which means that they are dealing with relative integers. This is necessarily in order to use the operators (e.g. < or +) on relative integers instead of using the associated Coq function or to declare a relative integer constant (e.g. 0%Z).

Next, we can use the `subst` tactic to automaticaly replace variables by terms to which they are equal (as stated by the hypotheses in the current environment) and clean the environment of replaced variables. Here, we can get rid of many variables at once with `subst o o1 result1 r11 r12 r21 r22 r23 r13.` (note the presence of the . at the end of each tactic). The new state is:

```
1 subgoal

  r1, r2, result : int
  h1 : in_range1 x
  h2 : in_range1 y
  h3 : in_range1 z
  h4 : (0 <= 2147483647)%Z -> in_range r1
  h5 : (0 <= 2147483647)%Z -> in_range r2
  h6 : (z < y)%Z
  h8 : in_range (x ÷ y)
  h9 : mk_int__ref result = mk_int__ref r1
  h12 : in_range (x ÷ z)
  _____(1/1)
  (x ÷ y <= x ÷ z)%Z
```

At this state, the hypotheses alone are not enough to prove the goal without proving properties about ÷ and < operators. It is necessary to use theorems from the Coq standard library. Coq provides a command `SearchAbout` to find theorems and definition concerning its argument. For instance, to find the theorems referring to the operator ÷, we use `SearchAbout Z.quot.`, where `Z.quot` is the underlying function for the ÷ operator. Among the theorems displayed, the conclusion (the rightmost term separated by -> operator) of one of them seems to match our current goal:

```
Z.quot_le_compat_l:
    forall p q r : int, (0 <= p)%Z -> (0 < q <= r)%Z -> (p ÷ r <= p ÷ q)%Z
```

The tactic `apply` allows the use of a theorem or an hypothesis on the current goal. Here we use: `apply Z.quot_le_compat_l.`. This tactic will try to match the different variables of the theorem with the terms present in the goal. If it succeeds, one subgoal per hypothesis in the theorem will be generated to verify that the terms matched with the theorem variables satisfy the hypotheses on those variables required by the theorem. In this case, p is matched with x, q with z and r with y and the new state is:

```
2 subgoals

  r1, r2, result : int
  h1 : in_range1 x
  h2 : in_range1 y
  h3 : in_range1 z
  h4 : (0 <= 2147483647)%Z -> in_range r1
  h5 : (0 <= 2147483647)%Z -> in_range r2
  h6 : (z < y)%Z
  h8 : in_range (x ÷ y)
  h9 : mk_int__ref result = mk_int__ref r1
  h12 : in_range (x ÷ z)
  _____(1/2)
  (0 <= x)%Z
  _____(2/2)
  (0 < z <= y)%Z
```

As expected, there are two subgoals, one per hypothesis of the theorem. Once the first subgoal is proved, the rest of the script will automatically apply to the second one. Now, if we look back at the SPARK code, X is of type `Positive` so X is greater than 0 and `in_rangeN` (where N is a number) are predicates generated by SPARK to state the range of a value from a ranged type interpreted as a relative integer in Coq. Here, the predicate `in_range1` provides the property needed to prove the first subgoal which is that "All elements of type positive have their integer interpretation in the range 1 .. (2^{31} - 1)". However, the goal does not match exactly the predicate, because one is a comparison with 0, while the other is a comparison with 1. Transitivity on "lesser or equal" relation is needed to prove this goal, of course this is provided in Coq's standard library:

```
Lemma Zle_trans : forall n m p:Z, (n <= m)%Z -> (m <= p)%Z -> (n <= p)%Z.
```

Since the lemma's conclusion contains only two variables while it uses three, using tactic `apply Zle_trans.` will generate an error stating that Coq was not able to find a term for the variable m. In this case, m needs to be instantiated explicitly, here with the value 1: `apply Zle_trans with (m:= 1%Z)`. There are two new subgoals, one to prove that `0 <= 1` and the other that `1 <= x`:

```
3 subgoals

  r1, r2, result : int
  h1 : in_range1 x
  h2 : in_range1 y
  h3 : in_range1 z
  h4 : (0 <= 2147483647)%Z -> in_range r1
  h5 : (0 <= 2147483647)%Z -> in_range r2
  h6 : (z < y)%Z
  h8 : in_range (x ÷ y)
  h9 : mk_int__ref result = mk_int__ref r1
  h12 : in_range (x ÷ z)
  _____(1/3)
  (0 <= 1)%Z
  _____(2/3)
  (1 <= x)%Z
  _____(3/3)
  (0 < z <= y)%Z
```

To prove that `0 <= 1`, the theorem `Lemma Zle_0_1 :   (0 <= 1)%Z.` is used. `apply Zle_0_1` will not generate any new subgoals since it does not contain implications. Coq passes to the next subgoal:

```
2 subgoals

  r1, r2, result : int
  h1 : in_range1 x
  h2 : in_range1 y
  h3 : in_range1 z
  h4 : (0 <= 2147483647)%Z -> in_range r1
  h5 : (0 <= 2147483647)%Z -> in_range r2
  h6 : (z < y)%Z
  h8 : in_range (x ÷ y)
  h9 : mk_int__ref result = mk_int__ref r1
  h12 : in_range (x ÷ z)
  _____(1/2)
  (1 <= x)%Z
  _____(2/2)
  (0 < z <= y)%Z
```

This goal is now adapted to the `in_range1` definition with `h1` which does not introduce subgoals, so the subgoal 1 is fully proved, and all that remains is subgoal 2:

```
1 subgoal

  r1, r2, result : int
```

```
h1 : in_range1 x
h2 : in_range1 y
h3 : in_range1 z
h4 : (0 <= 2147483647)%Z -> in_range r1
h5 : (0 <= 2147483647)%Z -> in_range r2
h6 : (z < y)%Z
h8 : in_range (x ÷ y)
h9 : mk_int__ref result = mk_int__ref r1
h12 : in_range (x ÷ z)
_____ (1/1)
(0 < z <= y)%Z
```

Transitivity is needed again, as well as `in_range1`. In the previous subgoal, every step was detailed in order to show how the tactic `apply` worked. Now, let's see that proof doesn't have to be this detailed. The first thing to do is to add the fact that `1 <= z` to the current environment: `unfold in_range1 in h3.` will add the range of z as an hypthesis in the environment:

```
1 subgoal

  r1, r2, result : int
  h1 : in_range1 x
  h2 : in_range1 y
  h3 : (1 <= z <= 2147483647)%Z
  h4 : (0 <= 2147483647)%Z -> in_range r1
  h5 : (0 <= 2147483647)%Z -> in_range r2
  h6 : (z < y)%Z
  h8 : in_range (x ÷ y)
  h9 : mk_int__ref result = mk_int__ref r1
  h12 : in_range (x ÷ z)
  _____ (1/1)
  (0 < z <= y)%Z
```

At this point, the goal can be solved simply using the `omega.` tactic. `omega` is a tactic made to facilitate the verification of properties about relative integers equalities and inequalities. It uses a predefined set of theorems and the hypotheses present in the current environment to try to solve the current goal. `omega` either solves the goal or, if it fails, it does not generate any subgoals. The benefit of the latter way is that there are less steps than with the previous subgoal for a more complicated goal (there are two inequalities in the second subgoal) and we do not have to find the different theorems we need to solve the goal without omega.

Finally, here is the final version of the proof script for the postcondition:

```
Theorem WP_parameter_def :
  forall (r1:Z) (r2:Z) (o:Z) (o1:Z) (result:Z)
         (r11:Z) (result1:Z) (r21:Z) (r12:Z) (r22:Z)
         (r13:Z) (r23:Z),
    ((in_range1 x)
    /\ ((in_range1 y)
    /\ ((in_range1 z)
    /\ (((0%Z <= 2147483647%Z)%Z -> (in_range r1))
    /\ (((0%Z <= 2147483647%Z)%Z -> (in_range r2))
    /\ ((z < y)%Z
    /\ (((((o = (ZArith.BinInt.Z.quot x y))
    /\ (in_range (ZArith.BinInt.Z.quot x y)))
    /\ (((mk_int__ref result) = (mk_int__ref r1))
    /\ (r11 = o)))
    /\ (((o1 = (ZArith.BinInt.Z.quot x z))
    /\ (in_range (ZArith.BinInt.Z.quot x z)))
    /\ ((result1 = r2)
```

```
       /\  (r21 = o1))))
       /\  (((r21 = r22)
       /\  (r11 = r12))
       /\  ((r23 = r21)
       /\  (r13 = r11))))))))))) ->
       (r12 <= r22)%Z.

  intros r1 r2 o o1 result r11 result1 r21 r12 r22 r13 r23
  (h1,(h2,(h3,(h4,(h5,(h6,((((h7,h8),(h9,h10)),((h11,h12),
  (h13,h14))),((h15,h16),(h17,h18))))))))).

subst o o1 result1 r11 r12 r21 r22 r23 r13.
apply Z.quot_le_compat_l.
  apply Zle_trans with (m:=1%Z).
    (* 0 <= 1 *)
    apply Zle_0_1.
    (* 1 <= x *)
    unfold in_range1 in h1.
    apply h1.
  (* 0 < z <= y *)
  unfold in_range1 in h3.
  omega.
Qed.
```

To check and save the proof:

```
gnatprove -P <prj_file>.gpr --limit-line=nonlinear.
adb:4:11:VC_POSTCONDITION --prover=Coq --report=all
```

Now running GNATprove on the project should confirm that all checks are proved:

```
nonlinear.adb:4:11: info: postcondition proved
nonlinear.adb:7:12: info: range check proved
nonlinear.adb:7:12: info: division check proved
nonlinear.adb:8:12: info: range check proved
nonlinear.adb:8:12: info: division check proved
```

Manual Proof Using GPS

This section presents a simple example of how to prove interactively a check with the manual proof feature. We reuse here the example presented in section *Manual Proof Using Coq*. We launch the Manual Proof on the failed check at:

```
nonlinear.adb:4:11:VC_POSTCONDITION
```

Right click on the corresponding location in the Locations terminal of GPS and select the menu *SPARK → Start Manual Proof*. The manual proof interface immediately starts. Both the Proof Tree and the Verification Condition (VC) appear in separate windows. In particular, the VC ends with the following:

```
axiom H : dynamic_property first last X

axiom H1 : dynamic_property first last Y

axiom H2 : dynamic_property first last Z

axiom H3 : first1 <= last1 -> dynamic_property1 first1 last1 R14

axiom H4 : first1 <= last1 -> dynamic_property1 first1 last1 R23
```

```
axiom H5 : Y > Z

axiom H6 : o1 = div X Y /\ in_range1 (div X Y)

axiom H7 : result = R1

axiom H8 : R13 = o1

axiom H9 : o = div X Z /\ in_range1 (div X Z)

axiom H10 : result1 = R23

axiom H11 : R22 = o

axiom H12 : R22 = R21

axiom H13 : R13 = R12

axiom H14 : R2 = R22

axiom H15 : R11 = R13

goal WP_parameter def : R12 <= R21
```

The Verification Condition is very similar to the one generated for Coq (as expected: the check is the same). As soon as the menus appear, the user can start using transformations to simplify the goal thus helping automatic provers. We will start the description of a complete proof for this lemma using only `altergo`. At first, we want to remove the equalities between constants that make the VC very difficult to read. These equalities were generated by the weakest precondition algorithm. They can be safely removed by `subst` and `subst_all`. In `Manual Proof` console, type:

```
subst_all
```

The transformation node was added to the Proof Tree and the current node is now changed making your transformation appear and the new Verification Condition to prove has been simplified:

```
axiom H : dynamic_property first last X

axiom H1 : dynamic_property first last Y

axiom H2 : dynamic_property first last Z

axiom H3 : first1 <= last1 -> dynamic_property1 first1 last1 R14

axiom H4 : first1 <= last1 -> dynamic_property1 first1 last1 R23

axiom H5 : Y > Z

axiom H6 : o1 = div X Y /\ in_range1 (div X Y)

axiom H7 : o = div X Z /\ in_range1 (div X Z)

--------------------------- Goal ---------------------------

goal WP_parameter def : o1 <= o
```

We should also have replaced the value of `o1` and `o` in the goal. These were not replaced because `H6` and `H7` are conjunctions. We can destruct both hypotheses `H6` and `H7` in order to make the equalities appear at toplevel:

```
destruct H6
```

Then:

```
subst o1
```

After simplifications, the goal is the following:

```
axiom H2 : dynamic_property first last X

axiom H3 : dynamic_property first last Y

axiom H4 : dynamic_property first last Z

axiom H5 : first1 <= last1 -> dynamic_property1 first1 last1 R14

axiom H6 : first1 <= last1 -> dynamic_property1 first1 last1 R23

axiom H7 : Y > Z

axiom H1 : in_range1 (div X Y)

axiom H : in_range1 (div X Z)

--------------------------- Goal ---------------------------

goal WP_parameter def : div X Y <= div X Z
```

This is more readable but `altergo` still does not manage to prove it:

```
altergo
```

answers `Unknown` as seen in the Proof Tree.

We need to investigate further what we know about `div`, and what would be useful to prove the goal:

```
search div
```

returns in the `Manual Proof` console:

```
function div (x:int) (y:int) : int = div1 x y

axiom H1 : in_range1 (div X Y)

axiom H : in_range1 (div X Z)
```

So, `div` is actually a shortcut for a function named `div1`. Let's search for this one:

```
search div1
```

Now, we get a lot of axioms about `div` and `mod` as expected. In particular, the axiom `Div_mod` looks interesting:

```
axiom Div_mod :
   forall x:int, y:int. not y = 0 -> x = ((y * div1 x y) + mod1 x y)
```

Perhaps, it is a good idea to instantiate this axiom with X and Y (respectively X and Z) and see what is provable from there:

```
instantiate Div_mod X,Y
```

A new hypothesis appears in the context:

```
axiom Div_mod : not Y = 0 -> X = ((Y * div1 X Y) + mod1 X Y)
```

After some struggling with those hypotheses, it looks like they won't actually help proving the goal. Let's remove these hypotheses:

```
remove Div_mod
```

Alternatively, we can go back to the node above the current one in the Proof Tree by clicking on it. We can also remove the transformation node corresponding to the use of instantiate by selecting it and writing in Manual Proof console:

```
Remove
```

The actual proof is going to use an additional lemma that we are going to introduce with assert. The Coq proof uses this exact same lemma inside the proof of Z.quot_le_compat_1. We could have expected altergo to have this lemma inside its theories but, currently, it does not:

```
assert (forall q a b:int. 0<b -> 0<a -> b*q <= a -> q <= div1 a b)
```

So, two new nodes appear below the current one (the first to prove the formula we just wrote and the second adding it as an hypothesis). We are going to prove this assert by induction on the unbounded integer q (the base case is 0):

```
induction q from 0
```

Both new goals can be discharged by altergo: this small lemma is proven. Now, we can use it in our proof. We begin by unfolding div to make div1 appear:

```
unfold div
```

Then we can apply our new lemma:

```
apply h
```

We are left with the following three subgoals to prove:

```
goal G : (Z * div1 X Y) <= X

goal G : 0 < X

goal G : 0 < Z
```

altergo proves the positivity of X and Z easily but it does not find a proof for the first subgoal. We are going to prove this one by transitivity of less or equal using Y * div1 X Y. Currently, we don't have a transformation to apply the transitivity directly so we assert it:

```
assert ((Y * div1 X Y <= X && Z) * ((div1 X Y) <= Y * div1 X Y))
```

To make two goals of this conjunction, we are using:

```
split_goal_wp
```

The left part is provable by altergo. On the second part, we are going to apply an axiom CompatOrderMult we found by querying what is known about the multiplication:

```
search (*)
```

We apply it to the current goal:

```
apply CompatOrderMult
```

The remaining goals can all be proven by `altergo`. This closes the proof. A popup should appear asking if the user wants to save and exit. Answer no because we want to make the proof cleaner (you can still save it by writing `Save` in `Manual Proof` console). Select a node and type:

```
clean
```

All attempted proof that did not succeed are erased and only the successful proofs remain. The proof can now be saved and manual proofs menus closed by clicking on *SPARK → Exit Manual Proof* from the menu. The proof is complete and GNATprove can be called again on the whole project to check that the former failing check is now understood as proved by GNATprove.

List of Useful Transformations and Commands

The transformations all contain a specific documentation through the `list-transforms` command and `help transform_name` command. The most useful transformations/commands are the following:

- `apply`: apply an hypothesis to the current goal. For example: `H : x > 0 -> not x = 0` can be applied on the goal `G : not x = 0`. After the application you will be left to prove a new goal `x > 0`.

- `assert`: adds a new lemma you can use for proving the current Verification Condition. For example: `assert x = 0` will generate two new subgoals. In the first one you have to prove that x is indeed equal to 0. In the second one, you can use this hypothesis.

- `case`: takes a formula and perform an analysis by case on its boolean value. You will have to prove your Verification Condition once with this formula asserted to true and once asserted to false.

- `clean`: removes unsuccessful proof attempts below proved goals.

- `clear_but`: removes all hypotheses except the one provided by the user as argument. Removing unused context helps the provers. For example, `clear_but H,H2,h` will remove everything but hypotheses H H2 and h.

- `compute_in_goal`: performs possible computations in goal.

- `destruct`: destruct the head constructor of a formula (`/\` , `\/` or `->`). With `H: A /\ B`, applying `destruct H` make two new hypotheses (`H: A` and `H1: B`). With `H: A \/ B`, applying `destruct H` duplicates the goal which has to be proved with `H: A` and `H: B` independently. With `H: A -> B`, `destruct H` creates a new subgoal for A and simplify to `H: B` in the current one.

- `eliminate_epsilon`: sometimes the goal appears as `epsilon [...]`. This transforms epsilons into adapted logic.

- `exists`: allows the user to provide a term that instantiates a goal starting with an existential.

- `help`: with no arguments, return basic commands that can be used. If a transformation is given as argument, it displays a small description of the transformation.

- `induction`: performs an induction on the unbounded integer specified.

- `instantiate`: instantiates a `forall` quantification at the head of an hypothesis with a term given by the user (a list of terms can be provided).

- `intros`: introduces a list of constants/hypotheses. This transformation should not be necessary but it can be used to rename constants/hypotheses.

- `left`: In a goal, transforms A \/ B into A.

- `list-provers`: gives a list of the provers available on your machine. You should have at least `altergo`.

- `list-transforms`: list transformations.

- `pose`: defines a new constant equal to a given term.

- `print`: prints the definition of a name.

- `remove`: removes a list of hypotheses.

- `replace`: replace a term by another and create a subgoal asking the user to show that they are equivalent.

- `rewrite`: rewrites an equality in a goal or hypothesis. For example, with `H: x = 0` and goal `y = x`, `rewrite H` transforms the goal into `y = 0`.

- `right`: In a goal, transforms A \/ B into B.

- `search`: search all occurrences of a name in the context.

- `split_*`: a set of transformations that split the goals/hypotheses. For example, `split_goal_wp` transforms the goal A /\ B into two new subgoals A and B.

- `subst`: try to find an equality that could be used for a given constant and replace each occurrence of this constant by the other side of the equality. It then removes said constant.

- `subst_all`: do all possible substitutions.

- `unfold`: unfolds the definition of a function in an hypothesis or a goal.

Recommendations

- As for proofs with an external interactive prover, the user should set the attribute `Proof_Dir` so that proofs can be saved under version control.

- The `Proof_Dir` is recommended to be under a version control system (git or svn for example). The proofs can be tedious to rewrite so it is better not to lose them.

- There is currently no way to adapt stuff that are proven in the current version to potential future ones. The update will have to be done manually but we hope to automate the process in the future,

- This feature is experimental and we currently recommend to keep the proof as short as possible.

Tips

- If the goal contains epsilons, they can be removed by using `eliminate_epsilon`.

- Manual provers can be launched during the edition of the proof like other provers. The user can select a goal node and type `coq` for example.

- The command line remembers what is typed. Arrow keys can be used to get the lasts queried commands.

7.10 Examples in the Toolset Distribution

Further examples of SPARK are distributed with the SPARK toolset. These are contained in the `share/examples/spark` directory below the directory where the toolset is installed, and can be accessed from the IDE (either GPS or GNATBench) via the *Help → SPARK → Examples* menu item.

These examples range from single subprograms to demo programs with dozens of units. In this section, we describe briefly the code in each example, the properties specified, and the results of GNATprove's analysis.

7.10.1 Individual Subprograms

These examples contain usually a single subprogram, and are typically very small (a few dozens slocs).

`binary_search` and `binary_search_unconstrained`

These programs search for a given value in an ordered array. The postcondition of the main function `Binary_Search` expresses that the search is successful if-and-only-if the array contains the value searched, and if so the index returned is one at which the array contains this value. GNATprove proves all checks on these programs. The version with an unconstrained array is the same as the one presented in the section on *How to Write Loop Invariants*, and used in a series of two articles published by Johannes Kanig in Electronic Design to compare dynamic and static verification techniques (see http://blog.adacore.com/testing-static-formal).

`euclidian_division`

This program implements the Euclidian division of two integers `Dividend` and `Divisor`, returning their quotient and remainder in `Quotient` and `Remainder` respectively. The postcondition of procedure `Linear_Div` expresses the expected mathematical relation between inputs and outputs. GNATprove proves all checks on this program.

`gcd`

This program computes the greatest common divisor between two positive numbers. The postcondition of function `GCD` checks that the number returned is indeed the greatest common divisor of its arguments. Four versions of the function are provided:

- a simple version that searches linearly for the GCD.
- a modification of the simple version with a more mathematical expression of divisibility in the contract of GCD.
- a modification of the simple version that optimizes the search to skip half the candidates for GCD.
- Euclid's algorithm for computing the GCD.

Each successive version makes use of more complex *Ghost Code* to prove that the implementation of GCD satisfies its contract. GNATprove proves all checks on this program, except for some elementary lemmas on modulo operator. This is detailed in the following post on SPARK 2014 Blog: http://www.spark-2014.org/entries/detail/gnatprove-tips-and-tricks-proving-the-ghost-common-denominator-gcd

`intro`

This program computes the price of a basket of items. The postcondition of the main function `Price_Of_Basket` checks that the resulting price is at least the price of the most expensive item. GNATprove proves all checks on this program.

linear_search

This program searches for a given value in an unordered array. The postcondition of the main function `Linear_Search` expresses that if the search is successful then the index returned is one at which the array contains the value searched. GNATprove proves all checks on this program. This program is the same as the one presented in the *SPARK Tutorial*.

longest_common_prefix

This program computes the length of the longest common prefix between two substrings of a common text. The postcondition of the main function `LCP` expresses this property. GNATprove proves all checks on this program. This program was proposed as a formal verification challenge during VerifyThis Verification Competition in 2012 (see http://fm2012.verifythis.org/).

pair_insertion_sort

This program performs a variant of insertion sort, that inserts in place two elements of an array at each loop iteration. This program was proposed as a formal verification challenge during VerifyThis Verification Competition in 2017 (see http://www.pm.inf.ethz.ch/verifythis.html). The postcondition of the main function `Sort` expresses both that the array is sorted on exit, and that it is a permutation of its input value. GNATprove proves all checks on this program. The process to progress through all levels of software assurance with SPARK on this example is detailed in the following post on SPARK 2014 Blog: http://www.spark-2014.org/entries/detail/verifythis-challenge-in-spark

search_linked_list

This program searches for a given value in an unordered linked list. The postcondition of the main function `Search` expresses that the search is successful if-and-only-if the list contains the value searched, and if so the cursor returned is one at which the list contains this value. GNATprove proves all checks on these programs.

string_search

This example contains multiple variants of substring search:

- a simple brute force search in `Brute_Force` and `Brute_Force_Slice`.
- a more efficient algorithm called quick search in `QS`.

The postcondition of all variants expresses that the search is successful if-and-only-if the string `Haystack` contains the substring `Needle` searched, and if so the index returned is one at which the string contains this substring. GNATprove proves all checks on these programs. A detailed account of the development and verification of this example is given in the following post on SPARK 2014 Blog: http://www.spark-2014.org/entries/detail/applied-formal-logic-searching-in-strings

trajectory_computation

This example contains code from an embedded safety-critical software, which computes the speed of a device submitted to gravitational acceleration and drag from the atmosphere around it. This program was used as challenge example in the article *"Automating the Verification of Floating-Point Programs"* published at VSTTE 2017 conference.

The Ada files contain multiple variants of the example in increasing order of difficulty, see README file for details. The challenge example used in the article corresponds to files `simple_trajectory.ads` and `simple_trajectory.adb`. In this version, only the speed is updated, not the distance. Both absence of run-time errors (including overflows) and safe bounds on the computed speed are proved by using a combination of provers. A dozen intermediate assertions are needed to benefit from this combination, so that different provers can prove different parts of the property.

7.10.2 Single Units

These examples contain a single unit, and are usually small (a few hundreds slocs at most).

adacore_u

This folder contains the complete source code of the small examples used in the quiz of the SPARK 2014 course available from the AdaCore University website (at http://university.adacore.com/courses/spark-2014/). They include unannotated units, examples with formally verified data flow, functional, or abstraction contracts, as well as erroneous programs, on which GNATprove detects failing checks.

Opening the example in GPS or GNATbench opens an aggregate project, with separate sub-projects for each lecture.

allocators

This program demonstrates how the specification of a SPARK program can be formalized using an abstract model and how the refinement relation between the model an its implementation can be verified using GNATprove. It is described in the article *"Abstract Software Specifications and Automatic Proof of Refinement"* published at RSSRail 2016 conference (at http://www.spark-2014.org/uploads/rssrail.pdf).

The example contains three versions of an allocator package. They are specified in terms of mathematical structures (sequences and sets). The refinement relation between the mathematical model and the implementation is expressed as a ghost function `Is_Valid` and enforced through contracts. It can be verified automatically using GNATprove.

- `Simple_Allocator` features a naive implementation of the allocator, storing the status (available or allocated) of each resource in a big array. It is specified using a ghost function `Model` which always returns a valid refinement of the allocator's data. The refinement relation is verified only once, as a postcondition of the `Model` function. The functional contracts on modifying procedures as well as the refinement relation are straightforward and can be verified easily at level 2 in a few seconds.

- `List_Allocator` introduces a free list to access more efficiently the first available resource. Here not every possible state of the allocator data can be refined into a valid model. To work around this problem, the model is stored in a global ghost variable which is updated along with the allocator's data and the refinement relation is expressed as an invariant that must be verified as a postcondition of each modifying procedure. The functional contracts on modifying procedures are straightforward but the refinement relation is now more complicated, as it needs to account for the implementation of the free list. They can be verified at level 4 in less than one minute overall.

- `List_Mod_Allocator` features the same implementation and contracts as `List_Allocator`, but its model is returned by a ghost function like in `Simple_Allocator` instead of being stored in a global ghost variable. As not every possible state of the allocator can be refined into a valid model, the refinement relation is not expressed as a postcondition of Model, but as an invariant, as in `List_Allocator` and must be verified as a postcondition of each modifying procedure. The functional contracts and the refinement relation resemble those of `List_Allocator`. However, as we don't construct explicitly the new model after each modification, the proof of the allocator's functional contracts requires induction, which is beyond the reach of automatic solvers. The induction scheme is given here manually in an auto-active style through calls to ghost procedures. The whole program can then be verified automatically at level 4 in less than one minute overall on an 8-cores machine, or in a few minutes on a single core.

See the relevant sections for more details on *Ghost Code* and *Manual Proof Using Ghost Code*.

database

This program implements a toy interface to a bank account database, with procedures to deposit and withdraw money, and functions to query the account balance and information. This program was used as running example in the article *"Integrating Formal Program Verification with Testing"* (at http://www.open-do.org/wp-content/uploads/2011/12/hi-lite-erts2012.pdf). The API is annotated with full functional contracts, as well as test cases expressed with aspect `Test_Case`. GNATprove proves all checks on this program.

evoting

This program implements a toy e-voting interface, to get candidates and votes from a file, compute the winner of the vote and print it. The API is annotated with functional contracts, some partial and some complete. GNATprove proves all checks on this program, except for initialization of an array initialized piecewise (known limitation of flow analysis) and an array access in a string returned by the standard library function `Get_Line` (which would require using a wrapper with contracts).

formal_queue

This program implements a queue of integers using a doubly linked list, with full functional contracts on the API of the queue. GNATprove proves all checks on this program.

natural

This program implements an interface to manipulate sets of natural numbers, stored in an array. Contracts on the interface subprograms express partial correctness properties, for example that the set contains an element after it has been inserted. GNATprove proves all checks on this program.

n_queens

This program implements the solution to the N queens problem, to place N queens on an N x N chess board so that no queen can capture another one with a legal move. The API is annotated with full functional contracts. GNATprove proves all checks on this program. This program was proposed as a formal verification challenge during VSTTE Verification Competition in 2019 (see https://sites.google.com/a/vscomp.org/main/).

patience

This program implements the game of Patience Solitaire, taking cards one-by-one from a deck of cards and arranging them face up in a sequence of stacks. The invariant maintained when playing is a complex relation between multiple arrays storing the current state of the game. GNATprove proves all checks on this program, when using provers CVC4, Alt-Ergo and Z3. This program was proposed as a formal verification challenge during VSTTE Verification Competition in 2014 (see http://vscomp.org/).

`prime_numbers`

This program implements two functions `Nearest_Number` and `Nearest_Prime_Number` which respectively find the closest coprime number and prime number for a given argument value and a given searching mode among three possibilities: above the value only, below the value only, or both. The spec of both functions is expressed in a `Contract_Cases` aspect, and proved automatically with GNATprove. GNATprove also proves automatically the functional contract of `Initialize_Coprime_List` which initializes the list of coprimes for a given argument, using Euclid's method, and returns this list to be used with `Nearest_Number`. The list of prime numbers is initialized at package elaboration using the sieve of Erathosthenes, a procedure which is currently not fully proved by GNATprove, due to the use of non-linear integer arithmetic and floating-point square root function.

This program offers a nice display of many SPARK features in a simple setting:

- *State Abstraction*
- *Subprogram Contracts*
- *Specification Features*
- *Loop Invariants*
- *Ghost Code*

The original code was contributed by Guillaume Foliard.

`red_black_trees`

This example demonstrates *Type Invariants* and *Manual Proof Using Ghost Code* on an implementation of red black trees. It features a minimalist library of trees providing only membership test and insertion. The complexity of this example lies in the invariants that are maintained on the data-structure. Namely, it implements a balanced binary search tree, balancing being enforced by red black coloring.

The implementation is divided in three layers, each concerned with only a part of the global data structure invariant. The first package, named `Binary_Trees`, is only concerned with the tree structure, whereas `Search_Trees` imposes ordering properties and `Red_Black_Trees` enforces balancing. At each level, the relevant properties are expressed using a `Type Invariant`. It allows to show each independent invariant at the boundary of its layer, assuming that it holds when working on upper layers.

The example features several particularities which make it complex beyond purely automated reasoning. First, the tree structure is encoded using references in an array, which makes it difficult to reason about disjointness of different branches of a tree. Then, reasoning about reachability in the tree structure requires induction, which is often out of the reach of automatic solvers. Finally, reasoning about value ordering is also a pain point for automatic solvers, as it requires coming up with intermediate values on which to apply transitivity.

To achieve full functional verification of this example, it resorts to manually helping automatic solvers using auto-active techniques. For example, ghost procedures are used to introduce intermediate lemmas, loop invariants are written to achieve inductive proofs, and assertions are introduced to provide new values to be used for transitivity relations.

This program and the verification activities associated to it are described in *"Auto-Active Proof of Red-Black Trees in SPARK"*, presented at NFM 2017 (at http://www.spark-2014.org/uploads/dross_moy_nfm_2017.pdf).

`railway_signaling`

This program implements a simple signaling algorithm to avoid collision of trains. The main procedure `Move` moving a given train along the railroad should preserve the collision-free property `One_Train_At_Most_Per_Track` and the correctness of signaling `Safe_Signaling`, namely that:

- tracks that are occupied by a train are signalled in red, and

- tracks that precede an occupied track are signalled in orange.

As the algorithm in Move relies on the correctness of the signaling, the preservation of the collision-free property depends also on the the correctness of the signaling. *Pragma Assume* is used to express an essential property of the railroad on which correctness depends, namely that no track precedes itself. GNATprove proves all checks on this program, when using provers CVC4, Alt-Ergo and Z3.

`ring_buffer`

This program implements a ring buffer stored in an array of fixed size, with partial contracts on the API of the ring buffer. GNATprove proves all checks on this program. This program was proposed as a formal verification challenge during VSTTE Verification Competition in 2012 (see https://sites.google.com/site/vstte2012/compet).

`segway`

This program implements a state machine controlling a segway states. The global invariant maintained across states is expressed in an expression function called from preconditions and postconditions. GNATprove proves all checks on this program.

`spark_book`

This collection of examples comes from the book *Building High Integrity Applications with SPARK* written by Prof. John McCormick from University of Northern Iowa and Prof. Peter Chapin from Vermont Technical College, published by Cambridge University Press:

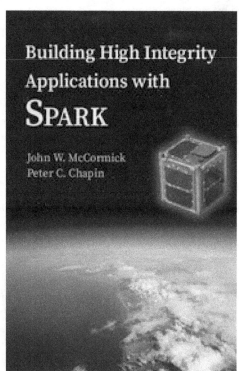

The examples follow the chapters of the book:

1. Introduction and overview

2. The basic SPARK language

3. Programming in the large

4. Dependency contracts

5. Mathematical background

6. Proof

7. Interfacing with SPARK

8. Software engineering with SPARK

9. Advanced techniques

Opening the example in GPS or GNATbench opens a project with all sources. Projects corresponding to individual chapters are available in subdirectories and can be opened manually.

The original source code is available from the publisher's website at http://www.cambridge.org/us/academic/subjects/ computer-science/programming-languages-and-applied-logic/building-high-integrity-applications-spark

tetris

This program implements a simple version of the game of Tetris. An invariant of the game is stated in function `Valid_Configuration`, that all procedures of the unit must maintain. This invariant depends on the state of the game which if updated by every procedure. Both the invariant and the state of the game are encoded as *Ghost Code*. The invariant expresses two properties:

1. A falling piece never exits the game board, and it does not overlap with pieces that have already fallen.

2. After a piece has fallen, the complete lines it may create are removed from the game board.

GNATprove proves all checks on the full version of this program found in `tetris_functional.adb`. Intermediate versions of the program show the initial code without any contracts in `tetris_initial.adb`, the code with contracts for data dependencies in `tetris_flow.adb` and the code with contracts to guard against run-time errors in `tetris_integrity.adb`. The complete program, including the BSP to run it on the ATMEL SAM4S board, is available online (see http://blog.adacore.com/tetris-in-spark-on-arm-cortex-m4).

tictactoe

This program implements a game of tic-tac-toe. A human player and the computer take turns. Subprograms `Player_Play` and `Computer_Play` in `tictactoe.ads` have partial contracts stating that the number of free slots decreases by one after each play.

GNATprove proves all absence of run-time errors on this program, and that the subprogram contracts are correctly implemented. Interestingly, no loop invariants are needed, although the program contains many loops, thanks to the use of *Automatic Unrolling of Simple For-Loops* in GNATprove.

traffic_light

This program implements two small simulators of traffic lights:

- Unit `Road_Traffic` defines safety rules for operating traffic lights over a crossroads. All procedures that change the state of the lights must maintain the safety property.

- Unit `Traffic_Lights` defines a concurrent program for operating traffic lights at a pedestian crossing, using two tasks that communicate over a protected object, where the invariant maintained by the protected data is expressed using a type predicate.

GNATprove proves all checks on this program, including the safe usage of concurrency (absence of data races, absence of deadlocks).

7.10.3 Multi-Units Demos

These examples contain larger demo programs (of a few hundreds or thousands slocs).

`autopilot`

This program was originally a case study written in SPARK 2005 by John Barnes, presented in section 14.3 of his book *"High Integrity Software, The SPARK Approach to Safety and Security"* (2003) and section 15.1 of the updated book *"SPARK: The Proven Approach to High Integrity Software"* (2012). For details on this case study, see one of the above books. The program in the toolset distribution is the SPARK 2014 version of this case study.

The program considers the control system of an autopilot controlling both altitude and heading of an aircraft. The altitude is controlled by manipulating the elevators and the heading is controlled by manipulating the ailerons and rudder.

The values given by instruments are modelled as *External State Abstraction* with asynchronous writers (the sensors) in package `Instruments`. The states of controllers are modelled as a *State Abstraction* called `State` in package `AP`, which is successively refined into finer-grain abstractions in the child packages of `AP` (for example `AP.Altitude` and `AP.Altitude.Pitch`). The actions on the mobile surfaces of the plane are modelled as *External State Abstraction* with asynchronous readers (the actuators) in package `Surfaces`.

Data and flow dependency contracts are given for all subprograms. GNATprove proves all checks on this program, except for 4 runtime checks related to scaling quantities using a division (a known limitation of automatic provers).

`bitwalker`

This program was originally a case study in C from Siemens rewritten by the Fraunhofer FOKUS research group for applying the Frama-C formal verification tool to it. It was later on rewritten in SPARK and formally proved correct with GNATprove (with 100% of checks automatically proved). This work is described in the article *"Specification and Proof of High-Level Functional Properties of Bit-Level Programs"* published at NFM 2016 conference (at https: //hal.inria.fr/hal-01314876).

This program introduces a function and procedure that read and respectively write a word of bits of a given length from a stream of bytes at a given position. It heavily uses bitwise arithmetic and is fully specified with contracts and automatically proved by GNATprove. In addition, two test procedures call read-then-write and write-then-read and GNATprove is able to prove the expected properties on the interplay between reading and writing.

In this program we use an external axiomatization in order to lift some operators from the underlying Why3 theory of bitvectors to SPARK. In particular the `Nth` function, at the core of the specification of the program, lets us check if a specific bit in a modular value is set or not. Note that while such a function could be easily implemented in SPARK, using the one defined in the Why3 theory leads to more automatic proofs because it lets the provers use the associated axioms and lemmas.

`crazyflie`

This program is a translation of the stabilization system of the Crazyflie 2.0, a tiny drone released by Bitcraze AB in 2013 and originally based on an open-source firmware written in C.

This SPARK code interfaces with the other parts of the firmware (ST peripheral libraries, FreeRTOS libraries, Crazyflie sensors and actuators), which remained in C, by using Ada capabilities for multi-language programs.

The goal was to prove absence of runtime errors on the most critical code parts of the drone's firmware. The techniques used to achieve this aim were presented in a post on the AdaCore Blog: http://blog.adacore.com/how-to-prevent-drone-crashes-using-spark

Data dependency contracts are given for most subprograms, specially in the `Stabilizer_Pack` package which uses *State Abstraction* to specify this type of contracts.

heatingsystem

This program is a standard example of controller, turning on and off the heating depending on the value of the current temperature read by a thermostat and the current mode of operation. Interfaces to the physical world are modelled as *External State Abstraction* for sensors and actuators. Data and flow dependency contracts are given for all subprograms. GNATprove proves all checks on this program.

ipstack

This program is an implementation of a TCP/IP stack targeted at bare-board embedded applications in certifiable systems. The API is an event driven architecture (based on LWIP design), with an application interface based on callbacks. The protocols supported are:

- IPv4
- ARP
- UDP
- TCP
- ICMP

This TCP/IP stack can be used either on a PowerPC bare-board system or on a Linux host as a native process. In the latter case, the TAP device is used for communication between the stack and the host system. For more details, see the corresponding README file.

Data dependency contracts are given for most subprograms. These contracts are proved by GNATprove flow analysis, which also proves the absence of reads of uninitialized data.

openETCS

This program is a case study performed by David Mentré in the context of the openETCS European project aiming at making an open-source, open-proof reference model of ETCS (European Train Control System). ETCS is a radio-based train control system aiming at unifying train signaling and control over all European countries. The results of this case study are described in the article *"Rail, Space, Security: Three Case Studies for SPARK 2014"*.

Package `Section_4_6` models a subset of the transitions allowed in the overall state automaton that the system should follow. Guards for transitions are expressed by using *Expression Functions*, and the disjointness of these guards is expressed by using *Contract Cases*. GNATprove proves all checks on this part of the program.

Package `Step_Function` implements piecewise constant functions used to model for example speed restrictions against distance. Full functional contracts are given for all the services of this package. GNATprove proves all checks on this part of the program, except the more complex postcondition of procedure `Restrictive_Merge`.

`sparkskein`

This program is an implementation of the Skein cryptographic hash algorithm (see http://www.skein-hash.info/). This implementation is readable, completely portable to a wide-variety of machines of differing word-sizes and endianness. This program was originally written in SPARK 2005 by Rod Chapman as a case study for the applicability of SPARK to cryptographic code. For details on this case study, see the article *"SPARKSkein: A Formal and Fast Reference Implementation of Skein"* (at http://www.adacore.com/knowledge/technical-papers/sparkskein/). The program in the toolset distribution is the SPARK 2014 version of this case study.

Compared to the original version written for the previous generation of the SPARK toolset, this version requires much less work to obtain complete assurance of the absence of run-time errors. In the following, we call a *precondition element* a conjunct in a precondition, *postcondition element* a conjunct in a postcondition and *loop invariant element* a conjunct in a loop invariant. The number of such elements in a verified program is directly related (usually proportional) to the verification effort, as each such element requires the user to write it, to debug it, and finally to prove it.

- Contrary to GNATprove, the previous toolset did not include *Generation of Dependency Contracts*. This required writing 17 non-trivial `global` contracts and 24 non-trivial `derives` contracts. With GNATprove, no data dependency or flow dependency is needed at all. We have kept 17 trivial null data dependency contracts and a single non-trivial data dependency contract for documentation purposes. Similarly, we have kept 11 trivial null flow dependency contracts for documentation purposes.

- SPARK naturally supports nesting of subprograms, which allows a natural top-down decomposition of the main operations into local procedures. This decomposition aids readability and has a negligible impact on performance, assuming the compiler is able to inline the local procedures, but it previously had a very costly impact on formal verification. The previous toolset required the user to write functional contracts on all local subprograms to be able to prove absence of run-time errors in these subprograms. On the contrary, GNATprove performs *Contextual Analysis of Subprograms Without Contracts*, which allows us to save the effort of writing 19 precondition elements and 12 postcondition elements that were needed in the original version.

- The previous toolset required the insertion of lengthy *Loop Invariants*, totalling 43 loop invariant elements (some of them quite complex), while GNATprove currently requires only 1 simple loop invariant stating which components of a record are not modified in the loop. This is partly due to GNATprove now being able to generate loop invariants for unmodified record components (see *Automatically Generated Loop Invariants*).

- The previous toolset generated a logical formula to prove for each path leading to a run-time check or an assertion. This lead to the generation of 367 formulas overall on the original version, almost 5 times more than the 78 checks generated by GNATprove on the new version. This difference is impressive, given that everything was done in the original version to control the explosion of the number of formulas, with the insertion of 24 special annotations in the source code similar to *Pragma Assert_And_Cut* in SPARK 2014, while no such work was needed in the new version. Despite this and other differences in efficiency between the two toolsets, the analysis time to ensure complete absence of run-time errors is similar between the two toolsets: 5 min with the previous toolset, half of that with GNATprove.

- Out of the 367 generated formulas, 29 were not proved automatically with the previous toolset: 6 formulas required the insertion of user-defined lemmas in the theorem prover, and 23 formulas required manual proof in a proof assistant. With GNATprove and provers CVC4, Z3 and Alt-Ergo, all checks are proved automatically.

`spark_io`

This program is an example wrapping of Ada standard input output library in a SPARK compatible library interface. For example, the standard unit `Ada.Text_IO` is wrapped in a unit called `SPARK.Text_IO` that provides the same services, but uses normal control flow to signal errors instead of exceptions. A type `File_Status` decribes either a normal status for a file (`Unopened` or `Success`) or an error status (`Status_Error`, `Mode_Error`, etc.). The standard type for a file `Ada.Text_IO.File_Type` is wrapped into a record type `SPARK.Text_IO_File_Type` together with the status described above.

Wrapper units are also given for most children of the Ada standard input output library `Ada.Text_IO`, for example the generic unit `SPARK.Text_IO.Integer_IO` wraps the services of the standard unit `Ada.Text_IO.Integer_IO`. Partial function contracts are expressed on all subprograms. GNATprove proves all checks on the implementation of these wrapper units.

text_io_get_line

This program is a simplified extracted version of the standard library function `Ada.Text_IO.Get_Line`, which reads a line of text from an input file. The various versions of `Ada.Text_IO.Get_Line` (procedures and functions) are specified with respect to a simplified model of the file system, with a single file `The_File` opened at a location `Cur_Location`. The low-level functions providing an efficient implementation (`fgets`, `memcpy`, etc.) are also specified with respect to the same model of the file system.

GNATprove proves automatically that the code is free of run-time errors (apart from a few messages that are either intentional or related to the ghost code instrumentation) and that subprogram bodies respect their functional contracts. The story behind this work was presented in a post on the AdaCore Blog: http://blog.adacore.com/formal-verification-of-legacy-code

thumper

This program is a secure time stamp client/server system that implements RFC-3161 (see https://www.ietf.org/rfc/rfc3161.txt). It allows clients to obtain cryptographic time stamps that can be used to later verify that certain documents existed on or before the time mentioned in the time stamp. Thumper is written in a combination of Ada 2012 and SPARK 2014 and makes use of an external C library. Thumper was developed as a SPARK technology demonstration by Prof. Peter Chapin from Vermont Technical College and his students. It is used as a case study in the book *Building High Integrity Applications with SPARK* written by Prof. John McCormick from University of Northern Iowa and Prof. Peter Chapin, published by Cambridge University Press (see section 8.5).

The program in the toolset distribution is a snapshot of the Thumper project and a supporting project providing ASN.1 support named Hermes, whose up-to-date sources can be obtained separately from GitHub:

- Thumper at https://github.com/pchapin/thumper
- Hermer at https://github.com/pchapin/hermes

The verification objectives pursued in both projects are currently to *Address Data and Control Coupling* with a focus on ensuring secure information flows (especially important for a cryptographic application) and to *Prove Absence of Run-Time Errors (AoRTE)*.

tokeneer

This program is a highly secure biometric software system that was originally developed by Altran. The system provides protection to secure information held on a network of workstations situated in a physically secure enclave. The Tokeneer project was commissioned by the US National Security Agency (NSA) to demonstrate the feasibility of developing systems to the level of rigor required by the higher assurance levels of the Common Criteria. The requirements of the system were captured using the Z notation and the implementation was in SPARK 2005. The original development artifacts, including all source code, are publicly available (see http://www.adacore.com/sparkpro/tokeneer).

The program in the toolset distribution is a translation of the original Tokeneer code into SPARK 2014. The core system now consists of approximately 10,000 lines of SPARK 2014 code. There are also approximately 3,700 lines of supporting code written in Ada which mimic the drivers to peripherals connected to the core system.

Data and flow dependency contracts are given for all subprograms. Partial functional contracts are also given for a subset of subprograms. GNATprove currently proves automatically 90% of all checks in Tokeneer.

APPLYING SPARK IN PRACTICE

SPARK tools offer different levels of analysis, which are relevant in different contexts. This section starts with a description of the main *Objectives of Using SPARK*. This list gathers the most commonly found reasons for adopting SPARK in industrial projects, but it is not intended to be an exhaustive list.

Whatever the objective(s) of using SPARK, any project fits in one of four possible *Project Scenarios*:

- the *brown field* scenario: *Maintenance and Evolution of Existing Ada Software*

- the *green field* scenario: *New Developments in SPARK*

- the *migration* scenario: *Conversion of Existing SPARK Software to SPARK 2014*

- the *frozen* scenario: *Analysis of Frozen Ada Software*

The end of this section examines each of these scenarios in turn and describes how SPARK can be applied in each case.

8.1 Objectives of Using SPARK

8.1.1 Safe Coding Standard for Critical Software

SPARK is a subset of Ada meant for formal verification, by excluding features that are difficult or impossible to analyze automatically. This means that SPARK can also be used as a coding standard to restrict the set of features used in critical software. As a safe coding standard checker, SPARK allows both to prevent the introduction of errors by excluding unsafe Ada features, and it facilitates their early detection with GNATprove's flow analysis.

Exclusion of Unsafe Ada Features

Once the simple task of *Identifying SPARK Code* has been completed, one can use GNATprove in check mode to verify that SPARK restrictions are respected in SPARK code. Here we list some of the most error-prone Ada features that are excluded from SPARK (see *Excluded Ada Features* for the complete list).

- All expressions, including function calls, are free of side-effects. Expressions with side-effects are problematic because they hide interactions that occur in the code, in the sense that a computation will not only produce a value but also modify some hidden state in the program. In the worst case, they may even introduce interferences between subexpressions of a common expression, which results in different executions depending on the order of evaluation of subexpressions chosen by the compiler.

- Handling of exceptions is not permitted. Exception handling can create complex and invisible control flows in a program, which increases the likelihood of introducing errors during maintenance. What is more, when an exception is raised, subprograms that are terminated abnormally leave their variables in a possibly uninitialized or inconsistent state, in which data invariants may be broken. This includes values of out parameters, which additionnally are not copied back when passed by copy, thus introducing a dependency on the parameter mode chosen by the compiler.

- The use of access types and allocators is not permitted. Pointers can introduce aliasing, that is, they can allow the same object to be visible through different names at the same program point. This makes it difficult to reason about a program as modifying the object under one of the names will also modify the other names. What is more, access types come with their own load of common mistakes, like double frees and dangling pointers.

- SPARK also prevents dependencies on the elaboration order by ensuring that no package can write into variables declared in other packages during its elaboration. The use of controlled types is also forbidden as they lead to insertions of implicit calls by the compiler. Finally, goto statements are not permitted as they obfuscate the control flow.

Early Detection of Errors

GNATprove's flow analysis will find all the occurrences of the following errors:

- uses of uninitialized variables (see *Data Initialization Policy*)

- aliasing of parameters that can cause interferences, which are often not accounted for by programmers (see *Absence of Interferences*)

It will also warn systematically about the following suspicious behaviors:

- wrong parameter modes (can hurt readability and maintainability or even be the sign of a bug, for example if the programmer forgot to update a parameter, to read the value of an out parameter, or to use the initial value of a parameter)

- unused variables or statements (again, can hurt readability and maintainability or even be the sign of a bug)

8.1.2 Prove Absence of Run-Time Errors (AoRTE)

With Proof Only

GNATprove can be used to prove the complete absence of possible run-time errors corresponding to:

- all possible explicit raising of exceptions in the program,

- raising exception `Constraint_Error` at run time, and

- all possible failures of assertions corresponding to raising exception `Assert_Error` at run time.

AoRTE is important for ensuring safety in all possible operational conditions for safety-critical software (including boundary conditions, or abnormal conditions) or for ensuring availability of a service (absence of DOS attack that can crash the software).

When run-time checks are enabled during execution, Ada programs are not vulnerable to the kind of attacks like buffer overflows that plague programs in C and C++, which allow attackers to gain control over the system. But in the case where run-time checks are disabled (in general for efficiency, but it could be for other reasons), proving their absence with GNATprove also prevents such attacks. This is specially important for ensuring security when some inputs may have been crafted by an attacker.

Few subprogram contracts (*Preconditions* and *Postconditions*) are needed in general to prove AoRTE, far fewer than for proving functional properties. Even fewer subprogram contracts are needed if types are suitably constrained with *Type Contracts*. Typically, 95% to 98% of run-time checks can be proved automatically, and the remaining checks can be either verified with manual provers or justified by manual analysis.

GNATprove supports this type of combination of results in *The Analysis Results Summary Table*. Multiple columns display the number of checks automatically verified, while the column *Justified* displays the number of checks manually justified. The column *Unproved* should be empty for all checks to be verified.

With a Combination of Proof and Test

It is not always possible to achieve 100% proof of AoRTE, for multiple reasons:

1. Formal verification is only applicable to the part of the program that is in SPARK. If the program includes parts in Ada that are not in SPARK, for example, then it is not possible to prove AoRTE on those parts.

2. Some run-time checks may not be proved automatically due to prover shortcomings (see *Investigating Prover Shortcomings* for details).

3. It may not be cost-effective to add the required contracts for proving AoRTE in a less critical part of the code, compared to using testing as a means of verification.

For all these reasons, it is important to be able to combine the results of formal verification and testing on different parts of a codebase. Formal verification works by making some assumptions, and these assumptions should be shown to hold even when formal verification and testing are combined. Certainly, formal verification cannot guarantee the same properties when part of a program is only tested, as when all of a program is proved. The goal then, when combining formal verification and testing, is to reach a level of confidence as good as the level reached by testing alone.

At the Level of Individual Run-Time Checks

One way to get confidence that unproved run-time checks cannot fail during execution is to exercise them during testing. Test coverage information allows to guarantee a set of run-time checks have been executed successfully during a test run. This coverage information may be gathered from the execution of a unit testing campaign, an integration testing campaign, or the execution of a dedicated testsuite focussing on exercizing the run-time checks (for example on boundary values or random ones).

This strategy is already applied in other static analysis tools, for example in the integration between the CodePeer static analyzer and the VectorCAST testing tool for Ada programs.

Between Proof and Integration Testing

Contracts can also be exercised dynamically during integration testing. In cases where unit testing is not required (either because proof has been applied to all subprograms, or because the verification context allows it), exercizing contracts during integration testing can complement proof results, by giving the assurance that the actual compiled program behaves as expected.

This strategy has been applied at Altran on UK military projects submitted to Def Stan 00-56 certification: AoRTE was proved on all the code, and contracts were exercised during integration testing, which allowed to scrap unit testing.

Between Proof and Unit Testing

Contracts on subprograms provide a natural boundary for combining proof and test:

- If proof is used to demonstrate that a subprogram is free of run-time errors and respects its contract, this proof depends on the precondition of the subprogram being respected at the call site. This verification can be achieved by proving the caller too, or by checking dynamically the precondition of the called subprogram during unit testing of the caller.

- If proof is used to demonstrate that a subprogram is free of run-time errors and respects its contract, and this subprogram calls other subprograms, this proof depends on the postconditions of the called subprogram being respected at call sites. This verification can be achieved by proving the callees too, or by checking dynamically the postcondition of the called subprograms during their unit testing.

Thus, it is possible to combine freely subprograms that are proved and subprograms that are unit tested, provided subprogram contracts (*Preconditions* and *Postconditions*) are exercised during unit testing. This can be achieved by compiling the program with assertions for testing (for example with switch `-gnata` in GNAT), or by using GNATtest to create the test harness (see section 7.10.12 of GNAT User's Guide on *Testing with Contracts*).

When combining proof and test on individual subprograms, one should make sure that the assumptions made for proof are justified at the boundary between proved subprograms and tested subprograms (see section on *Managing Assumptions*). To help with this verification, special switches are defined in GNAT to add run-time checks that verify dynamically the assumptions made during proof:

- `-gnateA` adds checks that parameters are not aliased

- `-gnateV` adds checks that parameters are valid, including parameters of composite types (arrays, records)

- `-gnatVa` adds checks that objects are valid at more places than -gnateV, but only for scalar objects

This strategy is particularly well suited in the context of the DO-178C certification standard in avionics, which explicitly allows proof or test to be used as verification means on each module.

8.1.3 Prove Correct Integration Between Components

In New Developments

GNATprove can be used to prove correct integration between components, where a component could be a subprogram, a unit or a set of units. Indeed, even if components are verified individually (for example by proof or test or a combination thereof), their combination may still fail because of unforeseen interactions or design problems.

SPARK is ideally equiped to support such analysis, with its detailed *Subprogram Contracts*:

- With *Data Dependencies*, a user can specify exactly the input and output data of a subprogram, which goes a long way towards uncovering unforeseen interactions.

- With functional contracts (*Preconditions* and *Postconditions*), a user can specify precisely properties about the behavior of the subprogram that are relevant for component integration. In general, simple contracts are needed for component integration, which means that they are easy to write and to verify automatically. See section on *Writing Contracts for Program Integrity* for examples of such contracts.

When using data dependencies, GNATprove's flow analysis is sufficient to check correct integration between components. When using functional contracts, GNATprove's proof should also be applied.

In Replacement of Comments

It is good practice to specify properties of a subprogram that are important for integration in the comments that are attached to the subprogram declaration.

Comments can be advantageously replaced by contracts:

- Comments about the domain of the subprogram can be replaced by *Preconditions*.

- Comments about the effects of the subprogram can be replaced by *Postconditions* and *Data Dependencies*.

- Comments about the result of functions can be replaced by *Postconditions*.

- GNATprove can use the contracts to prove correct integration between components, as in new developments.

Contracts are less ambiguous than comments, and can be accompanied by (or interspersed with) higher level comments than need not be focused on the finer grain details of which variables must have which values, as these are already specified concisely and precisely in the contracts.

In Replacement of Defensive Coding

In existing Ada code that is migrated to SPARK, defensive coding is typically used to verify the correct integration between components: checks are made at the start of a subprogram that inputs (parameters and global variables) satisfy expected properties, and an exception is raised or the program halted if an unexpected situation is found.

Defensive code can be advantageously replaced by preconditions:

- The dynamic checks performed by defensive code at run time can be performed equally by preconditions, and they can be enabled at a much finer grain thanks to *Pragma Assertion_Policy*.

- GNATprove can use the preconditions to prove correct integration between components, as in new developments.

8.1.4 Prove Functional Correctness

In New Developments

GNATprove can be used to prove functional correctness of an implementation against its specification. This strongest level of verification can be applied either to specific subprograms, or specific units, or the complete program. For those subprograms whose functional correctness is to be checked, the user should:

1. express the specification of the subprogram as a subprogram contract (see *Preconditions* and *Postconditions*);

2. use GNATprove to prove automatically that most checks (including contracts) always hold; and

3. address the remaining unproved checks with manual justifications or testing, as already discussed in the section on how to *Prove Absence of Run-Time Errors (AoRTE)*.

As more complex contracts are required in general, it is expected that achieving that strongest level of verification is also more costly than proving absence of run-time errors. Typically, SPARK features like *Quantified Expressions* and *Expression Functions* are needed to express the specification, and features like *Loop Invariants* are needed to achieve automatic proof. See section on *Writing Contracts for Functional Correctness* for examples of such contracts, and section on *How to Write Loop Invariants* for examples of the required loop invariants.

When the functional specification is expressed as a set of disjoint cases, the SPARK feature of *Contract Cases* can be used to increase readability and to provide an automatic means to verify that cases indeed define a partitioning of the possible operational contexts.

In Replacement of Unit Testing

In existing Ada code that is migrated to SPARK, unit testing is typically used to verify functional correctness: actual outputs obtained when calling the subprogram are compared to expected outputs for given inputs. A *test case* defines an expected behavior to verify; a *test procedure* implements a *test case* with specific given inputs and expected outputs.

Test cases can be used as a basis for functional contracts, as they define in general a behavior for a set of similar inputs. Thus, a set of test cases can be transformed into *Contract Cases*, where each case corresponds to a test case: the test input constraint becomes the guard of the corresponding case, while the test output constraint becomes the consequence of the corresponding case.

GNATprove can be used to prove this initial functional contract, as in new developments. Then, cases can be progressively generalized (by relaxing the conditions in the guards), or new cases added to the contract, until the full functional behavior of the subprogram is specified and proved.

8.1.5 Ensure Correct Behavior of Parameterized Software

In some domains (railway, space), it is common to develop software which depends on parameterization data, which changes from mission to mission. For example, the layout of railroads or the characteristics of the payload for a spacecraft are mission specific, but in general do not require developing completely new software for the mission. Instead, the software may either depend on data definition units which are subject to changes between missions, or the software may load at starting time (possibly during *elaboration* in Ada) the data which defines the characteristics of the mission. Then, the issue is that a verification performed on a specific version of the software (for a given parameterization) is not necessarily valid for all versions of the software. In general, this means that verification has to be performed again for each new version of the software, which can be costly.

SPARK provides a better solution to ensure correct behavior of the software for all possible parameterizations. It requires defining a getter function for every variable or constant in the program that represents an element of parameterization, and calling this getter function instead of reading the variable or constant directly. Because GNATprove performs an analysis based on contracts, all that is known at analysis time about the value returned by a getter function is what is available from its signature and contract. Typically, one may want to use *Scalar Ranges* or *Predicates* to constrain the return type of such getter functions, to reflect the operational constraints respected by all parameterizations.

This technique ensures that the results of applying GNATprove are valid not only for the version of the software analyzed, but for any other version that satisfies the same operational constraints. This is valid whatever the objective(s) pursued with the use of SPARK: *Prove Absence of Run-Time Errors (AoRTE)*, *Prove Correct Integration Between Components*, *Prove Functional Correctness*, etc.

It may be the case that changing constants into functions makes the code illegal because the constants were used in representation clauses that require static values. In that case, compilation switch -gnatI should be specified when analyzing the modified code with GNATprove, so that representation clauses are ignored. As representation clauses have no effect on GNATprove's analysis, and their validity is checked by GNAT when compiling the original code, the formal verification results are valid for the original code.

For constants of a non-scalar type (for example, constants of record or array type), an alternative way to obtain a similar result as the getter function is to define the constant as a deferred constant, whose initial declaration in the visible part of a package spec does not specify the value of the constant. Then, the private part of the package spec which defines the completion of the deferred constant must be marked SPARK_Mode => Off, so that clients of the package only see the visible constant declaration without value. In such a case, the analysis of client units with GNATprove is valid for all possible values of the constant.

8.1.6 Safe Optimization of Run-Time Checks

Enabling run-time checks in a program usually increases the running time by around 10%. This may not fit the timing schedule in some highly constrained applications. In some cases where a piece of code is called a large number of times (for example in a loop), enabling run-time checks on that piece of code may increase the running time by far more than 10%. Thus, it may be tempting to remove run-time checking in the complete program (with compilation switch -gnatp) or a selected piece of code (with pragma Suppress), for the purpose of decreasing running time. The problem with that approach is that the program is not protected anymore against programming mistakes (for safety) or attackers (for security).

GNATprove provides a better solution, by allowing users to prove the absence of all run-time errors (or run-time errors of a specific kind, for example overflow checks) in a piece of code, provided the precondition of the enclosing subprogram is respected. Then, all run-time checks (or run-time errors of a specific kind) can be suppressed in that piece of code using pragma Suppress, knowing that they will never fail at run time, provided the precondition of the enclosing subprogram is checked (for example by using *Pragma Assertion_Policy*). By replacing many checks with one check, we can decrease the running time of the application by doing safe and controlled optimization of run-time checks.

8.1.7 Address Data and Control Coupling

As defined in the avionics standard DO-178, data coupling is *"The dependence of a software component on data not exclusively under the control of that software component"* and control coupling is *"The manner or degree by which one software component influences the execution of another software component"*, where a software component could be a subprogram, a unit or a set of units.

Although analysis of data and control coupling are not performed at the same level of details in non-critical domains, knowledge of data and control coupling is important to assess impact of code changes. In particular, it may be critical for security that some secret data does not leak publicly, which can be rephrased as saying that only the specified data dependencies are allowed. SPARK is ideally equiped to support such analysis, with its detailed *Subprogram Contracts*:

- With *Data Dependencies*, a user can specify exactly the input and output data of a subprogram, which identifies the *"data not exclusively under the control of that software component"*:

  - When taking the subprogram as component, any variable in the data dependencies is in general not exclusively under the control of that software component.

  - When taking the unit (or sets of units) as component, any variable in the data dependencies that is not defined in the unit itself (or the set of units) is in general not exclusively under the control of that software component.

- With *Flow Dependencies*, a user can specify the nature of the *"dependence of a software component on data not exclusively under the control of that software component"*, by identifying how that data may influence specific outputs of a subprogram.

- With *Flow Dependencies*, a user can also specify how *"one software component influences the execution of another software component"*, by identifying the shared data potentially written by the subprogram.

- With functional contracts (*Preconditions* and *Postconditions*), a user can specify very precisely the behavior of the subprogram, which defines how it *"influences the execution of another software component"*. These contracts need not be complete, for example they could describe the precedence order rules for calling various subprograms.

When using data and flow dependencies, GNATprove's flow analysis is sufficient to check that the program implements its specifications. When using functional contracts, GNATprove's proof should also be applied.

8.1.8 Ensure Portability of Programs

Using SPARK enhances portability of programs by excluding language features that are known to cause portability problems, and by making it possible to obtain guarantees that specific portability problems cannot occur. In particular, analyses of SPARK code can prove the absence of run-time errors in the program, and that specified functional properties always hold.

Still, porting a SPARK program written for a given compiler and target to another compiler and/or target may require changes in the program. As SPARK is a subset of Ada, and because in general only some parts of a complete program are in SPARK, we need to consider first the issue of portability in the context of Ada, and then specialize it in the context of SPARK.

Note that we consider here portability in its strictest sense, whereby a program is portable if its observable behavior is exactly the same across a change of compiler and/or target. In the more common sense of the word, a program is portable if it can be reused without modification on a different target, or when changing compiler. That is consistent with the definition of portability in WikiPedia: "Portability in high-level computer programming is the usability of the same software in different environments". As an example of a difference between both interpretations, many algorithms which use trigonometry are portable in the more common sense, not in the strictest sense.

Portability of Ada Programs

Programs with errors cause additional portability issues not seen in programs without errors, which is why we consider them separately.

Portability of Programs Without Errors

The Ada Reference Manual defines precisely which features of the language depend on choices made by the compiler (see Ada RM 1.1.3 "Conformity of an Implementation with the Standard"):

- *Implementation defined behavior* - The set of possible behaviors is specified in the language, and the particular behavior chosen in a compiler should be documented. An example of implementation defined behavior is the size of predefined integer types (like `Integer`). All implementation defined behaviors are listed in Ada RM M.2, and GNAT documents its implementation for each of these points in section 7 "Implementation Defined Characteristics" of the GNAT Reference Manual.

- *Unspecified behavior* - The set of possible behaviors is specified in the language, but the particular behavior chosen in a compiler need not be documented. An example of unspecified behavior is the order of evaluation of arguments in a subprogram call.

Changes of compiler and/or target may lead to different implementation defined and unspecified behavior, which may or not have a visible effect. For example, changing the order of evaluation of arguments in a subprogram call only has a visible effect if the evaluation of arguments itself has some side-effects.

Section 18.4 "Implementation-dependent characteristics" of the GNAT Reference Manual gives some advice on how to address implementation defined behavior for portability.

A particular issue is that the Ada Reference Manual gives much implementation freedom to the compiler in the implementation of operations of fixed-point and floating-point types:

- The small of a fixed-point type is implementation defined (Ada RM 3.5.9(8/2)) unless specified explicitly.

- The base type of a fixed-point type is implementation defined (Ada RM 3.5.9(12-16)), which has an impact on possible overflows.

- The rounded result of an ordinary fixed-point multiplication or division is implementation defined (Ada RM G.2.3(10)).

- For some combinations of types of operands and results for fixed-point multiplication and division, the value of the result belongs to an implementation defined set of values (Ada RM G.2.3(5)).

- The semantics of operations on floating-point types is implementation defined (Ada RM G.2). It may or may not follow the IEEE 754 floating point standard.

- The precision of elementary functions (exponential and trigonometric functions) is implementation defined (Ada RM G.2.4).

Section 18.1 "Writing Portable Fixed-Point Declarations" of the GNAT Reference Manual gives some advice on how to reduce implementation defined behavior for fixed-point types. Use of IEEE 754 floating-point arithmetic can be enforced in GNAT by using the compilation switches "-msse2 -mfpmath=sse", as documented in section 8.3.1.6 "Floating Point Operations" of the GNAT User's Guide.

Note that a number of restrictions can be used to prevent some features leading to implementation defined or unspecified behavior:

- Restriction `No_Fixed_Point` forbids the use of fixed-point types.

- Restriction `No_Floating_Point` forbids the use of floating-point types.

- Restriction `No_Implementation_Aspect_Specifications` forbids the use of implementation defined aspects.

- Restriction `No_Implementation_Attributes` forbids the use of implementation defined attributes.

- Restriction `No_Implementation_Pragmas` forbids the use of implementation defined pragmas.

Note: SPARK defines a few constructs (aspects, pragmas and attributes) that are not defined in Ada. While GNAT supports these constructs, care should be exercised to use these constructs with other compilers, or older versions of GNAT. This issue is detailed in section *Portability Issues*.

Portability of Programs With Errors

In addition to the portability issues discussed so far, programs with errors cause specific portability issues related to whether errors are detected and how they are reported. The Ada Reference Manual distinguishes between four types of errors (see Ada RM 1.1.5 "Classification of Errors"):

- *Compile-time errors* - These errors make a program illegal, and should be detected by any Ada compiler. They do not cause any portability issue, as they must be fixed before compilation.

- *Run-time errors* - These errors are signaled by raising an exception at run time. They might be a cause of portability problems, as a change of compiler and/or target may lead to new run-time errors. For example, a new compiler may cause the program to use more stack space, leading to an exception `Storage_Error`, and a new target may change the size of standard integer types, leading to an exception `Constraint_Error`.

- *Bounded errors* - These errors need not be detected either at compiler time or at run time, but their effects should be bounded. For example, reading an uninitialized value may result in any value of the type to be used, or to `Program_Error` being raised. Like for run-time errors, they might be a cause of portability problems, as a change of compiler and/or target may lead to new bounded errors.

- *Erroneous execution* - For the remaining errors, a program exhibits erroneous execution, which means that the error need not be detected, and its effects are not bounded by the language rules. These errors might be a cause of portability problems.

Portability issues may arise in a number of cases related to errors:

- The original program has an error that is not detected (a run-time error, bounded error or erroneous execution). Changing the compiler and/or target causes the error to be detected (an exception is raised) or to trigger a different behavior. Typically, reads of uninitialized data or illegal accesses to memory that are not detected in the original program may result in errors when changing the compiler and/or the target.

- The original program has no error, but changing the compiler and/or target causes an error to appear, which may or not be detected. Typically, uses of low-level constructs like `Unchecked_Conversion` which depend on the exact representation of values in bits may lead to errors when changing the compiler and/or the target. Some run-time errors like overflow errors or storage errors are also particularly sensitive to compiler and target changes.

To avoid portability issues, errors should be avoided by using suitable analyses and reviews in the context of the original and the new compiler and/or target. Whenever possible, these analyses and reviews should be automated by tools to guarantee that all possible errors of a given kind have been reported.

Benefits of Using SPARK for Portability

The *Language Restrictions* in SPARK favor portability by excluding problematic language features (see *Excluded Ada Features*):

- By excluding side-effects in expressions, SPARK programs cannot suffer from effects occurring in different orders depending on the order of evaluation of expressions chosen by the compiler.

- By excluding aliasing, the behavior of SPARK programs does not depend on the parameter passing mechanism (by copy or by reference) or the order of assignment to out and in-out parameters passed by copy after the call, which are both chosen by the compiler.

- By excluding controlled types, SPARK programs cannot suffer from the presence and ordering of effects taking place as part of the initialization, assignment and finalization of controlled objects, which depend on choices made by the compiler.

As permitted by the SPARK language rules (see section 1.4.1 "Further Details on Formal Verification" of the SPARK Reference Manual), GNATprove rejects with an error programs which may implicitly raise a `Program_Error` in parts of code that are in SPARK. For example, all static execution paths in a SPARK function should end with a return statement, a raise statement, or a `pragma Assert (False)`. GNATprove's analysis can be further used to ensure that dynamic executions can only end in a return.

GNATprove reduces portability issues related to the use of fixed-point and floating-point values:

- GNATprove supports a subset of fixed-point types and operations that ensures that the result of an operation always belongs to the *perfect result set* as defined in Ada RM G.2.3. Note that the perfect result set still contains in general two values (the two model fixed-point values above and below the perfect mathematical result), which means that two compilers may give two different results for multiplication and division. Users should thus avoid multiplication and division of fixed-point values for maximal portability. See *Tool Limitations*.

- GNATprove assumes IEEE 754 standard semantics for basic operations of floating-point types (addition, subtraction, multiplication, division). With GNAT, this is achieved by using compilation switches "-msse2 -mfpmath=sse". Users should still avoid elementary functions (exponential and trigonometric functions) for maximal portability. See *Semantics of Floating Point Operations*.

Additionally, GNATprove can detect all occurrences of specific portability issues in SPARK code (that is, parts of the program for which SPARK_Mode=On is specified, see section on *Identifying SPARK Code*) when run in specific modes (see *Effect of Mode on Output* for a description of the different modes):

- In all modes (including mode `check`), when switch `--pedantic` is set, GNATprove issues a warning for every arithmetic operation which could be re-ordered by the compiler, thus leading to a possible overflow with one compiler and not another. For example, arithmetic operation `A + B + C` can be interpreted as `(A + B) + C` by one compiler, and `A + (B + C)` (after re-ordering) by another compiler. Note that GNAT always uses the former version without re-ordering. See *Parenthesized Arithmetic Operations*.

- In modes `flow`, `prove` and `all`, GNATprove issues high check messages on possible parameter aliasing, when such an aliasing may lead to interferences. This includes all cases where the choice of parameter passing mechanism in a compiler (by copy or by reference) might influence the behavior of the subprogram. See *Absence of Interferences*.

- In modes `flow`, `prove` and `all`, GNATprove issues check messages on possible reads of uninitialized data. These messages should be reviewed with respect to the stricter *Data Initialization Policy* in SPARK rather than in Ada. Hence, it is possible when the program does not conform to the stricter SPARK rules to manually validate them, see section *Justifying Check Messages*.

- In modes `prove` and `all`, GNATprove issues check messages on all possible run-time errors corresponding to raising exception `Constraint_Error` at run time, all possible failures of assertions corresponding to raising exception `Assert_Error` at run time, and all possible explicit raising of exceptions in the program.

The analysis of GNATprove can take into account characteristics of the target (size and alignment of standard scalar types, endianness) by specifying a *Target Parameterization*.

How to Use SPARK for Portability

GNATprove's analysis may be used to enhance the portability of programs. Note that the guarantees provided by this analysis only hold for the source program. To ensure that these guarantees extend to the executable object code, one should independently provide assurance that the object code correctly implements the semantics of the source code.

Avoiding Non-Portable Features

As much as possible, uses of non-portable language features should be avoided, or at least isolated in specific parts of the program to facilitate analyses and reviews when changing the compiler and/or the target.

This includes in particular language features that deal with machine addresses, data representations, interfacing with assembler code, and similar issues (for example, language attribute Size). When changing the compiler and/or the target, the program logic should be carefully reviewed for possible dependences on the original compiler behavior and/or original target characteristics. See also the section 18.4.5 "Target-specific aspects" of the GNAT Reference Manual.

In particular, features that bypass the type system of Ada for reinterpreting values (Unchecked_Conversion) and memory locations (Address clause overlays, in which multiple objects are defined to share the same address, something that can also be achieved by sharing the same Link_Name or External_Name) have no impact on SPARK analysis, yet they may lead to portability issues.

By using the following restrictions (or a subset thereof), one can ensure that the corresponding non-portable features are not used in the program:

```
pragma No_Dependence (Ada.Unchecked_Conversion);
pragma No_Dependence (System.Machine_code);
```

Similarly, the program logic should be carefully reviewed for possible dependency on target characteristics (for example, the size of standard integer types). GNATprove's analysis may help here as it can take into account the characteristics of the target. Hence, proofs of functional properties with GNATprove ensure that these properties will always hold on the target.

In the specific case that the target is changing, it might be useful to run GNATprove's analysis on the program in proof mode, even if it cannot prove completely the absence of run-time errors and that the specified functional properties (if any) hold. Indeed, by running GNATprove twice, once with the original target and once with the new target, comparing the results obtained in both cases might point to parts of the code that are impacted by the change of target, which may require more detailed manual reviews.

Apart from non-portable language features and target characteristics, non-portability in SPARK may come from a small list of causes:

- Possible re-ordering of non-parenthesized arithmetic operations. These can be detected by running GNATprove (see *Benefits of Using SPARK for Portability*). Then, either these operations may not be re-ordered by the compiler (for example, GNAT ensures this property), or re-ordering may not lead to an intermediate overflow (for example, if the base type is large enough), or the user may introduce parentheses to prevent re-ordering.

- Possible aliasing between parameters (or parameters and global variables) of a call causing interferences. These can be detected by running GNATprove (see *Benefits of Using SPARK for Portability*). Then, either aliasing is not possible in reality, or aliasing may not cause different behaviors depending on the parameter passing mechanism chosen in the compiler, or the user may change the code to avoid aliasing. When SPARK subprograms are called from non-SPARK code (for example Ada or C code), manual reviews should be performed to ensure that these calls cannot introduce aliasing between parameters, or between parameters and global variables.

- Possible different choices of base type for user-defined integer types (contrary to derived types or subtypes, which inherit their base type from their parent type). GNATprove follows GNAT in choosing as base type the smallest multiple-words-size integer type that contains the type bounds. For example, a user-defined type ranging from 1 to 100 will be given a base type ranging from -128 to 127 by both GNAT and GNATprove. The choice of base types influences in which cases intermediate overflows may be raised during computation. The choice made in GNATprove is the strictest one among existing compilers, as far as we know, which ensures that GNATprove's analysis detects a superset of the overflows that may occur at run time.

- Issues related to errors. See section *Avoiding Errors to Enhance Portability*.

- Issues related to the use of fixed-point or floating-point operations. See section *Portability of Fixed-Point and Floating-Point Computations* below.

Avoiding Errors to Enhance Portability

Because errors in a program make portability particularly challenging (see *Portability of Programs With Errors*), it is important to ensure that a program is error-free for portability. GNATprove's analysis can help by ensuring that the SPARK parts of a program are free from broad kinds of errors:

- all possible reads of uninitialized data

- all possible explicit raise of exceptions in the program

- all possible run-time errors except raising exception `Storage_Error`, corresponding to raising exception `Program_Error`, `Constraint_Error` or `Tasking_Error` at run time

- all possible failures of assertions corresponding to raising exception `Assert_Error` at run time

When parts of the program are not in SPARK (for example, in Ada or C), the results of GNATprove's analysis depend on assumptions on the correct behavior of the non-SPARK code. For example, callers of a SPARK subprogram should only pass initialized input values, and non-SPARK subprograms called from SPARK code should respect their postcondition. See section *Managing Assumptions* for the complete list of assumptions.

In particular, when changing the target characteristics, GNATprove's analysis can be used to show that no possible overflow can occur as a result of changing the size of standard integer types.

GNATprove's analysis does not detect possible run-time errors corresponding to raising exception `Storage_Error` at run time, which should be independently assessed. Because access types and dynamic allocation are forbidden in SPARK, the only possible cause for raising exception `Storage_Error` in a SPARK program is overflowing the stack.

Portability of Fixed-Point and Floating-Point Computations

Portability issues related to the use of fixed-point or floating-point operations can be avoided altogether by ensuring that the program does not use fixed-point or floating-point values, using:

```
pragma Restrictions (No_Fixed_Point);
pragma Restrictions (No_Floating_Point);
```

When fixed-point values are used, the value of the small and size in bits for the type should be specified explicitly, as documented in section 18.1 "Writing Portable Fixed-Point Declarations" of the GNAT Reference Manual:

```
My_Small : constant := 2.0**(-15);
My_First : constant := -1.0;
My_Last  : constant := +1.0 - My_Small;

type F2 is delta My_Small range My_First .. My_Last;
for F2'Small use my_Small;
for F2'Size  use 16;
```

The program should also avoid multiplication and division of fixed-point values to ensure that the result of arithmetic operations is exactly defined.

When floating-point values are used, use of IEEE 754 standard semantics for basic operations of floating-point types (addition, subtraction, multiplication, division) should be enforced. With GNAT, this is achieved by using compilation switches "-msse2 -mfpmath=sse".

The program should also avoid elementary functions (exponential and trigonometric functions), which can be ensured with a restriction:

```
pragma No_Dependence (Ada.Numerics);
```

If elementary functions are used, subject to reviews for ensuring portability, GNATprove's proof results may depend on the fact that elementary functions can be modeled as mathematical functions of their inputs that always return the same result when taking the same values in arguments. GNAT compiler was modified to ensure this property (see http://www.spark-2014.org/entries/detail/how-our-compiler-learnt-from-our-analyzers), which may not hold for other Ada compilers.

8.2 Project Scenarios

The workflow for using SPARK depends not only on the chosen *Objectives of Using SPARK*, but also on the context in which SPARK is used: Is it for a new development? Or an evolution of an existing codebase? Is the existing codebase in Ada or in a version of SPARK prior to SPARK 2014? We examine all these project scenarios in this section.

8.2.1 Maintenance and Evolution of Existing Ada Software

Although SPARK is a large subset of Ada, it contains a number of *Language Restrictions* which prevent in general direct application of GNATprove to an existing Ada codebase without any modifications. The suggested workflow is to:

1. Identify violations of SPARK restrictions.

2. For each violation, either rewrite the code in SPARK or mark it SPARK_Mode => Off (see section on *Identifying SPARK Code*).

3. Perform the required analyses to achieve the desired objectives (see section on *Formal Verification with GNATprove*), a process which likely involved writing contracts (see in particular section on *How to Write Subprogram Contracts*).

4. Make sure that the assumptions made for formal verification are justified at the boundary between SPARK and full Ada code (see section on *Managing Assumptions*).

Identifying Violations of SPARK Restrictions

A simple way to identify violations of SPARK restrictions is by *Setting the Default SPARK_Mode* to SPARK_Mode => On, and then running GNATprove either in check mode (to report basic violations) or in flow mode (to report violations whose detection requires flow analysis).

If only a subset of the project files should be analyzed, one should create a project file for *Specifying Files To Analyze* or *Excluding Files From Analysis*.

Finally, one may prefer to work her way through the project one unit at a time by *Using SPARK_Mode in Code*, and running GNATprove on the current unit only.

Rewriting the Code in SPARK

Depending on the violation, it may be more or less easy to rewrite the code in SPARK:

- Access types should in general be rewritten as private types of a package whose public part is marked SPARK_Mode => On and whose private part is marked SPARK_Mode => Off. Thus, the body of that package cannot be analyzed by GNATprove, but clients of the package can be analyzed.

- Functions with side-effects should be rewritten as procedures, by adding an additional out parameter for the result of the function.

- Aliasing should be either explicitly signed off by *Justifying Check Messages* or removed by introducing a copy of the object to pass as argument to the call.

- Goto statements should be rewritten into regular control and looping structures when possible.

- Controlled types cannot be rewritten easily.

- Top-level exception handlers can be moved to a wrapper subprogram, which calls the subprogram without handlers and handles the exceptions which may be raised. The callee subprogram (and any callers) can thus be analyzed by GNATprove, while the body of the wrapper subprogram is marked SPARK_Mode => Off. The same result can be obtained for exception handlers not at top-level by first refactoring the corresponding block into a subprogram.

Using SPARK_Mode to Select or Exclude Code

Depending on the number and location of remaining violations, SPARK_Mode can be used in different ways:

- If most of the codebase is in **SPARK**, *Setting the Default SPARK_Mode* to SPARK_Mode => On is best. Violations should be isolated in parts of the code marked SPARK_Mode => Off by either *Excluding Selected Unit Bodies* or *Excluding Selected Parts of a Unit*.

- Otherwise, SPARK_Mode => On should be applied selectively for *Verifying Selected Subprograms* or *Verifying Selected Units*. Violations are allowed outside the parts of the code marked SPARK_Mode => On.

- Even when most of the code is in **SPARK**, it may be more cost effective to apply SPARK_Mode => On selectively rather than by default. This is the case in particular when some units have non-**SPARK** declarations in the public part of their package spec (for example access type definitions). Rewriting the code of these units to isolate the non-**SPARK** declarations in a part that can be marked SPARK_Mode => Off may be more costly than specifying no SPARK_Mode for these units, which allows **SPARK** code elsewhere in the program to refer to the **SPARK** entities in these units.

When analyzing a unit for the first time, it may help to gradually mark the code SPARK_Mode => On:

1. Start with the unit spec marked SPARK_Mode => On and the unit body marked SPARK_Mode => Off. First run GNATprove in flow mode, then in proof mode, until all errors are resolved (some unproved checks may remain, as errors and checks are different *Categories of Messages*).

2. Continue with the both the unit spec and body marked SPARK_Mode => On. First run GNATprove in flow mode, then in proof mode, until all errors are resolved.

3. Now that GNATprove can analyze the unit without any errors, continue with whatever analysis is required to achieve the desired objectives.

8.2.2 New Developments in SPARK

In this scenario, a significant part of a software (possibly a module, possibly the whole software) is developed in SPARK. Typically, SPARK is used for the most critical parts of the software, with less critical parts programmed in Ada, C or Java (for example the graphical interface). A typical development process for this scenario might be:

1. Produce the high level (architectural) design in terms of package specifications. Determine which packages will be in **SPARK**, to be marked SPARK_Mode => On.

2. Alternatively, if the majority of packages are to be **SPARK**, *Setting the Default SPARK_Mode* to SPARK_Mode => On is best. Those few units that are not **SPARK** should be marked SPARK_Mode => Off.

3. Add *Package Contracts* to SPARK packages and, depending on the desired objectives, add relevant *Subprogram Contracts* to the subprograms declared in these packages. The package contracts should identify the key elements of *State Abstraction* which might also be referred to in *Data Dependencies* and *Flow Dependencies*.

4. Begin implementing the package bodies. One typical method of doing this is to use a process of top-down decomposition, starting with a top-level subprogram specification and implementing the body by breaking it down into further (nested) subprograms which are themselves specified but not yet implemented, and to iterate until a level is reached where it is appropriate to start writing executable code. However the exact process is not mandated and will depend on other factors such as the design methodology being employed. Provided unimplemented subprograms are stubbed (that is, they are given dummy bodies), GNATprove can be used at any point to analyze the program.

5. As each subprogram is implemented, GNATprove can be used (in mode `flow` or `proof` depending on the objectives) to verify it (against its contract, and/or to show absence of run-time errors).

8.2.3 Conversion of Existing SPARK Software to SPARK 2014

If an existing piece of software has been developed in a previous version of SPARK and is still undergoing active development/maintenance then it may be advantageous to upgrade to using SPARK 2014 in order to make use of the larger language subset and the new tools and environment. This requires more efforts than previous upgrades between versions of SPARK (SPARK 83, SPARK 95 and SPARK 2005) because the new version SPARK 2014 of SPARK is incompatible with those previous versions of the language. While the programming language itself in those previous versions of SPARK is a strict subset of SPARK 2014, the contracts and assertions in previous versions of SPARK are expressed as stylized comments that are ignored by GNATprove. Instead, those contracts and assertions should be expressed as executable Ada constructs, as presented in the *Overview of SPARK Language*.

The SPARK Language Reference Manual has an appendix containing a *SPARK 2005 to SPARK 2014 Mapping Specification* which can be used to guide the conversion process. Various options can be considered for the conversion process:

1. *Only convert annotations into contracts and assertions, with minimal changes to the executable code* - Note that some changes to the code may be required when converting annotations, for example adding with-clauses in a unit to give visibility over entities used in contracts in this unit but defined in another units (which was performed in previous versions of SPARK with `inherit` annotations). This conversion should be relatively straightforward by following the mapping of features between the two languages.

   The SPARK tools should be used to analyze the work in progress throughout the conversion process (which implies that a bottom-up approach may work best) and any errors corrected as they are found. This may also be an occasion to dramatically simplify annotations, as GNATprove requires far fewer of them. See the description of the conversion of SPARKSkein program in the section about *Examples in the Toolset Distribution*, for which a majority of the annotations are not needed anymore.

   Once the conversion is complete, development and maintenance can continue in SPARK.

2. *In addition to converting annotations, benefit from the larger language and more powerful tools to simplify code and contracts* - SPARK 2014 is far less constraining than previous versions of SPARK in terms of dependencies between units (which can form a graph instead of a tree), control structures (for example arbitrary return statements and exit statements are allowed), data structures (for example scalar types with dynamic bounds are allowed), expressions (for example local variables can be initialized with non-static expressions at declaration). In addition, useful new language constructs are available:

   - *Contract Cases* can be used to replace complex postconditions with implications.

   - *Predicates* can be used to state invariant properties of types, so that they need not be repeated in preconditions, postconditions, loop invariants, etc.

   - *Expression Functions* can be used to replace simple query functions and their postcondition.

   - *Ghost Code* can be used to mark code only used for verification.

- *Loop Variants* can be used to prove the termination of loops.

Changing the code to use these new features may favor readability and maintenance. These changes can be performed either while converting annotations, or as a second stage after all annotations have been converted (the case discussed above). Like in the previous case, the SPARK tools should be used to analyze the work in progress throughout the conversion process (which implies that a bottom-up approach may work best) and any errors corrected as they are found. Once the conversion is complete, development and maintenance can continue in SPARK.

3. *Gradually convert annotations and code* - It is possible to keep annotations in comments for the previous versions of SPARK while gradually adding contracts and assertions in SPARK 2014. The latest version of the SPARK 2005 toolset facilitates this gradual migration by ignoring SPARK pragmas. Thus, new contracts (for example *Preconditions* and *Postconditions*) should be expressed as pragmas rather than aspects in that case.

Typically, annotations and code would be converted when it needs to be changed. The granularity of how much code needs to be converted when a module is touched should be considered, and is likely to be at the level of the whole package.

The latest version of the SPARK 2005 toolset can be used to continue analyzing the parts of the program that do not use the new features of SPARK 2014, including units which have the two versions of contracts in parallel. GNATprove can be used to analyze parts of the program that have contracts in SPARK 2014 syntax, including units which have the two versions of contracts in parallel.

Note that some users may wish to take advantage of the new SPARK contracts and tools whilst retaining the more restrictive nature of SPARK 2005. (Many of the restrictions from SPARK 2005 have been lifted in SPARK because improvements in the tools mean that sound analysis can be performed without them, but some projects may need to operate in a more constrained environment.) This can be achieved using `pragma Restrictions (SPARK_05)`. For further details of this restriction please see the GNAT Reference Manual.

8.2.4 Analysis of Frozen Ada Software

In some very specific cases, users may be interested in the results of GNATprove's analysis on an unmodified code. This may be the case for example if the only objective is to *Ensure Portability of Programs* for existing Ada programs that cannot be modified (due to some certification or legal constraints).

In such a case, the suggested workflow is very similar to the one described for *Maintenance and Evolution of Existing Ada Software*, except the code cannot be rewritten when a violation of SPARK restrictions is encountered, and instead that part of the code should be marked `SPARK_Mode => Off`. To minimize the parts of the code that need to be marked `SPARK_Mode => Off`, it is in general preferable to apply `SPARK_Mode => On` selectively rather than by default, so that units that have non-SPARK declarations in the public part of their package spec (for example access type definitions) need not be marked `SPARK_Mode => Off`. See *Using SPARK_Mode to Select or Exclude Code* for details.

COMMAND LINE INVOCATION

GNATprove is executed with the following command line:

```
Usage: gnatprove -Pproj [switches] [-cargs switches]

proj is a GNAT project file
-cargs switches are passed to gcc

All main units in proj are analyzed by default. Switches to change this:
 -u [files]              Analyze only the given files
    [files]              Analyze given files and all dependencies
 -U                      Analyze all files (including unused) of all projects

gnatprove basic switches:
 -aP=p                   Add path p to project path
    --assumptions        Output assumptions information
    --codepeer=c         Enable or disable CodePeer analysis (c=on,off*)
    --clean              Remove GNATprove intermediate files, and exit
    --cwe                Include CWE ids in message output
 -f                      Force recompilation/analysis of all units
 -h, --help              Display this usage information
 -j N                    Use N parallel processes (default: 1; N=0 will use
                         all cores of the machine)
 -k                      Do not stop analysis at the first error
    --level=n            Set the level of proof (0 = faster to 4 = more powerful)
 -m                      Minimal reanalysis
    --mode=m             Set the mode of GNATprove (m=check, check_all, flow,
                         prove, all*, stone, bronze, silver, gold)
    --output-msg-only    Do not run any provers, output current flow and proof
                         results
 -q, --quiet             Be quiet/terse
    --replay             Replay proofs, do not attempt new proofs
    --report=r           Set the report mode of GNATprove (r=fail*, all,
                         provers, statistics)
 -v, --verbose           Output extra verbose information
    --version            Output version of the tool and exit
    --warnings=w         Set the warning mode of GNATprove
                         (w=off, continue*, error)

* Main mode values
  . check              - Fast partial check for SPARK violations
  . check_all, stone   - Full check for SPARK violations
  . flow, bronze       - Prove correct initialization and data flow
  . prove              - Prove absence of run-time errors and contracts
  . all, silver, gold  - Activates all modes (default)
```

```
* Report mode values
   . fail        - Report failures to prove checks (default)
   . all         - Report all results of proving checks
   . provers     - Same as all, plus prover usage information
   . statistics  - Same as provers, plus timing and steps information

* Warning mode values
   . off         - Do not issue warnings
   . continue    - Issue warnings and continue (default)
   . error       - Treat warnings as errors

gnatprove advanced switches:
 -d, --debug              Debug mode
 --debug-save-vcs         Do not delete intermediate files for provers
 --flow-debug             Extra debugging for flow analysis (requires graphviz)
 --limit-line=f:l         Limit analysis to given file and line
 --limit-line=f:l:c:k     Limit analysis to given file, line, column and kind of
                          check
 --limit-subp=s           Limit analysis to subprogram defined by file and line
 --memcached-server=host:portnumber
                          Specify a memcached instance that will be used for
                          caching of proof results.
 --no-axiom-guard         Do not generate guards for axioms defining contracts of
                          functions
 --no-counterexample      Do not generate a counterexample for unproved formulas
 --no-global-generation
                          Do not generate Global and Initializes contracts from
                          code, instead assume "null". Note that this option also
                          implies --no-inlining.
 --no-inlining            Do not inline calls to local subprograms for proof
 --no-loop-unrolling      Do not unroll loops with static bounds and no
                          (in)variant for proof
 --output-header          Add a header with extra information in the generated
                          output file
 --pedantic               Use a strict interpretation of the Ada standard
 --proof=g[:l]            Set the proof modes for generation of formulas
                          (g=per_check*, per_path, progressive) (l=lazy*, all)
 --prover=s[,s]*          Use given provers (s=altergo, cvc4*, z3, ...)
 --RTS=dir                Specify the Ada runtime name/location
 --steps=nnn              Set the maximum number of proof steps (prover-specific)
                          Use value 0 for no steps limit.
 --timeout=nnn            Set the prover timeout in seconds
                          Use value 0 for no timeout.
 --why3-conf=f            Specify a configuration file for why3

* Proof mode values for generation
   . per_check   - Generate one formula per check (default)
   . per_path    - Generate one formula per path for each check
   . progressive - Start with one formula per check, then split into
                   paths when needed

* Proof mode values for laziness
   . lazy        - Stop at first unproved formula for each check
                   (most suited for fully automatic proof) (default)
   . all         - Attempt to prove all formulas
                   (most suited for combination of automatic and manual proof)

* Prover name values
```

```
(Default prover is cvc4.)
(Provers marked with [steps] support the --steps switch.)
. altergo          - [steps] Use Alt-Ergo
. cvc4             - [steps] Use CVC4
. z3               - [steps] Use Z3
. ...              - Any other prover configured in your .why3.conf file
```

ALTERNATIVE PROVERS

B.1 Installed with SPARK Pro

The provers Alt-Ergo, CVC4 and Z3 are installed with the SPARK tool. By default, GNATprove uses prover CVC4 only. Switch `--level` changes the default to use one or more provers depending on the chosen level (see *Running GNATprove from the Command Line*). Switch `--prover` allows to use another prover, or a list of provers. Prover names `altergo`, `cvc4` and `z3` are used to refer to the versions of provers Alt-Ergo, CVC4 and Z3 that are installed with the SPARK toolset. The string `alt-ergo` can also be used to refer to Alt-Ergo. More information on Alt-Ergo, CVC4 and Z3 can be found on their respective websites:

- Alt-Ergo: http://alt-ergo.ocamlpro.com

- CVC4: http://cvc4.cs.nyu.edu

- Z3: https://github.com/Z3Prover/z3

B.2 Installed with SPARK Discovery

In this case, only prover Alt-Ergo is installed with the SPARK tool. Hence, by default GNATprove only uses prover Alt-Ergo. In particular, switch `--level` has no impact on the use of different provers. If provers CVC4 and Z3 are separately installed by the user and available on the execution path, then GNATprove will use them as documented in this User's Guide. In particular, CVC4 will then become the default prover instead of Alt-Ergo. Sources and binaries for provers CVC4 and Z3 can be found on their respective websites:

- CVC4: http://cvc4.cs.stanford.edu

- Z3: https://github.com/Z3Prover/z3 (search for "releases")

B.2.1 Installing CVC4 and Z3 for SPARK Discovery

- Download the latest version of CVC4 or Z3 from the websites specified above.

- Rename the executable file of the download to `cvc4` or `z3` (with `.exe` suffix on Windows). In the case of CVC4, you can simply rename the file you downloaded to `cvc4` (or `cvc4.exe` on Windows). In the case of Z3, you need to unzip the downloaded file. The executable file is in `bin/z3`.

- Add the location of the executable file to your `PATH` variable.

Note: If you are using SPARK Discovery GPL 2017, a known problem with CVC4 is that its options have changed. In order to use a current (un)stable CVC4 build, you should modify the file `<spark-install>/share/spark/`

`config/why3.conf` to remove `--boolean-term-conversion-mode=native` at the 4 places where it occurs.

B.3 Other Automatic or Manual Provers

B.3.1 Updating the Why3 Configuration File

GNATprove can call other provers, as long as they are supported by the Why3 platform (see complete list on Why3 webpage). To use another prover, it must be listed in your Why3 configuration file.

To create or update automatically a Why3 configuration file, call the command `<spark2014-install>/ libexec/spark/bin/why3config --detect-provers`. It searches your `PATH` for any supported provers and adds them to the default configuration file `.why3.conf` in your `HOME`, or a configuration file given in argument with switch `-C <file>`. This file consists of a few general settings and a section for each prover which is supported.

GNATprove reads the default configuration file `.why3.conf` in your `HOME`, or the configuration file given in argument with switch `--why3-conf=<file>`. Any prover name configured in this configuration file can be used as an argument to switch `--prover`.

Note that using this mechanism, you cannot replace the definitions provided with the SPARK tools for the provers `altergo`, `cvc4` and `z3`.

If more than one prover is specified, the provers are tried in order on each VC, until one of them succeeds or all fail. Interactive provers cannot be combined with other provers, so must appear on their own.

B.3.2 Sharing Libraries of Theorems

When GNATprove is used with a manual prover, the user can provide libraries of theorems to use during the proof process.

To do so, the user will need to set a proof directory (see *Project Attributes* for more details on this directory). The user needs to create a folder with the same name as the chosen manual prover (the casing of the name is the same as the one passed to the switch `--prover`) and put the library sources inside this folder.

Finally, some additional fields need to be added to the prover configuration in the Why3 configuration file (a basic example of prover configuration can be found in the section on *Coq*):

- `configure_build`: this field allows you to specify a command to configure the compilation of the library of theorems. This command will be called each time a source file is added to the library.

- `build_commands`: this field allows you to specify a set of command which will be called sequentially to build your library. These commands will be called each time GNATprove runs the corresponding manual prover. (In order to define multiple commands for this field, just set the field multiple times with different values, each time the field is set it adds a new element to the set of `build_commands`).

Inside these commands, pattern `%f` refers to the name of the library file considered, and `%o` to the name of the main `gnatprove` repository generated by GNATprove. This allows referring to the path of the compiled library of theorems inside these commands with `%o/user/<prover_name>`.

B.4 Coq

`gnatprove` has support for the Coq interactive prover, even though Coq is not part of the SPARK distribution. If you want to use Coq with SPARK, you need to install it yourself on your system and put it in your `PATH` environment variable. Then, you can simply provide `--prover=coq` to `gnatprove`. Note that the only supported version currently is Coq 8.5.

PROJECT ATTRIBUTES

GNATprove reads the package `Prove` in the given project file. This package is allowed to contain the following attributes:

- `Switches`, which defines additional command line switches that are used for the invokation of GNATprove. As an example, the following package in the project file sets the default report mode of GNATprove to `all`:

```
package Prove is
    for Switches use ("--report=all");
end Prove;
```

  Switches given on the command line have priority over switches given in the project file.

- `Proof_Dir`, which defines the directory where are stored the files concerning the state of the proof of a project. This directory contains a sub-directory `sessions` with one directory per source package analyzed for proof. Each of these package directories contains a Why3 session file. If a manual prover is used to prove some VCs, then a sub-directory called by the name of the prover is created next to `sessions`, with the same organization of sub-directories. Each of these package directories contains manual proof files. Common proof files to be used across various proofs can be stored at the toplevel of the prover-specific directory.

IMPLEMENTATION DEFINED PRAGMAS

D.1 Pragma SPARK_Mode

SPARK_Mode is a three-valued aspect. At least until we get to the next paragraph, a SPARK_Mode of On, Off, or Auto is associated with each Ada construct. Roughly, the meaning of the three values is the following:

- a value of On means that the construct is required to be in SPARK, and the construct will be analyzed by GNATprove.

- a value of Off means that the construct will not be analyzed by GNATprove, and does not need to obey the SPARK restrictions. The construct also cannot be referenced from other parts that are required to be in SPARK.

- a value of Auto means that the construct will not be analyzed, and GNATprove will infer whether this construct can be used in other SPARK parts or not.

We now explain in more detail how the SPARK_Mode pragma works.

Some Ada constructs are said to have more than one "section". For example, a declaration which requires a completion will have (at least) two sections: the initial declaration and the completion. The SPARK_Modes of the different sections of one entity may differ. In other words, SPARK_Mode is not an aspect of an entity but rather of a section of an entity.

For example, if a subprogram declaration has a SPARK_Mode of On while its body has a SPARK_Mode of Off, then an error would be generated if the subprogram took a parameter of an access type but not if the subprogram declared a local variable of an access type (recall that access types are not in SPARK).

A package is defined to have 4 sections: its visible part, its private part, its body declarations, and its body statements. A protected or task unit has 3 sections: its visible part, its private part, and its body. Other declarations which require a completion have two sections, as noted above; all other entities and constructs have only one section.

If the SPARK_Mode of a section of an entity is Off, then the SPARK_Mode of a later section of that entity shall not be On. [For example, a subprogram can have a SPARK declaration and a non-SPARK body, but not vice versa.]

If the SPARK_Mode of a section of an entity is Auto, then the SPARK_Mode of a later section of that entity shall not be On or Off.

The SPARK_Mode aspect can be specified either via a pragma or via an aspect_specification. In some contexts, only a pragma can be used because of syntactic limitations. In those contexts where an aspect_specification can be used, it has the same effect as a corresponding pragma.

The form of a pragma SPARK_Mode is as follows:

```
pragma SPARK_Mode [ (On | Off) ]
```

The form for the aspect_definition of a SPARK_Mode aspect_specification is as follows:

```
[ On | Off ]
```

For example:

```
package P
   with SPARK_Mode => On
is
```

The pragma can be used as a configuration pragma. The effect of such a configuration pragma is described below in the rules for determining the SPARK_Mode aspect value for an arbitrary section of an arbitrary Ada entity or construct.

Pragma SPARK_Mode shall be used as a local pragma in only the following contexts and has the described semantics:

Pragma placement	Affected construct	Alternative aspect form
Start of the visible declarations (preceded only by other pragmas) of a package declaration	Visible part of the package	As part of the package_specification
Start of the visible declarations (preceded only by other pragmas) of a task or protected unit	Visible part of the unit	As part of the declaration
Start of the private declarations of a package, a protected unit, or a task unit (only other pragmas can appear between the private keyword and the SPARK_Mode pragma)	Private part	None
Immediately at the start of the declarations of a package body (preceded only by other pragmas)	Body declarations of the package	As part of the package_body
Start of the elaboration statements of a package body (only other pragmas can appear between the begin keyword and the SPARK_Mode pragma)	Body statements of the package	None
Start of the declarations of a protected or task body (preceded only by other pragmas)	Body	As part of the protected or task body
After a subprogram declaration (with only other pragmas intervening). [This does not include the case of a subprogram whose initial declaration is via a subprogram_body_stub. Such a subprogram has only one section because a subunit is not a completion.]	Subprogram's specification	As part of the subprogram_declaration
Start of the declarations of a subprogram body (preceded only by other pragmas)	Subprogram's body	As part of the subprogram_body

A default argument of On is assumed for any SPARK_Mode pragma or aspect_specification for which no argument is explicitly specified.

A SPARK_Mode of Auto cannot be explicitly specified; the cases in which a SPARK_Mode of Auto is implicitly specified are described below. Roughly speaking, Auto indicates that it is left up to the formal verification tools to determine whether or not a given construct is in SPARK.

A SPARK_Mode pragma or aspect specification shall only apply to a (section of a) library-level package, generic package, subprogram, or generic subprogram. If a generic unit contains a SPARK_Mode pragma or aspect specification, then this rule also applies to the corresponding pragma or aspect specification which implicitly occurs within any instance of the generic unit. Except in one case described later in this section, this means that instances of such a generic shall only be declared at library level.

The SPARK_Mode aspect value of an arbitrary section of an arbitrary Ada entity or construct is then defined to be the following value (except if this yields a result of Auto for a non-package; see below):

- If SPARK_Mode has been specified for the given section of the given entity or construct, then the specified value;

- else for the private part of a public child unit whose parent unit's private part has a SPARK_Mode of Off, the SPARK_Mode is Off;

- else for the private part of a package or a protected or task unit, the SPARK_Mode of the visible part;

- else for a package body's statements, the SPARK_Mode of the package body's declarations;

- else for the first section (in the case of a package, the visible part) of a public child unit, the SPARK_Mode of the visible part of the parent unit;

- else for the first section (in the case of a package, the visible part) of a private child unit, the SPARK_Mode of the private part of the parent unit;

- else for any of the visible part or body declarations of a library unit package or either section of a library unit subprogram, if there is an applicable SPARK_Mode configuration pragma then the value specified by the pragma; if no such configuration pragma applies, then an implicit specification of Auto is assumed;

- else the SPARK_Mode of the enclosing section of the nearest enclosing package or subprogram;

- Corner cases: the SPARK_Mode of the visible declarations of the limited view of a package is always Auto; the SPARK_Mode of any section of a generic library unit is On. [Recall that any generic unit is in SPARK.]

If the above computation yields a result of Auto for any construct other than one of the four sections of a package, then a result of On or Off is determined instead based on the legality (with respect to the rules of SPARK) of the construct. The construct's SPARK_Mode is On if and only if the construct is in SPARK. [A SPARK_Mode of Auto is therefore only possible for (sections of) a package.]

In code where SPARK_Mode is On (also called "SPARK code"), the rules of SPARK are enforced. In particular, such code shall not reference non-SPARK entities, although such code may reference a SPARK declaration with one or more non-SPARK subsequent sections (e.g., a package whose visible part has a SPARK_Mode of On but whose private part has a SPARK_Mode of Off; a package whose visible part has a SPARK_Mode of Auto may also be referenced).

Similarly, code where SPARK_Mode is On shall, with some exceptions, not enclose code where SPARK_Mode is Off unless the non-SPARK code is part of the "completion" (using that term imprecisely, because we are including the private part of a package as part of its "completion" here) of a SPARK declaration. One major exception to this general rule is the (permitted) case of a library-level package (or generic package) visible part or private part having a SPARK_Mode of On which immediately encloses a declaration for which the initial section is explicitly specified to have SPARK_Mode of Off. There are also exceptions to this rule (described below) for protected units.

Code where SPARK_Mode is Off shall not enclose code where Spark_Mode is On. However, if an instance of a generic unit is enclosed by code where SPARK_Mode is Off and if any SPARK_Mode specifications occur within the generic unit, then the corresponding SPARK_Mode specifications occurring within the instance have no semantic effect. [In particular, such an ignored SPARK_Mode specification could not violate the preceding "Off shall not enclose On" rule because the Spark_Mode of the entire instance is Off. Similarly, such an ignored SPARK_Mode specification could not violate the preceding rule that a SPARK_Mode specification shall only apply to a (section of a) library-level entity.]

For purposes of both the "Off shall not enclose On" rule and the "On shall not enclose non-completion Off" rules just described, the initial section of a child unit is considered to occur immediately within either the visible part (for a public child unit) or the private part (for a private child unit) of the parent unit. In addition, the private part of a public child package is considered to occur immediately within the private part of the parent unit. [This follows Ada's visibility rules for child units. This means, for example, that if a parent unit's private part has a SPARK_Mode of Off, then the private part of a public child package shall not have a SPARK_Node of On. Note also that a SPARK_Mode configuration pragma which applies only to the specification (not the body) of a child unit is always ineffective; this is a consequence of the rules given above for determining the SPARK_Mode of the first section of a child unit.]

All of the above notwithstanding, the interactions between SPARK_Mode and protected units follow a slightly different model, not so closely tied to syntactic enclosure. Roughly speaking, the rules for a protected unit follow from the rules given for other constructs after notionally rewriting the protected unit as a package.

A protected unit declaration such as

```
protected type Prot
  with SPARK_Mode => On
is
   procedure Op1 (X : in out Integer);
   procedure Op2;
   procedure Non_SPARK_Profile (Ptr : access Integer)
     with SPARK_Mode => Off;
private
   Aaa, Bbb : Integer := 0;
end Prot;
```

can be thought of, for purposes of SPARK_Mode rules, as being a lot like

```
package Pkg
  with SPARK_Mode => On
is
   type Prot is limited private;
   procedure Op1 (Obj : in out Prot; X : in out Integer);
   procedure Op2 (Obj : in out Prot);
   procedure Non_SPARK_Profile (Obj : in out Prot; Ptr : access Integer)
     with SPARK_Mode => Off;
private
   type Prot is
     limited record
         Aaa, Bbb : Integer := 0;
     end record;
end Pkg;
```

which would be legal. The point is that a protected type which is in SPARK can have protected operation whose declaration is not in SPARK despite the fact that this violates the usual "On shall not enclose non-completion Off" rule. The declaration of the SPARK type no longer encloses the non-SPARK subprogram declaration after this notional rewriting, so this case is not considered to be a violation. [No such notional rewriting is needed for task units because task entries are not in SPARK.]

SPARK_Mode is an implementation-defined Ada aspect; it is not (strictly speaking) part of the SPARK language. It is used to notionally transform programs which would otherwise not be in SPARK so that they can be viewed (at least in part) as SPARK programs.

Note that if you would like to mark all your code in SPARK_Mode, the simplest solution is to specify in your project file:

```
package Builder is
   for Global_Configuration_Pragmas use "spark.adc";
end Builder;
```

and provide a file *spark.adc* which contains:

```
pragma SPARK_Mode;
```

EXTERNAL AXIOMATIZATIONS

E.1 What is it?

It is a feature of the SPARK toolset that allows to manually supply a WhyMl translation for the public specification of a library level package that is in SPARK. This feature is still experimental.

E.2 Why is it useful?

- For features that cannot easily be described using contracts, like transitivity, counting, or summation
- To link functions to the logic world, like trigonometry functions

E.3 How does it work?

- To say that a library package has an external axiomatization, we annotate it using:

```
pragma Annotate (GNATprove, External_Axiomatization);
```

- These packages should have SPARK_Mode On on their public specification and SPARK_Mode Off on their private part.
- The WhyMl translation for the package should be stored in a subdirectory named _theories of the proof directory specified for the project.

E.4 What should the translation look like?

- For each publicly visible entity E in the package P, it should provide the same elements (types as well as logic and program functions) as the automatic translation, all grouped in one single module named P__e. For example, the module for a function F should provide both a logic function declaration named f__logic and a program function declaration named f.
- For most types, a model module in defined in ada__model.mlw that can be cloned to get most of the required declarations.
- The manual translation may use any type, constant and function that is visible from the Ada package declaration.
- A good way to start an axiomatization file on a package is to launch the toolset on it and copy paste the modules created for each entity of the package. A WhyMl file created by the tool on a package P contains a module for every declaration visible from it, only declarations from P itself should be copied. The generated file usually

contains two modules for each entity, one named P__e and one named P__e__axiom. Both should be put together in P__e for the manual translation. The toolset will replace statically known expressions with their value. Beware that they might be architecture dependent.

E.5 Example

For example, let us consider the following package, stored in a file sum.ads, providing a summation function for slices of arrays of integers:

```ada
package Sums with SPARK_Mode is
   pragma Annotate (GNATprove, External_Axiomatization);

   subtype Extended_Index is Integer range 0 .. 2 ** 16;
   subtype Index is Integer range 1 .. Extended_Index'Last;

   subtype Vector_Element is
     Integer range Integer'First / Index'Last .. Integer'Last / Index'Last;

   type Vector is array (Index range <>) of Vector_Element;

   type Slice_Bounds is
      record
         Lo : Index;
         Hi : Extended_Index;
      end record;

   function Sum (X : Vector; Bounds : Slice_Bounds) return Integer with
     Pre => (Bounds.Lo > Bounds.Hi) or else
     (X'First <= Bounds.Lo and Bounds.Hi <= X'Last);

end Sums;
```

We can provide the following Why3 translation for it, that we should store in a file named sum.mlw:

```
module Sums__extended_index
 use import "_gnatprove_standard".Main
 use        "_gnatprove_standard".Integer
 use import "int".Int

 type extended_index

 function first : int = 0

 function last  : int = 65536

 predicate in_range (x : int) = first <= x /\ x <= last

 (* Clone of the model module for discrete types with static bounds *)
 clone export "ada__model".Static_Discrete with
 type t = extended_index,
 function first = first,
 function last = last,
 predicate in_range = in_range

 (* Type for mutable variables of type extended_index *)
 type extended_index__ref = { mutable extended_index__content : extended_index }
```

```
  val extended_index__havoc (x : extended_index__ref) : unit
    writes { x }

 (* All values of type extended_index are in range *)
 predicate dynamic_invariant (expr : int) bool bool bool  =
   dynamic_property first last expr

 (* We know nothing for default initialization of variables of type
    extended_index *)
 predicate default_initial_assumption int bool = true
end

module Sums__extended_index__rep
 use import Sums__extended_index
 use import "_gnatprove_standard".Main

 (* Projection functions from extended_index to int *)
 clone export "ada__model".Rep_Proj_Int with
   type t = extended_index,
   predicate in_range = in_range
end

module Sums__index
 use import "_gnatprove_standard".Main
 use         "_gnatprove_standard".Integer
 use import "int".Int

 type index

 function first : int = 1

 function last  : int = 65536

 predicate in_range (x : int) = first <= x /\ x <= last

 (* Clone of the model module for discrete types with static bounds *)
 clone export "ada__model".Static_Discrete with
 type t = index,
 function first = first,
 function last = last,
 predicate in_range = in_range

 (* Type for mutable variables of type index *)
 type index__ref = { mutable index__content : index }
 val index__havoc (x : index__ref) : unit
   writes { x }

 (* All values of type index are in range *)
 predicate dynamic_invariant (expr : int) bool bool bool  =
   dynamic_property first last expr

 (* We know nothing for default initialization of variables of type index *)
 predicate default_initial_assumption int bool = true

end

module Sums__index__rep
 use import Sums__index
```

```
  use import "_gnatprove_standard".Main

  (* Projection functions from index to int *)
  clone export "ada__model".Rep_Proj_Int with
    type t = index,
    predicate in_range = in_range
end

module Sums__vector_element
  use import "_gnatprove_standard".Main
  use        "_gnatprove_standard".Int_Division
  use import Standard__integer
  use import "int".Int

  type vector_element

  function first : int = Int_Division.div Standard__integer.first 65536

  function last  : int = Int_Division.div Standard__integer.last 65536

  predicate in_range (x : int)  = first <= x /\ x <= last

  (* Clone of the model module for discrete types with static bounds *)
  clone export "ada__model".Static_Discrete with
  type t = vector_element,
  function first = first,
  function last = last,
  predicate in_range = in_range

  (* Type for mutable variables of type vector_element *)
  type vector_element__ref = { mutable vector_element__content : vector_element }
  val vector_element__havoc (x : vector_element__ref) : unit
    writes { x }

end

module Sums__vector_element__rep
  use import Sums__vector_element
  use import "_gnatprove_standard".Main

  (* Projection functions from vector_element to int *)
  clone export "ada__model".Rep_Proj_Int with
    type t = vector_element,
    predicate in_range = in_range
end

(* Module for any array type ranging over signed integer types and
   containing vector_element *)
module Array__Int__Sums__vector_element
  use import "_gnatprove_standard".Main
  use import "int".Int
  use        Sums__vector_element
  use        Sums__vector_element__rep

  function one : int = 1

  type component_type = Sums__vector_element.vector_element
```

```
(* Clone of the model module for logical arrays containing vector_element
   and indexed by mathematical integers *)
clone export "_gnatprove_standard".Array__1 with
type I1.t = int,
predicate I1.le = Int.(<=),
predicate I1.lt = Int.(<),
predicate I1.gt = Int.(>),
function I1.add = Int.(+),
function I1.sub = Int.(-),
function I1.one = one,
type component_type = component_type

(* Primitive equality between arrays *)
function bool_eq (a:map) (af:int) (al:int) (b:map) (bf:int) (bl:int) : bool =
  (if af <= al
      then al - af = bl - bf
      else bf > bl) /\
        (forall idx : int. af <= idx <= al ->
            (get a idx) = (get b (bf - af + idx)))

(* Clone of the model module for comparison of arrays *)
clone export "ada__model".Array_Int_Rep_Comparison_Axiom with
type component_type = component_type,
function to_rep = Sums__vector_element__rep.to_rep,
type map = map,
type Index.t = int,
predicate Index.le = Int.(<=),
predicate Index.lt = Int.(<),
predicate Index.gt = Int.(>),
function Index.add = Int.(+),
function Index.sub = Int.(-),
function Index.one = one,
function get = get,
function bool_eq = bool_eq

end

module Sums__vector
 use import "int".Int
 use import "_gnatprove_standard".Main
 use        "_gnatprove_standard".Integer
 use import Standard__integer
 use import Sums__index
 use import Sums__vector_element
 use        Array__Int__Sums__vector_element
 use        Standard__integer__rep
 use        Sums__vector_element__rep

 predicate index_dynamic_property (first : int) (last : int) (x : int) =
     first <= x /\ x <= last

 (* Clone of the model module for unconstrained arrays *)
 type component_type  =
  Sums__vector_element.vector_element

 function id (x : int) : int = x

 (* Clone of the model module for unconstrained arrays *)
```

```
clone export "ada__model".Unconstr_Array with
type map = Array__Int__Sums__vector_element.map,
function array_bool_eq = Array__Int__Sums__vector_element.bool_eq,
type index_base_type = Standard__integer.integer,
type index_rep_type = int,
function to_rep = Standard__integer__rep.to_rep,
function rep_to_int = id,
predicate in_range_base = Standard__integer.in_range,
predicate index_dynamic_property = index_dynamic_property,
predicate index_rep_le = Int.(<=)

type vector  = __t

(* Type for mutable variables of type vector *)
type vector__ref = { mutable vector__content : vector }
val vector__havoc (x : vector__ref) : unit
  writes { x }

(* Helper function *)
function _get "inline" (v : vector) (i : int) : int =
           Sums__vector_element__rep.to_rep (Array__Int__Sums__vector_element.get
↪(to_array v) i)

(* If vectors are not empty, their bounds are between Index.first and
   Index.last *)
predicate dynamic_invariant (expr : vector) bool (skip_bounds : bool) bool  =
  (if skip_bounds then true
   else dynamic_property Sums__index.first Sums__index.last
         (first expr) (last expr))
end

module Sums__slice_bounds
 use import "int".Int
 use import "_gnatprove_standard".Main
 use        "_gnatprove_standard".Integer
 use import Sums__index
 use        Sums__index__rep
 use import Sums__extended_index
 use        Sums__extended_index__rep

 (* Fields for record type *)
 type __split_fields  =
  { rec__sums__slice_bounds__lo : index; rec__sums__slice_bounds__hi : extended_index
↪}

 type __split_fields__ref = { mutable __split_fields__content : __split_fields }
 val __split_fields__havoc (x : __split_fields__ref) : unit
   writes { x }

 (* Record type *)
 type slice_bounds  =
  { __split_fields : __split_fields }

 (* Type for mutable variables of type slice_bounds *)
 type slice_bounds__ref = { mutable slice_bounds__content : slice_bounds }
 val slice_bounds__havoc (x : slice_bounds__ref) : unit
   writes { x }
```

```
(* Helper function *)
function _rec__lo "inline" (b : slice_bounds) : int =
          Sums__index__rep.to_rep (rec__sums__slice_bounds__lo (__split_fields
   (b)))

(* Helper function *)
function _rec__hi "inline" (b : slice_bounds) : int =
          Sums__extended_index__rep.to_rep (rec__sums__slice_bounds__hi (__split_
   fields (b)))

(* Condition to be allowed to access Lo *)
predicate sums__slice_bounds__lo__pred (a : slice_bounds) =
 true

val rec__sums__slice_bounds__lo_
  (a : slice_bounds)  :Sums__index.index
 requires { sums__slice_bounds__lo__pred a }
 ensures  { result = a.__split_fields.rec__sums__slice_bounds__lo }


(* Condition to be allowed to access Hi *)
predicate sums__slice_bounds__hi__pred (a : slice_bounds) =
 true

val rec__sums__slice_bounds__hi_
  (a : slice_bounds)  :Sums__extended_index.extended_index
 requires { sums__slice_bounds__hi__pred a }
 ensures  { result = a.__split_fields.rec__sums__slice_bounds__hi }


(* Equality function over slice_bounds *)
function bool_eq (a : slice_bounds) (b : slice_bounds) : bool =
 _rec__lo a = _rec__lo b /\ _rec__hi a = _rec__hi b

function dummy : slice_bounds

(* No particular property applies to all values of types slice_bounds *)
predicate dynamic_invariant slice_bounds bool bool bool = true

(* We know nothing for default initialization of variables of slice_bounds *)
predicate default_initial_assumption slice_bounds bool = true
end

module Sums__sum
 use import "int".Int
 use import "_gnatprove_standard".Main
 use         "_gnatprove_standard".Integer
 use         "_gnatprove_standard".Array__1
 use import Sums__slice_bounds
 use import Sums__index
 use         Sums__index__rep
 use import Standard__integer
 use import Sums__extended_index
 use         Sums__extended_index__rep
 use import Sums__vector

 (* Logic complete function for sum *)
 function sum__logic
```

```
    (x : vector) (bounds : slice_bounds)  :int

(* Helper function *)
function _sum "inline" (x : vector) (bounds : slice_bounds)  :int =
            sum__logic x bounds

(* Axiom for defining the sum function *)
axiom sum_def:
    forall v : vector, b : slice_bounds
      [sum__logic v b].
      Standard__integer.in_range (sum__logic v b) /\
      (* Case of the empty slice *)
      (_rec__lo b > _rec__hi b -> _sum v b = 0) /\

      (* Case of a non-empty slice  *)
      (first v <= _rec__lo b <= _rec__hi b <= last v ->

          (* If the slice only contains one element *)
          (_rec__lo b = _rec__hi b -> _sum v b = _get v (_rec__lo b)) /\

          (* Link to smaller slices of the same vector *)
          (forall b1 : slice_bounds [sum__logic v b1].

              (* Ending at the same index *)
              ((_rec__hi b1 = _rec__hi b /\ _rec__lo b < _rec__lo b1 <= _rec__hi b) ->
              let b2 = {__split_fields =
                            {rec__sums__slice_bounds__lo = rec__sums__slice_bounds_
↪_lo (__split_fields b);
                            rec__sums__slice_bounds__hi = Sums__extended_index__rep.of_
↪rep ((_rec__lo b1) - 1)}} in
                  _sum v b = _sum v b1 + _sum v b2) /\
              (* Sartind at the same index *)
              ((_rec__lo b1 = _rec__lo b /\ _rec__lo b <= _rec__hi b1 < _rec__hi b) ->
              let b2 = {__split_fields =
                            {rec__sums__slice_bounds__lo = Sums__index__rep.of_rep_
↪((_rec__hi b1) + 1);
                            rec__sums__slice_bounds__hi = rec__sums__slice_bounds__hi (_
↪_split_fields b)}} in
                  _sum v b = _sum v b1 + _sum v b2)))

(* Program partial function with a precondition for sum *)
val sum (x : vector) (bounds : slice_bounds)  :int
 requires { _rec__lo bounds > _rec__hi bounds \/
            first x <= _rec__lo bounds /\ _rec__hi bounds <= last x }
 ensures  { result = sum__logic x bounds }

end
```

GNATPROVE LIMITATIONS

F.1 Tool Limitations

1. The Global contracts generated automatically by GNATprove for subprograms without an explicit one do not take into account indirect calls (through access-to-subprogram and dynamic binding) and indirect reads/writes to global variables (through access variables).

2. A subset of all Ada conversions between array types is supported:

   - element types must be exactly the same

   - matching index types must either be both modular with a base type of the same size, or both non modular

3. A subset of all Ada fixed-point types and fixed-point operations is supported:

   - fixed-point types must have a small that is a negative power of 2 or 10

   - multiplication and division between different fixed-point types and universal real are rejected

   - multiplication and division whose result type is not the same fixed-point type as its fixed-point argument(s) are rejected, except for the special case of dividing a fixed-point value by the small of its type (T'Small) to yield an integer result which is always exact.

   - conversions from fixed-point types to floating-point types are rejected

   These restrictions ensure that the result of fixed-point operations always belongs to the *perfect result set* as defined in Ada RM G.2.3.

4. Multidimensional array types are supported up to 4 dimensions.

5. Loop_Invariant and Loop_Variant pragmas must appear before any non-scalar object declaration.

6. Inheriting the same subprogram from multiple interfaces is not supported.

7. Formal object parameters of generics of an unconstrained record type with per-object constrained fields are badly supported by the tool and may result in crashes in some cases.

8. Quantified expressions with an iterator over a multi dimensional array (for example `for all Elem of Arr` where `Arr` is a multi dimensional array) are not supported.

9. Constrained subtypes of class-wide types and 'Class attributes of constrained record types are not supported.

10. Abstract states cannot be marked `Part_Of` a single concurrent object (see SPARK RM 9(3)). An error is raised instead in such cases.

11. Classwide Global and Depends contracts as defined in SPARK RM 6.1.6 are not supported.

12. Task attributes Identity and Storage_Size are not supported.

13. Type_Invariant and Invariant aspects are not supported:

- on private types declared in nested packages or child packages

- on protected types

- on tagged types

- on components of tagged types if the tagged type is visble from inside the scope of the invariant bearing type.

14. Calls to protected subprograms and protected entries whose prefix denotes a formal subprogram parameter are not supported. Similarly, suspension on suspension objects given as formal subprogram parameters is not supported.

F.2 Legality Rules

1. SPARK Reference Manual rule 4.3(1), concerning use of the box symbol "<>" in aggregates, is not currently checked.

2. The elaboration order rules described in the SPARK Reference Manual 7.7 are not currently checked.

3. The rule concerned with asserting that all child packages which have state denoted as being Part_Of a more visible state abstraction are given as constituents in the refinement of the more visible state is not checked (SPARK Reference Manual rule 7.2.6(6)).

4. GNATprove does not permit formal parameters to be mentioned in the input_list of an Initializes Aspect, contrary to SPARK Reference Manual 7.1.5(4). This limitation is only relevant for packages that are nested inside subprograms. This limitation is corrected in versions of the toolset based on GNAT Pro 7.2.2, GPL 2014, or later.

5. The case of a state abstraction whose Part_Of aspect denotes a task or protected unit is not currently supported.

6. The case of a Refined_Post specification for a (protected) entry is not currently supported.

7. The use Ada.Synchronous_Barriers.Synchronous_Barrier type is not currently allowed in SPARK.

8. Entry families are not currently allowed in SPARK.

F.3 Flow Analysis Limitations

1. Flow dependencies caused by record assignments is not captured with perfect accuracy. This means that the value of one field might incorrectly be considered to participate in the derivation of another field that it does not really participate in.

F.4 Proof Limitations

1. Postconditions of recursive functions called in contracts and assertion pragmas are not available, possibly leading to unproved checks. The current workaround is to use a non-recursive wrapper around those functions.

2. Attribute 'Valid is currently assumed to always return True.

3. Values read from an external source are assumed to be valid values. Currently there is no model of invalidity or undefinedness. The onus is on the user to ensure that all values read from an external source are valid. The use of an invalid value invalidates any proofs associated with the value.

4. The following attributes are not yet supported in proof: Adjacent, Aft, Bit_Order, Body_Version, Copy_Sign, Definite, Denorm, First_Valid, Fore, Last_Valid, Machine, all Machine_* attributes, Model, all Model_* attributes, Partition_Id, Remainder, Round, Safe_First, Safe_Last, Scale, Scaling, Small, Unbiased_Rounding, Version, Wide_Image, Wide_Value, Wide_Width, Wide_Wide_Image, Wide_Wide_Value, Wide_Wide_Width, Width.

   The attributes First_Bit, Last_Bit and Position are supported but if there is no record representation clause then we assume that their value is nonnegative.

5. The 'Update attribute on multidimensional unconstrained arrays is not yet fully supported in proof. Checks might be missing so currently an error is emitted for any use of the 'Update attribute on multidimensional unconstrained arrays.

6. The difference between the floating-point values +0 and -0 (as defined in IEEE-754 standard) is ignored in proof. This is correct for all programs that do not exploit the difference in bit-pattern between +0 and -0. For example, the following specially crafted program is proved by GNATprove but fails at run time due to a division by zero, because function Magic exploits the difference of bit-pattern between +0 and -0 by using Unchecked_Conversion to return a different integer value for arguments +0 and -0.

```ada
pragma SPARK_Mode;

with Ada.Unchecked_Conversion;

procedure Zero_And_Unchecked is
   procedure Crash (A, B : Float) is
      function Magic is new Ada.Unchecked_Conversion (Float, Integer);
      X : Integer;
   begin
      if A = B then
         if Magic (B) /= 0 then
            X := 100 / Magic (A);
         end if;
      end if;
   end Crash;

   type UInt32 is mod 2 ** 32;
   function Convert is new Ada.Unchecked_Conversion (UInt32, Float);

   Zero_Plus : constant Float := Convert (16#0000_0000#);
   Zero_Neg  : constant Float := Convert (16#8000_0000#);
begin
   Crash (Zero_Plus, Zero_Neg);
end Zero_And_Unchecked;
```

7. GNATprove does not follow the value of tags for tagged objects. As a consequence, tag checks are currently unprovable in most cases.

8. Constants declared in loops before the loop invariant are handled as variables by the tool. This means in particular that any information about their values needed after the loop invariant must be stated explicitly in the loop invariant.

9. Preconditions on arithmetic and conversion operators (including Time_Of) in Ada.Execution_Time and Ada.Real_Time packages described in SPARK Reference Manual 9.19 are not yet implemented.

10. Preconditions on arithmetic and conversion operators (including Time_Of) in Ada.Calendar package are not yet implemented.

PORTABILITY ISSUES

To execute a SPARK program, it is expected that users will compile the program (as an Ada program) using an Ada compiler. The SPARK language definition defines a number of implementation-defined (with respect to the Ada language definition) aspects, attributes, pragmas, and conventions. Ideally a SPARK program will be compiled using an Ada compiler that supports all of these constructs. Portability problems may arise if this is not the case.

This section is a discussion of the strategies available for coping with this situation.

Probably the most important rule is that pragmas should be used instead of aspect_specification syntax wherever this option is available. For example, use pragma Abstract_State rather than specifying the Abstract_State aspect of a package using aspect_specification syntax. Ada specifies that unrecognized pragmas shall be ignored, as opposed to being rejected. This is not the case for (syntactic) aspect specifications (this terminology is a bit confusing because a pragma can be used to specify an aspect; such a pragma is semantically, but not syntactically, an aspect specification). Furthermore, aspect specification syntax was introduced in Ada 2012 and will be rejected if the program is compiled as, for example, an Ada 95 program.

Many SPARK-defined constructs have no dynamic semantics (e.g., the Global, Depends, and Abstract_State aspects), so the run-time behavior of a program is unaffected if they are ignored by a compiler. Thus, there is no problem if these constructs are expressed as pragmas which are then ignored by the Ada compiler.

Of those constructs which do have dynamic semantics, most are run-time assertions. These include Loop_Variant, Loop_Invariant, Assert_And_Cut, Contract_Cases, Initial_Condition, and Refined_Postcondition. Because SPARK requires that the success of these assertions must be statically proven (and that the evaluation of the asserted condition can have no side effects), the run-time behavior of a program is unaffected if they are ignored by a compiler.

The situation with pragma Assume is slightly different because the success of the given condition is not statically proven. If ignoring an Assume pragma at run time is deemed to be unacceptable, then it can be replaced with an Assert pragma (at the cost of introducing a source code difference between the SPARK program that is analyzed statically and the Ada program that is executed). An ignored Assume pragma is the only case where the use of a SPARK-specific construct can lead to a portability problem which is not detected at compile time. In all other cases, either the Ada compiler will reject (as opposed to ignore) an unrecognized construct or the construct can safely be ignored.

An Ada compiler which does not support convention Ghost will reject any use of this convention. Two safe transformations are available for dealing with this situation - either replace uses of convention Ghost with convention Ada or delete the entities declared with a convention of Ghost. Just as was mentioned above in the case of modifying an Assume pragma, either choice introduces an analyzed/executed source code difference.

There are two SPARK attributes which cannot be used if they are not supported by the Ada compiler in question: the Update and Loop_Entry attributes.

SPARK includes a rule that a package which declares a state abstraction requires a body. In the case of a library unit package (or generic package) which requires a body only because of this rule, an Ada compiler that knows nothing about state abstractions would reject the body of the package because of the rule (introduced in Ada 95) that a library unit package (or generic package) body is never optional; if it is not required then it is forbidden. In the unlikely event that this scenario arises in practice, the solution is to force the library unit package to require a body for some other reason, typically by adding an Elaborate_Body pragma.

If a SPARK program is to be compiled and executed as an Ada 95 program (or any other pre-2012 version of Ada), then of course any construct introduced in a later version of Ada must be avoided (unless it is expressed as a safely-ignored pragma). This seems worth mentioning because Ada 2012 constructs such as quantified expressions and conditional expressions are often heavily used in SPARK programs.

SEMANTICS OF FLOATING POINT OPERATIONS

SPARK assumes that floating point operations are carried out in single precision (binary32) or double precision (binary64) as defined in the IEEE-754 standard for floating point arithmetic. You should make sure that this is the case on your platform. For example, on x86 platforms, by default some intermediate computations may be carried out in extended precision, leading to unexpected results. With GNAT, you can specify the use of SSE arithmetic by using the compilation switches "-msse2 -mfpmath=sse" which cause all arithmetic to be done using the SSE instruction set which only provides 32-bit and 64-bit IEEE types, and does not provide extended precision. SSE arithmetic is also more efficient. Note that the ABI allows free mixing of units using the two types of floating-point, so it is not necessary to force all units in a program to use SSE arithmetic.

SPARK considers the floating point values which represent positive, negative infinity or NaN as invalid. Proof obligations are generated that such values cannot occur.

SPARK considers rounding on floating point arithmetic operations to follow Round-Nearest-Even (RNE) mode, where a real result is rounded to the nearest floating point value, and ties are resolved to the floating-point with a zero in the last place. This mode of rounding should be forced if needed on the hardware to be able to rely on the results of GNATprove regarding floating point arithmetic.

SPARK ARCHITECTURE, QUALITY ASSURANCE AND MATURITY

I.1 Development Process and Quality Assurance

The SPARK development process and quality assurance are following the Adacore Quality Procedures in place for all development at AdaCore. This includes:

- The use of a report tracking system;

- Mechanisms for detecting and fixing defects;

- The usage of repositories and configuration management, the use of continuous integration technology, the stringent requirements on check-ins of source changes;

- The process for implementing new functionality;

- The process for maintaining user documentation;

- Ensuring quality of sources and technical documentation;

- Preparation of releases

As an extension to Chapter 2, section "AdaCore internal testsuite", SPARK contains its own testsuites:

- The SPARK main testsuite: This testsuite contains 1700 tests. These tests are specifically targeted at the SPARK software and cover typical use cases, often represented by code sent to us by customers, as well as specific features of the SPARK software.

- The ACATS testsuite in SPARK mode: A selection of the ACATS testsuite mentioned in the AdaCore Quality Procedures for the compiler is also used to test the SPARK tools.

These tests are run on various occasions (see also Chapter 2 of the Adacore Quality Procedures): * During nightly testing, once with assertions enabled, once without (the actual SPARK product); * After every check-in, during continuous integration; * To test a patch before check-in using the Mailserver technology.

I.2 Structure of the SPARK Software

At a high level, SPARK reads source files in the Ada programming language, with some annotations specific to SPARK, processes them, and in the end issues a report about errors found and proved or unproved properties. Looking more closely at how this is achieved, one can see this high-level structure of SPARK:

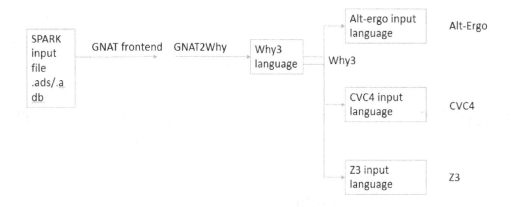

The development of the GNAT front-end and GNAT2Why components entirely follows the procedures outlined in AdaCore Quality Procedures and the previous section. The other components, however, are mostly developed by third parties. Their development process and the relationship to AdaCore and Altran will be outlined below.

For the nightly testing of SPARK, the GNAT and GNAT2Why components are updated every night according to the changes made during the day by AdaCore and Altran developers. The other tools, however, contain also check-ins by other persons. We update these tools in a controlled way, and after careful testing of the consequences. In other words, a check-in made e.g. to Z3 at some specific date, will not be part of the SPARK package of the same day, instead it will be integrated into SPARK after some time and after thorough testing in the SPARK environment.

I.2.1 GNAT front-end

SPARK shares its front-end (parsing and semantic analysis) with the GNAT compiler technology, which is very mature and has been used in countless projects for the last 20 years. The GNAT front-end is developed by AdaCore and follows the AdaCore quality procedures.

I.2.2 GNAT2Why

This part of SPARK serves two purposes:

- Implement Flow Analysis, the part of the SPARK analysis which detects uninitialized variables, and computes and checks the use of global variables and parameters.

- Translate the Ada source code to the Why language, for further processing by the Why3 tools. GNAT2Why is developed by AdaCore and Altran and follows the AdaCore quality procedures.

I.2.3 Why3

This part of SPARK takes the information in the Why language produced by GNAT2Why, translates it further into a format suitable for SMT solvers such as Z3 and CVC4, and runs these tools. The results are reported back to gnat2why.

History: Started around the year 2000 by Jean-Christophe-Filliâtre as "Why" (see Jean-Christophe Filliâtre. Why: a multi-language multi-prover verification tool. Research Report 1366, LRI, Université Paris Sud, March 2003), it has undergone a number of redevelopments until its current version Why3 (since 2010).

Track record: Apart from SPARK, it is used by Frama-C, Atelier B, and other program verification tools.

Relationship with AdaCore/Altran: The Inria team around Why3 has strong ties with AdaCore and Altran. A number of research projects have been and are being carried out in collaboration with this team. This includes the Hi-Lite project, which led to the current version of SPARK based on Why3, and the still ongoing project SOPRANO and joint laboratory ProofInUse. In addition, while Why3 is mainly developed at Inria, AdaCore and Altran have made important contributions to the technology, such as the so-called fast-WP, a more efficient implementation of the main algorithm of Why3, and the why3server, a more scalable method of running external tools such as SMT solvers.

- Main developers: Inria research institute

- Main website: http://why3.lri.fr

- Version Management: Git

- License: Open Source, LGPL 2.1

- Public mailing-list: why3-club@lists.gforge.inria.fr

- Bug tracking: https://gforge.inria.fr/tracker/?group_id=2990

I.2.4 Alt-Ergo

History: Started around the year 2005 at Inria by Sylvain Conchon and Evelyne Contejean as "Ergo" (see CC(X): Efficiently combining equality and solvable theories without canonizers. Sylvain Conchon, Évelyne Contejean, and Johannes Kanig. SMT Workshop, 2007). Starting from 2013, developed and distributed mainly by OCamlPro. Since then, OCamlPro issues every year a private release and a public release (lagging one year behind the private release). SPARK uses the public release of Alt-Ergo.

Track record: Apart from SPARK, it is used by Frama-C and Atelier B. In particular, used by Airbus for the qualification DO-178C of an aircraft [10].

Relationship with AdaCore/Altran: AdaCore and OCamlPro collaborate in the SOPRANO. AdaCore has contributed some minor changes to Alt-Ergo, including a deterministic resource limiting switch.

- Main developers: OCamlPro

- Main website: https://alt-ergo.ocamlpro.com/

- Version Management: Git

- License: CeCill-C (GPL compatible)

- Public mailing-list: alt-ergo-users@lists.gforge.inria.fr

- Bug tracking: https://github.com/OCamlPro/alt-ergo/issues

I.2.5 Z3

History: Started around the year 2007 at Microsoft Research by Leonardo de Moura and Nikolaj Bjørner (see Leonardo de Moura and Nikolaj Bjørner. Efficient E-Matching for SMT solvers. In Automated Deduction - CADE-21, 21st International Conference on Automated Deduction, Bremen, Germany, July 17-20, 2007, Proceedings, volume 4603 of Lecture Notes in Computer Science, pages 183-198. Springer, 2007). Released to open source under a very permissive license in 2015.

Track record: Apart from SPARK, used by Dafny and PEX projects inside Microsoft. Has won the SMT competition several times in several categories.

Relationship with AdaCore/Altran: AdaCore and Altran have provided bug reports, feature requests and small fixes to the Z3 team, in particular related to a deterministic resource limiting switch.

- Main developers: Microsoft

- Main website: https://github.com/Z3Prover/z3

- Version Management: Git

- License: MIT License

- Stackoverflow community: http://stackoverflow.com/questions/tagged/z3

- Bug tracking: https://github.com/Z3Prover/z3/issues/

I.2.6 CVC4

History: CVC4 is the fourth in the Cooperating Validity Checker family of tools, which dates back to 1996, but does not directly incorporate code from any previous version. CVC4 development started in 2012.

Track record: Very good results in various SMT competitions. Used in TNO tool.

Relationship with AdaCore/Altran: AdaCore and Altran have provided bug reports, feature requests and small fixes to the CVC4 team, in particular related to a deterministic resource limiting switch.

- Main developers: New York University

- Main website: http://cvc4.cs.nyu.edu/web/

- Version Management: Git

- License: Modified BSD License

- Mailing List: cvc-users@cs.nyu.edu

- Bug tracking: http://cvc4.cs.nyu.edu/bugs/

GNU FREE DOCUMENTATION LICENSE

Version 1.1, March 2000

Copyright (C) 2000 Free Software Foundation, Inc.

59 Temple Place, Suite 330, Boston, MA 02111-1307 USA

Everyone is permitted to copy and distribute verbatim copies of this license document, but changing it is not allowed.

J.1 PREAMBLE

The purpose of this License is to make a manual, textbook, or other written document 'free' in the sense of freedom: to assure everyone the effective freedom to copy and redistribute it, with or without modifying it, either commercially or noncommercially. Secondarily, this License preserves for the author and publisher a way to get credit for their work, while not being considered responsible for modifications made by others.

This License is a kind of 'copyleft', which means that derivative works of the document must themselves be free in the same sense. It complements the GNU General Public License, which is a copyleft license designed for free software.

We have designed this License in order to use it for manuals for free software, because free software needs free documentation: a free program should come with manuals providing the same freedoms that the software does. But this License is not limited to software manuals; it can be used for any textual work, regardless of subject matter or whether it is published as a printed book. We recommend this License principally for works whose purpose is instruction or reference.

J.2 APPLICABILITY AND DEFINITIONS

This License applies to any manual or other work that contains a notice placed by the copyright holder saying it can be distributed under the terms of this License. The 'Document', below, refers to any such manual or work. Any member of the public is a licensee, and is addressed as 'you'.

A 'Modified Version' of the Document means any work containing the Document or a portion of it, either copied verbatim, or with modifications and/or translated into another language.

A 'Secondary Section' is a named appendix or a front-matter section of the Document that deals exclusively with the relationship of the publishers or authors of the Document to the Document's overall subject (or to related matters) and contains nothing that could fall directly within that overall subject. (For example, if the Document is in part a textbook of mathematics, a Secondary Section may not explain any mathematics.) The relationship could be a matter of historical connection with the subject or with related matters, or of legal, commercial, philosophical, ethical or political position regarding them.

The 'Invariant Sections' are certain Secondary Sections whose titles are designated, as being those of Invariant Sections, in the notice that says that the Document is released under this License.

The 'Cover Texts' are certain short passages of text that are listed, as Front-Cover Texts or Back-Cover Texts, in the notice that says that the Document is released under this License.

A 'Transparent' copy of the Document means a machine-readable copy, represented in a format whose specification is available to the general public, whose contents can be viewed and edited directly and straightforwardly with generic text editors or (for images composed of pixels) generic paint programs or (for drawings) some widely available drawing editor, and that is suitable for input to text formatters or for automatic translation to a variety of formats suitable for input to text formatters. A copy made in an otherwise Transparent file format whose markup has been designed to thwart or discourage subsequent modification by readers is not Transparent. A copy that is not 'Transparent' is called 'Opaque'.

Examples of suitable formats for Transparent copies include plain ASCII without markup, Texinfo input format, La-TeX input format, SGML or XML using a publicly available DTD, and standard-conforming simple HTML designed for human modification. Opaque formats include PostScript, PDF, proprietary formats that can be read and edited only by proprietary word processors, SGML or XML for which the DTD and/or processing tools are not generally available, and the machine-generated HTML produced by some word processors for output purposes only.

The 'Title Page' means, for a printed book, the title page itself, plus such following pages as are needed to hold, legibly, the material this License requires to appear in the title page. For works in formats which do not have any title page as such, 'Title Page' means the text near the most prominent appearance of the work's title, preceding the beginning of the body of the text.

J.3 VERBATIM COPYING

You may copy and distribute the Document in any medium, either commercially or noncommercially, provided that this License, the copyright notices, and the license notice saying this License applies to the Document are reproduced in all copies, and that you add no other conditions whatsoever to those of this License. You may not use technical measures to obstruct or control the reading or further copying of the copies you make or distribute. However, you may accept compensation in exchange for copies. If you distribute a large enough number of copies you must also follow the conditions in section 3.

You may also lend copies, under the same conditions stated above, and you may publicly display copies.

J.4 COPYING IN QUANTITY

If you publish printed copies of the Document numbering more than 100, and the Document's license notice requires Cover Texts, you must enclose the copies in covers that carry, clearly and legibly, all these Cover Texts: Front-Cover Texts on the front cover, and Back-Cover Texts on the back cover. Both covers must also clearly and legibly identify you as the publisher of these copies. The front cover must present the full title with all words of the title equally prominent and visible. You may add other material on the covers in addition. Copying with changes limited to the covers, as long as they preserve the title of the Document and satisfy these conditions, can be treated as verbatim copying in other respects.

If the required texts for either cover are too voluminous to fit legibly, you should put the first ones listed (as many as fit reasonably) on the actual cover, and continue the rest onto adjacent pages.

If you publish or distribute Opaque copies of the Document numbering more than 100, you must either include a machine-readable Transparent copy along with each Opaque copy, or state in or with each Opaque copy a publicly-accessible computer-network location containing a complete Transparent copy of the Document, free of added material, which the general network-using public has access to download anonymously at no charge using public-standard network protocols. If you use the latter option, you must take reasonably prudent steps, when you begin distribution of Opaque copies in quantity, to ensure that this Transparent copy will remain thus accessible at the stated location until at least one year after the last time you distribute an Opaque copy (directly or through your agents or retailers) of that edition to the public.

It is requested, but not required, that you contact the authors of the Document well before redistributing any large number of copies, to give them a chance to provide you with an updated version of the Document.

J.5 MODIFICATIONS

You may copy and distribute a Modified Version of the Document under the conditions of sections 2 and 3 above, provided that you release the Modified Version under precisely this License, with the Modified Version filling the role of the Document, thus licensing distribution and modification of the Modified Version to whoever possesses a copy of it. In addition, you must do these things in the Modified Version:

- Use in the Title Page (and on the covers, if any) a title distinct from that of the Document, and from those of previous versions (which should, if there were any, be listed in the History section of the Document). You may use the same title as a previous version if the original publisher of that version gives permission.

- List on the Title Page, as authors, one or more persons or entities responsible for authorship of the modifications in the Modified Version, together with at least five of the principal authors of the Document (all of its principal authors, if it has less than five).

- State on the Title page the name of the publisher of the Modified Version, as the publisher.

- Preserve all the copyright notices of the Document.

- Add an appropriate copyright notice for your modifications adjacent to the other copyright notices.

- Include, immediately after the copyright notices, a license notice giving the public permission to use the Modified Version under the terms of this License, in the form shown in the Addendum below.

- Preserve in that license notice the full lists of Invariant Sections and required Cover Texts given in the Document's license notice.

- Include an unaltered copy of this License.

- Preserve the section entitled 'History', and its title, and add to it an item stating at least the title, year, new authors, and publisher of the Modified Version as given on the Title Page. If there is no section entitled 'History' in the Document, create one stating the title, year, authors, and publisher of the Document as given on its Title Page, then add an item describing the Modified Version as stated in the previous sentence.

- Preserve the network location, if any, given in the Document for public access to a Transparent copy of the Document, and likewise the network locations given in the Document for previous versions it was based on. These may be placed in the 'History' section. You may omit a network location for a work that was published at least four years before the Document itself, or if the original publisher of the version it refers to gives permission.

- In any section entitled 'Acknowledgements' or 'Dedications', preserve the section's title, and preserve in the section all the substance and tone of each of the contributor acknowledgements and/or dedications given therein.

- Preserve all the Invariant Sections of the Document, unaltered in their text and in their titles. Section numbers or the equivalent are not considered part of the section titles.

- Delete any section entitled 'Endorsements'. Such a section may not be included in the Modified Version.

- Do not retitle any existing section as 'Endorsements' or to conflict in title with any Invariant Section.

If the Modified Version includes new front-matter sections or appendices that qualify as Secondary Sections and contain no material copied from the Document, you may at your option designate some or all of these sections as invariant. To do this, add their titles to the list of Invariant Sections in the Modified Version's license notice. These titles must be distinct from any other section titles.

You may add a section entitled 'Endorsements', provided it contains nothing but endorsements of your Modified Version by various parties – for example, statements of peer review or that the text has been approved by an organization as the authoritative definition of a standard.

You may add a passage of up to five words as a Front-Cover Text, and a passage of up to 25 words as a Back-Cover Text, to the end of the list of Cover Texts in the Modified Version. Only one passage of Front-Cover Text and one of Back-Cover Text may be added by (or through arrangements made by) any one entity. If the Document already includes a cover text for the same cover, previously added by you or by arrangement made by the same entity you are acting on behalf of, you may not add another; but you may replace the old one, on explicit permission from the previous publisher that added the old one.

The author(s) and publisher(s) of the Document do not by this License give permission to use their names for publicity for or to assert or imply endorsement of any Modified Version.

J.6 COMBINING DOCUMENTS

You may combine the Document with other documents released under this License, under the terms defined in section 4 above for modified versions, provided that you include in the combination all of the Invariant Sections of all of the original documents, unmodified, and list them all as Invariant Sections of your combined work in its license notice.

The combined work need only contain one copy of this License, and multiple identical Invariant Sections may be replaced with a single copy. If there are multiple Invariant Sections with the same name but different contents, make the title of each such section unique by adding at the end of it, in parentheses, the name of the original author or publisher of that section if known, or else a unique number. Make the same adjustment to the section titles in the list of Invariant Sections in the license notice of the combined work.

In the combination, you must combine any sections entitled 'History' in the various original documents, forming one section entitled 'History'; likewise combine any sections entitled 'Acknowledgements', and any sections entitled 'Dedications'. You must delete all sections entitled 'Endorsements.'

J.7 COLLECTIONS OF DOCUMENTS

You may make a collection consisting of the Document and other documents released under this License, and replace the individual copies of this License in the various documents with a single copy that is included in the collection, provided that you follow the rules of this License for verbatim copying of each of the documents in all other respects.

You may extract a single document from such a collection, and distribute it individually under this License, provided you insert a copy of this License into the extracted document, and follow this License in all other respects regarding verbatim copying of that document.

J.8 AGGREGATION WITH INDEPENDENT WORKS

A compilation of the Document or its derivatives with other separate and independent documents or works, in or on a volume of a storage or distribution medium, does not as a whole count as a Modified Version of the Document, provided no compilation copyright is claimed for the compilation. Such a compilation is called an 'aggregate', and this License does not apply to the other self-contained works thus compiled with the Document, on account of their being thus compiled, if they are not themselves derivative works of the Document.

If the Cover Text requirement of section 3 is applicable to these copies of the Document, then if the Document is less than one quarter of the entire aggregate, the Document's Cover Texts may be placed on covers that surround only the Document within the aggregate. Otherwise they must appear on covers around the whole aggregate.

J.9 TRANSLATION

Translation is considered a kind of modification, so you may distribute translations of the Document under the terms of section 4. Replacing Invariant Sections with translations requires special permission from their copyright holders, but you may include translations of some or all Invariant Sections in addition to the original versions of these Invariant Sections. You may include a translation of this License provided that you also include the original English version of this License. In case of a disagreement between the translation and the original English version of this License, the original English version will prevail.

J.10 TERMINATION

You may not copy, modify, sublicense, or distribute the Document except as expressly provided for under this License. Any other attempt to copy, modify, sublicense or distribute the Document is void, and will automatically terminate your rights under this License. However, parties who have received copies, or rights, from you under this License will not have their licenses terminated so long as such parties remain in full compliance.

J.11 FUTURE REVISIONS OF THIS LICENSE

The Free Software Foundation may publish new, revised versions of the GNU Free Documentation License from time to time. Such new versions will be similar in spirit to the present version, but may differ in detail to address new problems or concerns. See http://www.gnu.org/copyleft/.

Each version of the License is given a distinguishing version number. If the Document specifies that a particular numbered version of this License 'or any later version' applies to it, you have the option of following the terms and conditions either of that specified version or of any later version that has been published (not as a draft) by the Free Software Foundation. If the Document does not specify a version number of this License, you may choose any version ever published (not as a draft) by the Free Software Foundation.

J.12 ADDENDUM: How to use this License for your documents

To use this License in a document you have written, include a copy of the License in the document and put the following copyright and license notices just after the title page:

```
Copyright (c)  YEAR  YOUR NAME.

Permission is granted to copy, distribute and/or modify this document
under the terms of the GNU Free Documentation License, Version 1.1
or any later version published by the Free Software Foundation;
with the Invariant Sections being LIST THEIR TITLES, with the
Front-Cover Texts being LIST, and with the Back-Cover Texts being LIST.
A copy of the license is included in the section entitled 'GNU
Free Documentation License'.
```

If you have no Invariant Sections, write 'with no Invariant Sections' instead of saying which ones are invariant. If you have no Front-Cover Texts, write 'no Front-Cover Texts' instead of 'Front-Cover Texts being LIST'; likewise for Back-Cover Texts.

If your document contains nontrivial examples of program code, we recommend releasing these examples in parallel under your choice of free software license, such as the GNU General Public License, to permit their use in free software.

www.ingramcontent.com/pod-product-compliance
Lightning Source LLC
Chambersburg PA
CBHW062104050326
40690CB00016B/3201